Children's Learning

Children's Learning

HAROLD W. STEVENSON

University of Michigan

PRENTICE-HALL, INC., Englewood Cliffs, New Jersey

Printed in the United States of America

ISBN: 0-13-132472-1

Library of Congress Catalog Card Number: 73-178272

10 9 8 7 6 5 4 3 2 1

ACKNOWLEDGMENTS:

Pages 9-10   Munn, N. L. Learning in children. In L. Carmichael (Ed.) *Manual of child psychology,* 2nd Ed. New York: Wiley, 1954.

Page 49   Watson, J. B. and Raynor, R. Conditioned emotional reactions. *Journal of Experimental Psychology,* 1920, 3.

Page 59   Leont'ev, A. N. Learning as a problem in psychology. In N. O'Connor (Ed.), *Recent Soviet Psychology.* New York: Liveright, 1961.

Pages 64-65   Luria, A. R. The genesis of voluntary movements. In N. O'Connor (Ed.), *Recent Soviet Psychology.* New York: Liveright, 1961.

Pages 69–70   Luria, A. R. The role of language in the formation of temporary connections. In B. Simon (Ed.), *Psychology in the Soviet Union.* Stanford: Stanford University Press, 1957.

Pages 150–151   Kendler, T. S. Development of mediating responses in children. In J. C. Wright & J. Kagan (Eds.), *Basic cognitive processes in children. Monographs of the Society for Research in Child Development,* 1963, 28, No. 2.

Page 232   Bijou, S. W., & Baer, D. M. *Child Development,* Vol. 1. New York: Appleton-Century-Crofts, 1961.

PRENTICE-HALL INTERNATIONAL, INC., *London*
PRENTICE-HALL OF AUSTRALIA, PTY. LTD., *Sydney*
PRENTICE-HALL OF CANADA, LTD., *Toronto*
PRENTICE-HALL OF INDIA PRIVATE LIMITED, *New Delhi*
PRENTICE-HALL OF JAPAN, INC., *Tokyo*

Preface

This book was started at the Center for Advanced Study in the Behavioral Sciences at Stanford, California in 1967–68. I began my year at the Center with the task of writing a chapter on children's learning for the third edition of the *Manual of Child Psychology* (Mussen, 1970). It rapidly became apparent that all of the relevant research could not be condensed into one chapter, and when the chapter was done, I wondered if I should try to develop the material into a book. I am grateful to Professor Lois Meek Stolz, a friend since my graduate student days at Stanford, who urged me to do it.

My major goal was to present the vast and diversified research in children's learning in as clear and meaningful a way as possible. Students who have had only an introductory course in psychology should be able to understand this material.

Most of the information in this book is recent and has been available only in journals and technical chapters. It is my hope that the book will serve students in psychology and education as a guide through the profusion of studies and divergent theoretical positions that are represented in the experimental literature on children's learning.

I am indebted to my colleagues, Herbert Pick and John Flavell, for reading sections of the book, and to Kenneth MacCorquodale for helpful comments about the whole manuscript. The typing was done by Geraldine Jaunty and Nancy Saros. My most continuingly helpful critic has been my wife, Nancy G. Stevenson. It is to her that I express my deepest gratitude. Of course, we have both learned the most about children from our own, Peggy, Janet, Andy, and Patty.

Publishers of the following journals and monographs kindly permitted the reproduction of figures and quotations: *American Journal of Mental Deficiency, American Journal of Psychology, Canadian Journal of Psychology, Child Development, Developmental Psychology, Journal of Abnormal and Social Psychology, Journal of Comparative and Physiological Psychology, Journal of the Experimental Analysis of Behavior, Journal of Experimental Psychology, Journal of Experimental Child Psychology, Journal of Experimental Research in Personality, Journal of Personality and Social Psychology, Minnesota Symposia on Child Psychology, Monographs of the Society for Research in Child Development, Psychological Review,* and *Science.*

Harold W. Stevenson

Contents

Plan of the Book

How can the literature on children's learning be organized? The most satisfying approach would be a theoretical one. However, psychologists have no broad theories of children's learning. Without such theories there can be no core around which to build an integrated body of knowledge. There is the possibility of using age as an organizing theme. This proves to be a forced and unproductive approach, however, for studies have not always been conducted with this variable in mind. We are left with a less elegant possibility. Psychologists have been driven by certain basic questions about how children learn. A natural approach, therefore, is to follow the lines along which research has developed, taking each question in turn and following the studies as they have evolved. We end up with an exposition that is disjointed, but that is nevertheless representative of the current status of our knowledge.

In seeking answers to basic questions about children's learning, psychologists have tended to concentrate on particular types of tasks. These tasks have been popular, not because they are especially important in themselves, but because they are convenient and meaningful ways of investigating the relation of crucial variables to the learning process. The research typically has begun with basic questions but often has emerged as detailed inquiry into particular types of tasks, such as transposition or paired-associates.

Too many studies have been done to allow the discussion to be all-inclusive. It is necessary, therefore, to be selective, to include only those studies that seem to be most substantial in terms of their contribution to knowledge about children's learning and most likely to weather methodological and procedural criticisms. Two large groups of studies are omitted because they are not relevant to the major purposes of the book. Generally, we will not examine studies that use abnormal or subnormal children as subjects. The excuse for this is that these studies tend to tell us more about the characteristics of these types of children than they do about how children learn. The child in school also has been studied, often in the context of projects on curricula or the use of mechanical and electronic aids in teaching. Such material has been omitted on the grounds that it appears to have greater implications for educational practice than it does for the understanding of learning.

The first chapter of this book is an historical introduction to research in learning. It summarizes the major developments of the last hundred years in the study of learning and relates these developments specifically to children's learning.

The main body of the text is divided into six major topics. Research on human infants is discussed in Chapters 2 and 3. When does the infant begin to learn, and what types of variables influence learning in its earliest, most primitive forms?

Chapters 4 through ten are concerned with language and learning. Language certainly is one of the most important acquisitions of the young child. An irrevocable break is produced when the child begins to span time and space through the use of words.

A section of five chapters deals with reinforcement and learning. How does the introduction of reward influence what the child will do and what he will learn?

Stimulus factors and attention are discussed in Chapters 16 through 20. Unless the child attends to the material he is supposed to learn, there is little possibility that learning will occur. Are there ways to construct and present stimuli that will capture the child's attention? Once he has attended to the stimuli, what other variables influence how much he will learn?

In Chapters 21 and 22 concept learning is discussed. Child psychologists, like all other investigators beginning a new area of exploration, have tended to tackle the relatively simple before looking at the complex questions. We have less information about how children learn concepts than about how they learn simple discriminations.

Individual differences in learning are discussed in Chapter 23. Learning is no more consistent among individuals than is any other form of behavior. What kinds of differences in learning exist? What characteristics of the individual have a significant influence on the rate and amount he will learn?

The last chapter is a summing-up, an effort to tease out the major developmental changes and the most powerful experimental variables. Looking to the future, an attempt is made to suggest the types of studies that may prove to be most productive in subsequent research.

Children's Learning

Development of Research in Children's Learning

To ask how children learn is to pose some of the most complex, basic, and compelling questions found in contemporary science. Children's behavior is marvelously intricate and ever changing. With great rapidity the human being is transformed from a helpless, somnolent newborn into a curious, active child. Trying to understand how early experiences might influence later behavior would be difficult enough if the child were a stable creature, but childhood is a period of continuous change. Principles that may be appropriate in discussing the behavior of the two-year-old give us an incomplete account of what happens at eight. Since research on children's learning is a relatively new undertaking, we should realize from the beginning that our answers to the basic questions are frequently tentative, sometimes superficial, and never complete. If we are willing to accept as our goal being able to ask increasingly sophisticated questions rather than expecting final solutions, our quest will not end in frustration. Having partial answers does not mean that we are helpless, nor does it keep us from attempting to put what we do know into practical application; it does mean that we must be aware of the limitations of our knowledge, of where facts leave off and beliefs begin.

Ten years ago, a comprehensive survey of what we knew about children's learning would have required only a chapter. Today, there is more than enough material to fill a book. Why did it take so long for the study of children's learning to become a serious topic of study? And why have the recent developments been so rapid? To see why this should have been the case, we must look briefly at the historical antecedents of the research in children's learning.

THE STUDY OF LEARNING

It is sometimes said that the study of learning is the nucleus about which the rest of psychology revolves. Because we know that so much of human behavior is learned, we realize that a science of human behavior must remain incomplete until we have a firm understanding of the learning process. As a consequence, learning has been one of the most intensively studied areas in psychology.

It usually is appropriate in introducing a topic to define terms. At first, it would seem to be relatively easy to define what we mean by learning. Everyone would agree that learning involves a change in behavior as a result of experience. But learning itself can never be observed. We must make inferences about learning from changes in performance. Because we must distinguish between learning and performance we get into trouble when we attempt to give a precise definition of what we mean by learning. Changes in performance may have many causes. Fatigue, drugs, level of motivation, surgery—all can lead to changes in performance but are not necessarily examples of learning. For the present, therefore, we must be satisfied with a rather broad definition, realizing that the more we find out about the conditions that lead to changes in performance, the more precise our definition of learning can become.

The Beginnings

There never has been a scarcity of ideas about how learning occurs. For many years people have watched animals learning tricks, children learning the alphabet, and adults learning new skills. From these observations came early commonsense ideas about learning. Sometimes the ideas were astute and insightful; often, they were intuitively reasonable. Elaborated by uncommon persons, they became the basis for theories of pedagogy and for philosophical discussions about the origins and nature of human knowledge. But they always were speculative. To be more than this the ideas would have to be based, not on observation alone, but on information collected in a systematic and reliable manner. Uncontrolled observation is an inefficient means of obtaining information and may lead to incomplete or misleading interpretations of what has been observed.

A turning point came in the late nineteenth century with the appearance of experimental psychology. Those interested in the study of human consciousness adopted the experimental method that had been applied so successfully for scores of years to investigations of the physical world and more recently to the study of human physiology. Observations still were the data, but they were made in controlled situations where the subjects' experiences could be carefully regulated and their responses evaluated in a standard manner. At first only adults were used as subjects in these studies. Children were not skillful in reporting their experiences and rarely were used in psychological research.

The primary interest of the early experimental psychologists was in sensation and perception. It did not take long, however, for them to become involved in the study of learning, especially as it was found in human adults and lower animals. Adults, mostly college students, were easily recruited as subjects, and the animal laboratory was a convenient place to do research. Ebbinghaus began his investigation of the acquisition and retention of verbal material before 1885. In 1898, Thorndike reported the first of his long series of studies of animal learning, and in 1906 Pavlov published his first studies of animal conditioning. During the early part of the twentieth century the majority of the research on learning was influenced by the lines of investigation initiated by these men. There were other investigators, of course, but their influence was less lasting. None of these psychologists worked with children. If they talked at all about children's learning, they were forced to extrapolate downward from the college sophomore or upward from the rat, cat, or pigeon.

Early Research with Children

Psychologists sometimes became curious about how children would perform in a particular type of task. Studies of conditioning were reported by Krasnogorski (1907); Hunter (1913) compared the learning of delayed reactions by children and animals; Hicks and Carr (1912) studied how rapidly children were able to learn their way through a maze. These studies were straightforward adaptations of tasks and procedures that had proved to be useful with animals. They were innovative only in that they used children as subjects. The studies were normative and descriptive, aimed at answering such questions as whether young children performed more effectively than animals and whether differences in age, intelligence, and sex resulted in differences in performance. They were, by necessity, empirical studies, for no theoretical positions of any complexity had yet been developed. In general, these studies had little influence on the psychology of learning or on developmental psychology. They represented unsystematic excursions by comparative psychologists into the human domain.

Watson

The picture changed abruptly with the entrance of John B. Watson, America's best known psychologist of the 1920s. Watson was a radical behaviorist, an undeviating environmentalist—and an influential advocate of both positions. He became an important figure in psychology because of his insistence on the necessity of studying behavior objectively. Early psychologists had used the method of introspection to analyse the qualities of experience. Watson was interested in studying the *effects* of experience, not on subjective states but on observable behavior. With this change in emphasis children became acceptable subjects for psychological study. The behavior of children could be studied as effectively as that of the mature organism.

Watson began doing research with infants and children himself, studying the reflexes of newborns, the development of emotions, and the basis for producing and eliminating fears in young children. Later, through his speeches and writings he began to exert a strong influence on child care practices. The key to effective child care, according to Watson, was to be found in the concept of the conditioned response. Behavior was assumed to be the product of a multitude of conditioned responses built up during the course of the child's life. If this is the case, then it follows that any type of behavior can be produced as long as the stimuli and responses are arranged in an appropriate fashion.

On the pervasive effects of environmental influences over inherited characteristics, Watson often stated his views in a dramatic manner. This well-known excerpt from his address at Clark University in 1925 on the topic, "What the nursery has to say about instincts," illustrates the kind of statement that stimulated enormous interest and controversy in the field:

Give me a dozen healthy infants, well-formed, and my own specified world to bring them up in and I'll guarantee to take any one at random and train him to be any type of specialist I might select—a doctor, lawyer, artist, merchant-chief, and, yes, even into beggarman and thief, regardless of his talents, penchants, tendencies, abilities, vocations, and race of his ancestors. (Watson, 1926, p. 10)

In making such claims Watson undoubtedly hoped to arouse the interest of others in the great possibilities for modifying behavior through appropriate arrangement of experience. His hopes were realized, and his imprint on American psychology still is visible. One of his continuing legacies is the long series of studies conducted by American psychologists on the problems of children's learning. Work on children's learning was influenced by many others, but Watson's bold and forceful proposals provided the impetus that was needed to get the inquiry underway.

Trial-and-error Learning

Watson was not alone in his advocacy of an objective psychology. Edward L. Thorndike, long-time professor at Columbia University, was one of America's leading learning theorists for many decades. We still see the influence of his interpretation of learning as a trial-and-error process, or, as he called it, learning by selecting and connecting. Whereas Watson had presented the outline of a theory, Thorndike tried to fill in some of the details. His views were expressed in the Law of Exercise (strengthening through use), Law of Disuse (weakening through disuse), and Law of Effect (strengthening through reward and weakening through punishment). These laws were vaguely stated and in the end Thorndike himself was in only partial agreement with his early formulations. Although Thorndike was not a child psychologist, it was for or against Thorndike's views that many of the early experiments in children's learning were performed. The demonstration by Thorndike of the facilitative effects of introducing rewards on the performance of animals and human adults led directly to investigations of whether similar effects would be found with children. Although there were differences in the relative effectiveness of different incentives when, for example, the performance of children was compared with that of adults, the results generally indicated a higher level of performance when the child was presented an incentive for correct response than when he was not (Abel, 1936; Hurlock, 1931).

Sensory-Motor Learning

Partially as a response to the proponents of conditioning such as Watson, and partially as a result of the inherent importance of the topic, many early investigators were concerned with the acquisition of sensory-motor skills. Many of the studies of sensory-motor learning were designed to answer the general question of whether a given amount of practice has comparable effects at all levels of maturation. Of these studies, perhaps the best known are those of Gesell and Thompson (1929), Hilgard (1932), and McGraw (1935). In these studies there typically were two groups of children: an experimental group that received intensive training on a particular skill over a period of time, and a control group that was given infrequent or no practice for the same period, followed by intensive training. The importance of both learning and maturation was clearly demonstrated, for when young children were given relatively simple tasks, such as learning to climb stairs, to cut, or to button, greater maturation resulted in increasingly greater effectiveness of a given amount of training. By the late 1930s, however, this point had been made repeatedly and interest in sensory-motor learning waned.

LEARNING THEORIES

Psychology was not ready in the 1920s for elaborate theories of learning. The field was too new; there was too little information. In the next decade, however, theoretical papers about learning began to appear. For the next twenty years the field was divided into camps, each proposing and attempting to defend a particular theory of learning. There were Gestaltists (Kohler, 1929), connectionists (Thorndike, 1932), purposivists (Tolman, 1932), behaviorists (Hull, 1935), and reinforcement theorists (Skinner, 1938). The objective was no longer simply empirical investigation, but rather the assessment of the validity of alternative theoretical interpretations. None of the theories explicitly discussed developmental changes in learning, but all proved to be valuable sources of ideas for research with children, and importantly, they elucidated the possible relevance of many variables in determining how children learn. Until recently, the research on children's learning was a derivative of the studies that had been conducted with animals and human adults in support of one or the other of these theories.

The Early Studies

What was the cumulative impact of the research that had been done with children, other than replicating the findings of earlier work with animals and human adults? Surprisingly little. Munn, in concluding his review of the research on children's learning conducted prior to 1954, summarized his impressions in the following way:

> So far as discovering anything fundamentally new about the learning process is concerned, the investigations on learning in children have failed. One possible reason for this is that such investigations have from the first been patterned too much after the lines of earlier research with animals and adults in the laboratory. A more likely reason, however, is that the phenomenon of learning is fundamentally the same whether studied in the animal, child, or adult. (Munn, 1954, p. 449)

While one may wish to qualify the second interpretation, Munn's general conclusion seems appropriate. Educational and child-rearing practices and research in learning with other types of subjects were not strongly influenced by the work that had been done with children. This does not mean, however, that teachers and parents were not influenced by psychological concepts in learning. Paradoxically, the influence came directly from studies of pigeons, rats, monkeys, and sophomores, rather than from studies with children.

The Modern Era

Theories of learning that had been developed to account for the behavior of animals and human adults proved to be capable of handling only a small portion of the information that had been collected with children. What seemed at one time to be an effective interpretation proved upon further investigation to be inadequate. Investigators had to begin giving closer attention to the characteristics of children that made them especially suitable for yielding new information about the learning process. It seems logical, and the studies offered support for such an argument, that the learning process would undergo changes as the child develops. Research became more productive and the study of children's learning vitalized when psychologists began to select children because of their distinctive characteristics and not merely because of curiosity about how children would perform in standard laboratory tasks or because they were readily available and cooperative.

An illustration of this shift in emphasis is found in the work of Margaret Kuenne in the mid-forties. Kuenne was a doctoral student at the University of Iowa, studying under Kenneth Spence, a leading stimulus-response theorist. The important point about her study is that it was an attempt to extend traditional stimulus-response notions to the discussion of developmental changes in the acquisition and transfer of a discriminative response. She assumed that young, verbally unsophisticated children would perform in a manner comparable to what Spence had proposed for nonverbal animals. Older children, beginning to use words as means of guiding their responses, should perform in a different manner. The results supported her contentions, and, as we shall see later, she was able to suggest a mechanism that enabled her to account for the developmental changes she observed (Kuenne, 1946).

Kuenne's study excited interest both because it was a lucid example of how theoretically based research could be conducted with children, and because it demonstrated how developmental studies might provide a means of bridging the chasm that separated the research with lower animals from that conducted with mature human adults. This kind of research required a concern with developmental processes, familiarity with theory, and a willingness to venture forth with new theoretical ideas that might differ from those developed in accounting for the behavior of lower animals or human adults.

During the past two decades, the study of children's learning has become one of the most lively and productive aspects of research on human learning. The recent and rapid growth of the field is evident in Figure 1-1, where the number of studies reported in English is plotted by decade. More information about children's learning has been accumulated since 1960 than in all the previous decades combined. This burst of activity does not mean we have as much information as we would like. It does mean, however, that we are beginning to be beyond the period where the charge can be made that the research only reaffirms what was already known, rather than opening up new ideas.

The rapid advance in knowledge is a result of many factors. The emergence of theories and the application of the experimental method were two important antecedents. But the critical step occurred when investigators began to select children because of their growing facility with language, their acquisition of social competence, their expanding systems of conceptualization, and their greater capacity for attentiveness. Without a theoretical base, this research would have devolved into normative studies. With a theoretical orientation, the research has attempted to integrate, with increasing analytic precision, the role of a multitude of variables including developmental level into the discussions of the learning process. There were other reasons, too. Advances in laboratory instruments provided the experimenter with precise and flexible electronic devices for the presentation of materials, the recording of responses, and for the arduous task of analysing the data. One also must acknowledge the great importance of the financial support that has been available. Without funds, rapid advances in research are impossible.

The interest now is in the analysis of the processes that seem to influence the ease and efficiency with which children learn. Current research typically is variable-oriented, in contrast to the problem orientation of earlier studies. It would be an overstatement to say that all learning

Figure 1-1.   Number of publications in English of studies of children's learning, plotted by decade. (Data from H. W. Stevenson, Studies of children's learning: A bibliography. *Psychonomic Monograph Supplements,* 1968, 2, Whole No. 27.)

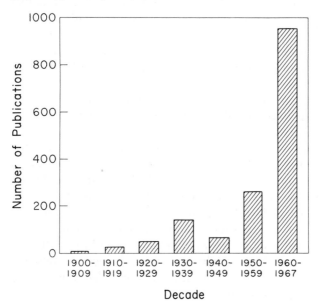

studies with children now seek to assess the significance of particular variables. Most commonly, however, questions are asked about how experimental variables influence learning either singly or in interaction, rather than about how long it takes children to learn a certain task, whether performance differs according to age, sex, and intelligence, and how the performance of children differs from that of lower animals. The degree to which the research has been successful can be evaluated only by looking at the studies that have been done. [Reviews of research on children's learning appear in Brackbill and Koltsova (1967), Stevenson (1970), and White (1963).]

2

Learning in Young Infants

Let us start at the beginning, with the very young baby. A visit to the newborn nursery of any hospital will reveal a group of warmly wrapped infants, most of them asleep, some with pursed mouths, wrinkled foreheads, and contorted arms, who open their eyes now and then, a few with very red faces crying vigorously. When the visitors leave and feeding time arrives, nearly all the babies are awake. Some surely are; their cries are beginning to turn into rage. Others have their eyes open, they move a bit, and then go back to sleep. Anyone looking at the babies wonders what is going on in their heads. Are they aware of the world about them? Does their experience have any significance for them? Is their behavior influenced by what goes on in the environment? We cannot ask the babies. We cannot even guess by looking at them, for they are so remote from anything with which we, as adults, can empathize.

What could we do to determine the effects of environmental events on the young infant? One possible approach to this question is to attempt to condition them. If the newborn can be conditioned we would know not only that he is responsive to external stimuli, but also that his later behavior was influenced by these stimuli.

Let us review briefly how a conditioned response is developed. Take any naturally occurring response, such as an eyeblink in response to a puff of air. In this case, the unconditioned (unlearned) response is an eyeblink to the unconditioned stimulus of a puff of air. Now, just before presenting the puff of air we might turn on a dim light—or present any other stimulus that does not ordinarily lead to an eyeblink. We can repeat this procedure a number of times, and then, as a test, turn on the light but do not present the air puff. The infant now blinks to the light. He did not do this at the beginning of the trials, but now he does. He has learned to anticipate the puff of air and blinks his eye upon the presentation of the neutral stimulus. We have conditioned the infant. The light now functions as a conditioned (learned) response. The process whereby an initially neutral stimulus becomes capable of eliciting a response that was made previously to another stimulus is known as *classical conditioning*. We know that this is a basic mechanism in learning, demonstrable across a wide variety of subjects, including both animals and human beings.

NEONATAL CONDITIONING

Whether or not a newborn infant can be conditioned is an important question, not only for persons with a particular interest in the young infant, but also for those who are attempting to construct theories of behavior. Any theory that posits an enduring effect of early experience on later behavior, as psychoanalysis does, assumes that the infant's behavior is modified by his experience. Other theories, such as those of the behaviorists, have proposed that conditioning is the basic mechanism for producing behavioral change. Behavior is assumed to be the product of a multitude of conditioned responses built up during the course of the individual's life. Behaviorists need to know whether or not the behavior of the infant can be explained on the basis of the principles of conditioning.

It would seem that the question could be answered readily. But infants are notoriously difficult subjects with whom to work, and their behavior does not always conform to the expectations of the adult experimenter. Not until very recently could definitive statements be made about infant conditioning. Before 1920, children had been used in only a few studies of conditioning and young infants not at all. Krasnogorski (1907), a Russian, and Mateer (1918), an American, had conducted successful studies of conditioning with older children. Somewhat later, Marquis (1931) and Wenger (1936) reported successful conditioning of neonates, but the validity of their results was questioned on the basis of their having had inadequate control groups.

The inclusion of appropriate control groups is of critical importance. Control groups are introduced to rule out alternative interpretations of the change in behavior found as a consequence of the conditioning procedure. Unless one can demonstrate that the change in behavior is not a result of maturation or of increased sensitivity to the conditioned stimulus, positive findings from the conditioning trials are meaningless as far as learning is concerned. It is necessary, therefore, to have at least three groups of infants: (a) an experimental group that undergoes the conditioning procedure; (b) a group controlling for the effects of maturation that is tested at the beginning and at the end of the experiment with no relevant intervening experience; and (c) a control group undergoing the "conditioning" procedure, but for which the conditioned stimulus is never coupled with the unconditioned stimulus.

A study by Wickens' and Wickens' (1940) presents a good illustration of the problems encountered in working with young infants. This study will be discussed in some detail, for it is a carefully conducted study and the results are in line, up to a point, with those obtained with more mature subjects. Had these investigators not included the appropriate control groups, their conclusions would have been less complex, but premature.

The Wickens' attempted to provided an appropriate design for their experiment by including three groups of infants, one experimental and two control. The unconditioned response selected for study was foot retraction to an electric shock (unconditioned stimulus). If a mild electric shock is applied to the sole of an infant's foot, he will retract his foot. The Wickens wished to find out whether they could bring about the retraction of the infant's foot with an initially neutral stimulus such as a buzzer by pairing it with the shock. Would the infant learn to retract its foot (conditioned response) when the buzzer sounded (conditioned stimulus), independent of the presentation of the shock? The 12 experimental subjects, all under ten days of age, were given 36 paired presentations of buzzer and shock, 12 each day on three successive days.

For the two control groups the experimenters did not associate the buzzer with the shock. One control group was given a preliminary test on the first day of the experiment to determine whether the buzzer alone was effective in eliciting foot retraction. It was not. The procedure for the second control group was identical to that of the experimental group, except that the buzzer was omitted entirely.

On the fourth day all three groups of babies were presented a series of test trials with the buzzer. Nine of the 12 experimental subjects who had experienced the buzzer with the shock showed clear evidence of conditioning; that is, they withdrew their foot upon hearing the buzzer alone. Of the 12 subjects in the first control group that had had no intervening experience with either the shock or buzzer, only one retracted its foot to the sound of the buzzer. The results for the second control group, where the infants had received 36 shocks to the bottoms of their feet, posed the problems. When these infants were presented the buzzer for the first time on the test trials, 11 showed foot retraction. What had happened? The infants in this control group appeared to have been "conditioned," even though the buzzer and shock never had been paired during the training trials.

Two interpretations of the findings have been offered. The first assumes that what appeared to be conditioning in the control group was a result of sensitization, whereby repeated stimulation by the shock lowered the threshold for eliciting foot retraction. According to this interpretation, the subsequent application of any strong stimulus, such as a buzzer, would be effective in producing the response. The more frequently cited interpretation is that conditioning *was* demonstrated in the second control group, but that the conditioned stimulus for this group was a sudden change in the stimulus situation. Both shock and the onset of a buzzer constitute such a change. This interpretation is both cumbersome and untestable. If neonates are so sensitive that any change in stimulation can function as a conditioned stimulus, it would seem unlikely that studies ever could be designed to assess the critical features of conditioning in neonates. Even more important perhaps is the fact that the adjustment of young infants would be excruciatingly difficult if any change in stimulation could function as an effective conditioned stimulus. The nonspecificity of such a stimulus would lead to chaotic, rather than organized and appropriate behavior. What would differentiate one change in stimulation from another? Interest in the whole problem rapidly dwindled, for no resolution of the problems of interpreting the results of the Wickens' study seemed apparent.

Adaptation

If the method of classical conditioning is full of problems, perhaps another approach to the study of learning capacity in neonates would be more effective. Infants gradually adapt to feeding schedules. Would it be possible to demonstrate that such adaptation can occur during the first weeks after birth? Marquis (1941) placed one group of breast-fed newborns on a three-hour feeding schedule and a second breast-fed group on a four-hour schedule for the first eight days of life. On the ninth day, the group that had been fed every three hours was changed to a four-hour schedule.

Activity level of young infants varies according to a U-shaped function; it is high both before and after feedings with a trough of inactivity somewhere between each feeding. If the infants had adapted to a three-hour schedule, an increase in bodily activity should appear after three hours in the infants whose feeding schedule had been modified. Marquis measured activity level by a stabilimeter, a device for recording the frequency of movement made by the infant as it lies in its crib. Shortly after the three hours had elapsed, a burst of activity began in the infants whose schedule had been changed. By the end of four hours their activity level exceeded anything found earlier in these infants and was far beyond that of the infants consistently fed on a four-hour schedule. The infants appeared to have been frustrated by the failure of milk to appear at the expected time. One means of expressing this frustration was a heightened level of bodily activity.

The results seem to be clear, but do they offer evidence of learning? The possibility cannot be ruled out that they reflect a form of physiological adaptation. The infants fed on a three-hour schedule may have consumed less milk at each feeding than did those on the four-hour schedule. At the end of three hours their stomachs may have been empty, and the level of excitability of the central nervous system may have been increased. In this way, the great increase in activity at the end of three hours may have had nothing to do with learning but may have been a somatic response to a lack of food.

A related study concerned the white blood cell (leucocyte) count in neonates. Normally, around the sixth day after birth, the leucocyte count increases an hour or so after the infant is fed—a reaction of the blood to the intake of food. However, Krachkovskaia (1967) observed an increased leucocyte count in eight-day-olds shortly *before* they were fed. The increase observed before feeding could be considered a conditioned response to the lapse of time between feedings. As such, it would be termed an example of temporal conditioning, with the passage of time functioning as the conditioned stimulus.

To test this observation experimentally, several infants, all over one month of age, were observed before and after they had been switched from a three- to a four-hour schedule. The infants adapted to the original schedule, and when it was changed there was a rapid adaptation to the new schedule. On the first day following the change, the leucocyte count increased at the end of the three-hour period. On the second day, however, the increase occurred at the end of the fourth hour—immediately preceding feeding. Leucocyte count had been modified as a function of the change in feeding schedule.

These results, as well as those of Marquis, may be examples of temporal conditioning, where the conditioned stimulus was the passage of a period of time. It still is not clear, however, that either set of results represents more than a form of physiological adaptation produced by biochemical changes in the digestive and circulatory systems. Whatever one's interpretation, both studies show that responses of young infants may be modified by changes in their routines.

HABITUATION

Another line of evidence supporting the view that the behavior of neonates can be changed through experience is found in studies of habituation. Habituation is a term used to describe the phenomenon whereby stimuli that initially are effective in producing a particular form of behavior become ineffective with repeated presentation. As with the studies of feeding schedules, there is disagreement about whether habituation is a form of learning or of sensory adaptation. The latter interpretation places the effect within the sensory system and attributes the decreased response to fatigue of the sensory receptors. The disagreement about interpretation does not reduce the importance of habituation as an example of the modifiability of neonatal response.

Work on neonatal habituation was stimulated by the report of a Russian study (Bronshtein, Antonova, Kamenetskaya, Luppova, & Sytova, 1958) that found positive results. These investigators placed a pacifier in the neonate's mouth and then sounded a tone or presented an odor. When the pacifier was inserted the infant began to suck, but the sucking ceased upon the presentation of the auditory or olfactory stimuli. Gradually, the introduction of an extraneous stimulus became ineffective in producing a cessation of sucking. Habituation had occurred.

The phenomenon has been demonstrated in several other studies. Keen (1964) repeated the Bronshtein et al. study under carefully controlled conditions, and although habituation occurred more slowly than it had in the earlier study, it did occur.

Habituation of heart activity to tones also has been found (Bartoshuk, 1962; Bridges, 1961). When the neonate hears a moderately intense sound, there is a rapid increase in heart rate. Evidence for habituation appears if the degree of acceleration in heart rate decreases with repeated presentations of the sound. Graham, Clifton, and Hatton (1968) asked whether habituation of heart rate would occur if the interval between presentations was quite long (90 seconds). If habituation was found, the results could not readily be attributed to sensory adaptation, for adaptation of the sense organs should dissipate within 90 seconds. Habituation did occur, but it was slow to develop and was not manifest on every trial. Furthermore, there was no evidence that the experience transferred from one day to the next during the five days of the experiment. On the one hand, the results seem to support the interpretation of habituation as a form of learning, but the failure to find any transfer between days diminishes the strength of this interpretation. Apparently, critical tests of the learning-adaptation interpretations must await a more complete understanding of physiological activity in the newborn.

Another approach to the study of neonatal habituation is found in the studies of the habituation of bodily activity to olfactory stimuli (Engen & Lipsitt, 1965; Engen, Lipsitt, & Kaye, 1963). When an odor, such as oil of anise, is placed before an infant's nostrils, there is a heightened level of bodily activity. It was found in these studies that when an odor was presented on a series of trials, the amount of activity decreased significantly—evidence of habituation. Furthermore, the effectiveness of a second odor, such as asafetida, in producing heightened bodily activity was lessened when it was presented after habituation had occurred to the first odor. There was, so to speak, some evidence of cross-odor habituation. But when the first odor was presented again after habituation occurred to the second odor, activity level increased again, although not to the degree it had on initial presentation of the odor. Thus, whether or not we wish to consider habituation a form of learning, the positive results of all these studies represent additional examples of how the responses of neonates may be modified by experience.

Procedures used in studies of habituation and conditioning have many common features. The major difference is the sequence in which the stimuli are presented. In studies of habituation the neutral stimulus is presented *after* the unconditioned stimulus, whereas in studies of conditioning the neutral (conditioned) stimulus is presented *before* the unconditioned stimulus. Or, looking at it in another way, in studies of habituation the neutral stimulus (e.g., tone) is presented while the unconditioned response (say, sucking) is being made, whereas in studies of conditioning the neutral stimulus is presented before the unconditioned response occurs. At first, it is hard to reconcile the fact that positive results were obtained in studies of habituation, while the results of the studies of conditioning were indeterminant. There is, however, a factor other than temporal order of stimuli that differed between the two sets of studies. Noxious stimuli (such as shock) were used in the studies of conditioning, whereas the stimuli in the studies of habituation were benign (such as tones). It is possible that stressful stimuli may lead to negative or unexpected results, whereas positive findings may be obtained when nonstressful stimuli are used. This suggestion is given some support by studies of appetitive conditioning.

APPETITIVE CONDITIONING

Appetitive conditioning deals with the conditioning of responses related to the intake of food. The most extensive work in this area has been done by Papoušek, a Czech pediatrician, at the Institute for the Care of Mother and Child in Prague (Papoušek, 1967a, 1967b). In contrast to the American investigator, who generally has ready access to neonates for only a few days after birth, Papoušek was fortunate in having infants available at the Institute from birth until they were six months old.

Having made the decision to study appetitive conditioning, Papoušek was faced with the problem of devising a technique for pursuing his research. Since even newborns are capable of turning their heads and since such movements can be quantified easily, the decision was made to use head-turning as the conditioned response. A head-cradle was constructed. As the infant rotated its head, the change in the position of the head-cradle was recorded via a connecting shaft and an electrical circuit as a deflection from a baseline on a moving piece of graph paper.

The procedure for presenting the unconditioned stimulus differed somewhat from those used in traditional studies of conditioning. A tone was sounded in the midline above the baby's head and if the baby turned his head to the left, milk was offered to him. If the baby did not turn his head, the research assistant touched the left corner of his mouth with a nipple, and if this was ineffective in producing head-turning the baby's head was turned to the left and the nipple placed in his mouth. The baby then was allowed to drink a quantity of the milk. The procedure was repeated for ten trials each day until the baby spontaneously made five consecutive head-turns to the left at the sound of the tone in a single day.

Three groups of infants, with average ages of 3, 86, and 142 days, were used as subjects. The youngest group is of interest for the present discussion. The first conditioned head-turn appeared in this group after an average of three days of training (32.2 trials). After an average of 177 trials, all 14 infants included in the group reached the criterion of learning. These results leave no doubt that neonates *can* be conditioned, even though individual babies differ in the amount of time it takes them to learn. Here, then, is the answer to the question we have been pursuing.

Neonates' responses were less stable than were those of older infants, and their rate of conditioning was slower. Older groups required an average of only 42.3 and 27.8 trials, respectively, to reach criterion. There also were marked individual differences among the neonates in their rate of learning. For example, the standard deviation of the number of trials to criterion for this group was 93.4 whereas in the other two groups the standard deviations were less than 20.0.

Some newborns learned the response in seven days, but others required more than a month of training. The differences appeared to be dependent primarily on differences in the maturity of the central nervous system. In a careful analysis of possible determinants of the individual differences in learning, such as sex, season of the year, and somatic and constitutional characteristics, only two factors were significantly related to rate of conditioning. Stouter babies, and, paradoxically, babies who had a lower daily intake of milk were conditioned more readily. Neither factor accounted for all of the individual differences in rate of learning. The message from these data is that anyone proposing a particular type of training for the newborn must expect that the training will be readily effective with some infants, but distressingly slow with others. From the beginning of life there are great differences among individuals in the rate at which they are able to learn.

Following the publication of Papoušek's study, several other successful efforts to condition neonates have been reported. Kaye (1965) worked with the Babkin reflex, a reflex in which pressure to the palms of a supine infant results in the infant's opening its mouth. The arms of two- to four-day-old infants were moved from the extended to the flexed position; when the arms were in the flexed position, pressure was applied to the palms. In tests following 35 training trials, the frequency of mouth opening to arm movement alone was significantly higher than during a baseline period and was consistently above that of other infants for whom arm movement never had preceded pressure to the palms.

Kaye's results were replicated by Connolly and Stratton (1969). These investigators pursued the matter further and asked whether a sound (white noise) could function as an effective conditioned stimulus for the Babkin response. Two problems would be settled if evidence of conditioning were obtained. First, as in Kaye's study, both the conditioned and unconditioned stimuli had involved kinesthetic stimuli resulting from bodily movement. Could conditioning occur when the conditioned stimulus was from a modality different from that of the unconditioned stimulus? That is, would auditory rather than kinesthetic stimuli be capable of eliciting the Babkin response? Second, Papoušek's study was not strictly a study of classical conditioning. In classical conditioning, the neutral (conditioned) stimulus is presented prior to the unconditioned stimulus and the two stimuli then are experienced concurrently by the subject for a short period. (Papoušek had deviated from this procedure by reinforcing the head-turning response.) Would positive results be found with neonates if the procedure did conform to the method of classical conditioning?

Infants 50 to 90 hours old were used in the study. During 25 training trials, pressure to the infant's palms (unconditioned stimulus) was applied within the first second of a three-second presentation of white noise (conditioned stimulus). Evidence of conditioning was assessed during 15 extinction, or test trials, in which only the sound was presented. The average number of positive responses during the test period was 5.4. This is significantly above the mean of 1.3 found for control groups who had experienced either 30 palm-presses and 15 presentations of the auditory stimulus or 5 palm-presses and 40 presentations of the auditory stimulus. Interestingly, an average of 10.7 positive responses were found in the 15 extinction trials for their first replication study, thus conditioning was more effective when both the conditioned and unconditioned stimulus were within the same sensory modality. At any rate, the results offer evidence of classical conditioning in the neonate.

A study closely related to that of Papoušek was conducted by Siqueland and Lipsitt (1966). Infants between one and four days of age were presented 30 trials in which tactile stimulation of the cheek preceded the presentation of a bottle by three seconds. When the infant rotated its head to the side of stimulation, it was allowed to drink a quantity of dextrose-water solution. This study differed from that of Papoušek in that Siqueland and Lipsitt sought to determine whether reinforcement would strengthen the head-turning response, rather than asking whether the head-turning response could be elicited by a previously neutral stimulus such as a tone.

The Siqueland and Lipsitt study is an example of *operant conditioning*.

In operant conditioning, conditions are arranged so that the desired be-havior (in this case, head-turning) occurs in the presence of the condi-tioned stimulus (touching the cheek), and when it does it is reinforced or rewarded. If the frequency of response increases with increasing fre-quency of reinforcement, conditioning is deemed to have occurred. The question is whether reinforcement increases the frequency of behavior *emitted* in the presence of the conditioned stimulus, rather than whether the conditioned stimulus becomes increasingly effective in *eliciting* the behavior, as is the case in classical conditioning. In the present study, the specific question is whether the administration of a nutritive substance would operate as a reinforcer to strengthen the head-turning response.

During the first few trials, approximately 30% of the infants turned their heads to the side on which their cheek was stroked. By the end of train-ing, over 80% of the infants did so (see Figure 2-1). Thus, the tactile stimulus, which was moderately effective in eliciting a head-turning re-sponse at the onset of training was transformed through the application of reinforcement into a highly effective means of evoking this response. The increase in percentage of infants turning their heads was far greater than might occur by chance, and was much greater than that found in a control group of infants of the same ages who underwent the same pro-

Figure 2-1.   Mean percent responses during the training and extinc-tion trials made to the eliciting stimulus by the experimental and con-trol groups. (From E. R. Siqueland and L. P. Lipsitt, Conditioned head turning in human newborns. *Journal of Experimental Child Psy-chology,* 1966, 3, 360, © 1966 Academic Press.)

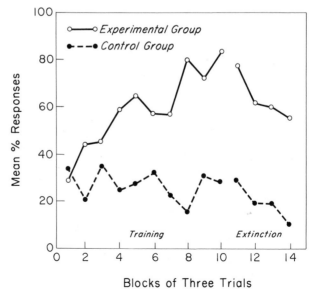

cedure but for whom reinforcement was not dependent upon headturn-ing (see Figure 2-1).

Following the training trials, 12 trials were given in which a head-turn to tactile stimulation never was reinforced. If the reinforcement of a response increases the strength of a response, withdrawal of reinforcement should weaken it. The progressive weakening of a response through non-reinforcement is known as *extinction*. Siqueland and Lipsitt found typical extinction effects. By the end of the 12 trials fewer than 60% of the infants rotated their heads to the tactile stimulus. Reinforcement had increased the frequency of head-turning and the withdrawal of reinforcement had resulted in a diminution in the frequency of this response.

The types of results found in the aforementioned study are not limited to the head-turning response. Lipsitt, Kaye, and Bosack (1966) found that when the insertion of a rubber tube in the mouths of one- to four-day-old infants was followed by reinforcement with a dextrose solution, the rate of sucking increased significantly. When reinforcement was omitted during extinction trials, the rate decreased. Thus rate of suck-ing was significantly altered by the presentation and withdrawal of re-inforcement.

By far the most complex problem presented to newborns is found in a

Figure 2-2. Percentage of responses to positive (S+) and negative (S−) stimuli during training and reversal trials. (From E. R. Sique-land and L. P. Lipsitt, Conditioned head turning in human newborns. *Journal of Experimental Child Psychology*, 1966, 3, 370, © 1966 Academic Press.)

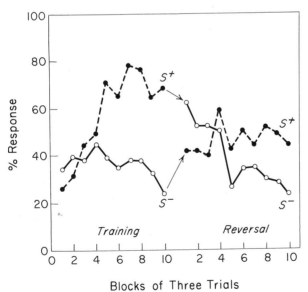

Blocks of Three Trials

second study by Siqueland and Lipsitt (1966). In the previous study by these authors an auditory stimulus (buzzer) was introduced, in part, to maintain a stable level of arousal or wakefulness during the experiment. In this study, auditory stimuli functioned as positive and negative stimuli for evoking the conditioned response. The subjects were two- to five-day-old infants. Head turns preceded by the positive stimulus (buzzer) were reinforced with dextrose solution, and those preceded by the negative stimulus (tone) were not. After 60 trials the pattern or reinforcement was reversed for a second series of 60 trials. That is, after 60 trials the buzzer, which previously had been the negative auditory stimulus, became the positive stimulus (i.e., it led to reinforcement) and the tone, which previously had been the positive auditory stimulus became the negative stimulus (i.e., it no longer led to reinforcement). The results are presented in Figure 2-2.

Clear evidence of the infants' ability to discriminate between reinforced and nonreinforced stimuli was found; not only did the frequency of responses to the positive stimulus increase during the first 60 trials, but by the end of the reversal trials the frequency of responses to the previously negative stimulus exceeded that to the previously positive (now negative) stimulus. The infants had learned the appropriate cue for head-turning and had modified this response when the significance of the cues was reversed. [Additional discussions of infant learning may be found in Brackbill and Koltsova (1967), Horowitz (1968), Lipsitt (1967), and Sameroff (1971).]

CONCLUSIONS

The ability to learn is characteristic of the human being from the earliest days of life. Whether all types of experience are equally conducive to learning is still an open question. In the studies we have reviewed, experience appears to have different effects, depending upon whether it leads to aversive or appetitive stimuli. When pleasant stimuli are used the neonate seems to be able to learn rather quickly. When noxious stimuli are used, the results are difficult to interpret, probably because noxious stimuli increase the infant's general state of arousal.

Large individual differences among neonates in their rate of learning impose important restrictions on the effects that any type of experience may have. For some, there may be notable effects, but for others, the experience may be of only minimal importance. These individual differences in rate of learning apparently reflect differences among infants in their maturity at a given age. But the general immaturity of all neonates makes any effort, at best, less likely to produce smooth and articulated responses than will be possible at later ages.

Both behaviorists and psychoanalysts welcome the results of these studies. The results are in line with the behaviorists' assumption that behavioral change can occur during early infancy through the process of conditioning, and, as the psychoanalysts have assumed, the infant is responsive to events that occur in his environment from the earliest days. We do not know whether naturally occurring conditioning situations are the primary means whereby the newborn learns, nor do we know whether the experiences of the young infant have enduring influences on behavior. Such questions can be answered only with further research, both on conditioning and on other possible forms of early learning.

3

Conditioning in Older Infants

Some years ago a controversy raged in psychology about the role of maturation versus learning in the development of behavior. Some writers seemed to say that if one waited long enough the behavior would emerge, regardless of training. Others wrote as if training in itself was the necessary and sufficient condition for behavioral change. In the end, neither of these extreme positions proved to be tenable. If training was begun too early, some progress was evident—but it was achieved only with great investment of time and effort. By waiting until the individual was more mature, the same effects could be obtained rapidly and with ease. Learning and maturation are interdependent processes. There is a time when the individual is more capable of learning than he is earlier in his life. This is what we mean when we talk of "readiness" for learning.

PAPOUŠEK'S STUDY

There are data in Papoušek's study of infants' head-turning that are relevant to this controversy. As we have seen, neonates can be conditioned, but stable conditioning is more difficult to establish with them than with older infants. What has not been pointed out is that the process of conditioning goes through more noticeable and protracted changes with neonates than with older infants. Papoušek found that during the initial trials, the tone, which was the conditioned stimulus, often produced signs of distress in the neonates, seen in facial grimaces and unhappy vocalizations. At this stage, the neonate's motor responses were diffuse. The conditioned stimulus often resulted in wider opening of the eyes and changes in breathing, rather than a turn of the head. Then came a period of unstable response in which the conditioned response sometimes appeared and sometimes did not. Ultimately, stable conditioning was achieved. The differences between the younger and older subjects in their rates of progress through these stages appear to be due to differences in the level of maturation of the central nervous system, especially those portions producing greater specificity of motor response.

Papoušek did not stop with establishing the conditioned response. After the infants had learned to turn their heads to the left at the sound of the tone, extinction trials were begun; that is, head-turning was no longer reinforced with milk. The conditioned response extinguished rapidly, but, inexplicably, the rate of extinction did not differ according to age. Each group had reached the criterion of extinction (five consecutive trials in which they did *not* turn their heads to the left at the sound of the tone) in between 25 to 27 trials. We do not know why the neonates showed such rapid extinction after having been so slow to condition. Only in the group of neonates (now, on the average, 32 days old) was there a significant relation between rate of conditioning and rate of extinction. The slower conditioners were the fastest to extinguish. That is, those who were the slowest in learning to turn their heads were the fastest in learning not to turn their heads. It may be that the learned response was less stable in the slow learners and disintegrated rapidly when reinforcement was withdrawn.

The subjects then were given a series of re-learning or re-conditioning trials, again learning to turn the head to the left at the signal of the tone. The youngest group reached criterion in an average of 43 trials, a decrease of 134 trials over the average required in original learning. The rapid re-conditioning must be attributed to their greater maturity *and* to their prior experience. These infants, now averaging 38 days of age, reached criterion in approximately the same number of trials as was required by the 86-day-old infants in original learning (mean = 42 trials).

The Papoušek study is interesting, not only as a source of information about infant conditioning, but also as an example of the role of maturation in learning. Learning was possible at an early age, but in reaching the same level of performance younger infants required many more trials than did older infants and more than they did themselves at a later age. A reasonable question to be asked before a specific training procedure is undertaken with infants is whether the consequences—at this age—merit the effort that will be required.

CONDITIONING OF VOCALIZATION

Being able to condition head-turning in young infants is of theoretical significance, but most persons would not regard this finding of great importance in the discussion of the behavior of infants outside the laboratory. A study that does have important practical implications is that of Rheingold, Gewirtz, and Ross (1959) on the conditioning of vocalizations in three-month-old infants. The purpose of this study was to determine whether the frequency of vocalization could be increased by reinforcement and then decreased by the withdrawal of reinforcement.

Before proceeding we should define more precisely what we mean by a reinforcer. Defining a reinforcer is an empirical problem. A reinforcer is any stimulus event that increases the strength of a response. This may sound circular. We are interested in finding stimuli that will strengthen a response and are told that such stimuli are those that strengthen a response. The circularity of this definition is relieved, however, by the fact that a stimulus that is capable of reinforcing one category of responses also should be capable of reinforcing other categories of responses. Once isolated, a stimulus should have broad utility as a reinforcing agent.

Three-month-olds generally have a moderate rate of vocalization and it is easy to establish a baseline measure of this response. A baseline rate of response is that rate occurring prior to any experimental intervention. The experimenter simply stands impassively in front of the infant and counts the number of vocalizations that occur during a specified period of time. After obtaining the baserate of response, Rheingold et al. rein-

Figure 3-1. Mean number of vocalizations on consecutive experimental days for first (Experiment 1) and replication (Experiment 2) groups. (From H. L. Rheingold, J. L. Gewirtz, and H. W. Ross, Social conditioning of vocalizations in the infant. *Journal of Comparative and Physiological Psychology,* 1959, 52, 70. Reprinted by permission of the American Psychological Association.)

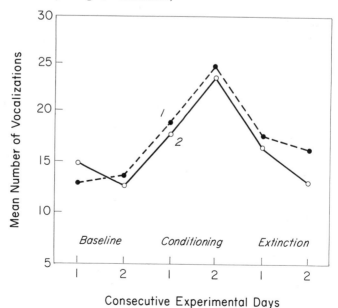

forced subsequent vocalizations with a complex of social acts, including smiling, making "tssk" sounds, and touching the baby's abdomen. The experiment was conducted with two groups of infants in nine daily three-minute sessions over six days. The procedure was identical for both groups; the second group was tested to determine whether the results could be replicated. As can be seen in Figure 3-1, by the end of the second day of conditioning the frequency of vocalizations was nearly twice the baseline rate. When vocalization was no longer reinforced during the two days of extinction, vocalization declined to approximately the baseline level.

The results are simple and straightforward. If a particular form of behavior has utility, if it leads to some consequence, the likelihood that it will be performed is increased. If it does not lead to a meaningful change in the stimulus situation, the rate will remain at a baseline level or will be decreased. This is the core of an important principle for the regulation and control of behavior. Its significance often is underestimated because it is such a simple point, but as we shall see, it has many important practical applications.

Before we can accept the results of the Rheingold et al. study as a demonstration of conditioning, we must consider an alternative interpretation of their results. It is possible that the form of reinforcement used in this study had an arousing effect on the infants, so that the frequency of vocalization was a function of level of arousal rather than a product of learning. In other words, the responses made by the adult in reinforcing the infant may have been exciting, and one of the ways in which the infant expressed his excitement was by increased vocalization. What appeared to be extinction may have been a result of the return of the level of arousal to a more normal state when reinforcement was discontinued. To preclude the possibility that the results were due to differences in the infants' level of arousal, it would be necessary to demonstrate that the same social acts (smiling, touching abdomen, etc.) given when the baby was not vocalizing would not incite the baby to vocalize at a rate greater than the baserate. Another way of saying this is that the reinforcement should be *noncontingent*.

Reinforcement is noncontingent if it is given independent of the emission of the desired response. If the frequency of vocalization did not increase with noncontingent reinforcement, it could be concluded that the increase found in the Rheingold et al. study with contingent reinforcement was a result of learning.

A study was designed by Weisberg (1963) to investigate this possibility. The conditions of the previous study were replicated, and several other conditions were added. Six groups of infants were used. The two groups of central interest were those in which social reinforcement was presented following vocalization (contingent reinforcement) and independently of vocalization (noncontingent reinforcement). Two additional groups were included to ascertain whether the effects were restricted to social reinforcement. For these groups a non-social stimulus (chime) was presented either contingently or noncontingently of vocalization. In addition, to rule out the possibility that simply seeing an adult might be arousing, a group was tested in the presence of a nonresponsive adult. A final group was observed when no adult was visible and no reinforcement of vocalization occurred. The frequency of vocalization increased significantly within the experimental period in only one group—the group that received social reinforcement as a consequence of vocalization. The chime was not an effective reinforcer, nor did presentation of social reinforcement unrelated to vocalization produce an increase in the frequency of vocalization. The results of the Rheingold et al. study therefore must represent conditioning.

One more aspect of the Rheingold et al. results has been investigated. Since the social reinforcement provided by Rheingold et al. consisted of several components, visual, tactile, and auditory, the question may be raised whether all are necessary to produce effective conditioning. Todd and Palmer (1968) investigated this question with two groups of three-month-olds. The design of the study was essentially a replication of that used by Rheingold et al., except that each vocalization was followed by five seconds of tape-recorded auditory reinforcement, consisting of a woman's voice repeating such phrases as "pretty baby" and "hello baby." For half of the infants an adult was present and visible while the reinforcement was given, and for the other half the adult could not be seen. Further, the adult was not visible during the baseline and extinction periods, and when he did appear in the conditioning period he maintained an expressionless and impassive face. The basic purpose of the study, therefore, was to determine the degree to which the adult's presence is critical in the conditioning of infant vocalizations with auditory reinforcement.

Both groups of infants showed significant conditioning and extinction effects; the frequency of vocalization increased relatively consistently during the conditioning period and decreased to the baseline level when reinforcement was omitted. However, the effectiveness of the human voice as a reinforcing agent was enhanced if the infant could see an adult. There was a significantly greater frequency of vocalization during the conditioning period when the adult was present. We need more information about other types of stimuli, such as smiles from the adult or tactual stimulation, that may be effective reinforcers, but for the present it is clear that the human voice, presented in a contingent relation to the infant's vocalization, constitutes such a stimulus.

What would have happened had these studies been continued for many more weeks? Would the time of the appearance of the first word have been hastened? Would the infants have been more precocious in their use of words? We do not know. We do know that the infant's responsiveness can be increased if other persons in the environment reciprocate by responding to the infant. The impoverished behavior and retarded development of language described in studies of institutionalized infants and of others living under deprived conditions often can be attributed to the fact that these infants live in a nonresponsive world. It is important to note that although attentiveness by the adult may be an important factor in maintaining and increasing the infant's general responsiveness, the use of attention as a means of producing behavioral change seems to be restricted to its occurring *after* the desired response has been performed. In other words, we must distinguish between the use of attention as a stimulus and as a reinforcer. An effective mother is not only a responsive mother; she is also one who exerts some degree of control over the time and setting in which her responses to the infant occur.

PARTIAL REINFORCEMENT

Practically speaking, it is impossible to reinforce an infant every time a desired response is made. Will learning occur if the response is reinforced only a certain proportion of the time? The latter case, which is described as partial reinforcement, has been found to be an effective procedure for producing learning. In the Rheingold et al. study, for example, each vocalization was reinforced only during the initial trials; as the frequency of vocalization increased, every second and then every third vocalization was reinforced. This procedure, as was noted by these investigators, may produce a slight depression in the rate of conditioning, but it also produces a very high resistance to extinction. This point is illustrated clearly in a study by Siqueland (1968) on the conditioning of the head-turning response in newborn infants.

The infants ranged in age from 51 to 96 hours at the beginning of the study. During a three-minute baseline period the frequency with which the infants spontaneously rotated their heads was ascertained. The infant's head rested in a head-cradle of the type used by Papoušek, and a deflection of 10 degrees or more met the criterion of a head-turn. After the baseline period the infants were reinforced 10 times with the presentation of a non-nutritive nipple. This procedure was continued for 15 more trials for half of the infants, but for the other half reinforcement was delivered according to a fixed ratio of one reinforcement for every third head-turn. This was followed by a five-minute period of extinction in which no head-turn was reinforced, after which 15 more head-turns were reinforced on the schedule for the last 15 of the first conditioning period, and the experiment was terminated with a two-minute extinction period. Performance differed between the two groups in both extinction periods. Partial reinforcement resulted in a slower rate of extinction than did continuous reinforcement.

Similar results have been obtained by Brackbill (1958) in the conditioning of the smiling response in four-month-old infants. Two groups of infants were used. Both groups were given continuous reinforcement to smiling during the early trials. Reinforcement consisted of the experimenter's smiling, picking up the baby, patting and talking to the baby after the baby smiled. When the infants smiled four times in five minutes (a predetermined criterion) the subjects in one group were reinforced by the experimenter only one-fourth of the time (a partial reinforcement schedule). After 125 responses had been reinforced in this manner, reinforcement was discontinued. As can be seen in Figure 3-2, the group that received continuous reinforcement showed a rapid drop in rate of response when reinforcement was omitted. The partially reinforced babies

Figure 3-2.   Mean number of smiling responses made in successive five-minute intervals during extinction following continuous and intermittent reinforcement of the conditioned response. (From Y. Brackbill, Extinction of the smiling response in infants as a function of reinforcement schedule. *Child Development,* 1958, 29, 115. Copyright 1958 Society for Research in Child Development, Inc.)

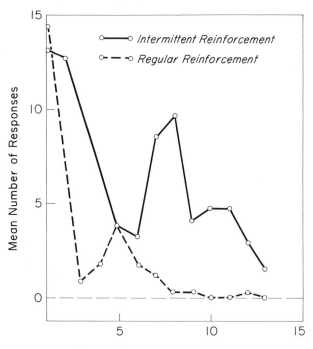

continued to smile at the experimenter for a longer period of time after the cessation of reinforcement.

Smiling was not the only behavior that changed during the course of conditioning and extinction. There were complementary changes in the amount of protest behavior (crying and fussing). As Papoušek had found in his study, Brackbill similarly found that the amount of distrust or protest behavior decreased as the conditioned response became more stable. In Brackbill's study, the amount of protest behavior increased again during extinction. (The greatest amount of protest behavior in the study of vocalization by Rheingold et al. also occurred on the first day of extinction.) Brackbill's infants who had received continuous reinforcement quickly learned in the extinction trials to avert their gaze when the experimenter came into view. They turned their heads to one side and ceased to fixate the experimenter's face. Presumably, withdrawal of reinforcement was frustrating and the infants' response to frustration was to avoid the source of their distress. When reinforcement was no longer available in the manner they expected, they withdrew into a more constricted, but more predictable world.

PUPILLARY CONDITIONING

It is contended by some writers that some disorders of infancy are of psychosomatic origin, that is, they may be traceable to the infant's response to distressing experiences. Disorders of digestion, elimination, and of circulation, all potentially with a psychosomatic basis, are mediated by the autonomic nervous system. We have seen that head-turning, sucking, vocalization, and smiling can be conditioned during the early months of infancy, but these responses are controlled by the somatic nervous system. (In general, the autonomic nervous system controls the internal environment of the organism, while the somatic nervous system conveys impulses from the sense organs to the central nervous system and motor impulses from the brain and spinal cord to the skeletal muscles of the body.) Can responses dependent upon the activity of the autonomic nervous system also be conditioned? If they can, the argument that disorders in infancy may be of psychosomatic origin gains in credibility.

A report by Brackbill, Fitzgerald, and Lintz (1967) deals with this problem. The responses selected for study were pupillary dilation and constriction—both of which are under autonomic control. The infants were between 25 and 85 days of age. To record the infants' responses, continuous photographic records were made on infra-red film. Three types of conditioned stimuli were used with different groups of infants. One stimulus was the mere passage of time (20 seconds). For a second group, the conditioned stimulus was a complex sound of moderate intensity. For the third group of infants the conditioned stimulus was the passage of time and the sound. In studying pupillary dilation the unconditioned stimulus was the offset of a bright light. In studying pupillary constriction the unconditioned stimulus was the onset of a light. The problem, then, was to determine whether the pupillary responses of dilation and constriction could be conditioned to the three types of stimuli.

Pupillary diameter changed significantly during the conditioning procedure, but only when the conditioned stimulus was time or time plus sound. No indication of conditioning was found for the sound alone. Two aspects of these results are especially noteworthy: the remarkable sensitivity of young infants to the passage of time and their insensitivity to the auditory stimulus. Both are without ready explanation. Although we do not know yet whether other autonomic responses are equally susceptible to conditioning, it seems reasonable to assume that they would be and that stimuli associated with unpleasant (or pleasant) experiences may become capable of eliciting the autonomic responses related to the affective state.

Another point should be made about these results and those of two other studies. The eyeblink has been conditioned in eight-day-olds (Dashkovskaia, 1953) and in older infants (Lintz, Fitzgerald, & Brackbill, 1967). In both of these studies the eyeblink (unconditioned response) was produced by a puff of air into the infant's eye. A puff of air to the eye or a change in brightness are mildly noxious stimuli; thus our conclusions in Chapter 2 about the use of noxious stimuli in conditioning must be modified slightly. Mildly noxious stimuli apparently can be used to produce effective conditioning. We still have no evidence, however, that intensely noxious stimuli produce more than indeterminate results. Nor do we know whether even mildly noxious stimuli will be effective if they are unrelated to responses that are adaptive for the organism, such as pupillary dilation or the eyeblink.

CONDITIONING EMOTIONAL RESPONSES

Two of the most famous children in child psychology are Albert and Peter, the subjects of early research on the genesis and elimination of children's fears (Watson & Raynor, 1920; Jones, 1924a, 1924b). Watson, by 1920, had done a series of studies on children's emotions and believed that he could isolate only three basic emotional responses during infancy: fear, rage, and love. If there were so few basic emotional responses, how is the elaborate range of emotions found in older children and adults established? Through conditioning, said Watson. To demonstrate his point he conducted a study with Albert, a stolid 11-month-old. Albert was not afraid of animals, but, as most children, showed a distinct fear of loud noises (in this case, hearing a steel bar struck with a sharp blow). Would it be possible to produce a fear of animals in Albert by following the presentation of a white rat with this loud sound? After two paired presentations of the white rat and the loud sound, the sight of the rat led Albert to withdraw himself and begin whimpering. With two more paired presentations, "The instant the rat was shown the baby began to cry. Almost instantly he turned sharply to the left, fell over on left side, raised himself on all fours and began to crawl away so rapidly that he was caught with difficulty before reaching the edge of the table" (Watson & Raynor, 1920, p. 5). A conditioned fear response had been established. Subsequently, the presentation of a rabbit, dog, cottonwool, and a Santa Claus mask also produced fear, demonstrating that the response had generalized to other stimuli similar to the conditioned stimulus, the white rat.

If fears can be produced by conditioning, it should be possible to eliminate fears by conditioning. The study of Peter by Mary Cover Jones showed that this was possible. Peter, a two-year-old enrolled in a daycare center, was afraid of white rats, rabbits, fur coats, and other similar objects. It was decided, therefore, to pair the presentation of a rabbit with food, a stimulus that produced a positive response. Peter was seated in a highchair and given food. The experimenter brought the rabbit in a wire cage into the room while Peter was eating. The distance between Peter and the rabbit was decreased gradually until by the end of the study Peter allowed the rabbit in the play pen with him, fondled the rabbit affectionately, and let the rabbit nibble his fingers. By pairing a pleasant stimulus with one that produced fear, a positive response came to replace the negative one. It is possible, of course, that the results could have been reversed. With a less sensitive experimenter, Peter might have developed an aversive response to food rather than a positive response to the rabbit.

Jones was not content to demonstrate that conditioning was an effective means of eliminating fears. She also explored, with other children, the effectiveness of several other techniques. Most were unsuccessful. Disuse (preventing the child from encountering the feared objects); verbal appeal (talking about the feared object in pleasant terms); negative adaptation (repeatedly presenting the feared object)—none of these techniques was effective in reducing young children's fears. Distracting the child in the presence of the feared object was moderately effective, as was the method of social imitation, whereby the child was shown the feared object in the presence of other children who had a positive rather than a negative response to the object. Thus, although the last two methods were useful, neither was more effective than conditioning.

These studies became well known as practical applications of the conditioning procedure. They were easy to understand and they were successful. Emotional response may result from a form of conditioning. By experiencing a neutral object in the presence of a feared object the neutral object may become capable of producing fear. In a parallel manner, emotional response may be decreased if the instigating stimulus is paired with a stimulus that leads to pleasure. As we shall see in a later chapter, much of the recent research in behavior modification has its root in these early studies.

CLINICAL APPLICATION

A ten-month-old is brought to a physician with the complaint that the infant is unresponsive. When the mother vocalizes the infant fails to seek out the source of the sound. Loud noises fail to produce a startle response; the infant lies immobile instead of tensing its muscles. One's first guess is that the infant is deaf. But it also is possible that the infant is severely retarded or autistic. Both retarded and autistic children may fail to respond appropriately to environmental events. How might one confirm or reject the possibility of deafness? Would the method of the conditioned response be applicable to this problem? Among the first to recognize that conditioning might be a useful technique was Aldrich (1928), an American pediatrician, and his work has been extended by many others (e.g. Statten & Wishart, 1956).

In most of the clinical studies shock has been used as the unconditioned stimulus, although other forms of stimulation could, and perhaps should be used. What ordinarily is considered a laboratory study of conditioning is, in this case, a clinical test. In a typical example, a tone of a given intensity is sounded just before a shock is delivered. The child makes a reflexive motor response to the unpleasant shock. This procedure is repeated a number of times and then the shock is omitted. Does the child make the response to the tone that previously had been made only following the shock? In other words, has the tone become a conditioned stimulus, eliciting the conditioned motor response? If the procedure is unsuccessful and there is no evidence of conditioning, more paired presentations of the tone and shock are given, and if this still is unsuccessful the intensity of the tone is increased. By lengthening the number of trials and varying the loudness and pitch of the sound the possibility of establishing a conditioned response to sounds is either confirmed or rejected. If the initial phase of the testing is successful, the limits of hearing can be established by testing the child with other sounds than that initially used as the conditioned stimulus. These trials constitute tests for stimulus generalization; that is, they are tests made to determine whether other stimuli, similar to the conditioned stimulus, are capable of eliciting the conditioned response. Conditioning usually is restricted to the most difficult clinical cases, but in such instances it is a valuable addition to other tests in diagnosing sensory disorders. Although it has been used primarily in cases of suspected deafness, the method obviously is applicable to other sensory modalities, such as vision.

CONCLUSIONS

Studies of infant learning have relied on the conditioning procedure, not because psychologists are unimaginative in thinking of other methods, but because the limited behavioral repertoire of infants makes it difficult to devise methods other than those dependent upon the modification of simple responses. The studies provide clear demonstrations that the infant is very competent at learning. And he will learn if his world is ordered in a consistent fashion and if his responses are followed by meaningful consequences.

As the infant matures, his learning proceeds with increasing efficiency and smoothness. Generally, procedures that are effective at an early age will be more effective at a later age. At any age there are large individual differences in the rate of learning, for the same situation may have different effects, depending upon the child. The studies with infants temper the enthusiasm of both the eager environmentalist and of the ardent maturationalist. As is so often the case, the truth appears to lie somewhere between the two extremes. A given set of experiences will not be equally effective with all children or with the same children at an earlier age, but without experience there is little likelihood that many types of behavior will ever emerge.

4

The First Words

In this chapter we will begin our discussion of language, one of the most important acquisitions of the older infant, and trace changes that occur in the learning process as the child becomes capable of using and responding to words. Our attention will be concentrated on the first three years, the period in which sounds are transformed into words and words come to represent abstractions of reality. As we have seen, prior to the acquisition of language, much of the child's learning can be explained economically by the principles of classical and operant conditioning. In the way he learns, the preverbal child often appears to be much more similar to lower animals than to other humans. However, with the emergence of language the child can learn with a speed and efficiency that is never even approached by the highest nonhuman primates. The child becomes capable of using words as substitutes for objects and actions, and is thereby freed from his dependence on the physical world as a means of organizing his behavior. Words begin to have a directive influence on behavior; verbal instructions, from himself and from others, become effective instigators of action.

In this discussion we will rely heavily on the work of Soviet investigators, for they have spent a great deal of time studying the influence of language on the behavior of the young child. We will begin by discussing how words become capable of evoking response—what the Soviets call the *second signal system*. We then will discuss developmental changes in the voluntary control of behavior, especially those related to the development of inhibition. These two groups of studies illustrate two functions of language: the use of language as a means of representing the world of objects and events, and of directing and controlling behavior.

THE EMERGENCE OF LANGUAGE

Somewhere around the end of the first year the infant utters its first word. Usually, the word is a duplicated monosyllable, such as "mama" or "wawa," made spontaneously or in imitation of adult speakers. By saying that the infant has uttered his first word, we are implying that it has learned to isolate discrete sounds and to make them in the presence of a particular person or object. Or, as is frequently the case, the sounds are made to general classes of stimuli; he may call any person "mama," and any liquid "wawa."

By the end of the first year the child can respond to verbal instructions. When told, "Come to mother," the infant can understand and comply. During this period, the words used by the infant are predominantly nouns and verbs. Language at this stage has a "signal" function. Words are used to express what the infant wants or what he perceives. "Doggy," says the infant, and we immediately assume that he either wants his toy dog or sees a dog passing by. Words represent the here and now; there are no past and future tenses for the young infant. Only later are words used as symbols, expressing abstract states and functioning as inner representations of sequences of actions and events.

The few isolated words of the young infant form the antecedents of true communicative language. How this transition from naming to speaking occurs is still a matter of argument, but sometime before the second birthday, we usually hear the first simple sentence. The infant begins to use words to elicit behavior in others—"Go bye-bye!" And words may be used in the absence of the desired object, as when the infant calls its mother from an adjoining room. These are important steps. The physical stimulus does not need to be present to elicit the words. They are spoken in response to what goes on in the infant's own body, or, more significantly, to what goes on in the infant's own head.

The Second Signal System

Since the time of Pavlov, Soviet investigators have distinguished three types of stimuli that are effective in eliciting responses in human beings. We already have discussed two of these: unconditioned stimuli and conditioned stimuli. As we have seen in the discussion of classical conditioning, an initially neutral stimulus, if followed by an unconditioned stimulus, becomes capable of eliciting the response, or a portion of it, that was made earlier only to the unconditioned stimulus. The neutral stimulus then is designated as the conditioned stimulus. At this level, the organism is said to be under the control of the first signal system. This system is considered to be the primary basis of learning in lower animals and the first basis of learning in the human being.

For the human, however, sounds develop into words, and words develop meanings. Words as sounds may function as conditioned stimuli for lower animals. A dog can learn to come to his food dish when it hears the word *food*. Words as conveyors of meaning are assumed to be effective only with human beings. Only human beings appear to be able to use words as conceptual abstractions of reality. When this stage of development is reached the human child is said to come under the control of what the Soviet investigators call the second signal system. With the development of the second signal system, relations between stimuli and responses become much more complex. Because the second signal system is dependent upon a higher order of activity of the nervous system than is involved in establishing conditioned responses in the first signal system, studies of the second signal system are known as studies of higher order conditioning.

How does behavior come under the control of the second signal system? In much the same way that other types of conditioned responses are established. The procedure is as follows: After a stable conditioned response is developed, the presentation of the conditioned stimulus is preceded by a verbal signal. Eventually, the verbal signal becomes capable of eliciting the conditioned response. The second signal system activates the first signal system.

The whole process can be readily understood if we look at a typical study, in this case a study by Degtiar (1962; cited by Brackbill, 1967), who worked with children from 1½ to 3 years of age. In line with the results of other studies, Degtiar had no difficulty in developing a conditioned response (eyeblink) to the sound of a bell or the onset of a dim light. Once the conditioned response had been established, the words *bell* and *lamp* were spoken by the experimenter before presenting the auditory and visual stimuli. In time, the verbal stimuli alone were capable of eliciting the eyeblink. A primitive form of the second signal system was at work; concrete verbal representations were effective substitutes for the conditioned stimuli. Thus far, the results are unexciting, but when abstract verbal representations of the conditioned stimuli were used, namely, the Russian words for *sound* and *light*, there was immediate generalization of the conditioned response to these words for the older subjects. The younger subjects had given evidence prior to the experiment of knowing the meaning of these abstract words, but the words were not effective with these subjects in producing the conditioned response.

Look at what has happened. The eyeblink is no longer dependent upon the sounding of a bell; words are sufficient to elicit the response. With older children, even abstract words are effective. As the associative network among words continues to develop, even more complex relations among words become possible. The concept of the second signal system offers a means of explaining how behavior, once under the control of physical stimuli, eventually can be elicited by abstract words designating a class of stimuli of which the conditioned stimulus was a specific instance. Though this may sound mechanical, a great deal more is implied in the operation of the second signal system than the mere substitution of words for physical stimuli. Leont'ev (1961) has characterised the importance of the second signal system in the following manner:

> The stimuli of the second signal system are not therefore merely conditioned stimuli of the second order. They differ from the first signal system conditioned stimuli in that they represent in material form, capable of acting on man, the properties and relationships of objects in their generalized grouping and detached from the actual objects. It is for this reason that these stimuli form for men a special system of reality (Leont'ev, 1961, p. 235).

A second study further illustrates the operation and significance of the second signal system and introduces some of the variables that may enhance or reduce the system's effectiveness.

Koltsova (1967) worked with two-year-olds, again using eyelid conditioning. Two sets of stimuli were used with one group of subjects: geometrical forms and common objects. The presentation of geometrical forms was accompanied by the experimenter's saying the word thing and delivering a puff of air to the eye. When the common objects were presented, they never were followed by the word or the air-puff. One stimulus was presented at a time and a new stimulus was introduced only after stable conditioning (consistent eyeblink to the forms) or inhibition of response (consistent inhibition of the response to the objects) was established.

The subjects rapidly developed a conditioned discrimination; they learned to blink when the forms appeared and to inhibit the blink to the objects. By the time the fifth stimulus was presented, only one trial was needed to elicit an eyeblink to the forms or inhibition of this response to the figures. The word *thing* had generalized to all types of geometrical forms. (A more definitive test would have been devised, of course, if Koltsova had said *thing* in some of the trials without presenting the forms.) Another test of generalization was given after the completion of the conditioning trials. The children were shown a variety of geometrical forms and common objects, including some that had been used in the conditioning trials. When the children were asked to pick out a *thing*, clear differentiation was found. They picked out only geometrical figures. Koltsova concluded that the conditioned response had generalized across a class of stimuli, inhibition of response had occurred to members of a second class, and generalization of the word *thing* to new objects was affirmed in the postexperimental session.

The results for a second group of two-year-olds were quite different. For this group, small skeins of yarn of different colors were used as the conditioned stimuli, and a puff of air to the eye followed the presentation of each skein. The word *thing* accompanied only those skeins in which yellow predominated. For this group of two-year-olds, the verbal stimulus was irrelevant as a means of differentiating whether or not a stimulus would be followed by a puff of air. (It is not clear why Koltsova chose to use different stimuli for these subjects from those she had used for the first group of subjects.)

As in the first group, conditioning occurred with increasing rapidity as each new skein of yarn was presented—but only for the first few skeins. By the time the tenth skein of yarn had been presented the eyeblink became weak and unstable, and by the fifteenth, the conditioned eyeblink had been extinguished. A form of habituation had occurred; the monotonous and unchanging procedure had reduced the effectiveness of the stimuli as elicitors of the conditioned response. Furthermore, in tests of generalization made after the conditioning trials, no discrimination was found for the class of objects (the yellow skeins) denoted by the word 'thing.' The children chose any skein of yarn or the largest and brightest objects they could find. Their training had not been without effect, but the word *thing* had an imprecise meaning. Koltsova's results illustrate that learning to generalize is not independent of learning to discriminate. An abstract word can come to encompass a class of objects for the child if he learns the types of stimuli that comprise the class represented by the abstract word, and the types of stimuli that fall outside this class.

The Soviet account of the second signal system is a logical extension of their long tradition of attempting to discuss behavior in terms of classical conditioning. Whether or not we wish to accept their views, it must be said that something like the second signal system is operative in young children. Words are capable of producing responses that previously were produced only by a physical stimulus, and eventually abstract designations of concrete objects become effective stimuli. It is reasonable to assume that during the early years this occurs through the words being associated with the physical stimuli: the word *table* with a certain type of furniture, *kitty* with a certain type of animal, and so forth. But there seem to be limits in the degree to which classical conditioning is effective with young children. From the discussion thus far, one might assume that classical conditioning is a ubiquitous phenomenon. It is not. After early childhood it becomes increasingly difficult to establish stable responses through classical conditioning. Although conditioned responses can be established with older children, classical conditioning does not occur so readily as it does before the ages of four or five. To be assured that a conditioned response will appear with older children, investigators frequently must distract them or instruct them not to inhibit response. For example, Ross (1966) has shown that eyelid conditioning can be accomplished successfully with older children if, during the course of conditioning, they are distracted from the experimental procedure by viewing an interesting film. As far as the children are concerned, the experiment thereby becomes an incidental aspect of their presence in the experimental setting.

How can this change in susceptibility to classical conditioning be interpreted? It is not coincidental that conditionability wanes at about the time the child begins to be proficient in the use of language. What appears to happen is that the child interprets the conditioning situation as a test of his ability to control his behavior. He shows this control by making voluntary responses or by inhibiting responses to the conditioned stimulus. In eyelid conditioning, for example, voluntary responses can be readily distinguished from nonvoluntary responses in that the voluntary responses are more regular and are made more rapidly. Whereas language may facilitate other forms of learning, it is a means by which the child can disrupt the process of conditioning.

Voluntary Inhibition

The parent of a newborn can demonstrate how "strong" the baby is by placing a thin rod in the baby's palm. The baby grasps the rod and as the parent tugs the grasp becomes more and more firm. The baby may pull himself off the mattress if the parent persists in tugging.

The nine-month-old infant pulls himself to a standing position in his playpen. After a few moments he begins to scream. The parent finds he can calm the child by lowering him to a sitting position.

What have these observations in common? Let us look at the first example. The grasping reflex is a primitive response to stimulation of the infant's palm. As the stimulus input becomes more intense, the firmness of the grasp increases until it is finally weakened by fatigue. The mechanism for release of the grasp has not yet developed. In the second example the infant can pull himself up, but again, he is unable to reverse the process. There may be a notable lag between the time a child is capable of making a response and the time he is able to inhibit or reverse it. This lag between excitation and inhibition of response also is operative as the child begins to develop voluntary control of his own behavior. He can carry out an act as instructed before he is capable of complying with instructions to inhibit the act.

Of all the adaptations adults must make in interacting with young children, perhaps the most difficult is learning how to deter a child from performing a response the adult views as being undesirable. The verbally sophisticated adult can comply with the instruction *not* to do something as readily as with the instruction to pursue a particular act. Consequently, in their interactions with children, adults tend to expect that either form of instruction will be effective, "I have told you and told you," says the mother, "not to hit your baby sister!" But the two-year-old brother fails to heed the mother's demand.

A. R. Luria, one of the most influential Soviet psychologists, has described the early role of speech in directing the behavior of young children in the following way:

It would appear as if the power to respond to speech as a stimulus does not develop until the beginning of the second year. If we say to a child of one and a half years "hold out your hand" or "clap your hands," it is easy to obtain the appropriate response. However, careful observation will show that at this stage the effect of speech is still very limited, and if there is any conflict with some act the child may have started already, the order may be quite ineffectual. Following Shchelovanov we may tell a child who is putting on a stocking to take it off, or one who is taking rings off a stick to put them back, and it will be seen that the intended effect on the original act is not produced, but that on the contrary the action proceeds more vigorously. At this stage of development, a child's actions are dominant and adult speech has merely a release function; it is not able to suppress an act already begun and still less to deflect a child from one task to another (Luria, 1961, p. 166).

Many studies have been conducted by Luria and his associates indicating that the young child's failure to comply with negative instructions is a result of his immaturity, rather than his perversity. The studies by S. V. Yakovleva (discussed by Luria, 1961) offer useful illustrations of the stages through which the child is assumed to go before he is capable of voluntary inhibition of response. A young child is given a rubber bulb and told to squeeze it. The 1½-year-old has no difficulty in carrying out this instruction. The child then is told "Stop pressing," but at this age the instruction is ineffective. The child does not inhibit his response and rather than stop pressing, actually may press the bulb more vigorously.

Now let the instruction be changed slightly: "When the light comes on, squeeze the bulb." Since the child has shown that he is capable of complying with a direct positive instruction, this might be considered an insignificant modification of the original instruction. But we cannot reach this conclusion too quickly. By asking the child to wait until the light comes on, we are asking him to inhibit response until the appropriate signal has appeared. If inhibition of response is difficult for the child at this age, the modified instruction should be extremely difficult to follow. This is found to be the case; the child cannot carry out the instruction. He either presses the bulb harder, or ceases to respond.

These examples illustrating the ineffectiveness of instructions in producing inhibition of response would seem to imply that the adult is powerless in his attempts to dissuade the child from making an undesired response. Not completely. Would it not be possible to instruct the child to perform another response that is incompatible with the undesired response, rather than instructing him to inhibit the response? This was easily accomplished in the situation we have been discussing. The child was instructed to squeeze the bulb and then move his hand away. The child squeezed the bulb, and, in following the second aspect of the instruction, was forced to cease squeezing the bulb. Could the mother, in our earlier example, have been successful in halting her son's hitting by instructing him to perform another, incompatible response, such as rocking the baby's crib? Many parents and preschool teachers have found this type of practice to be effective with young children. Books on child care often emphasize the importance of giving the child an alternative positive instruction rather than relying so frequently on instructions involving *do not*. Studies such as the one just discussed offer a rationale for this advice.

Let use now introduce a three-year-old to the bulb-pressing task. In contrast to the younger child, the three-year-old is capable of following the instructions to press the bulb, to stop pressing, and to wait until a signal appears before pressing. When the instructions are a bit more complicated, however, he also fails. For example, he is unable to follow the instruction: "when the lamp lights, press twice." The child cannot regulate his behavior by this instruction and perseverates after the second press. If, however, he has been taught to count "One, two," and is instructed to count as he presses, he will be able to follow the instruction successfully.

Another example illustrates the tenuous control words have over the behavior of the three-year-old. Two lights are used. The child is trained to say "I must press" to one light, (the positive light) and "I must not press" to the second light (the negative light). Later, when the lights are presented in a random fashion, the child makes the appropriate verbal response, but presses to both lights. Saying "I must not press" did not result in inhibition of pressing. Then the procedure is changed slightly. The child is taught to say "I must press" to the positive light and to say nothing to the negative light. Appropriate response and inhibition of response occurs. Trying to follow the two instructions is confusing; a single positive instruction is adequate.

From these examples we can see that being able to follow positive and negative instructions are not complementary processes. The one-year-old is capable of the first, but not until the age of four or five is the second securely established. The young child's inability to inhibit response is not due to his failure to understand the meaning of the instructions. Words simply do not have the directive influence on behavior that they will when language is more fully developed. There are two important aspects to this development. With increasing age, the linguistic system becomes more elaborate and closer relations are established between words and actions. The child's opportunities for learning have an important influence on both, but regardless of the child's linguistic competence a certain level of maturation of the central nervous system appears to be necessary before voluntary inhibition of response is possible.

INTERNALIZED SPEECH

Responding to instructions from others is the first step toward the child's eventually being able to direct his own behavior. As the little girl approaches the street corner with her mother the mother says, "Look both ways." Later, when the child is at the corner by herself we hear her saying, "Look both ways," as she looks first in one direction and then the other. When she is older she will approach the corner, look both ways, but we no longer will hear her repeat the instruction. She has internalized the command; she performs correctly without the manifest aid of speech.

Luria (1957) has described the developmental changes in the process whereby the directive functions of speech become internalized in the following way:

Observations have also disclosed that the child's speech, which directs his solutions of a problem, is at first unabbreviated and full; but that later, as he masters his actions, it becomes increasingly abbreviated and contracted. First, the child ceases to say everything aloud and in full; his speech sinks to a whisper, its grammatical structure becomes contracted and broken, he begins to utter only separate words indicating necessary objects or actions at critical points; after a time his speech ceases, and he begins to perform his task in silence. Occasionally, when children utter stray remarks, the fact that speech has not disappeared, but has only taken new concealed forms, is revealed. Full, overt speech, therefore, gradually becomes transformed into contracted, internal speech. This internal speech, however, continues to fulfill the same function, that of mobilizing the systematic connections of past experience, which may be useful for orientation in the new conditions and for the regulation of future actions. The child's speech, in this contracted form, is indissolubly linked with his thinking, and continues to share in those forms of activity which the child now performs in silence (Luria, 1957, p. 117).

By the fourth or fifth year, the child is capable of organizing his behavior according to the meaning conveyed in instructions, rather than depending upon words as signals for response. At this time, instructions can determine the responses that will be made; the environment influences behavior primarily in providing the context for applying the instructions and in verifying the correctness of response. The smooth and silent performance of the five-year-old will break down, however, if the instructions prove to be too complex or confusing. This is characteristic not only of young children. Any adult receiving complicated directions in a strange city will find himself relying on explicit reiteration of the instructions as he attempts to carry them out.

AMERICAN STUDIES OF LURIA'S VIEWS

Even though we may accept Luria's general conclusion that the directive functions of language are slow to develop, we must be cautious in accepting his chronology of this development. Several American investigators have sought to replicate Luria's studies, but this has not proved to be an easy task, for Luria's reports are inexplicit about such essential details as the type and degree of preliminary experience given the children, the intensities and durations of the stimuli, and the children's levels of verbal facility. Because it is so difficult to reproduce Luria's experimental conditions, failures to replicate his results do not mean that his ideas are discredited, but they do raise serious questions about the generality of the hypotheses his studies are assumed to support.

One of the American studies (Beiswenger, 1968) is not a critical test of Luria's views, for although positive and negative instructions were given by the experimenter, none of the children were instructed to verbalize themselves. The children were told to depress a plunger in a clown's nose when a green light appeared, but not to make this response when the light was red. As might be expected, there was a rapid increase between the ages of 41 and 78 months in the children's ability to respond correctly to these instructions. Only 59% of the youngest children, but 96% of the oldest children, were able to do so.

Three other studies (Jarvis, 1968; Miller, Shelton & Flavell, 1970; Wilder, 1968) compared children's performance when they were required to verbalize positive and negative self-instructions with that occurring when no instructions to verbalize were given. These studies constitute more relevant tests of Luria's position, for according to Luria the different conditions should have different effects, depending upon the child's age. The results were negative. The major conclusions in each study were that performance improved in all conditions with increasing age, but that the effects of self-instructions did not differ according to the child's age. Since these are among the first non-Soviet studies to explore Luria's ideas they merit closer attention.

The first study (Jarvis, 1968) included four groups of children, with mean ages of 47, 59, 72, and 81 months. The children were shown a drawing of a rabbit's head that had eyes that lit up with colored lights. Below the head was a large button. One-third of the children at each age level performed silently, one-third were instructed to say "Push" when the correct color appeared (and prior to pressing the button), and one-third were instructed to say "Don't push" when the incorrect color appeared. Verbalizing had no distinctive effects on performance at any age level. The older children performed more effectively than the younger children, but as far as Luria's hypotheses were concerned, the results were negative.

A similar study, with similar results, was reported by Wilder (1968). Three- and five-year-olds were told to squeeze a clown's nose as fast as they could when they saw a particular light. There were trials in which only this light flashed and trials in which this light alternated with another, irrelevant light. Generally, five-year-olds were more efficient than three-year-olds, but saying "Go" before squeezing produced no greater difference in performance at three than it did at five. Interestingly, an analysis of mistakes indicated that the errors of the younger children were primarily ones of omission; that is, they failed to follow their verbal response with the motor response. For these children, speech tended to replace rather than facilitate the motor response.

By far the most extensive study is that of Miller, Shelton, and Flavell (1970). There were more children (160) and they were younger than those used in the other studies. The mean ages of the four groups of children included in the study were 3.2, 3.6, 4.1, and 4.9 years. The authors purposefully chose younger children on the assumption that the children in the preceding studies may have been too old to benefit from explicit self-instructions. This assumption proved to be incorrect, for no differential effects of the various experimental conditions were found at any age level. There were four conditions. One-fourth of the children at each age level performed silently, one-fourth were told to say "Squeeze" prior to responding to the correct light, one-fourth were told to say "Don't squeeze" to the incorrect light, and one-fourth were told to verbalize both statements. The authors frequently found it difficult to get the children to verbalize before making the motor response; many of the children squeezed and then repeated the self-instruction.

Where these studies leave Luria's hypotheses is not clear. At best, we must consider Luria's idea as more tentative than they may have appeared. It will take many more studies before we have a firm grasp of the intricate relations that exist between language and other forms of behavior. Luria's work may have had its greatest impact in stimulating others to investigate how these relations develop. [For a further discussion of this general topic, see Wozniak (1971.)]

CONCLUSIONS

This is the first of several chapters dealing with the role of language in learning. The primary emphasis in this chapter has been on the role of language in representing the external world and in directing behavior.

As we have seen, words exert a powerful influence on behavior, making the behavior of the young child more complex than any found in lower animals. Perhaps the major message in the discussion, however, is to point out how verbally sophisticated adults may be prone to overestimate how well the young child can control his behavior by means of words. It is no coincidence that educators have chosen the ages of five to six as the time for beginning school. Present evidence appears to indicate that not until this time can the average child utilize language effectively as a means of abstracting from his experience and of directing his own behavior. We will have a good deal more to say about this point in the next few chapters.

5

Words as Labels

A group of three-year-olds is seated with their nursery school teacher, looking at a book with illustrations of houses. There is a lively interchange between teacher and children: "What kind of a house is this? It is an apartment house. Where do we find apartment houses? That's right, in cities. And what kind of a house is this? Yes, an igloo. Who lives in igloos? And this is a . . . a what kind of house? A pueblo." The group proceeds through the book, naming each type of dwelling. Young children want to know the names of what they see. In looking at a book, they often appear to be more interested in knowing what is depicted in the illustrations than in following the narrative of the story.

We have discussed the role of words in eliciting and directing responses. In this chapter we will discuss the functions of words as labels and how the acquisition of such labels influences the learning process. As soon as the infant begins to be responsive to words, parents begin the long process of labeling. The parent holds up an object and says, "Ball. Ball. This is a ball." At first, the utterance serves primarily to call the infant's attention to the object being presented. When the parent speaks, the infant looks at the parent and at the object. Attending to the spoken word proves to be pleasurable; the sounds are varied, the objects are continually changing, and he has the attention of his parents.

Words begin to be used as a means of differentiating among objects: "Where's the ball? Where's the bunny?" The child learns not only to look at the object, but also to discriminate between objects on the basis of their labels. The object and word become tightly interrelated. It is no joke to the two-year-old to have the parent play word games with him by calling a ball a bunny. He responds with irritation: "No! That's a *ball.*" By the time the child is four or five, the game may be funny and it may be amusing for the child to initiate such games himself.

Labels serve many purposes. Among the more important is their influence on the ease with which children can identify and discriminate among objects. We can illustrate this point with an example. A child is looking at pictures of jungle animals. When asked to find the tiger he points correctly, but when asked about two other animals he makes errors. He points to the lion instead of the leopard and the leopard instead of the lion. Is the tiger easier to identify because it has a more distinctive name? Does the child confuse the lion and leopard partly because the two names sound more similar?

Figure 5-1. In the pretraining period in studies of acquired distinctiveness of cues, S_1 and S_1' are two different, but similar, stimuli to which distinctive verbal responses, R_a and R_b are learned. The distinctive stimuli, S_a and S_b, produced by these verbal responses form part of the total stimulus complexes to which the individual must learn new responses, R_1 and R_2, during the experimental period. If the response-produced stimuli are highly distinctive, the stimulus complexes will be more distinctive during the experimental task than would have been the case had no verbal responses been learned. For studies of acquired equivalence of cues, S_1 and S_2 are dissimilar stimuli to which two similar verbal responses, R_a and R_a' are learned. The similar stimuli, S_a and S_a', produced by these verbal responses form part of the total stimulus complexes to which the individual must learn new responses, R_1 and R_2. Performance in the experimental task should be impaired by the greater similarity of S_1 and S_2 produced by the addition of the similar verbally produced stimuli, S_a and S_a'.

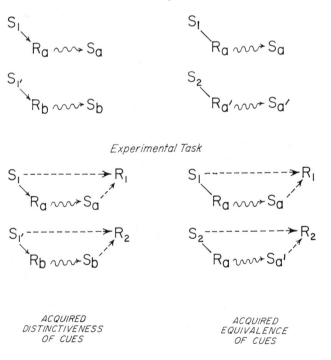

Pretraining

Experimental Task

ACQUIRED
DISTINCTIVENESS
OF CUES

ACQUIRED
EQUIVALENCE
OF CUES

In this chapter we will discuss the experimental evidence related to the question of whether labels increase the distinctiveness of objects and thereby modify the child's responses to them. The discussion is guided by two complementary hypotheses that have been offered to deal with this possibility: the hypotheses of *acquired distinctiveness* of cues and of *acquired equivalence* of cues.

The hypothesis of acquired distinctiveness of cues proposes that learning to respond to similar stimuli with highly distinctive names makes the total stimulus complex embodied in each cue more distinctive. The stimulus complex is viewed as consisting of the external stimulus and the stimuli produced by the distinctive verbal response (see Figure 5-1). For example, the stimuli could be similar but not identical drawings of girl's faces for which the names Lucy and Alma are learned. It is assumed in each case that the stimulus complex (picture plus name) is made more distinctive through learning the dissimilar names.

According to the hypothesis of acquired equivalence of cues, learning to respond to different stimuli with highly similar names is assumed to make the two stimulus complexes appear more similar. In this case, if the two drawings of girls' faces were labeled "Anne" and "Annie," their later identification would presumably be harder than if their names were Lucy and Alma, and also, theoretically, harder than if there were no labels. Applying similar names to the two stimuli is predicted to impair the efficiency with which the two stimuli can be discriminated in subsequent situations.

Before discussing these hypotheses further, it is of interest to point out that many persons faced with the practical problems of teaching children to read have adopted the hypothesis of acquired distinctiveness of cues, knowingly or not, in developing their training techniques. Learning to read is, in part, a matter of learning to discriminate among the letters of the alphabet. Proposals have been offered for increasing the distinctiveness of the different letters as a means of facilitating later learning. The distinctiveness is increased in these cases not by verbal labels, but by introducing stimuli related to other sensory modalities. Some persons have required the child to trace the outline of each letter as he says its name in an effort to add distinctive kinesthetic cues to the visual and auditory cues associated with each letter. It is assumed that the distinctiveness of the visual stimuli is increased by adding the kinesthetic cues. Other persons have constructed letters with different tactual qualities by attaching materials such as sandpaper and velvet to the tops of letters. Here, tactual as well as kinesthetic cues are present as the child traces each letter. Others have color-coded the alphabet. Vowels are painted different pastel colors and letters with hard sounds are coded in shades of blue or green. Common color groupings are used to emphasize the similarity of certain sounds and within these sound groups different hues are used to distinguish different letters. Behind all these techniques is the idea that later discrimination among letters will be facilitated if the differences among the letters are enhanced by the addition of other, distinctive attributes.

ACQUIRED DISTINCTIVENESS OF CUES

Studies investigating the hypothesis of acquired distinctiveness of cues have involved various elaborations of a basic procedure. The procedure for this type of study is divided into two parts, a pretraining period and a period of discrimination learning. During the pretraining period the child is shown a set of two or more relatively similar objects and is told their names. The names have been selected as being highly distinctive. When the child has learned the correct name for each object, the discrimination learning task is introduced. Learning labels for the objects during pretraining is hypothesized to aid the child later in learning to discriminate among the objects by increasing their distinctiveness.

Procedure for Studying Discrimination Learning

Before proceeding, the procedure used in discrimination learning tasks should be described in somewhat greater detail. From the child's point of view discrimination learning tasks may be difficult, but from the point of view of the experimenter such tasks are quite simple. The experimenter shows a child two or more objects, such as a circle and a square, and he tells the child he is going to hide a reward under one of the objects. The child is to try to find it. The experimenter consistently hides the reward under the square. Will the child learn to choose the square in preference to the circle? In other words, will he learn to discriminate between the two objects, selecting the correct one and rejecting the other?

The apparatus in a discrimination learning task typically consists of a tray containing wells into which rewards can be placed and a movable screen to shield the experimenter as he arranges the stimuli over the wells. The rewards may vary from a token used to designate correct response to a prize of some value. Prior to testing each child one stimulus is designated at random as the correct one and the child's choice of this stimulus yields the reward. In most studies the correct stimulus differs for different children. In the task described above, for example, half of the children would be rewarded for choices of the square and half would be rewarded for choices of the circle. During the experimental trials the positions of the stimuli and other irrelevant cues are randomized so that only a discrimination between the relevant aspects of the stimuli can result in consistently correct response. Most studies use the noncorrection method, whereby the child is given only one choice on each trial. If the choice is incorrect the trial is terminated and the child receives no reward. (In the correction method the child is allowed to continue to respond on each trial until he selects the correct stimulus.) Trials are continued until the correct stimulus is chosen so frequently that the child's performance cannot be attributed to chance.

Experimental Data

A typical experiment on acquired distinctiveness of cues is that of Norcross and Spiker (1957) in which preschool children were pretrained with pictures of faces. During the pretraining trials one group learned distinctive names ("Jean" and "Peg") for drawings of two female faces; a second learned distinctive names ("Jack" and "Pete") for drawings of two male faces; and a third had to respond to the pairs of the female faces by saying "same" or "different," depending upon whether or not the two faces presented on each trial were identical. Pretraining was continued for each group until 12 consecutive correct responses were made. Following pretraining the children were presented a discrimination learning task in which the two female faces were the discriminative stimuli. The children were shown the two faces mounted on wooden cubes and told that if they chose the correct one they would find a marble hidden underneath. The point of the game was to find as many marbles as possible, for at the end of the study the marbles could be exchanged for a prize.

Each group served a particular purpose. The labels, "Jean" and "Peg," learned by the first group presumably increased the distinctiveness of the two female faces the children were required to learn to discriminate between in the discrimination learning task. The second group that learned distinctive labels for male faces was introduced to test whether learning was facilitated by prior experience in learning names and in differentiating the relevant characteristics of stimuli. To discriminate between the male faces it was necessary to attend to the same characteristics (hair, eyes, and nose) that differentiated the two female faces. The third group of children had relevant experience in discriminating between the two female faces during pretraining, but they were given no opportunity to learn distinctive names for the two faces. Comparison of the performance of the first and third groups on later discrimination learning is perhaps the most crucial for evaluating the hypothesis of acquired distinctiveness. Both groups had pretraining experience with the female faces, but only the first group had learned distinctive names.

Thirty trials were given on the discrimination learning task. The group of children who had learned distinctive names for the female faces chose the correct face significantly more often than did the other two groups. The children who had learned distinctive labels for the discriminative stimuli thus performed more effectively in discrimination learning than did the children who had been given the other two forms of pretraining. The second and third groups did not differ significantly from each other in the frequency with which they chose the correct face. Learning to attend to the critical features of the discriminative stimuli (the third group) and pretraining in learning labels for a different set of stimuli (the second group) had equivalent effects on later discrimination learning. The results appear to support the hypothesis of acquired distinctiveness of cues.

A problem clouds the interpretation of these findings. The children found it more difficult to learn the names of the female faces in pretraining than to determine whether or not a pair of faces was identical. The mean number of pretraining trials differed (13.4 versus 5.5) for the first and third groups, the most important groups in assessing the validity of the hypothesis under investigation. This problem did not prove to be a critical one. When the study was repeated (Spiker & Norcross, 1962), equating the number of pretraining trials for the three groups, the results were comparable to those found in the original study.

Number of pretraining trials also was controlled in a study by Norcross (1958). Each child was required to learn distinctive names for one pair of stimuli and nondistinctive names for a second pair during pretraining. The stimuli were line drawings of Indian faces—a pair of boys' faces and a pair of girls' faces. The similar names were "zim" and "zam" and the distinctive names were "wug" and "kos." Half of the children learned the distinctive names for the boys' faces and the similar names for the girls' faces. The pairings were reversed for the other half of the subjects. Both pairs were presented during pretraining until the children were able to name each face correctly. Both pairs of faces were used in the discrimination learning task. The children had to learn which of the two boys' faces was correct and which of the two girls' faces was correct. As predicted from the hypotheses of acquired distinctiveness and equivalence of cues, performance on the discrimination learning task revealed more rapid learning for the pair of faces with distinctive names than for the pair with similar names.

There is little disagreement among these and other studies that discrimination learning is facilitated if the child learns distinctive names for the stimuli during pretraining and that the relative distinctiveness of the names significantly affects the degree of facilitation that will occur. [For a thorough review of these studies, see Cantor (1965).] The studies do not, however, provide definitive tests of the hypothesis that the stimulus characteristics are changed by the addition of verbal labels. Other interpretations may be made. For example, knowing names for the stimuli may make it possible for the child to spend the time between the discrimination learning trials rehearsing the response that is correct; that is, the child could tell himself, "Kos is correct" (Spiker, 1956). Errors in rehearsal would presumably be greater if the stimuli possessed similar names than if the names were distinctive. The confusion in this case would not be between the faces but between the names.

A more convincing demonstration of the tenability of the hypothesis of acquired distinctiveness of cues is found in a study by Katz (1963), who showed that the similarity of names given to different stimuli influenced both the difficulty of discrimination learning and the likelihood that children would show perceptual confusion. The study was conducted in three stages. Three experimental groups were constituted on the basis of the experience provided during the initial, pretraining stage. The children were seven- and nine-year-olds. In group I, the children learned to associate four nonsense syllables, RIC, JAN, SOL, and BUZ, with four irregularly shaped "nonsense" figures. A different nonsense syllable was associated with each figure. Only two of the nonsense syllables were used with Group II, and each was attached to two of the figures. Group III did not learn to name the figures, but merely counted the number of times the figures were presented during the pretraining period, which for all groups consisted of 150 trials. There were, then, three groups: one that learned distinctive labels for each figure, one that learned common labels for pairs of the figures, and a third group that learned no labels.

During the second stage the children were required to make judgments about whether pairs of figures were the same or different. All possible pairings of the figures were presented, and on each trial the child was to press buttons labeled "same" or "different," depending upon his perception of the figures. This is an important stage in the experiment. A test of perceptual discrimination offers somewhat more conclusive evidence that the words had an influence (or lack of influence) on perceptual processes than can be obtained by computing the number of correct or incorrect responses in discrimination learning.

The figures were presented by means of a tachistoscope, a device for controlling the rate of presentation and illumination of the figures. The figures were seen only briefly, 0.2 sec., on each of 28 trials. According to the hypotheses of acquired distinctiveness and equivalence of cues, the number of errors made by the children in the three groups should differ. The most relevant test of the hypotheses would be to determine the number of errors made on the 10 trials in which pairs of nonidentical figures were presented. Children who had learned common labels for pairs of figures should respond to the figures as being identical more frequently than should those who had learned distinctive labels. The results supported this prediction. Nearly twice as many errors (judging the different figures as being the same) were made on these 10 trials by the group possessing common labels than by the group possessing distinctive labels mean $= 4.3$ and 1.9, respectively). The group that had learned no labels made an intermediate number of errors (mean $= 3.1$). Verbal labels did seem to influence the perceptual characteristics of the stimuli in the manner proposed by the two hypotheses.

A series of discrimination learning trials constituted the third stage of the experiment. Three of the four figures were used on these trials; two necessarily were figures for which the children in Group II had learned a common label. The "correct" stimulus always was one of the latter two stimuli. The frequencies of correct response made by the three groups of children in 50 trials, the maximum allowed, were in line with the results of the earlier studies. When common labels had been learned in the first stage, there was an average of only 16.3 correct responses in the discrimination learning task; when distinctive labels had been learned, 25.9; and when no labels had been learned, 21.2. The presence of common or distinctive labels had significantly influenced the process of discrimination learning.

According to the hypothesis under investigation, the impairment or facilitation of performance in the discrimination learning task is attributable to the influence of labels on the perception of the figures—as opposed to the influence of labels as mediators or in the acquisition of associations. For example, the number of confusions between figures should be greater when two figures share a common label than when distinctive labels have been attached to these two figures. Since three figures were used in the discrimination learning task, it was possible to compute an index of this confusion. For this purpose, children's performance was assessed on the trial following each rewarded trial. If labels make the stimuli perceptually more similar, the children who learned common labels for pairs of figures should have a greater tendency than the children in the other groups to choose either the rewarded figure or the figure sharing the same name on the trial after a previous choice had led to reward. Support was found for this prediction. Children who had learned common labels tended to choose the second figure with the same label about as often as they chose the previously rewarded figures, approximately 40% of the time in each case. On the other hand, children who had learned distinctive labels for the three stimuli chose the rewarded stimulus approximately 80% of the time on the subsequent trial, and chose the figure which for the preceding group had a common label, less than 20% of the time. Intermediate percentages were found for the children who had not learned labels. The overall findings of this study indicate, therefore, that labels may have a significant effect on perception, as revealed both in judgments of stimulus similarity and in the types of errors made in discrimination learning. In a later study (Katz & Zigler, 1969) involving only the first two stages of the present design, verbal labels again were found to influence children's perceptual judgments. The effects were more pronounced with seven-year-olds than with nine-year-olds, and identical labels had a greater effect on the incidence of "same" judgments when the members of each pair of nonsense figures were highly dissimilar than when they were similar to each other. These two studies come as close as any that have been reported to providing critical tests of the hypotheses of acquired distinctiveness and equivalence of cues.

CONCLUSIONS

Results from the studies that have been discussed are in line with predictions from the hypotheses of acquired distinctiveness and equivalence of cues. This does not mean, however, that we can accept the hypotheses as the most effective means of interpreting the data. It is difficult in considering these hypotheses to decide at what level they are to be discussed. Do they imply, for example, that the children in the study by Katz really *perceived* the two figures with common labels as being similar? Did the distinctive or common labels enhance or reduce the perceptual differences among the stimuli, or were the differences in performance due to verbal, rather than perceptual factors? Might not the children have assumed the figures were functionally equivalent because they shared a common label? Could not the children's discriminative responses have been elicited by the verbal labels, rather than by the figures themselves? If this were the case, the same predictions would have been made, but the results would be attributed to the effects of labels as mediators of response and not to the effects of labels in modifying perceptual cues. We have little basis within these studies for deciding among these alternative explanations.

For the present, we must consider the hypotheses of acquired distinctiveness and equivalence of cues as convenient, but not as the sole means of summarizing a body of data. Perhaps future studies will show an alternative hypothesis to be more powerful. Despite these problems of interpretation, the present data leave us with the important fact that labels may aid or confuse us in discriminating among stimuli, depending upon the types of words that are selected as labels. We may expect that whatever is done to increase the distinctiveness of stimuli by means of verbal labels will be of help when we subsequently are required to respond differentially to these stimuli.

6

Words as Mediators of Response

Let us draw some figures on pieces of cardboard—a small square, a large square, and a middle-sized square, each on a separate card; a small circle, a large circle, and middle-sized circle; and so on, with triangles, rectangles, and ellipses. Let us now place one set of figures, say the three squares, before a three-year-old. "See these cards? One of the cards is a lucky card. Each time you point to the lucky card, I will give you one of these prizes." After the child makes his choice the cards are rearranged (to prevent his learning to choose a particular position rather than a particular card) and the child is given another trial. When the lucky card is chosen trial after trial in a consistent fashion, a new set of three figures is presented, now the three circles. Each time a new set of cards is introduced, the child must ascertain which two cards never are lucky and which one consistently yields a prize. A prize is given only for choices of the middle-sized figure. Three-year-olds learn this kind of problem very slowly. When we repeat the procedure with six-year-olds, he learns very rapidly. After a few sets of figures have been presented he is able to respond correctly on his first choice. Before he leaves, we ask him how he knew which was the lucky card. "Well," he replied, "it was always the middle-sized picture."

The six-year-old has given us a clue about another important function of words—their utility as mediators of response. We assume the child told himself, as he told us, "It is always the middle-sized picture." By knowing the term "middle-sized" and by learning its relevance for this task, he was eventually able to respond correctly the first time a new set of figures was presented. It was unnecessary for him to go through the laborious process of finding out which figure in each set of three was the lucky one. His response was determined principally by the words he used, rather than by the figures he saw.

The three-year-old did not appear to have learned the relevance of the term "middle-sized" for the solution of the problem. To our parting question he answered, "I knew it was the lucky card because you gave me a prize." A repetition of the question produced bewilderment: "I just knew." He could tell us nothing about the characteristic of the cards that had been critical for correct response. Being unable to apply the term "middle-sized," or perhaps by not knowing it, he was forced to respond to each set of cards as if they constituted a new problem, finding out what he could through trial and error.

When the child's experiences can be summarized or coded by means of words, learning can occur with greater rapidity, effectiveness, and generality. Words enable the child to form rules. They become a dominant factor in thinking. Concepts gain firmness and durability when they can be put in the form of words. Before the child can use words to govern his behavior, he must act in order to know. Later, he may use words to short-circuit action; behavior may be guided by the application of rules, concepts, or other components of the inner world of thought.

The period between the ages of three and six is a transition period. During very early childhood language has not been acquired. Later, words may be understood but are not easily used. By the age of six or seven, most children are able to use words with facility and dispatch. The development between the ages of about three and six of the ability to use words as substitutes for action is one of the most significant accomplishments of childhood. Because of its importance, this period has received a great deal of attention by child psychologists. Many writers have discussed this period, and a number of different interpretations of the influences of language on behavior have been offered. In this and the next few chapters we will be concerned with one of these interpretations, that embodied in the hypothesis of verbal mediation. This hypothesis was proposed by stimulus-response theorists as a means of discussing the relation between language and learning.

Mediation theory is not restricted to verbal mediation, but it is to the studies of verbal mediation that we will direct our attention here. Several large bodies of research are based on this hypothesis, among them studies of transposition, reversal and nonreversal shifts, and verbal learning. Each group of studies will be discussed in turn in the next several chapters. Our purpose will be to trace the development of the hypothesis in studies of children's learning and to evaluate its success in accounting for the experimental data. Before turning to the larger groups of studies, it is desirable to describe the hypothesis in detail, together with illustrative experiments.

VERBAL MEDIATION

What do we mean when we suggest that words may be mediators of response? Generally, we mean that overt response to a stimulus is based on verbalizations which are in turn controlled by the stimulus.

Something like the concept of mediation has been used frequently to account for the fact that certain acts, intervening between perception and overt response, have a determining influence on the form that overt response will take. Mediational theories regard a mediator as a response or series of responses evoked by the external stimulus that intercede between the perception of the external stimulus and overt response. Mediating responses usually are assumed to be covert or implicit, although in some cases they may be observable. In studies of verbal mediation, it is assumed that the external stimuli evoke the verbal mediator and that the stimuli produced by the mediator lead to, or become associated with, the overt response.

As can be seen in Figure 6-1, the components of the verbal mediation paradigm are the same as those depicted in Figure 5-1 illustrating the hypothesis of acquired distinctiveness of cues. The important factor distinguishing these two hypotheses is the role assigned to the response-produced stimuli. In the hypothesis of acquired distinctiveness the response-produced stimuli are incorporated in the stimulus complex, while in the verbal mediation hypothesis they are assigned a mediating function. The two hypotheses offer different interpretations of the effects of words on performance, which, as we have seen in the previous chapter, may sometimes lead to similar predictions.

The Intermediate-size Problem

We began our discussion with an anecdotal account of children's performance on an intermediate-size problem. We do not need to rely on anecdotes, however, for this problem has been investigated extensively in the context of the hypothesis of verbal mediation. Our discussion was based on the assumption that the older, successful child was capable of

Figure 6-1. This figure illustrates the hypothesized differences between the young, "preverbal" child and the older, "verbal" child. The overt response (R) of the preverbal child is assumed to be dependent on the characteristics of the external stimulus (S). The overt response of the "verbal" child, however, may be produced by the external stimulus or through the process of verbal mediation. In the latter case, the external stimulus is assumed to elicit a verbal response (R_V) and the stimuli (S_V) produced by this response may elicit, or be associated with the overt response.

"Preverbal" child   *"Verbal" child*

$$S \longrightarrow R \qquad\qquad S \longrightarrow R$$
$$R_V \rightsquigarrow S_V$$

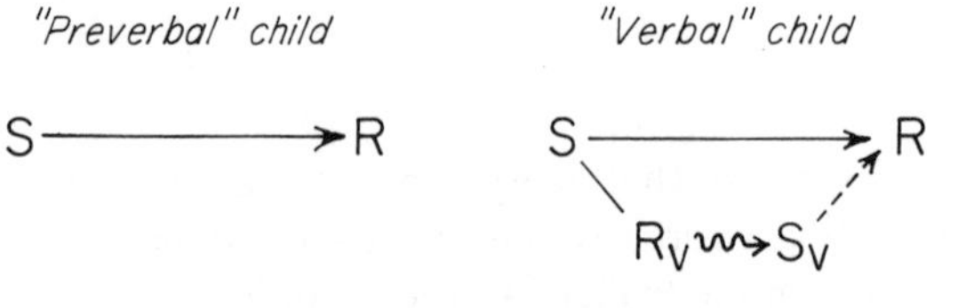

using verbal mediation to guide his performance, while the younger child was not. One of the first studies to test the validity of such an assumption was reported by Spiker, Gerjuoy, and Shepard (1956).

The study by Spiker et al. was designed to determine whether children's performance in the intermediate-size problem would differ according to whether or not they possessed an appropriate verbal label. Two groups of children were selected on the basis of their performance in a preliminary test. In this preliminary test children between the ages of 40 and 67 months were shown sets of cards bearing figures of different relative sizes. In an effort to elicit the term "middle-sized' or "medium-sized," they were told, "This is the big one, this is the little one, and this is the _____." If the child was unable to use the term he was asked to point to the middle-sized card. From 84 children tested, the experimenters selected 30 who responded consistently with the correct term and 30 who were unable to use the term or to point correctly on instruction. On the average the children who possessed the concept of middle-size were 5½ months older than those who did not.

Several days after the preliminary test the children who had been selected for the study were brought back for the experimental trials. Thirty cards, each containing three black squares, were constructed for these trials. Seven different squares were used; the smallest square had an area of ¼ square inch and the largest, 16 square inches. On each card the ratio of the areas of the squares was 1:2:4. With seven squares it is possible to construct five such sets of squares. One card, for example, would contain squares of 2, 4, and 8 square inches; another, squares of ¼, ½, and 1 square inch. Six linear arrangements of three squares are possible (e.g., from left to right: large, small, medium; large, medium, small; medium, large, small; etc.); therefore, for each of the five sets of three squares there were six cards, each with a different linear arrangement. There was, then, a total of 30 different cards (five sets of squares, each in six linear arrangements). These cards were used to form two tasks. In Task A each child was presented only one of the five possible sets of squares. Each of the six cards containing this set of squares was presented five times, generating a series of 30 trials. In Task B, each of the 30 cards was presented once. Correct response in all cases required pointing to the middle-sized square. Half of the children were given Task A and half, Task B.

Task A is relatively easy. The children merely had to learn which of three squares was correct, ignoring differences in their relative position on the card. Task B is more difficult. Solution of this task on a trial and error basis would be tedious. It would devolve into a much simpler problem, however, if the child could apply the term "middle-sized" in the course of his performance. The results were in line with the hypothesis that ease of learning is increased when children are capable of relevant mediation. On Task A there was relatively little difference in the mean number of correct responses for children who had and had not been able to use the term "middle-sized" (mean = 24.6 and 22.6, respectively). On Task B, however, the two groups performed in a widely divergent manner. Those who had been able to use the term "middle-sized" correctly in the preliminary test performed nearly as well on this task as did the comparable group of children tested with Task A, but children who had not demonstrated such knowledge performed at only a chance level. The mean numbers of correct responses for the two groups were 21.4 and 10.2, respectively. The results appear to indicate that although verbal mediation may have a modest effect in learning a simple task, failure to mediate may prevent children from learning when the task is made more complex.

The hypothesis was tested in a somewhat different fashion by Stevenson and McBee (1958). Again a size discrimination was used, but in this case the stimuli were three cubes with sides of 2, 2½, and 3 inches. The subjects were four- and six-year-olds and all were given a maximum of 40 trials. For one-third of each age group choices of the large cube were deemed to be correct; for one-third, choices of the middle-sized cube; and for one-third, choices of the small cube. Six-year-olds presumably know all three relevant terms and should be capable of performing at a high level, regardless of which stimulus is correct. Four-year-olds, however, should have more difficulty in using words to assist them in learning, especially when the correct stimulus is the middle-sized block. As can be seen in Figure 6-2, the results are in line with these expectations. The six-year-olds performed at about the same level, regardless of which block was correct. The four-year-olds did surprisingly well when either the large or small blocks were correct, but their performance dropped to approximately a chance level when the middle-sized block was correct. None of the four-year-olds, but many of the six-year-olds, showed evidence of having learned the middle-sized problem by meeting a relatively strict criterion of learning (five consecutive correct responses). The four-year-olds clearly could discriminate among the three blocks, but their responses were unstable when the correct response was represented by a term with which they were less familiar.

A third and final illustrative study of the role of verbal mediation in the solution of the intermediate-size problem was reported by Reese (1966). Reese required children to discriminate between three squares with areas of 16, 32, and 64 square inches. He instituted an unorthodox procedure for half of his subjects. On each trial the children were told, "It (the prize) is under the medium one," and if they then made an error they were shown the correct block and told again, "No, it's under the medium one." The other half of the subjects were tested under a standard procedure. No directions were given to them about which block would be correct, but after an error they were told, "No, it's under this one," and were shown the correct block. If children cannot direct their responses on the basis of verbal labels, the instructions should be of little help. If they are capable of verbal mediation, the problem should be quite simple. Two groups of preschool children were tested, three-year-olds and four-year-olds.

Neither group appeared to show spontaneous verbal mediation, for without instruction the problem was difficult for children at both ages. But the four-year-olds were able to utilize a verbal cue when it was available, while the three-year-olds were not. The mean number of trials required to reach a criterion of nine correct responses on 10 successive trials was about the same for the younger subjects, regardless of whether or not they had received instructions about which stimulus was correct (mean = 20.4 and 22.9, respectively). The four-year-olds were able to benefit from the instructions. Those who were told which block was cor-

Figure 6-2.   Mean numbers of correct responses made by four- and six-year-old children when small, middle-sized, and large stimuli were correct in a three-choice size discrimination problem. (From H. W. Stevenson and G. McBee, The learning of object and pattern discriminations by children. *Journal of Comparative and Physiological Psychology*, 1956, 51, 753. Reprinted by permission of the American Psychological Association.)

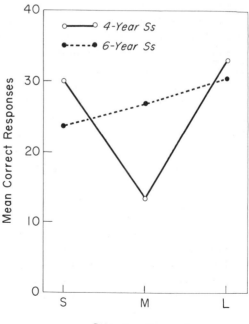

rect learned the problem in an average of 9.8 trials; those who were not told required an average of 29.1 trials.

These studies of the intermediate-size problem all point to the same conclusion. When children are able to use a word to describe a relation that exists within a set of stimuli they prove to be more efficient in learning to select the stimulus denoted by this word than do less mature or less verbally facile children who cannot use, or do not know, the relevant word.

Production Deficiency

As we have seen, the asquistion of language does not automatically mean that words will be used as verbal mediators. The very young child cannot use verbal mediation because he does not know the relevant words, but later, when he does know the relevant words, there still may or may not be mediation. Reese (1962) has called the stage of development in which verbal responses do not serve as mediators a period of "mediational deficiency." Even though the child is capable of using words, he demonstrates a deficiency in verbal mediation. An example of what is meant by this was seen in the last study discussed, where three-year-olds, told the relevant response, were unable to utilize this information in the solution of the problem.

Another basis for the young child's poor performance may be that he knows the relevant words but fails to produce them at the appropriate time. The latter view has been termed the *production deficiency hypothesis* by Flavell, Beach, and Chinsky (1966). There is a very fine distinction between these two proposals. Both assume that the young child is ineffective in verbal mediation. The first points to the possibility that, for some reason, verbal stimuli are not yet effective for the young child as mediators of response. The second proposes that words may be effective but cannot operate as mediators because the child fails to produce them at the proper time. The two proposals are not mutually incompatible, of course, for depending upon the child and the problem, each may offer a valid interpretation of the experimental findings.

At this point we should discuss some of the evidence that has been presented in support of the production-deficiency hypothesis. [A thorough review of these studies is available in Flavell (1970).] Support for this hypothesis requires evidence that young children actually engage in verbal mediation less frequently and less appropriately than do older children. Some measure of the presence or absence of mediation must be obtained within the experimental session. Pre-experimental testing and postexperimental questioning are inappropriate; we cannot infer from measures obtained before or after the experiment whether the child failed to produce the words or whether he produced them and they were ineffective. Some means must be devised for determining whether mediation occurred. In our preceding discussion we pointed out that mediation typically is an implicit process. Fortunately, when verbal mediation is implicit, it often is not without external manifestations. Children, and sometimes adults, move their lips as they verbalize to themselves. Why not "read" children's lips in the course of their performance and use the incidence of lip movement as an indication of the operation of verbal mediation? This is what Flavell, Beach and Chinsky did.

After becoming proficient in lip-reading, they began an investigation of children's performance on a task that required the recall of a sequence of items. This type of serial memory task was chosen in preference to others because it seemed likely that children would engage in verbal rehearsal in an effort to improve their performance. Seven pictures of common objects were arranged in a horizontal display in front of the child. The experimenter then pointed to a subset of these pictures (e.g., three) in a random order. All of the pictures were removed and a duplicate set of pictures was spread out in a new order. The child was asked to point to the subset of three pictures in the same order he had seen demonstrated. To be sure the children understood the directions they were given preliminary experience in a similar but simpler task. On successive trials the number of pictures in the subset (i.e., the number to be remembered) increased from two to five, with the maximum number of pictures depending upon the child's age and his degree of success. The children were five- and eight-year-olds.

How can you stare intently at a child, trying to lip-read, without making the child unduly sensitive? Put him in a space helmet! The visor of the helmet was raised to reveal each display, and between presentations the visor was down. Although the experimenter could see the child's lips in the intervening period—the time when he was most likely to engage in spontaneous verbal rehearsal—the child could not see the experimenter.

The younger children knew words for all of the objects, but failed to utilize this knowledge in their performance. Of the 20 five-year-olds, 18 gave no evidence of moving their lips to form relevant words or of showing lip movements that could be judged as labeling. In contrast, only 8 of the 20 eight-year-olds failed to indicate such activity. If one is willing to assume that the incidence of lip movement is a valid measure of verbal mediation, and it seems reasonable to make such an assumption, the results must be interpreted as supporting the contention that young children's difficulties in verbal mediation may be due, in part, to their failure to employ words as mediators of response. Why they fail to do this is not clear. Is it because they know the words but do not know how to use them? Or is it due to a more general cognitive immaturity that prevents them from comprehending the intellectual requirements of the task? The information from a second study provides some clarification of these questions.

Only seven-year-olds were used in the second study (Keeney, Cannizzo, & Flavell, 1967). By selecting an age level between those used in the first study, it was hoped that subgroups of subjects could be obtained, one that showed spontaneous verbal rehearsal and one that did not. The procedure was essentially the same as that used in the preceding study, except that all children were given ten experimental trials with sets of stimuli containing pictures of between two and five common objects. Of the 89 children tested, 24 were found to show perceptible lip movements on either nine or ten of the trials and 17 showed such movements on none or only one of the trials. The first group was classified as "producers" and the second as "nonproducers."

By comparing the performance of these two groups the authors were able to answer an important question: Do children who spontaneously produce verbal mediators recall more items in the correct order than do children of the same age who do not produce these verbalizations? The answer is yes. The recall scores of the producers were significantly above those of the nonproducers.

Six weeks later the two groups of children were brought back to the testing situation. The results from the first trial made it possible to ascertain whether the children's tendency to engage in verbal rehearsal was an enduring characteristic. Of those who previously had been classified as producers, 19 of the 24 showed verbal rehearsal on this trial, while only 1 out of 17 of those who had been classified as nonproducers did so. At least over this period of time, there were reliable differences between the groups in their tendency to produce verbal mediators.

After the initial trial an attempt was made to determine whether the nonproducers could be trained to engage in verbal mediation, and if so, whether their recall scores would be comparable to those who used mediation spontaneously. The experimenter told the children he was going to point to the pictures and they were to whisper the names out loud when the visor of the space helmet was down. Ten trials comparable to those of the original session were given, wherein the child was required to repeat the names of the objects that were presented on each trial. The results were clear-cut. The recall scores of the nonproducers who were instructed to verbalize were at the same level as those of two subgroups of children classified as producers, half of whom also had received the instruction to verbalize and half of whom had not.

The study was concluded with a third set of three trials. Before these trials the children were told they did not have to say the words unless they wanted to. The recall scores of the nonproducers dropped; there was no significant deterioration in the performance of the producers.

Left to their own techniques, the nonproducers reverted to their earlier, less effective mode of performance. The nonproducers had proved to be relatively incorrigible; when instructed to verbalize their performance improved, but this training had no lasting effect. Without instructions they failed to demonstrate verbal mediation.

The results indicate that part of the young child's difficulty in learning and remembering appears to be due to his failure to use words appropriately in the course of his performance. The results do not necessarily mean that a failure to produce words at the appropriate time constitutes the sole basis of the young child's difficulties. Even though the results of the second set of trials revealed that when the words were produced they had a facilitative effect on performance, we cannot conclude that the performance of still younger children would be influenced in a comparable manner. It is possible that a preschool child, for example, might be able to produce the words at the appropriate time, but still be unable to grasp the relation between what he was saying and what he was supposed to do.

Several studies with preschool children offer some evidence concerning this point. The mean age of the children in each of the studies was approximately five years and each study assessed children's ability to remember a sequence of items. On the assumption that having names available would aid recall, half of the children in each study were required to verbalize the name of each stimulus as it was presented. Hagen and Kingsley (1968a) showed children eight cards, one at a time, depicting common animals. After the child saw the picture the card was turned over and placed in front of the child. With all eight cards in front of him, he was asked to point to the card bearing a particular animal. Children who had labeled the animals performed no more effectively than children who had not. (However, labeling did improve the performance of six-, seven-, and eight-year-olds included in this study.) On the other hand, Bernbach (1967) found that labeling facilitated the performance of preschool children. He used four cards rather than eight, with each card a different color. Better recall scores were obtained by children who had labeled the colors than by those who had not.

Why should the results of the two studies be in conflict? One possibility is that the effect of labeling differs, depending upon the number of stimuli. A long sequence of names may be more readily forgotten by preschool children than by older children. Some evidence supporting this possibility was obtained by Hagen and Kingsley when they analyzed their results according to the relative recency with which a particular card had been presented. Whereas labeling had no effect on recalling the location of cards that were among the first shown the child, it did produce better recall for the last few cards. Thus labeling may aid performance when there are few items, as was the case in Bernbach's study, or when the items are among the most recently presented from a longer list.

More general facilitating effects of labeling on preschool children's performance also can be produced. Hagen and Kingsley (1968*b*) found improved performance when preschool children were instructed—and required—to rehearse the names of the stimuli (again, pictures of animals) after they had been presented. This procedure forces the child to continue to verbalize the names of the items in the total array, that is, to keep all of the names in mind. On his own he may have no tendency to do so and may recall the names of only those that have been most recently presented. In contrast to groups of children who merely labeled the stimuli or who whispered the labels to themselves, children who engage in overt labeling and rehearsed the labels performed at a higher level than the group given no instructions to label. The results seem to point to the conclusion that preschool children, like older children, may benefit from labeling under certain conditions, but that unlike older children, they are less likely to adopt the strategy of verbal rehearsal unless they are required to do so.

Before leaving this group of studies we should recognize that they represent a special case of verbal mediation. Verbal rehearsal of the very materials that are to be reproduced or recalled may have quite different effects from what would be found when the mediating responses are not so similar to the overt responses that must be made. It would be interesting to know whether the effects are comparable in the two types of situations.

Developmental Studies

The discussion thus far may be interpreted as implying that, at least with older children, the application of verbal mediators inevitably results in more effective performance. This is not necessarily true. It always is possible that the child is capable of mediating and bases his response on some type of verbal mediation, but the whole mediational process is inappropriate for the solution of the problem. Two studies may be used to illustrate this point.

As part of a more extensive study, Stevenson, Iscoe, and McConnell (1955) presented a two-choice discrimination learning task to subjects varying in age from the preschool through college years. The subjects were shown two wooden squares that differed in size. They were told that the experimenter would hide an object and the point of the task was to find the object as often as possible. For half of the subjects at each age level the object was hidden under the smaller square, and for the other half, under the larger square. According to the verbal mediation hypothesis, and in line with common sense, the subjects should learn the problem with greater and greater ease with increasing age. As can be seen in Figure 6-3, the results are consistent with this prediction through grades 5 to 8. These children needed fewer than one-third the number of trials required by preschool children to learn the problem to a criterion of nine consecutive correct responses. But then the prediction went awry. Tenth graders and college students required nearly as many trials to learn as did the children in the two youngest groups. How can this be explained? The findings made sense when the subjects were questioned about their performance at the end of the experiment. The two oldest groups indicated that they expected a much more difficult problem and tried to find a solution in the form of a complex sequence of positions or stimulus patterns. Or, in some cases, they reported that they assumed success depended on chance and there was no solution at all. In other words, they showed no failure to mediate, in the sense that their be- havior was guided by some form of implicit response. But by responding on the basis of presumed sequences or patterns, they performed in a manner that was inappropriately complex for the simple task with which they were confronted.

Similar effects have been found in somewhat more difficult problems. Weir and Stevenson (1959) presented children of ages three, five, seven, and nine with a task in which they were required to discriminate the cor- rect member of five pairs of pictures of common animals, such as a

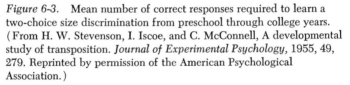

Figure 6-3.   Mean number of correct responses required to learn a two-choice size discrimination from preschool through college years. (From H. W. Stevenson, I. Iscoe, and C. McConnell, A developmental study of transposition. *Journal of Experimental Psychology*, 1955, 49, 279. Reprinted by permission of the American Psychological Association.)

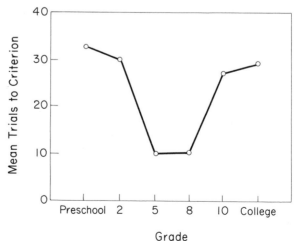

monkey and a cat, and an elephant and a dog. The children were given 140 trials; each pair of pictures appeared once in each block of 5 trials. Only about half of the total number of responses made by the three-year-olds were correct. As one might expect, performance improved for the five-year-olds. At this age, children should be more capable of using the names of the animals as a basis for remembering which animals in each pair was correct. But at age seven performance dropped, and by age nine the children, on the average, made only one more correct response in the 140 trials than did the three-year-olds. The children's comments at the end of the experiment gave a ready explanation of this decline. The older children made such statements as, "I thought that it was going to be a pattern," and "I thought you were going to change them all around." Their complex hypotheses had hindered their development of the more simple, correct solution.

These two studies are extreme cases. The performance of children does not often decline with increasing age. The studies serve, however, to point out that if the mediational processes are not in concordance with the level of difficulty of the problem, the facilitative effects of mediation are lost; performance may be less efficient than that found with children at a lower developmental level.

CONCLUSIONS

This chapter is the first of four concerned with verbal mediation, a construct used by stimulus-response theorists to account for the manner in which the acquisition of language may influence children's learning. Young children, less proficient in the use of language than older children, have difficulty in learning, especially when the solution of the problem can be translated into words. Their difficulties may arise from at least two possible sources: they are less capable of producing words at the appropriate times, and even when the words are produced they may demonstrate deficiencies in comprehending the significance of words for the solution of the problem. It is assumed that if appropriate words are produced and utilized, learning will be more efficient. At the same time, if the words lead the child to unnecessarily complex or irrelevant responses they may be a deterrent rather than an aid to good performance.

The results of studies stimulated by the hypothesis of verbal mediation are of practical interest. If the child is to be able to summon words to assist him at important times, he must have extensive experience in using words. Without appropriate models and without instruction, the child's learning of language is retarded, and unless he has had experience in labeling, describing, and summarizing his experience by means of language it is likely that his learning in many other situations will be impaired.

7

Transposition

We will concentrate our attention in the next two chapters on studies of transposition, a type of problem that has proved to be particularly valuable in assessing the relation between verbal ability and learning. To illustrate what we mean by transposition we can use a two-choice discrimination learning task of the type discussed in the preceding chapter. Children are presented two squares, a small one and a large one, with choices of the larger square always being rewarded. After this discrimination has been learned, the smaller of the original pair of squares is replaced by a third, still larger square for the test trials. The child is not told that such a change has been made and the procedure for presenting the stimuli remains unchanged. Which square will the child choose? Will he choose the square that was correct in the training phase, which is now the smaller of the two, or will he choose the larger square of the test pair? If he chooses the larger of the new pair of stimuli, he is judged to have transposed. Transposition occurs, then, when the child chooses the stimulus in a new set of stimuli that bears the same relation to this set as was held by the correct stimulus in the training set. In other words, transposition involves the transfer of a differential response associated with one set of stimuli to new sets of stimuli differing in the same property.

Organisms generally do transpose in this type of problem. We can say this because the effect has been found in tests with chickens, rats, monkeys, chimpanzees, children, and human adults, and with stimuli differing on one of many dimensions, such as size, brightness, or pitch.

Psychologists have been interested in studying transposition ever since the first study on it was published by Kinnamon in 1902. There are several reasons why it has been considered to be such an interesting and important topic. Learning theorists have been interested in transposition because it represents a form of transfer of training, a problem of great concern to all who hope to understand how learning in one situation may influence learning in new situations. Because different theorists have made specific, and sometimes opposing predictions about the conditions under which such transfer should occur, studies of transposition often have been used to test various theoretical positions [see Hebert & Krantz (1965) and Reese (1968) for thorough reviews of the literature on transposition]. Child psychologists have had a special interest in transposition because of the marked changes in performance on this problem that occur between the early and later years of childhood.

THEORETICAL BACKGROUND

Gestalt psychologists, who contend that learning consists of developing an understanding of the relations that exist among stimuli, interpreted the results from studies of transposition as strong support for their views. The fact that transposition occurs was considered to constitute evidence of the subjects' strong predispositions to learn the relations that exist among stimuli rather than particular stimulus-response connections, as behaviorists assume. Would not the latter position have to predict that subjects would choose the smaller stimulus of the test set, the one that had yielded reward during the training trials, rather than make a relational response? The Gestalt interpretation seemed to hold the upper hand for many years; a relational theory offered a ready explanation of experimental results that stumped the behaviorists.

One aspect of the results from studies of transposition was always an embarrassment to the Gestalt theorists, however. A relational interpretation was satisfactory in explaining the results as long as the test stimuli and the training stimuli were very similar to each other. When tests were made with stimuli further removed from the training pair, the frequency of subjects transposing decreased. Subjects no longer made a relational response when the test stimuli were markedly different in their absolute characteristics from those used in training. On such tests the subjects either responded randomly or chose the stimulus nearer the training pair. This finding posed problems for the relational theorist. If learning consists of understanding the relations that exist among stimuli, why should transposition not occur when the stimuli are remote from the training pair but the relation between the stimuli is maintained?

Spence's Model

Spence (1937), a leading exponent of the stimulus-response approach, proposed a theoretical model capable of predicting the experimental results. Before discussing this model, however, it is helpful to extend our description of the procedure used in studies of transposition. The example used above, where one of the training stimuli was retained for the test trials, has been called a *near* test of transposition with stimuli *one-step* removed from the training pair. Tests are referred to as *far* tests of transposition when the test stimuli are more distant from the training stimuli on the relevant stimulus dimension. The number of steps by which the test stimuli are removed from the training stimuli is defined by the number of pairs of stimuli that intervene between the training and test stimuli. This can be illustrated by means of an example. Assume that six squares are constructed with area-ratios of 2 : 1, the smallest having an area of 1 square inch and the largest, 32 square inches. Ratios and areas of any size could, of course, be used. Subjects are trained with the pair of squares with areas of 1 and 2 square inches. Choices of the larger square are rewarded. Test trials with the 2 and 4 square inch squares would be defined as a near test one-step removed; test trials using the squares with areas of 16 and 32 square inches would be a far test four-steps removed.

Figure 7-1. The subject is assumed to have been trained to select the square of 160 square centimeters in preference to one of 100 square centimeters. The solid line represents the generalization gradient of excitatory tendencies and the dashed line represents the generalization gradient of inhibitory tendencies. Intervening values are the hypothetical strengths of the net excitatory tendencies resulting from the subtraction of inhibitory tendencies from the excitatory tendencies associated with each stimulus. The value of 51.7 for the positive stimulus is above that of 29.7 for the negative stimulus, reflecting the fact that the discrimination has been learned. By comparing the relative strengths of the net excitatory strength for successive pairs of stimuli, performance in the transfer task can be predicted. Transposition should occur for stimuli one step removed (256 versus 160 square centimeters), for at the end of training the net strength for the larger stimulus of this pair is greater. For the pair of stimuli with areas of 655 and 409 square centimeters, however, transposition should not occur; the smaller stimulus should be chosen. (The stimulus members indicated on the base line are placed at equal intervals on a logarithmic scale.) (From K. W. Spence, The differential response in animals to stimuli varying within a single dimension. *Psychological Review*, 1937, 44, 433. Reprinted by permission of the American Psychological Association.)

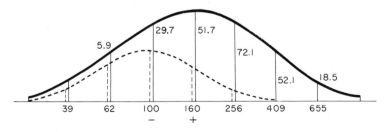

Stimulus size – sq. cm.

Spence's model makes it possible to predict both the high frequency of transposition that occurs on near tests and the decrease in frequency of transposition found on far tests. The details of the model are presented in Figure 7-1. This has been termed an *absolute* model, in the sense that it is concerned with the absolute characteristics of the stimuli rather than their relation to each other. Essentially, Spence assumed that discrimination learning is a cumulative process wherein reward strengthens the tendency to approach the positive (correct) stimulus and nonreinforcement increases the tendency to avoid or inhibit response to the negative (incorrect) stimulus. The strength of the response made to the positive stimulus during training (excitatory tendency) generalizes to other stimuli along the same dimension, as does the strength of the tendency to inhibit response to the negative stimulus (inhibitory tendency). By summing the excitatory and inhibitory tendencies algebraically at different points along the stimulus continuum, and assuming that a positive response subsequently will be made to the stimulus with the greater net excitatory strength, it is possible to predict that transposition will occur for the near pair of stimuli and will drop to a chance level for increasingly far pairs of stimuli. The latter prediction is not easily provided by a relational theory. Stimulus-response theorists, on the other hand, hail the evidence of a decrease in the incidence of transposition as the test stimuli become more remote from the training pair (the *distance effect*) as an indication of the greater power of a stimulus response or *absolute* theory.

RESEARCH WITH CHILDREN

How does all of this apply to children? Kuenne, a student of Spence, pursued the question. Kuenne assumed that the incidence of transposition should differ, depending upon the child's linguistic competence. Spence's model dealt with nonverbal organisms. Are the mechanisms governing the performance of young children similar to those proposed for nonverbal animals? If so, should not the performance of young children who are incapable of verbalizing the relations among stimuli conform to Spence's model? Kuenne predicted an affirmative answer would be obtained to both questions. However, older children who can verbalize relations such as "larger than" should rely upon verbal cues to guide their responses. Their performance should be less dependent upon the absolute characteristics of the test stimuli. Kuenne assumed that the older children would spontaneously apply verbal labels to the stimuli and would learn a response such as "Pick the big one" during the course of the training trials. They then should apply this verbal mediator to the test stimuli and make a relational response, regardless of the differences in absolute size between the training and test pairs. Freed from the constraints imposed by the absolute characteristics of the stimuli, older, verbally mediating children should show rapid learning and consistently high frequencies of transposition.

Kuenne predicted, therefore, that the incidence of transposition would be high for both younger and older children when the test stimuli were adjacent to the training stimuli. Both should transpose on near tests, younger children because of the generalization of excitatory and inhibitory tendencies and older children because of verbal mediation. The near test, therefore, does not provide a clear basis for differentiating between these two mechanisms. With the far test, however, younger children who are incapable of verbalizing the relations among the stimuli should not transpose, while older children, who presumably are capable of verbal mediation, should transpose at a high level. The performance of children at intermediate stages of development should fall between these two extremes.

To test these predictions, Kuenne conducted a developmental study of transposition, including children at four levels of mental age: three, four, five, and six years. Mental age was used as the basis for selecting children on the assumption that this measure provides a rough indication of the degree to which behavior may be controlled by verbal responses. The children were trained to choose the smaller of two squares differing in size (see Figure 7-2). Half of the children at each mental age level were tested with stimuli one step removed and half with stimuli five steps removed. As can be seen in Figure 7-3, transposition remained at a high level across all mental ages for the near stimuli, but decreased consistently for the far stimuli as mental age decreased.

The verbalizations of the subjects during and after the experiment provided additional support for Kuenne's proposals. Practically none of the children at the three-year level were able to verbalize the size relation that existed within the pairs of stimuli and nearly all at the five- and six-year levels were able to verbalize the principle either spontaneously or

Figure 7-2.   Stimuli used by Kuenne (1946) in training and test trials, drawn to scale.

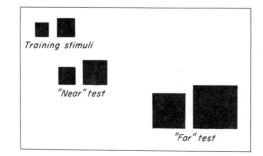

upon questioning. There were other children, however, who were able to identify the stimuli as "little" and "big," but who failed to verbalize the relation of size to the solution of the problem. These were predominantly younger children who, on the far test of transposition, performed at chance level. Being able to apply labels was not sufficient to produce mediation.

The study was repeated with minor modifications by Alberts and Ehrenfreund (1951), who selected children on the basis of chronological age. Different subgroups of children were tested with pairs of stimuli one, two, four, and five steps removed from the training pair. By including the intermediate steps it was possible to obtain gradients of transposition that provided intermediate values between the near and far tests. The results are presented in Figure 7-4. Transposition remained high across all test pairs for the older children (4½- to 5½-year-olds) but decreased consistently for the younger children (3-year-olds) as the number of steps between the training and test pairs increased. Again, the older children tended to verbalize the relation embodied in the stimuli while the younger children did not.

These studies were greeted with enthusiasm. They were well done and they offered a rather compelling account of developmental changes in the learning process. Both sets of results appeared to provide support for the

Figure 7-3.   Mean number of relational responses made during 10 test trials on near and far tests of transposition, plotted according to mental age of the children. (From M. R. Kuenne, Experimental investigation of the relation of language to transposition behavior in young children. *Journal of Experimental Psychology,* 1946, 36, 483. Reprinted by permission of the American Psychological Association.)

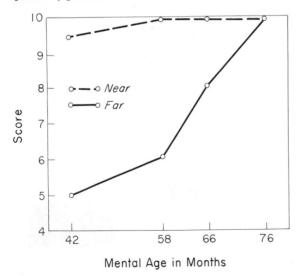

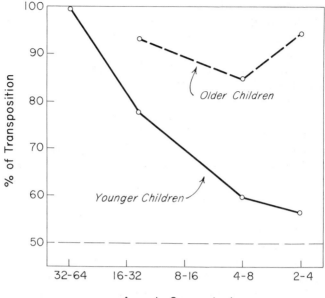

Figure 7-4.   Percentage of transposition obtained by younger and older children at various steps tested. (From E. Alberts and D. Ehrenfreund, Transposition in children as a function of age. *Journal of Experimental Psychology*, 1951, 41, 35. Reprinted by permission of the American Psychological Association.)

two-process model outlined by Kuenne. Children responded relationally if they could verbalize the relevant relation. Otherwise, they appeared to respond in a manner similar to nonverbal animals. But more data were to come. Research that followed the publication of these two studies showed that Spence's ideas were not capable of providing a satisfactory explanation of the experimental results. An interpretation of young children's learning on the basis of his ideas proved to be inadequate.

Relational Learning

Several studies with young children demonstrated that Spence's model could predict neither the form of original learning nor the effect of prior experience on subsequent response. In these studies the performance of the young child did not appear to be determined by the operation of excitatory and inhibitory processes. From an early age children respond to the relations that exist among stimuli, rather than to their absolute characteristics. Even two- and three-year-olds who are incapable of verbal mediation show a strong tendency toward relational response. A model that does not predict such results must be based on erroneous premises. The first of the studies leading to such a conclusion was concerned with testing Spence's predictions about the acquisition of a discriminative response.

If learning is a matter of building up the strength of the response to one stimulus and decreasing the strength of the tendency to choose an alternate stimulus, it should be more difficult for young children to learn to select a stimulus that varies across trials than one that reappears on every trial. To test this possibility, Graham, Ernhart, Craft, and Berman (1964) presented pairs of squares to children between the ages of 2 and 4½ years. Each pair consisted of a common square and a second square larger or smaller than the first. For some children, response to the relation between the stimuli was rewarded (e.g., choice of the larger square in each pair were reinforced) and for other children choices of the square that was common across pairs was reinforced. Since 2-year-olds may be considered to be incapable of verbalizing relations among stimuli, the Spence model predicts they would learn the absolute problem more easily than the relational problem. By 4½ years of age, when children are more effective at verbal mediation, the relational problem should be learned more easily.

The results failed to support these predictions. The relational problem was learned more readily at all ages and performance was nearly maximal by the age of three. The study was repeated with a slightly more difficult task. Four pairs of squares were used. Again, on each trial the pair consisted of a common square and a second square, larger or smaller than the first. The child now had to learn either an absolute response or a relation that existed within four pairs of squares. The results were similar to those found in the first study. The tendency to respond to relations between stimuli appears, therefore, to be a primitive form of behavior that may take precedence over an absolute pattern of response even in the absence of verbal mediation.

Further evidence against Spence's model came from a study (Berman & Graham, 1964) investigating the effect of a single reinforcement on subsequent response in a two-choice size discrimination. Two- and four-year-olds were presented two squares; a choice of either square was reinforced. On the second trial the square chosen on the first trial and a second square were presented. The size of the new square, relative to the squares used on the first trial, depended on the child's choice on the first trial. It was smaller than the first two if the child had chosen the smaller square on the first trial and larger if the child had chosen the larger square. On the second trial, then, the child could make either an absolute or a relative response. This procedure precludes the operation of gradients posited by Spence, for by giving only one reinforced trial a gradient of inhibitory tendencies could not develop. The model must predict, therefore, that the previously reinforced stimulus would be chosen on the second trial, for this would be the stimulus with the greater excitatory strength (or, if sufficient excitatory strength was not produced by a single reinforcement, the choices should be random). Contrary to the prediction, children chose the square of the same relative size more often than they chose the previously reinforced square.

The results are not restricted to visual stimuli. Riley, McKee, Bell, and Schwartz (1967) asked first and third graders to make absolute or relative judgments concerning tones differing in loudness and pitch. The children followed the relative instructions better than the absolute instructions and appeared, in fact, to discriminate between loudness almost exclusively on a relational basis. The authors point out that a relational discrimination requires that the child learn no more than a general relation, while an absolute discrimination is dependent upon the retention of information about a specific stimulus. Relational responding may be a more primitive mode of response because it requires less differentiation of the specific attributes of the stimuli and is less dependent upon memory.

Effects of Procedural Modifications

Studies demonstrating children's early and strong tendencies toward relational responding are not the only ones failing to support Spence's model. Other studies have shown that the incidence of transposition on far tests, where young children are predicted to do poorly, may be altered radically by making seemingly minor modifications in the experimental procedure. The heightened ability of young children to transpose in these studies does not appear to be due to verbal mediation, but to the manner in which the original training, or in some cases the test trials, are conducted.

Johnson and Zara (1960) were among the first to show how transposition may depend upon the procedure used during the training trials. The study was designed to find out whether transposition could be increased by instituting a training procedure that emphasized the relevance of relative size for the solution of the problem. This was accomplished by presenting children multiple discrimination problems, rather than the single discrimination task used in the previous studies. Accordingly, half of the children were trained with one pair of stimuli and half with two pairs of stimuli. The stimulus of the same relative size within each pair was correct in all cases. The subjects were three- and five-year-olds. When only one pair of stimuli was presented on the training trials, a distance effect was found on the tests for transposition. The incidence of transposition decreased from approximately 80% for stimuli one step removed to 50% for stimuli five steps removed. Following training with two pairs of stimuli, the children transposed at a high level regardless of the distance between the training and test sets. Not only was transposition more frequent in the latter case, but the double discrimination problem was learned more rapidly than the single discrimination problem. Young children, presented multiple problems that could be solved by the same principle, were able to perform in much the same manner as the older children in previous studies who were capable of verbal mediation. The results have been replicated by Sherman and Strunk (1960).

A different approach was taken by Tighe and Tighe (1969), who asked whether the distance effect might be due in part to the child's failure to identify the training and test stimuli as belonging to the same stimulus continuum. For adults it may be easy to abstract a common dimension, such as size, and order even widely divergent examples on that dimension. This is more difficult for children. In the transposition experiment, therefore, the child's failure to demonstrate transfer between the training and test trials may be derived from his failure to perceive the training and test stimuli as members of the same stimulus continuum. Transposition may fail to occur because the training and test stimuli are responded to as different classes of stimuli.

Would it be possible to increase children's tendencies to perceive a common dimension among stimuli by providing relevant experience during pretraining trials? Tighe and Tighe sought to do this with six-year-olds. The stimuli were cylinders differing in height. A stimulus was presented and the child was asked whether a comparison stimulus looked "exactly the same" as the stimulus just seen. Only two stimuli were used during these pretraining trials for some children; for others there were three different stimuli. For a third group, two stimuli were used as standards, but the comparison stimulus varied continuously. In this case, the child had to tell the experimenter when the comparison stimulus was of the same height as the preceding standard stimulus. After 16 pretraining trials, a two-choice discrimination task was presented, again using stimuli differing in height (4 versus 5½ inches). When this was learned, transposition was assessed with stimuli differing markedly from the training pair (heights of 10¾ and 15 inches).

Pretraining with only two values did not increase the incidence of transposition over that found for children who had no relevant pretraining, but nearly all children in the other two pretraining conditions transposed. Experience during pretraining with either three stimulus values or with continuous variation of the dimension apparently had increased the children's sensitivity to the relevance of height as a differentiating characteristic among stimuli.

Another novel procedure was introduced by Cole, Dent, Eguchi, Fujii, and Johnson (1964). Children, and other subjects, make few errors in learning a discrimination if one stimulus is much more dominant than the others. One means by which such dominance can be achieved is by presenting a full representation of the correct stimulus, but gradually "fading-in" the incorrect stimulus. In this study the correct stimulus, a large square, was complete on all trials. The negative stimulus was represented initially by a thin line that gradually evolved through the 30 training trials into a smaller square. The procedure was successful. Only 7 of the 26 three-year-olds used in the study made more than one error, and these children were eliminated as subjects. As was pointed out by Berman and Graham (1964), these conditions preclude the generation of inhibitory potential, and according to Spence transposition should not be found, even on test trials one-step removed from the training stimuli. But it did occur. Over 70% of the responses on test trials presented immediately or after 15 or 30 overtraining trials were relational responses.

Examples also are available to illustrate how seemingly slight changes in the testing procedure may influence the incidence of transposition shown by young children. Stevenson and Langford (1957), for example, argued that any procedure that increased the difficulty of discrimination between the sets of stimuli used in the training and test trials should result in a higher frequency of transposition. Since the test trials in Kuenne's study were presented 24 hours after the termination of training, the high incidence of transposition on the near test may have been due to a failure to recognize that a new stimulus had been substituted in the original pair. If this were the case, near transposition may result partly from children's failure to discriminate between the pairs of stimuli used in the training and test trials.

Three-year-olds, who were unable to verbalize the principle involved in the solution of the problem, were required to learn a two-choice size discrimination and were tested, either immediately or after 24 hours, with sets of stimuli one, two, three, or four steps removed from the training pair. It was predicted that the incidence of transposition would be lower with immediate than with delayed testing because of the greater likelihood in the first case that children would be aware of the change in stimuli following the training trials. A distance effect was found for both groups, but the frequency of transposition was significantly higher with delayed than with immediate testing.

Tighe and Tighe (1969), on the other hand, have suggested that transposition on *far* tests also may be influenced by the manner in which the test trials are conducted. They sought to create testing procedures that would increase the child's awareness of the common dimension existing between the training and test stimuli, in this case, height. Three conditions were used during the test trials: (a) the children (six-year-olds) saw only the test stimuli; (b) the training stimuli were reintroduced alternately with the test stimuli; (c) the training and test stimuli were present on each test trial. (The training procedure was identical to that described in their preceding study discussed above.) The opportunity to see the training and test stimuli simultaneously on the test trials should greatly increase the salience of height as a common dimension and thereby produce greater transfer from training to test trials. The results supported this argument; of the 12 children in each of the three testing conditions, the number transposing on a *far* test were 1, 6, and 12, respectively.

Trying to predict whether young children will transpose has proved to be much more complicated than Spence, or anyone else, might have expected. Clearly, the application of Spence's model for nonverbal organisms is inappropriate in discussing the performance of young children. The studies described above and numerous others (e.g., Hunter, 1952; Johnson & Bailey, 1966; Rudel, 1958; Stevenson & Iscoe, 1954; Stevenson, Iscoe, & McConnell, 1955) indicate we must give up the model. It was explicit, stimulating, but ineffective. Children's learning would have been easier to interpret if the evidence had been more supportive of the assumptions underlying this position. But we must resign ourselves to the fact that any effort to understand children's learning is bound to be more difficult than the already complex task of trying to account for learning by lower animals.

In many ways these conclusions are negative. We cannot be entirely satisfied when one of the primary contributions of a group of studies is to present evidence that a particular view is untenable. In this case, however, negative evidence does constitute an important contribution. Psychology has been strongly influenced by the stimulus-response viewpoint represented by Spence. Since studies of transposition are concerned with central postulates of this view, evidence that they do not lead to a satisfactory interpretation of children's learning forces us to abandon such an approach and seek new, more effective theories. The factors these theories must encompass will gain additional clarity as we continue our discussion of transposition and related topics.

The Mediation Hypothesis

Thus far, the verbal mediation hypothesis has escaped relatively unscathed. The studies have shown that verbal mediation may not be the necessary condition for transposition, but it does seem to be a sufficient condition. Do the results of any studies challenge this conclusion?

Several studies are relevant to this question. The first was a developmental study of children's ability to use verbal responses as mediators. Marsh and Sherman (1966) trained two groups of children (mean age 3.2 and 4.6 years) to discriminate between a pair of squares differing in both size and brightness. The two dimensions were relevant and redundant in that, for example, a large black square was positive and a small white square was negative. The children were instructed about one of the two relevant dimensions and were required to tell the experimenter which square the reward was under before they were allowed to pick it up. The instructions took the following form: "These are the blocks we're going to play with. Which one is the big one? Which one is the little one? Good. Now, *which* is this one? And what's this one?" For half of the children size was verbalized, as in the preceding example, and for the other half, brightness. The children were tested with the previously positive stimulus and a new stimulus that differed both in size and brightness (e.g., the large black square and a still larger white square).

The incidence of transposition differed, depending upon the dimension that had been verbalized. At both ages the proportion of children who transposed was greater in the groups that verbalized size than in those that verbalized brightness. When the performance of the very youngest children was analysed, it was found that they did not transpose above chance on the test trials when size had been verbalized and tended to choose the previously positive stimulus when brightness had been verbalized.

The study was repeated with two-year-olds, now including a group that received no instructions. The incidence of transposition was not significant in any of the groups; the children tended to choose the previously positive stimulus. The activation of a verbal response through instructions was not sufficient to ensure that performance of young children would be influenced significantly by such verbalization. McKee and Riley (1962) reported similar results for auditory transposition. Labeing tones as "high" or "low" did not facilitate transposition along a pitch dimension.

These results are not out of line with our previous discussion of verbal mediation and are, in fact, a reaffirmation of the conclusions reached by Kuenne. According to Kuenne (1946), the young child is "able to make differential verbal responses to appropriate aspects of the situation, but his verbalization does not control or influence his overt choice behavior. Later, such verbalizations gain control and dominate choice behavior" (p. 488). In transposition, therefore, a certain level of development is necessary before the child is able to benefit from his own verbalizations or those of others.

This does not mean that verbally competent children always behave as if they were using mediational processes. In a study by Zeiler (1966a), for example, presenting children a difficult task appeared to inhibit the development of appropriate verbal mediators. Zeiler worked with four- and five-year-olds, all of whom could verbalize the relations of small and large in postexperimental questioning. The stimuli were squares with area-ratios of either 1.96 : 1 or 1.4 : 1, thus the differences within the first set of the stimuli were much more readily discernible than were those in the second set. Test trials were conducted with stimuli 1, 2, 3, and 4 steps removed from the training pair. A uniformly high level of transposition was found for stimuli from the first set, but a distance effect, similar to those found in previous studies with preverbal children, was obtained when the area-ratio of the stimuli was 1.4 : 1. We can assume, both from the slower original learning and from the decrease in transposition on far tests, that children did not employ verbal mediators when faced with stimuli from the latter set. Difficult problems may require close attention to the stimuli and thereby reduce the child's opportunities to engage in verbal mediation.

CONCLUSIONS

The chapter began with the proposals that (a) performance of young children in the transposition problem is under the control of mechanisms similar to those governing the behavior of nonverbal animals and (b) with increasing age performance is more and more strongly influenced by children's ability to produce verbal mediators. The first proposal proved to be untenable. Models developed to account for the performance of lower animals in the transposition problem appear to have limited applicability in predicting children's performance. Although we still do not have a satisfactory means of accounting for the performance of young children in the transposition problem, the mechanisms appear to be much more complex than those governing the behavior of lower animals.

With slight exceptions, the data tend to be in line with the second proposal, that dealing with verbal mediation. Around the ages of four to six, most normal children appear to develop the capacity to use words as abstract designations of the physical world that are capable of directing the course of their behavior. Merely knowing words is insufficient; the two- and three-year-old may know the words but be unable to relate them to action. Not until around the age of six are most children, by themselves, capable of seeing the relation between what is said and what they must do. Through the use of language the child gains independence from the characteristics of a particular setting, he learns more readily, and is able to transfer this learning over a broader range of situations.

This is not to say that the older child always mediates or that the younger child always performs in a manner different from older children. When training in the transposition problem is given with a difficult problem, older children may behave like non-mediators. Similarly, if the training is given with stimuli that emphasize their relational properties, younger children may perform as well as older children. Generally, however, these studies appear to indicate that language is an important aid, in both learning and transfer.

8

Transposition of Intermediate Size

Information about children's performance in transposition tasks does not end with the discussion of the two-choice problem. There have been many studies of the transposition of intermediate size. Although intermediate values of dimensions other than size could be represented, only size problems have been used in studies with children. The general procedure is much the same as that for the two-choice problem. Sets of three stimuli are presented during the training and test trials, and during training only choices of the stimulus of intermediate size are rewarded. The question is whether children then will demonstrate transposition by choosing the stimulus of intermediate size in the test set.

The initial line of argument in this chapter follows that of the preceding chapter. Spence (1942) extended his model to include the three-choice problem and the first studies to be described were undertaken to assess its applicability to the performance of young children. This model fared only slightly better than its counterpart had in the two-choice problem. If the discussion were to consist only of a reiteration of the fact that a model formulated in the discussion of animal learning is inappropriate in the study of children's learning, we would add little to our previous conclusions. But the intermediate-size problem is more difficult than the two-choice problem, thereby presenting greater opportunity for more complex mechanisms to become operative. This is seen most vividly in studies with older children. Older children tend to show a greater incidence of far transposition than younger children in some of the studies but, in general, linguistic competence appears to be less critical a variable in transposition of intermediate size than in the two-choice problem. If language is not of primary significance, then what processes are important?

SPENCE'S MODEL

Spence's discussion of the intermediate-size problem is a straightforward extension of the basic ideas proposed in his consideration of the two-choice problem. To derive predictions for the intermediate-size problem we have only to draw a second gradient of inhibition with its apex over the third member of the training set of three stimuli (see Figure 8-1). Predictions about the rate of learning and type of transfer can be made by subtracting the sum of the two generalized inhibitory tendencies from the excitatory tendencies associated with each stimulus. If this is done, two predictions can be made: the intermediate-size problem should be difficult to learn and transposition should *never* occur with nonverbal organisms.

The second prediction is derived in the following manner. According to this model, the net excitatory strength always is greatest for the stimulus in the test set that is nearest in size to the stimulus reinforced during training. In tests one step removed this would be the previously reinforced stimulus; in far tests of transposition it would be the smallest or largest of the test stimuli, depending upon whether the tests were conducted with sets of stimuli larger or smaller than the training set. In either case, it is predicted that the subject will not transpose.

Figure 8-1. Spence's model for transposition of intermediate size. The solid line represents the generalization gradients of excitatory tendencies and the dashed lines represent the generalization gradients of inhibitory tendencies. The numerical values are the hypothetical strengths of the net excitatory tendencies. It is apparent from these curves that among possible test sets the stimulus with the greatest net excitatory strength is the stimulus nearest the previously positive stimulus, thereby leading to the prediction that transposition of intermediate size will not occur. (From K. W. Spence, The basis of solution by chimpanzees of the intermediate-size problem. *Journal of Experimental Psychology,* 1942, 31, 268. Reprinted by permission of the American Psychological Association.)

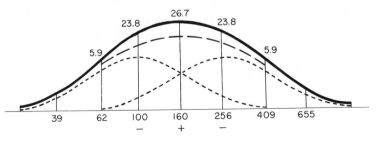

Stimulus size – sq. cm.

STUDIES WITH CHILDREN

One of the first studies that produced results in conflict with Spence's predictions was published by Stevenson and Bitterman (1955). Although the four- and five-year-old children in this study could solve the intermediate-size problem, only 4 of the 24 later could explain the significance of the middle-sized stimulus for the solution of the problem. For purposes of classification, then, the children may be considered to be preverbal in the sense that they could not supply appropriate labels for the stimuli and gave no evidence of using verbal mediators. (The term *preverbal* will be used in the remainder of this chapter to designate such children.)

Test trials were conducted with sets of stimuli one and five steps removed from the training set. The results were not discrepant with those previously found with preverbal children for the two-choice problem, but were directly opposed to what Spence might predict for the three-choice problem. Transposition of intermediate size occurred for stimuli one step removed and a distance effect was obtained.

Stevenson and Bitterman attempted to explain their findings, as well as those obtained in studies of the two-choice problem. They assumed that in the course of the training trials children learn something about the absolute properties of the stimuli as well as the relation between the positive and negative stimuli. That is, they learn something about what all of the stimuli are like, as well as which stimulus yields reward. The verbal ability of older children enables them to transfer their learning from one situation to others differing greatly in their absolute properties. Younger children may learn a relational response, but in being unable to form an abstract representation of this relation, the stability of their performance on test trials will be impaired if they recognize that a new set of stimuli has been introduced. According to this view, transposition by preverbal children is highly dependent upon perceptual processes. The probability that preverbal children will transpose on near tests is assumed to depend on the degree to which the stimuli used in testing are discriminably different from those used in training. Preverbal children should not transpose on far tests, for here they should be able to discriminate between the training and test sets with relative ease, and faced with a "new" set of stimuli fail to show transfer from training to test trials. It should be pointed out that the discrimination of a difference between training and test sets of stimuli is not as simple as might be assumed. As in all discrimination learning problems, the stimuli are presented in different horizontal arrays on successsive trials. Since in the intermediate-size problem there are six possible horizontal arrays of the three stimuli, discrimination of differences between sets of stimuli is more difficult than would be the case if the stimuli simply were presented in order of increasing size.

Effect of Area-ratio

One way in which these deductions can be evaluated is by looking at the results of studies that have used stimuli with different area-ratios. Area-ratio is the ratio by which the size of successive stimuli in the set differs. If training stimuli are highly similar to each other (have a low area-ratio) transposition should be more likely to occur than if they are dissimilar (have a high area-ratio), since between-set differences are necessarily more difficult to discriminate when within-set differences are small. For example, if the area-ratio is 2 : 1 and the training stimuli have areas of 16, 8, and 4 square inches, the replacement of the 16 square inch stimulus by a 2 square inch stimulus in the test trials is more likely to be noticed than if the area-ratio of the stimuli were 1.2 : 1. In the latter case the areas of the comparable training stimuli would be very similar to each other (e.g., 4.0, 4.8, and 5.8 square inches) and to a new stimulus (3.3 square inch) that might be used in the test trials.

Area-ratio has been varied in several studies (Reese, 1961, 1962, 1964; Rudel, 1957). There was a tendency in these studies for the frequency of transposition one step removed to vary inversely with the area-ratio; transposition was frequent when the area-ratio was small and decreased as the area-ratios increased. Transposition was found in 80% or more of the cases when the area-ratio was 1.3 : 1 or 1.5 : 1; when the area-ratios were 1.6 : 1 or 2 : 1, it never exceeded 60%; and when the area-ratio was as high as 3 : 1 transposition declined to less than 25%. On far tests of transposition three or more steps removed, transposition never occurred in more than 20% of the cases, regardless of the area-ratio of the stimuli. [A further discussion of the data used in this analysis may be found in Reese (1965).]

What happens when children do not transpose? Are their responses made at random? No; in tests one step removed they tend to choose the previously positive stimulus, and in far tests, the stimulus most similar to the training set. Here, then, is a curious situation. Stevenson and Bitterman make no explicit provision for the absolute mode of responding found when children do not transpose. The Spence position, on the other hand, reveals a fundamental weakness in failing to account for the occurrence of transposition, but offers a satisfactory basis for predicting how children will respond when they fail to transpose. A successful model must be able to handle both sets of results. As yet, none has been able to do this.

Even so, transposition by preverbal children must not be *just* a matter of failing to discriminate the test stimuli as being different from those used in training. If this were the case, a change in an irrelevant but salient aspect of the stimuli between the training and test trials should produce a decrease in the frequency of near transposition. For example, changing the color or shape of the stimuli (while maintaining the same size relations) surely should indicate to the child that the test stimuli are different from those used in the training trials. When Hansen and Cole (1968) did this, however, there was no significant decrease in the incidence of transposition. A distance effect was found whether or not the test stimuli differed in color or shape from the training stimuli, but the frequency of near transposition was unaffected by the change in color or shape. Thus a noticeable change in an irrelevant aspect of the stimuli does not reduce the incidence of transposition.

Training with Extreme Sets of Stimuli

Another implication of Stevenson and Bitterman's position is that young children may fail to transpose on far tests because they do not understand that the relational response is applicable over a broad range of stimuli. Preschool children generally have limited experience in situations where relations are maintained, even though the absolute properties of the stimuli are changed. The confusion of the four-year-old about the continuity of relations is seen when he asks such questions as "were you *always* my mother?" It is difficult for him to comprehend that a relation that exists here and now also existed in the past and will endure in the future.

If a child's failure to transpose is due, in part, to his failure to realize that a relational response learned in one situation may be applicable in other situations, it should be possible to devise a procedure which clarifies that the relation is not limited to a particular set of stimuli. A study by Gonzales and Ross (1958) demonstrated this could be done. Four-year-olds were trained with two sets of squares selected from the opposite ends of a size continuum. Thirteen squares were constructed for the study, the smallest with an area of 1 square inch and the remaining squares increased by a ratio of 1.3 : 1. The three smallest and the three largest squares were used in the training trials. This should afford extreme examples of how the middle-sized stimulus may be correct, regardless of the absolute size of the training set. Testing was conducted with a set of stimuli intermediate in size between the two training sets. Following this type of training, preverbal children showed a high incidence of transposition of intermediate size on far tests.

It will be recalled, however, that far transposition on the two-choice problem was obtained by Johnson and Zara (1960) when training was conducted with two sets of stimuli that did not represent extremes on the stimulus dimension. Are the results discussed above dependent on training with extreme sets of stimuli, or could they also be obtained following training with any two sets of stimuli, as might be suggested by the Johnson and Zara results? That is, is the effect dependent upon the range of examples or can it be obtained merely by increasing the number of examples in which the relational response is correct? Two studies have investigated this question (Beatty & Weir, 1966; Caron, 1966). Three- and four-year-old children were used in both studies and only children who failed to comprehend the term "middle-sized" were retained as subjects.

In each study there were two groups of children, each trained with two sets of stimuli. One group received "extreme-set" training with one set of stimuli from each extreme of a size distribution. The second group received "multiple-set" training with two adjacent sets of stimuli selected from one extreme. The procedure will be described in some detail. Beatty and Weir used 16 squares with area-ratios of 1.3 : 1. (For purposes of notation we will number the squares from 1 through 16 in order of increasing size.) The subjects in the "extreme-set" group were trained with squares 4-5-6 and 14-15-16 and in the "multiple-set" group with squares 1-2-3 and 4-5-6. Both groups, therefore, were trained with two sets of stimuli, but in the first case they were adjacent sets while in the second case they represented extremes in the range of stimuli. Tests were conducted with squares 9-10-11, which provided a far test of transposition for all subjects. Caron used 9 squares with area-ratios of 1.8 : 1. Training was given with squares 1-2-3 and 7-8-9 in the "extreme-set" group and with squares 1-2-3 and 4-5-6 in the "multiple-set" group. The subjects in the first group were tested with squares 4-5-6, and in the second group, with squares 7-8-9.

The incidence of transposition was greater in both studies following extreme-set training than following multiple-set training. Of the 20 children in each of Beatty and Weir's two conditions, 16 transposed on the first test trial after extreme-set training, while only 3 transposed after multiple-set training. The corresponding figures for the Caron study were 46 out of 90 in the first case and 20 out of 90 in the second case. The transposition of intermediate size by preverbal children may depend upon the types of examples presented during training. The results do not necessarily contradict the findings of Johnson and Zara, for it seems reasonable to assume that more extreme examples may be necessary in the three-choice problem to emphasize the generality of the relation learned during training than is necessary in the easier two-choice problem.

These studies offer interesting insights into means by which transfer in young children can be increased. It appears that an important basis of their failure to transfer what they have learned from one situation to another lies in their difficulty in recognizing the comparability of two situations whose absolute properties differ. If the child is shown through appropriate examples that the response being learned is not restricted to stimuli with particular absolute properties, a high degree of transfer—in the apparent absence of verbal mediation—can be obtained.

Verbal Mediation

The verbal mediation hypothesis would lead us to expect that transposition in the intermediate-size problem gradually comes under verbal control. Older, verbally competent children should transpose on both near and far tests. Despite the fact that a number of studies have been concerned with this problem, we still are unable to reach any firm conclusions.

Only one study (Caron, 1967) has found clear evidence that children who possess a term denoting middle-size show a greater frequency of transposition in the intermediate-size problem than do children who do not know such a term. The study included 288 four-year-olds. Prior to the experiment children were assigned to Concept or No-Concept groups on the basis of their ability to provide an appropriate label for the middle-sized of three squares. Of the children included in the study, half were in each group. Tests of transposition were conducted 1, 3, or 6 steps removed from the training set. Transposition was found with children who did not know a term for middle-size, but relatively few children who knew this term failed to transpose. Of 167 children who responded relationally on the first test trial, 110 were Concept subjects and 57 were No-Concept subjects. When asked to verbalize the principle of solution in post-test questioning, however, only 36 children (33 Concept and 3 No-Concept) were able to explain the basis of their responses.

In the remaining studies (Caron, 1966; Reese, 1961, 1962; Reese & Fiero, 1964; Rudel, 1957; Zeiler, 1963a) no consistent relations appeared between children's ability to verbalize the concept of middle-size and their performance on test trials. It is not clear why this was the case. It may reflect certain procedural problems. In some studies the number of subjects was so small that no definitive relations could be established, and the testing procedure differed across the studies. Although the only uncontaminated test of transposition is the performance on the first test trial (since later trials may reflect learning on the test rather than the training trials), most of these studies report the results for a series of test trials. In some cases any response on the test trials was rewarded while in others reward was given only for choices of the middle-sized stimulus. Each procedure may have significant, but different, effects on the incidence of transposition. Whatever the basis for these findings, the best that can be said is that the relation between verbalization and transposition is less striking than was the case with the two-stimulus problem. There appears to be a complex, and at times tenuous, relation between knowing a term for middle-sized, transposing, and being able to use a relevant term in the description of performance.

Supplying Labels

In the last chapter we found that merely supplying a label for the correct stimulus was not sufficient to insure that young children would use the labels in the test trials. What if preverbal children were supplied with the labels during the training trials, and also were told, prior to each response, which stimulus would be correct? This procedure should be effective in increasing the frequency of transposition, for it not only provides a potential mediator, but also should clarify the relevance of the mediator for the solution of the problem.

Reese (1966) followed this procedure in a study with three- and four-year-olds. (A portion of this study was discussed in Chapter 6.) In Group I, the experimenter labeled the middle-sized block as the "medium" one, told the children before each response on the training trials that the reward would be under the "medium" one, and following errors repeated, "No, it's under the medium one." In Group II, the children were told, "It's not under the big one or the little one," and after an error, "No, it's not under the big one or the little one." The labels were omitted in Group III and the children were told, "It's under one of the blocks." The experimenter did not make any comments during the test trials, but simply asked the children, "Which one is it under?" The area-ratio of the stimuli was 2 : 1 and test trials were conducted with stimuli one and three steps removed from the training set.

Children who had received instructions about the correct stimulus showed more frequent transposition than did those who had received no instructions. On the first test trial 39% of the children in Group I, 50% in Group II, and 18% in Group III transposed. Telling the children which stimuli were not correct actually produced a slightly higher frequency of transposition than telling the children which stimulus was correct. Even with such explicit provision of labels, however, at least half of the children did not transpose. Young children show a remarkable intransigence about accepting the fact that what is said may have utility in directing what they should do. It is interesting to contemplate what the results might have been had the experimenter preceded the training trials with a more explicit illustration of how words may have general applicability in solving problems. This could be done quite easily by combining the techniques of Johnson and Zara or Gonzales and Ross with those used in the present study. It may require multiple examples before the young child understands that a word may be useful in selecting the response to be made to stimuli wiith different absolute characteristics.

Ratio Theory

If developmental differences in transposition of intermediate size are so nebulous, perhaps a theory would be more successful if the variable of verbal mediation were ignored. Zeiler (1963*a*) attempted to do this in proposing a ratio theory, which derives its predictions about the intermediate-size problem solely on the basis of the characteristics of the stimuli present in the training and test situations. For a while this appeared to be an attractive theory, for it offered a quantitative approach to the transposition problem. Basically, it is an application of Helson's (1964) theory of adaptation level. The details do not need to be discussed here, but, in general, it is assumed that an adaptation level is established during the training trials that is a sum of the geometric mean of the values of the stimuli present and of a residual adaptation level derived from prior experience. The child learns to select a stimulus that has a particular ratio to this adaptation level. During the test trials, it is predicted that the stimulus will be chosen whose ratio to the adaptation level for the test trials is most similar to the ratio of the original positive stimulus to the training adaptation level. Zeiler (1963*a*, 1963*b*) presented a series of studies with children that seemed to be in line with these predictions. Shortly afterward, Riley, Sherman, and McKee (1966) replicated the conditions used by Zeiler in his studies, but found it impossible to obtain certain of Zeiler's findings. After discussing the instances where the theory was and was not upheld, Zeiler (1966*b*) found it necessary to conclude that ". . . the ratio theory is also unconvincing (p. 260)."

Individual Differences

In some respects the results of the studies we have discussed are discouraging, for our efforts to produce tidy generalizations about the transposition of intermediate size are not fulfilled. We are left with a large amount of data and no convincing theoretical interpretation. Although partial support for each theory can be found, none of the theories provides an adequate and comprehensive basis for predicting the results. Could it be that we are demanding too great consistency in our results? Perhaps different children learn different things about the stimuli, and our efforts to separate children by age or possession of the concept of middle-size give us an incomplete description of the differences among children that vitally influence how and what they will learn. Perhaps no theory will be capable of predicting children's performance if we fail to provide more effective means of classifying our subjects.

If we were to conclude that individual differences among children preclude theoretical analyses of their learning we would be creating an inappropriately bleak outlook for the construction of satisfactory theories. If, however, we assume that individual differences among children impose limiting conditions upon the applicability of theories, we would be pointing out an important way in which theories can go wrong.

If we are to study individual differences we must determine what characteristics that differ among children are important for learning. One approach would be to discover what kinds of differences in learning and transfer exist, and then attempt to uncover some means of predicting when the differences will occur. An initial step has been taken by Zeiler and Salten (1967) in a study of 20 five- and six-year-old children. The children were presented a standard intermediate-size problem, and all children were given both near and far tests of transposition. Separate gradients of transposition were plotted for each child; these gradients were of four distinct types. Six children showed uniform transposition across all sets of training stimuli; seven showed predominantly absolute choices; three showed decreasing gradients as the test stimuli became more remote; and four showed inconsistent choices. The authors concluded: "The most parsimonious conclusion is that different children were controlled by different aspects of the stimuli and therefore produced the variety of choice gradients. These data are the first which indicate basically different choice gradients among children of the same age (p. 183)." Why were different children controlled by different aspects of the stimuli? The authors had no clue. Thus tantalized, we are left to wonder.

CONCLUSIONS

The transposition problem has proved to be a hearty one. Study after study has attempted to penetrate the bases whereby children transpose (or fail to transpose) a relational response across sets of stimuli differing in their absolute properties. In the intermediate-size problem we still have no means of predicting with a high degree of accuracy when transposition will occur. In fact, one of the more provocative results was the finding that different children seem to learn different things about the stimuli during the course of training. The separation of children into preverbal and verbal categories anticipated the fact that children's modes of learning may differ, depending upon factors other than their experience in the training and testing situations. It remains for future research to clarify what, other than verbal ability, may be related to differences among children in their performance on transfer tasks.

When young children do not understand the meaning of the term "middle-size" they are not likely to transpose in the intermediate-size problem unless (a) the test stimuli are perceptually very similar to the training stimuli or (b) training is given with extreme sets of stimuli that emphasize the broad applicability of a relational response. Without a readily available concept of middle-size, young children find it hard to realize that a relational response existing within one set of stimuli may be applicable to other, dissimilar sets. Even when they are told the basis of correct response they may need multiple examples of how this solution is applicable over a broad range of stimuli. Possessing a concept of middle-size is not the critical factor in transposition, however, for there are enough instances where children knew the concept of middle-size and failed to transpose that we can be sure that verbal mediation is less influential as a factor in the performance of four- through six-year-olds than it was in the two-choice problem. Perhaps it will be shown that the complexity of the relation involved in the concept of middle-size is such that verbal mediation becomes a powerful aid in transfer at a somewhat later age.

This chapter concludes the discussion of transposition. It does not conclude our discussion of the tangled and controversial research on verbal mediation and transfer, however. Although we know that the hypothesis of verbal mediation does not offer the clear and direct explanation of discrimination learning that seemed so appealing just a few years ago, it is useful, nevertheless, to pursue the arguments arising from consideration of the hypothesis with another group of studies dealing with transfer of training. In showing how verbal mediation is not a sufficient explanation of developmental changes in transfer, we will discover other processes that do have significant effects, either by themselves or in interaction with verbalization.

9

Discrimination-shift Problems

One case of transfer of training is transposition. Several other types of transfer problems that have captured a great deal of interest are those dealing with discrimination-shifts. Behind these studies is the same question asked in studies of transposition: Will performance in the various types of shifts differ, depending upon children's capabilities in the use of language? As you will see, this research is difficult to read. The experimental procedures are complicated and a maze of variables emerge as significant determinants of children's performance. In fact, the research on discrimination-shifts is among the most difficult to follow in the literature of child psychology. Why have child psychologists selected these problems? Because they seemed to be a particularly sensitive means of obtaining information about how language may be used in directing behavior.

REVERSAL AND NONREVERSAL SHIFTS

Our discussion will begin with a consideration of reversal and nonreversal shifts. These tasks were taken directly from studies of problem-solving with human adults and of discrimination learning with rats. College students had been found to behave one way in these problems, rats another way. In the first studies with children, it seemed that very young children performed more like rats and older children performed more like college students. If so, there must be a period during childhood of transition from one form of learning to the other. Could this be the period when the child acquires language, before which his performance does not depend on verbal mediation and after which it does? The story sounds familiar. It is the same argument that led to the developmental studies of transposition. Only the experimental tasks are different.

Designing a study to investigate reversal-shifts is relatively simple. The study consists of two parts. During training the child must learn to choose Stimulus A in preference to Stimulus B. After he has mastered this task the transfer task is introduced. The child finds an abrupt change in the relation between response and reward. He must reverse his responses, for choices of B rather than A now lead to reward.

When we talk about reversal and nonreversal shifts, however, the procedure becomes more complicated. The tasks still are presented in two stages, but the stimuli differ on two dimensions rather than on just one. For example, figures may be used that differ in both color and form. One dimension is relevant for the solution of the training problem and one is irrelevant. Form may be the relevant dimension and choices of a triangle rather than a square are rewarded, regardless of their color. In the second phase of the task the child must learn either a reversal or a nonreversal shift. In a reversal shift the relevant dimension (form) remains relevant but the pattern of reinforcement is reversed. Choices of the square now are rewarded, regardless of their color. In a nonreversal shift the previously irrelevant dimension becomes relevant. Whereas form had been the relevant dimension during training, color becomes the relevant dimension during a nonreversal shift. Choices of one of the colors are rewarded, regardless of the form bearing the color. The basic question asked in such studies is whether the performance of verbally competent children will differ on reversal and nonreversal shifts from that of younger children who are less facile in their use of language. To see how predictions about performance are related to the child's level of language development we will look at the theoretical notions and experimental work of Tracy and Howard Kendler, whose writings have stimulated much of the research on reversal and nonreversal shifts with children.

Theoretical Background

The basic paradigm for the study of reversal and nonreversal shifts is presented in Figure 9-1. This paradigm and the predictions made from stimulus-response (single-unit) and mediation theory espoused by the Kendlers have been described in the following manner:

If a subject is initially trained on stimuli that differ simultaneously in brightness (black vs. white) and size (large vs. small) by being rewarded to responses to black regardless of size, a reversal shift would consist of learning to respond to white, and a nonreversal shift would consist of learning to respond to small. Comparisons between these two types of shifts are of particular interest because theories based on single-unit vs. mediated S-R connections yield opposed predictions about their relative efficiency. A single-unit theory assumes a direct association between the external stimulus and the overt response and would predict a reversal shift to be more difficult than a nonreversal shift. This is because reversal shift requires the replacement of a response that has previously been consistently reinforced with a response that has previously been consistently extinguished. In a nonreversal shift previous training has reinforced responses to the newly positive and negative stimuli equally often. Strengthening one of these associations does not require as much extinction of its competitor as in a reversal shift and should, therefore, be acquired more easily.

A theory that includes a mediating link (or links) between the external stimulus and the overt response leads to a different prediction. The mediating link is conceived of as a perceptual or verbal response, often covert, to the relevant dimension, which produces cues that elicit the overt response. In a reversal

Figure 9-1. In the first discrimination the black stimulus is correct (see text). According to a single-unit theory the excitatory tendency (habit strength) developed to "black" will be increased with each reinforcement. "Large" will share in this reinforcement half of the time and "small" half of the time. Since rate of extinction is assumed to be a function of habit strength, it will require a larger number of trials to extinguish the response to "black" than to either "large" or "small." Since the new response cannot be learned until the prior response has been extinguished, it is predicted that a reversal problem will require more trials than a nonreversal for nonmediating children. If the children have made some response, such as "It's the black one" during the training trials, it should be easier for them to shift to a second value on this dimension ("It's the white one") than to begin to verbalize a new dimension. Mediating children, therefore, should learn the reversal problem more readily than the nonreversal problem.

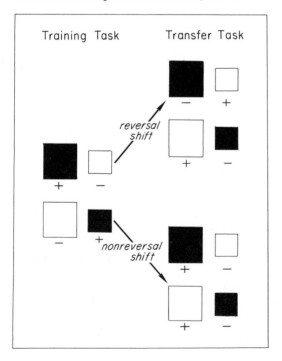

shift, the initial dimension maintains its relevance, hence, so does the mediated response. Only the overt response needs to be changed, and since the experimental situation provides only one alternative overt response, the problem presents no difficulty. In a nonreversal shift the previously acquired mediation is no longer relevant, consequently both the mediating and overt response must be replaced, making the task more difficult than a reversal shift. It is therefore to be expected that for subjects who mediate, a reversal shift will be acquired more easily than a nonreversal shift (Kendler, 1963, pp. 35-36).

This position is much the same as the one we encountered in Kuenne's (1946) discussion of transposition. If children are incapable of using verbal mediators their shift performance should be in line with stimulus-response notions about relative rates of extinction and acquisition following different patterns of reinforcement. The ease of changing overt responses should be dependent upon changes in patterns of reinforcement between the training and shift trials. When verbal mediators are used, children's performance should be determined by what they say, rather than by the pattern of reinforcement they receive in responding to the absolute characteristics of the stimuli. For these children, the ease of changing overt responses should depend upon whether the mediator remains relevant or is changed. Reversal and nonreversal shifts have become interesting problems, then, because they enable us to test predictions based on assumptions concerning the relative ease of changing overt responses as contrasted to changing verbal mediators.

The Kendlers' Studies

Perhaps the first question that should be asked is whether children will learn a reversal faster than a nonreversal problem, or vice versa. The first study comparing the ease of learning reversal and nonreversal shifts was undertaken by the Kendlers (1959) with five- and six-year-olds. The children were given a task of the type described above. After learning the original discrimination, half were shifted to a reversal problem and half to a nonreversal problem. Overall, one type of shift was not learned more rapidly than the other, apparently contradicting predictions made from both single-unit and mediational theories.

In reflecting upon their findings, the Kendlers hypothesized that their failure to achieve results consonant with either theory might be because children of the age levels represented in the study were at a transitional period. Some might be operating in a single-unit manner, others might be employing verbal mediation. Consequently, the subjects were separated according to the ease with which they had learned the initial discrimination (above and below the median number of training trials). Those who had been slow to learn the original discrimination were found to learn the nonreversal shift more rapidly than the reversal shift; the fast learners learned the reversal shift more rapidly than the nonreversal shift. The results fall in line with predictions if it is assumed that the fast learners had approached the task with a verbal label for the correct stimuli, while the slow learners had not. If this were the case, the more rapid original learning and the greater ease in learning the reversal than the nonreversal shift would be in line with mediation theory. Children who showed slower original learning and greater difficulty in learning the reversal than the nonreversal shift would seem to be performing in line with single-unit theory.

Post hoc interpretations are never conclusive. The next step, therefore, was to attempt to clarify and strengthen the deductions made in the first study by testing younger children. Since it was assumed that children below the ages of five or six are unlikely to utilize verbal mediators spontaneously, they should have more difficulty in learning a reversal than a nonreversal shift. This prediction was supported when the earlier procedure was repeated with three- to five-year-olds (Kendler, Kendler, & Wells, 1960). The interpretation of the results is obscured, however, when we compare the performance of the children (half of the subjects) who had been required to verbalize the basis of response during the terminal phase of the training trials with that of those who had not been instructed to verbalize. The performance of the two groups did not differ, even though the use of verbal labels had been assumed to be helpful in reversal learning. The authors were forced to conclude that at this stage "verbal responses, though available, do not readily mediate between external stimuli and overt responses, but rather form parallel connections with little or no interaction (p. 87)." These results were used by Reese (1962) in his formulation of the mediational deficiency hypothesis (see Chapter 6).

Relevant verbalization also failed to produce faster reversal learning with four- and seven-year-olds in a subsequent study (Kendler & Kendler, 1961). Children at each age were divided into three groups. In the training problem all groups were presented a large black square and a small white one, with choices of the first being reinforced. During these trials the children either (a) were required to verbalize the relevant dimension ("large"), (b) were required to verbalize the to-be irrelevant dimension ("black"), or (c) were not required to verbalize. On the reversal trials choices of the small stimuli were reinforced, regardless of their brightness. The results are presented in Figure 9-2. As far as the central purpose of the study is concerned, the results are ambiguous. The seven-year-olds did not benefit from verbalizing the relevant dimension, but they probably should not since they are assumed to be capable of spontaneous mediation. The four-year-olds (forgetting the mediational deficiency hypothesis for the moment) were expected to benefit from relevant verbalization. There was a trend in this direction, but it was not statistically significant. Verbalizing the irrelevant dimension during the training trials retarded learning on the second problem at both age levels, and the effect was about as great with four-year-olds as with seven-year-olds. It began to appear that the standard reversal-nonreversal task was not as effective as the Kendlers had hoped.

To pursue the quest for developmental changes in performance on discrimination-shift problems, Kendler, Kendler, and Learnard (1962) applied a new method, known as the optional-shift technique. Optional shift studies are conducted in three phases (see Figure 9-3). During initial training children are presented two pairs of stimuli whose members differ, for example, in size and brightness. (For purposes of simplification only one of the possible arrangements of stimuli and reinforcement is used in this example.) One attribute of one dimension is reinforced; say, black. One pair of the original stimuli is retained in a second phase, but now white is reinforced. Since in this example the white stimulus also is the small stimulus, children could be responding in the second phase on the basis of brightness (reversal shift) or size (nonreversal shift). A test then is conducted with the two original pairs of stimuli. For one of

Figure 9-2.   Mean number of trials required by four- and seven-year-olds to learn a reversal-shift problem after having verbalized the relevant dimension during the preceding trials on the original task, after no verbalization, and after having verbalized the irrelevant dimension during the original task. (From H. H. Kendler and T. S. Kendler, Effect of verbalization on discrimination reversal shifts in children. *Science*, 1961, 134, 1619. Copyright 1961 by the American Association for the Advancement of Science.)

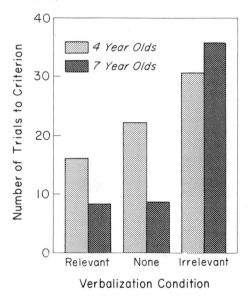

the pairs choices of either the large white stimulus or the small black stimulus are reinforced. Since responses to either stimulus in this pair are reinforced, consistent choices of one stimulus must be determined by the dimensions on which the stimuli differ (brightness or size) rather than by the consequences of response (reward or nonreward). The child is classified as having shown a reversal shift if his choices are predominantly (eight of ten choices) of the white stimulus, and a nonreversal shift if his choices are predominantly of the black (small) stimulus. In the first case it is assumed that the child had responded to brightness in the second phase of the task; in the second case, it is assumed that he had responded to size. If he had been responding to brightness he should choose the white (large) square, while if he had been responding to size he would choose the small (black) square. We do not know that this is what occurred, but infer that it was from his choices made in the third phase of the task.

Kendler, Kendler, and Learnard (1962) selected children at five age levels for their study; the mean ages were three, four, six, eight, and ten years. The percentage of children classified as showing reversal shifts increased with increasing age, from approximately 40% at age three to 60% at age ten. The increase is not dramatic, but is in the predicted direction. Contrary to prediction, the percentage of children demonstrating non-reversal shifts did not change; it remained around 30% at all ages. The remaining children responded inconsistently, showing a predominance of neither reversal nor nonreversal shifts. At the completion of the study the children were asked what the "winner" looked like. In line with the expectation that reversal shifts would be shown by children who are

Figure 9-3.   An illustration of a typical arrangement of stimuli and reinforcement used in the optional-shift technique. (From T. S. Kendler, H. H. Kendler, and B. Learnard, Mediated responses to size and brightness as a function of age. *American Journal of Psychology,* 1962, 75, 575, © 1962 *American Journal of Psychology.*)

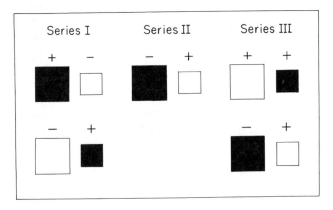

capable of mediating, 85% of the "reversers" verbalized the correct dimension. (The percentage of children who verbalized appropriately increased from around 40% at age three to over 80% at age ten, thus there is a parallel between ability to verbalize the relevant dimensions and the frequency of reversal shifts). Of the children who were classified as "nonreversers," however, 67% gave a correct verbal description of the stimuli. This finding was not expected, for nonreversers should not be so effective at verbalization. In general, the findings gave only partial support for the Kendlers' single-unit and mediational interpretation of shift performance.

A study then was conducted (Kendler, 1964) in which kindergarten children were told the basis for correct response and were required to verbalize prior to making each choice during the training trials of the optional-shift problem. Again, there was an unsystematic relation between verbalization and performance. The frequency of reversal shifts was increased by requiring the children to verbalize the basis of their response. But during the second phase of the task many children continued to verbalize the previously appropriate statements, while making the opposite choice from that contained in their verbalizations. For example, "a child who made no adjustment in the words he spoke would be saying, 'Black is the winner and white is the loser,' while he consistently chose the white square" (p. 431). (It should be pointed out that in this, as in all of the studies, the training conditions were counter-balanced so that each value of each dimension was relevant for one-fourth of the children.) When the study was repeated and only relevant verbalization was permitted in the second, optional shift phase, the incidence of reversal shifts again was higher in the verbalizing than in the nonverbalizing groups—but only when brightness was the initially relevant dimension. When it was shape, there was no significant difference between the verbalizers and nonverbalizers. Here we find one of the first hints that performance in these types of tasks may differ, depending upon the particular types of stimuli chosen for the study.

As the data accumulated, alternative interpretations of the effects were suggested. One of these concerned the influence of the number of training trials on reversal learning. According to a stimulus-response analysis, rate of extinction, hence rate of reversal learning, should be retarded as the number of training trials is increased. Since rate of extinction is assumed to depend on the number of prior reinforced responses, overtraining should retard extinction of the original response and thereby increase the number of trials required for learning the reversal. The slow learners of the Kendler and Kendler (1959) study and the younger children in the Kendler, Kendler, and Learnard (1962) study might have shown slower reversal learning, not because they were incapable of verbal mediation, but because they had had more training trials than the faster or older subjects.

To determine whether large amounts of training would produce a lower incidence of reversal learning, Kendler and Kendler (1966) gave half of their subjects 16 and half 36 trials on the original discrimination before presenting optional shift trials. The frequency of reversal shifts was not influenced by overtraining. While these data might be interpreted as supporting the Kendlers' position, it should be noted that their subjects were four- and nine-year-olds. Four-year-olds should be operating in a single-unit fashion. If this were the case, overtraining should have resulted in greater perseveration on the previously correct response, thereby reducing their tendency to show reversal shifts.

Would an entirely different technique produce more stable results? Kendler, Kendler, and Marken (1969) have attempted to answer this question. The subjects were between four and eighteen years old. They were shown, for example, pictures of fruit and of clothing. Each time a fruit appeared it was necessary to press one button to obtain a reward, and each time an article of clothing appeared, a second button had to be pressed. After this discrimination was acquired, the relation between stimulus and response was reversed for all of the pictures, or the relation was reversed for only half of the pictures in each category. The first is an example of a reversal shift, and the second was termed a half-reversal shift (since a reversal was required for only half of the items). If the subjects possess a well-organized mediating response, it should be relatively easy to reverse the stimulus-response relation for all of the items, but more difficult when the new "rule" pertained to only half of the items. If, on the other hand, the subjects were responding in a single-unit fashion, the half-reversal should be relatively easier, since it required learning a new relation for only half of the items. As predicted, the reversal shift became increasingly easier than the half-reversal with increasing age. At age four, however, the two types of reversal were learned with equal ease. The new technique thus provided only partial support for the distinction between single-unit responding and mediated behavior. Older subjects seemed to be directing their responses on the basis of a mediating process related to category of stimulus, but the youngest children did not necessarily seem to be learning each of the stimulus-response relations in a single-unit fashion.

This is the core of the Kendlers' work with children. It is central in the discussion of developmental changes in performance on discrimination-shift problems, although it comprises only a small portion of the research with children that has been done. The Kendlers have been vigorous in the pursuit of information that would bear on their hypotheses. In the end, however, the hypotheses could not withstand the barrage of experimental data. Words alone were insufficient for effective mediation in the young child. At the same time, the performance of preverbal children did not conform with great consistency to a single-unit analysis. Older children at times appeared to mediate and their performance on reversal tasks seemed to be in line with the verbal mediation hypothesis. Even so, the effects were dependent upon the dimension that happened to be relevant for original learning and the tendency to show reversal shifts was not always characteristic of "verbal" children. The equivocal nature of these findings demanded recognition of the fact that a satisfactory interpretation of performance on discrimination-shift problems would require a more elaborate structure than the Kendlers proposed. [Recently, however, the Kendlers have attempted to extend their model. (Kendler & Kendler, 1970.)]

METHODOLOGICAL CRITICISMS

It is useful at this point to review some of the criticisms that have been made of the methodology used in studies of discrimination-shifts. This research contains many perplexing problems in experimental design, and criticisms of the methodology began as soon as the first studies were published. Bit by bit they amounted to a devastating attack. Slamecka (1968) has written a penetrating analysis of these methodological difficulties, and the following discussion relies heavily upon his points. A reply, and further discussion of these issues, has been made by the Kendlers (Kendler & Kendler, 1969).

reversal - no reinforcement
nonreversed - ration or interval

Partial Reinforcement

Let us compare the pattern of reinforcement on the transfer task in reversal and nonreversal shifts. It is clear in Figure 9-1 that in the reversal shift there is consistent nonreinforcement of responses to the previously correct stimuli. For the nonreversal shift, the pattern of reinforcement changes for only one of the two pairs of stimuli. For the other pair, the pattern of reinforcement is the same in the transfer task as it was in the training task. In short, there is 0% reinforcement of responses to the previously correct stimuli in the reversal shift and approximately 50% reinforcement of responses to the previously correct stimuli in the nonreversal shift. This awkward state of affairs leads to several difficulties.

According to either a single-unit or mediational interpretation, partial reinforcement should make nonreversal learning more difficult than reversal learning. There is a vast literature indicating that partial reinforcement of a previously correct response leads to greater difficulty in learning a new response to the same stimuli than does consistent nonreinforcement of the previously correct response. Whether one is responding to the absolute characteristics of the stimuli or on the basis of verbal mediation, partial confirmation of a response should result in greater reluctance to abandon it than would be the case when the response no longer receives any confirmation. The design therefore biases the results toward more rapid learning of the reversal than the nonreversal shift.

Developmental changes in the frequency of reversal shifts also may be related to the partial reinforcement effect. In the reversal shift, the sudden and total cessation of reinforcement of the previously correct response should aid the child in detecting that the problem has changed and provide a strong cue that new, completely different responses must be made. It is reasonable to assume that older children would detect the change in the pattern of reinforcement more readily and would use this information more effectively than would younger children. In the non-reversal shift, the necessity for changing response and the form of the new response are less obvious. Since the previous solution continues to receive partial confirmation, even older children would have some difficulty in detecting that the problem had changed. On these bases alone, an increase in the ease of learning reversal shifts and less pronounced developmental changes in performance on nonreversal shifts would be predicted.

In the face of these difficulties experimenters adopted the optional-shift technique, where, during the third phase of the task, all responses to the critical stimuli are reinforced. This procedure also poses formidable problems, for there is no means by which the type of shift can be manipulated experimentally. In such a "free" response design, one is left with co-relations (e.g., older children make more reversal shifts), but knowledge that two variables are co-related does not provide the desired information about causation. We need to know why older children make more reversal shifts, not merely that they do.

The confounding effects of partial reinforcement can be eliminated in a simple manner—by using new stimuli on the shift trials. If the training stimuli differ in color and shape, for example, the stimuli in the transfer task also would differ in color and shape, but the colors and shapes would be different from those used in constructing the training stimuli. A shift comparable to the reversal shift can be introduced by requiring the child to respond to color (and not to shape) in both training and transfer trials. A form of nonreversal shift would occur if the basis of response were changed from color to shape. The first has been termed an intradimensional shift and the second, an extradimensional shift. These two types of shift will be described further in the following pages.

Cue Preference

In looking at Figure 9-1 the first thing I notice is that the squares differ in brightness. Someone else might notice first that they differ in size. I probably would be more ready to label the squares in terms of "black" and "white"; the other person, in terms of "large" and "small." If I happen to be tested on a reversal task with brightness as the relevant dimension, I would be likely to label the squares appropriately during both the training and transfer trials and would show rapid learning during both periods. If, on the other hand, I were presented a nonreversal shift and size became the relevant dimension, my tendency to label the squares in terms of brightness would be inappropriate. The results of discrimination-shift problems may be influenced, therefore, by differences among individuals in their tendencies to respond to different dimensions represented in the stimuli. This is not an especially novel argument, of course, for Zeiler and Salten (1967) made a similar point in their discussion of transposition, where different children appeared to be responding to different aspects of the stimuli.

Depending upon the conditions under which the children are tested, differences in cue preference or cue dominance may bias response towards faster learning of reversal or nonreversal shifts. This is an especially important problem in developmental studies, for children at different ages tend to show different preferences for particular aspects of stimuli, such as color, pattern, size, shape, brightness, or height. Whether learning will be fast or slow may depend upon whether the dimension to which the child first responds happens to be relevant in the solution of the problem. If it is, the initial discrimination will be learned rapidly, and, in turn, the children will be more likely to respond to a second value on this dimension (reversal shift) than to a value on the nonpreferred dimension (nonreversal shift). Children may show faster reversal or nonreversal learning, depending on differences in cue preferences rather than upon their ability to mediate.

Children's preferences for particular cues cannot be controlled experimentally. Their effects on performance can be taken into account, however, by selecting children, prior to the experiment, who evidence particular preferences and by including an evaluation of the effects of these preferences in the analysis of the data.

Intradimensional and Extradimensional Shifts

In view of the preceding criticisms, the results of a study by Eimas (1966) are of special interest, for this was the first study of discrimination-shifts with children that used different stimuli in the training and transfer trials. The stimuli differed in color and form. The subjects were kindergarteners with a mean age of 5½ years and second graders with a mean age of 8 years. Training on the original discrimination was carried either to criterion (20 out of 25 responses correct in a daily session) or 50 overtraining trials were given. For half of the children the transfer task was an intradimensional shift and for the other half, an extradimensional shift.

The older children learned the training task more rapidly than did the younger children, and form cues were easier to discriminate than color cues. On the transfer tasks, as can be seen in Figure 9-4, the intradimensional shift was learned more rapidly than the extradimensional shift at both ages, and overtraining facilitated the learning of both types of shifts. These results were confirmed in a study by Mumbauer and Odom (1967) to be discussed later.

The failure to find age differences in the ease of learning the two types of shift is not in accord with the Kendlers' position. To interpret his results, Eimas relied on a theory of discrimination learning proposed by Zeaman and House (1963), who have discussed the discrimination-shift problems in terms of mediating attentional responses. In this case, the mediator is a nonverbal observing response that is transferred from the training to the transfer task. That is, the child learns to respond to (observe) one dimension during training and transfers this observing response to the transfer task. We will leave further discussion of nonverbal mediation to a later chapter.

Figure 9-4.   The mean number of errors made in learning intradimensional and extradimensional shifts as a function of relevant dimension, age, and overtraining. (Data from P. D. Eimas, Effects of overtraining and age on intradimensional and extradimensional shifts in children. *Journal of Experimental Child Psychology,* 1966, 3, 352.)

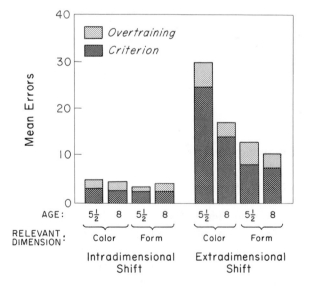

STUDIES OF CUE PREFERENCES

An incidental aspect of both the Kendler (1964) and Eimas (1966) studies was that the results were dependent upon which stimulus dimension was correct. In view of these findings and in light of our previous discussion, studies directly investigating cue preferences are of crucial interest. One of the first investigations was reported by Smiley and Weir (1966). The stimuli differed on color and form, two dimensions for which children are known to have different preferences. Before the training problem was presented, two series of trials were given, on the basis of which children (of kindergarten age) could be classified as color or form dominant. Equal numbers (32) of form dominant and color dominant children were selected for the study. During the training trials of the optional-shift procedure either the dominant or nondominant dimension was reinforced. In the test series, 25 children for whom the dominant dimension had been correct, but only 8 children for whom the nondominant dimension had been correct, showed reversal shifts. The corresponding numbers of children who showed nonreversal shifts were 5 and 10, respectively. It is interesting here to note that when the nonreversal shift involved shifting the children from their nondominant to their dominant dimension, twice as many children showed a nonreversal shift as when they were shifted from a dominant to a nondominant dimension.

In contrast to earlier findings, the rate of learning the original task was not related to the incidence of reversal shifts, but was significantly faster for children whose preferred dimension had been reinforced. Only 2 children whose dominant dimension had been reinforced failed to learn the second, optional-shift phase of the problem, but 13 children whose nondominant dimension had been reinforced failed to do so. The results strongly suggest that dimensional dominance has a determining influence both on rate of learning and frequency of reversal shifts, such that both are increased if there is a fortuitous assignment of children to the condition in which their preferred dimension is reinforced.

Other studies have found similar effects. The effect of stimulus preferences is clearly evident in a study by Tighe and Tighe (1966) with three- and four-year-olds. The stimuli differed in height (flat versus raised square) and in pattern (horizontal versus vertical stripes). Children for whom height was the relevant dimension learned the initial discrimination in an average of 4.3 trials, while those for whom pattern was correct required nearly twenty times as many trials (an average of 73.4). All 16 children trained to criterion on the height discrimination showed a reversal shift in the optional shift procedure, but only 2 of the 16 children trained to criterion on the pattern discrimination showed reversal shifts. When height was the relevant dimension the tendency to show reversal shifts was not altered by 100 overtraining trials, but the frequency of reversal shifts among four-year-olds was increased by overtraining when pattern was the relevant dimension. In other words, overtraining had no influence on performance when the dominant dimension was correct but appeared to heighten the salience of the nondominant dimension.

Eimas (1967) also found differences in the frequency of reversal shifts by eight- and ten-year-olds, depending upon the dimension that was relevant during the training trials. The frequency of reversal shifts was greater when the relevant dimension was size than when it was brightness. We are led to conclude, therefore, that the frequency of reversal shifts may be highly dependent on the particular dimension that happens to be relevant and is reinforced.

Although it may be impossible to modify children's preferences for particular cues, the salience of such cues can be heightened by appropriate pretraining experiences. Tighe (1965), for example, assumed that the ease of learning a reversal shift would be increased if the child were given experience during pretraining in isolating and utilizing the to-be-relevant stimulus dimensions. Five- and six-year-olds who made same-different judgments with the training stimuli during pretraining later learned a reversal shift more rapidly than did children who were given irrelevant pretraining or who were presented a nonreversal shift. The number of dimensions represented in the pretraining stimuli may be an important variable. Five- and six-year-olds showed faster reversal learning when all four values (two of height and two of brightness) were represented in the pretraining experience than when the stimuli differed only in height or brightness (Tighe & Tighe, 1968). Similarly, Vaughter and Cross (1965) found that prior experience with both stimuli used in a reversal task produced more rapid learning than when the experience was limited to one of the stimuli or when no preliminary experience was given.

Being able to order stimuli on a dimension also may facilitate the ease of learning reversal shifts. The children in a study by Johnson and White (1967) who were above the median in performance on a task involving the dimensional ordering of stimuli made significantly fewer errors in learning a reversal shift than did those below the median on the ordering task. Whatever we may call it—cue preference, cue dominance, stimulus saliency, or ordering ability—whenever the stimulus dimensions are differentiated by the subject prior to the experimental task, the ease of learning a reversal shift is significantly increased. The interpretation of any set of data is obscured unless this factor is taken into account.

Before leaving the discussion of cue preferences the results of a complex but elucidating study by Mumbauer and Odom (1967) should be reviewed. This study assessed the roles of dimensional preference, verbalization, and overtraining in reversal, intradimensional, and extradimensional shifts with preschool children. The incorporation of so many variables in a single experiment complicates the discussion of the results, but such a design provides a powerful means of assessing the effects of each variable in isolation and in interaction with the other variables. Relying on the fact (Suchman & Trabasso, 1966) that preschool children differ in their preferences for form and color (generally preferring form to color after the age of four), the stimuli were designed to vary on these two dimensions. Initial learning was faster when the children (mean age, five years) were tested with form as the relevant dimension and when they verbalized prior to responding. A significant interaction between verbalization and dimension indicated that verbalizing had no influence on rate of learning the training problem when the preferred dimension (form) was relevant, but facilitated performance when the nonpreferred dimension (color) was relevant.

On the shift trials, learning was faster when form was correct, when the children had verbalized the relevant dimension during the training trials, and on intradimensional or reversal shifts. (To assess the magnitude of these effects see Table 9-1, containing the mean number of trials required to learn the shifts under the various conditions.) There were numerous significant interactions. The general pattern in these interactions was for the performance of one of the groups included in the comparisons to diverge from that of all the other groups entering into the interaction. The outcome of these interactions leads to several conclusions. Of central importance is the fact that the various types of shifts were learned with equal ease, except when children were required to make an extradimensional shift from their preferred dimension. It was more difficult to shift from a form-relevant to a color-relevant problem than from a color-relevant to a form-relevant problem. Verbalization had no significant effect when the preferred dimension had been correct but the combination

Table 9-1.   Mean numbers of trials required to reach criterion (9 out of 10 correct responses) on intradimensional, reversal, and extradimensional shift problems under the various experimental conditions (6 subjects per cell)

Overtraining	Shift	Verbalization		No Verbalization	
		Form	Color	Form	Color
	Intra-	10.2	11.5	11.3	22.0
0	Reversal	10.5	10.8	12.0	47.2
	Extra-	17.3	40.2	20.0	105.0
	Intra-	9.3	18.3	9.5	11.5
25	Reversal	10.2	10.3	12.5	13.0
	Extra-	35.3	38.2	20.2	49.3

Data from C. C. Mumbauer and R. D. Odom, Variables affecting the performance of preschool children in intradimensional, reversal and extradimensional shifts. *Journal of Experimental Psychology*, 1967, 75, 184.

of a nonpreferred dimension and nonverbalization retarded learning for the various types of shifts. A similar effect was found for overtraining; the groups that had not been overtrained and were shifted to a color discrimination required more trials to learn the various shifts than did children who were shifted to a form discrimination or who were overtrained and shifted to a color discrimination. Finally, overtraining and verbalization had equivalent but not cumulative effects. Children who had not verbalized and were not overtrained performed more poorly than the groups that had verbalized, received overtraining, or both.

In the presence of so many significant interactions it becomes necessary to qualify statements about the effects of the experimental variables. Each may have strong or minimal effects, depending upon the operation of another variable. For the most part, their influence was dependent upon whether or not training had been conducted with a preferred or nonpreferred dimension.

The methodological problems of the earlier studies have, for the most part, been resolved in the studies just discussed. These studies contribute two important findings: First, extradimensional shifts are not easier for preverbal children to solve than intradimensional shifts. Second, the characteristics of the stimuli have a strong determining influence on the ease with which discrimination shifts are made. The first finding is contrary to predictions based on the single-unit interpretation, and the second leads one to question whether verbal mediation is the necessary or sufficient explanation of the rapid learning of reversal shifts by older children. The studies do not disprove the validity of the verbal mediation hypothesis, but are clear illustrations of how behavior that once was considered to be verbally mediated may be found in the apparent absence of such mediation.

ADDITIONAL STUDIES

It is impossible, and unnecessary, to discuss the remaining studies in detail, for by now scores of studies with children have appeared in the discrimination-shift literature. The most efficient means of acknowledging their contributions is to present summary statements of the experimental results. Because the different studies have used different procedures, most of which are subject to the methodological criticisms discussed above, it is possible to make comments only about the general directions of the results. Some inconsistencies in the findings are to be expected, for as we have seen, seemingly minor differences in experimental design may produce marked differences in performance. [For exhaustive reviews of the discrimination-shift studies with children, see Hale (1968) and Wolff (1967).]

Age

Do the remaining studies indicate that younger children learn extradimensional (or nonreversal) shifts more rapidly than intradimensional (or reversal) shifts and that older children show the opposite effects? Of six studies with preschool children, the results of four are in the predicted direction (Marsh, 1964; Saravo, 1967; Tighe & Tighe, 1967; Trabasso, Deutsch, & Gelman, 1966); and two are not (Cobb & Price, 1966; Dickerson, 1966). With older children intradimensional shifts were learned more easily than extradimensional shifts in nine studies (Furth & Youniss, 1964; Heal, 1966; Hochman, 1966; Sanders, Ross, & Heal, 1965; Saravo, 1967; Suzuki, 1961; Trabasso, Deutsch, & Gelman, 1966; and Youniss, 1964); while in five studies they were not (Tighe & Tighe, 1967; Trabasso, Deutsch, & Gelman, 1966; Viney & Varner, 1967; Youniss & Furth, 1965; and Willer, 1963). In general, then, the results offer some support for positions positing age differences in performance, but the developmental differences are not strikingly consistent.

Before reaching any conclusions about developmental changes, a study by Jeffrey (1965) should be considered. Jeffrey has shown how a slight change in the testing procedure can produce results that have a destructive effect on any theory postulating changes with age in the ease of learning reversal shifts. The study included four-, six- and eight-year-olds and college students. The subjects were trained on a color discrimination and after reaching criterion the previously nonreinforced stimulus was reinforced. In addition to changing the pattern of reinforcement, the form of the stimuli was changed from circles to squares. With this procedure, there were no developmental changes in ease of reversal learning. These results may be interpreted as indicating that young children have difficulty in reversal learning because they are less capable than older children in abstracting a common dimension within the training and test stimuli. Changing one aspect of the cues between the training and test trials apparently emphasized this commonality, thereby increasing the ease of learning the reversal shift by younger children. We are left, then, with the possibility of wiping out all developmental changes in performance by introducing procedures that were not considered in early discussions of developmental changes in shift behavior.

Verbalization

Does verbalization increase the tendency to show reversal shifts? In studies where verbalization was manipulated directly, the results turn out to be elusive. The results of Silverman (1966) offer clear support for the facilitative effects of verbalization; both three- and four- and seven- and

eight-year-olds learned a reversal shift more rapidly when they were required to verbalize the relevant dimension during training than when
they were not. No overall facilitating effects of verbalization were reported by Morse and Shepp (1967) for kindergarten and first-grade children. Among the intradimensional shift subjects, however, those who
spontaneously continued to verbalize during the shift problem learned
more rapidly than did those who abandoned verbalization after the training trials. For the older children, verbalization impeded the learning of
extradimensional shift problems. Unexpectedly, the kindergarten children
who verbalized during the training period later learned both types of
problems more slowly than did those who did not verbalize. Blank
(1966), who informed half of her preschool subjects of the solution to the
training problem, found that such information did not help them significantly on the reversal problem, for their performance was similar to that
of groups for whom the correct responses were not labeled. Similarly,
Cobb and Price (1966) found no differences in the performance of preschool children who were given pretraining in learning relevant or irrelevant labels for the discriminative stimuli. Whatever the ultimate resolution
of the sources of discrepancies among these studies, it is obvious that verbalization does not necessarily result in more effective learning of reversal and intradimensional shift problems.

Overtraining

A third variable is overtraining. In the studies discussed thus far overtraining has had an indecisive effect on discrimination-shift performance.
A more definitive statement can be obtained from Wolff (1967), who has
discussed the results of 30 comparisons produced from studies investigating the effects of overtraining on discrimination-shift performance by
children (pp. 384-391). From his analysis, Wolff concluded that overtraining had little effect on children's performance in extradimensional-
shift problems. For intradimensional and reversal shifts, overtraining was
more likely to facilitate shifts involving stimuli varying in visual qualities
(e.g., color), but not when the stimuli varied in the spatial dimension
(e.g., left, middle, right). Generally, then, overtraining given prior to intradimensional or reversal shifts had an effect on performance similar to
that postulated for verbal mediation, namely, increasing the frequency of
reversal or intradimensional shifts. Whether overtraining increases the
saliency of the stimuli, strengthens an observing response, or increases
the likelihood of verbal mediation remains open to question.

CONCLUSIONS

The investigation of discrimination-shift problems seemed to be a
straightforward means of investigating the relation of language and trans-

fer at the time the Kendlers published their first studies. Whatever hope these studies held out that discrimination-shift problems would produce a definitive resolution of the issues related to developmental changes in verbal mediation was quickly lost as, with each study, the interpretation of the data became more tortuous and complex. For some, this is a frustrating and burdensome area of research. Judging by the deluge of recent publications, however, many have considered the analysis of children's performance on discrimination shifts to pose interesting and exciting problems.

What have we learned from these studies? Perhaps the most important conclusion that can be drawn is that equating verbal mediation with the acquisition of words is untenable. The ability to generate verbal solutions to problems involves much more than possessing relevant words. Verbalization is not the beginning, but it may be the end-product of a long series of cognitive activities involved in the solution of a discrimination-shift problem. The child must attend to the relevant dimension, abstract the significance of this dimension for the solution of the problem, and utilize the conceptual scheme resulting from this abstraction in new and modified situations. In the process of doing this, he may or may not code his activities in terms of words, and in the end, may or may not be able to describe in words what he has done. The evidence seems to undermine analyses of learning that consider words simply as stimuli mediating between the perception of the stimulus and overt response. Whenever supplying verbal labels to young children has had a facilitating effect on transfer, the results can be explained parsimoniously by assuming that the labels were effective in directing the child's attention to the relevant aspects of the stimuli. This is not to say that language does not influence the performance of older children; it does imply, however, that the mechanistic consideration of words simply as stimuli is an inadequate statement of the multifaceted role that language may have on learning.

It seems doubtful that continued research on developmental changes in discrimination-shift behavior is merited. A few studies have shown that extradimensional shifts may be learned more rapidly by younger children than intradimensional shifts, but the major contribution of these studies has been to demonstrate how reversal or intradimensional shifts may be increased in frequency or made easier to learn. If the subject can verbalize the relevant dimension, if he has had prior experience in isolating the relevant dimensions, if the correct dimension is one he prefers, and if he is given overtraining on the initial problem—each of these variables seems to contribute to increasing the ease of learning reversal shifts. Are we to conclude that these variables all act to increase the probability that the child will use verbal cues in the solution of the problem, or are we to conclude that they all operate to increase the child's attentiveness to the relevant dimension? This is the crux of the current controversy concerning the necessity of verbal mediation in reversal learning. It seems unlikely that we will be able to obtain conclusive evidence in favor of either view. It is a difficult, if not impossible problem to ascertain whether or not the child has used covert verbalization in the course of his performance. Asking the child at the end of the study or getting the child to verbalize during the course of the study have been found to be insufficient approaches to this question. Nor is looking at lip movements or other overt indications sufficient, for subjects capable of verbal mediation do not always show such overt manifestations of verbal activity. Perhaps other techniques will be devised. Until they are, it is unlikely that the controversy will be resolved.

We are left, then, with a hypothesis whose support is at best controversial. We cannot reject the hypothesis that language is an important aide in learning and transfer. We can, however, continue to pursue the analysis of how language is facilitating, and how other processes may influence behavior in a manner similar to that found with the use of language. No one reading these studies can continue to accept the assumption that making a verbal utterance is equivalent to comprehending the significance and meaning of the utterance.

We still are plagued by the fundamental dilemma of whether thought arises from language, or whether language is only a means of communicating thought. Are we to follow Piaget, who "asserts very strongly that representational thought does not begin with and result from the incorporation of verbal signs from the social environment" (Flavell, 1963, p. 155), or can we still regard something like the hypothesis of verbal mediation as an over-simplified, but viable, approach to understanding symbolic behavior? Perhaps in the coming decades we can make a better guess than we can at this stage of knowledge in developmental psychology.

10

Paired-associate Learning

Thus far, we have concentrated primarily on the role of language in learning nonverbal responses. Our conclusions might be different if we were to look at studies of verbal learning, for here the potential mediator and the response lie in the same domain of behavior. Spontaneous or instructed application of words may have more direct influence on the learning of new relations among other words than on the learning of discriminative motor responses. We will begin our discussion, therefore, with a review of studies investigating verbal mediation and then proceed to a more general discussion of how naturally acquired language may facilitate or interfere with verbal learning in formal experimental tasks. Practicallly all of the studies relevant to this discussion have used one type of verbal learning, the learning of paired associates. [Reviews of this literature may be found in Goulet (1968) and Keppel (1964).]

Learning to associate words and objects, names and places, dates and events are common experiences in everyday life. All involve learning paired-associates. Given the object can we name the word? Given the word can we locate the object? Or, given a word can we produce a word with which it has been associated in the past?

Although paired-associate learning has had a long and venerable history in psychology, few of the early studies included children as subjects. It has become apparent, however, that children may be ideal subjects for this type of research. Not only do they make it possible to study developmental changes, but the results of studies with children often tend to be less ambiguous than those found with adults. Children possess less complexly interrelated networks of verbal associations and because of this they may be more strongly influenced by their experiences in the experimental situation than are adults.

METHODOLOGY

In a list of paired associates each pair consists of a stimulus element and a response element which embodies the response the child is to learn. The anticipation method is used in most studies. In this method the stimulus element appears, followed after a brief pause by the paired presentation of both the stimulus and response elements. The child is instructed to attempt to anticipate the response element by verbalizing it prior to its appearance. Training is continued until the child correctly anticipates each response element before it is presented with the stimulus elements. Many studies use designs (paradigms) developed in studies of verbal mediation with adults. It is necessary to become familiar with some of these paradigms to understand the research.

Some paradigms attempt to build in mediators by requiring the child to learn successive lists of associations, while others capitalize on the child's natural language habits. In the first, an effort is made to develop the verbal mediator within the experimental session. In a commonly used three-stage paradigm, children are required to learn three lists of paired associates. They learn to associate A with B in the first stage, B with C in the second stage, and finally A with C in the third stage (A-B, B-C, A-C). For example, to the stimulus element "house" the child must learn to respond "car." After learning this he must learn to respond "tree" to "car." Finally, he must learn to respond "tree" to "house." The word "car" is assumed to function as a potential mediator which, if effective, would facilitate the learning of the association "house-tree" in the third stage of the study (i.e., house-*car*, *car*-tree). This example delineates the sequence for only one of the several pairs of associates that would be constructed for each list. Two common characteristics of this form of paired-associate learning are evident in this example. The stimulus and response elements are coupled arbitrarily, rather than on the basis of a meaningful relation between the words. Further, there is no question of whether the child "knows" the potential mediator; he is forced to learn it and cannot progress through the lists until he has mastered each list. These studies are concerned, therefore, with the question of whether associations learned in early lists may function as effective links in learning a new set of verbal associations.

By arranging the lists in different ways we can produce conditions that, according to mediation theory, should produce interference, as well as facilitation. Interference should be produced if the pairings in the third list are arranged so that the potential mediator elicits incorrect responses. For example, whereas learning the A-C list may be facilitated if the pairings for all items are consistent across all three lists, interference may be produced if the A-C relations are incompatible with the stimulus-response relations that have been learned in the previous lists. If the sequence for the three lists were "house-car, car-tree, house-pen," we would expect that in the third list "house" would elicit the associate "car," which in turn would elicit "tree." In this case, "tree" would be an incorrect response to "house" and the tendency to say "tree" would interfere with the learning of the correct response "pen."

A second type of procedure eliminates the first of the three stages by selecting words for the A-B associations from high frequency associates in word-associate norms. Other techniques for providing potential mediators between the stimulus and response elements involve linking the two elements by verbal and pictorial means and varying the syntactical relations embodied in the mediating words or pictures. These procedures will be discussed in detail in later sections.

CLASSICAL MEDIATION PARADIGMS

It is a puzzle to wade through the intricate paradigms of the studies to be discussed, but when we do we find the results are remarkably consistent. It seems to be relatively easy to arrange paired-associate tasks to produce what appears to be mediated facilitation or interference. Even four-year-olds who have been characterized in other contexts as demonstrating a deficiency in mediation benefit from training that provides a mediating link between two associations. Although young children generally learn lists of paired associates more slowly than do children at later ages, mediational processes, at least in the paradigms to be discussed, do not appear to differ across ages—after the ages of seven or eight years. Therefore, even though words may be ineffective at times in mediating responses in nonverbal tasks, they are capable of functioning as useful links in the formation of chains of verbal associations.

Developmental Studies

We should now look at the studies that lead to these conclusions. One of the first questions to be asked was whether the acquisition of a potential mediator would influence subsequent learning by young children. With five- and six-year-olds, Norcross and Spiker (1958) were able to demonstrate both facilitation and interference with the three-stage paradigm described above. Then can mediation be demonstrated in still younger children? To answer this question, Boat and Clifton (1968) tested four-year-olds with the same three-stage paradigm. The lists consisted of five pairs of colored pictures representing unrelated words, such as "dress-rabbit." A control group learned the sequence A-B, D-C, A-C. Since D always was a new word that appeared only in the second list there was no possibility of using the D-C associations to facilitate learning the A-C list. When the performance of the two groups was compared, the mean number of correct responses on the A-C list was consistently higher in the experimental than in the control group. Learning the mediating B-C links facilitated subsequent learning of the A-C associations. Four-year-olds therefore appear to be capable of effective mediation in paired-associate learning when the potential mediator is embedded within the training experience. In this form of verbal learning preschool children do not appear to have a deficiency in the ability to mediate.

The presence of potential mediators is of benefit not only to young children, but to older children and adolescents as well. In fact, there is some evidence that the degrees of facilitation and interference produced by the acquired mediator are similar across a wide span of ages. Davis (1966) tested children at grades 2, 4, 6, 8, and college students on nine-item lists. Nouns of high frequency in everyday language were arranged to produce facilitation, interference, and control conditions, with three items in each list representing each condition. An example of such lists is presented in Table 10-1. This is a sensitive type of design, for measures of facilitation and interference are obtained for each child, rather than for different groups of children. Facilitation and interference were found for the subjects at each developmental level. There was no significant interaction between age and condition. Even though rates of learning differed at the different ages, the experimental conditions had equivalent effects across all ages included in the study.

A study by Palermo (1962), using children in grades 3 through 6, also

Table 10-1.   Examples of items arranged to produce facilitation, interference, and control conditions in a paired-associate task (as in the study by Davis, 1966)

	List 1	List 2	List 3
Facilitation	A-B	B-C	A-C
	cat-mop	mop-sun	cat-sun
	eye-ham	ham-ant	eye-ant
	jet-boy	boy-nut	jet-nut
Interference	A-B	B-C	A-C (rearranged)
	sea-pig	pig-gas	sea-bug
	arm-ice	ice-gun	arm-gas
	hat-fog	fog-bug	hat-gun
Control	A-B	B-D	A-C
	air-man	man-owl	air-jam
	bed-sky	sky-bun	bed-hat
	box-fur	fur-lid	box-fly

failed to find significantly different effects of the experimental conditions at the different age levels. Only A-B and A-C lists were presented. The design was of the following form: there were six stimulus elements and three response elements in each list. After the A-B list was learned, new responses were paired with the old stimuli to produce facilitation, interference, or no effect. Using the facilitation arrangement as an example, the response "scissors" was paired with both "stool" and "shoe" in the first list. In the second list both "stool" and "shoe" were associated with the same response "house." Since both stimulus elements were associated with the same response in each stage, the strengthening of each association in the second stage should facilitate the learning of the other because of the tendency for each to elicit the common mediator "scissors" (i.e., "stool-*scissors*-house"; "shoe-*scissors*-house").

Pairings were arranged to produce potential interference by switching the stimulus-response relations in the second (A-C) list. For example, the common mediator "scissors" learned in the first list to both "stool" and "shoe" should elicit incorrect intrusions into the learning of the second list if one of the stimulus elements has a new associate (e.g., the sequence "stool-*scissors*-house" might be elicited when the now-correct association is "stool-basket"). Children at each grade learned the A-C list more effectively in the facilitation than in the interference condition, but, unpredictably, the level of performance of both groups was below that found in a control condition. It is unclear why the performance of both experimental groups was depressed. Nevertheless, the conditions designed to produce mediated associations did result in differential effects on the amount of transfer evident in learning the A-C lists, and the effects were similar at the different ages.

The number of developmental studies using classical paradigms is small and the conclusions would be more tentative if similar effects were not found in other studies using different approaches to paired-associate learning. Before discussing these studies, however, it is of interest to review the results of several other studies, for they provide examples of how other classical paradigms have been found to produce evidence supportive of the hypothesis of verbal mediation.

Other Paradigms

Another approach to investigating possible effects of mediation in paired-associate learning was reported by Nikkel and Palermo (1965). Here, the first stage of the three-stage paradigm was omitted and words were selected for the A-B association because of their high association value as ascertained from word-association norms. For example, the word "blossom" has a strong tendency to elicit "flower." Thus, the A-B associations were derived from pairings existing in the child's natural language. Training began, therefore, with the second stage of an A-B, C-A, C-B paradigm. In this stage, a nonsense syllable such as DIT was used as the stimulus element and "blossom" as the response element (C-A). In the third, or test stage, DIT as a stimulus was associated with the response "flower" (C-B). It was assumed that facilitation would occur because of the tendency for DIT to elicit "blossom," which already had a strong tendency to elicit "flower." When both this and the A-B, B-C, A-C paradigms were used, sixth graders showed the fastest learning of the C-B and A-C lists when the conditions were arranged to produce facilitation and the slowest learning when the conditions were arranged to produce interference.

These findings have been replicated with more complex designs, including ones relying on the development of backward associations (e.g., lists of the form, B-C, B-A, and A-C). Palermo (1966) found the relative differences among the facilitation, control, and interference conditions to be as great with sixth graders when one or two backward associations were necessary for mediation to occur, as they were in the previous studies that involved only forward associations. Further work by Shapiro and Palermo (1968) with aural presentation of the materials to fourth-grade children found significantly better performance in facilitation conditions compared to interference or control conditions. Linkages between words in natural language may be of aid or hindrance to paired-associate learning, depending upon the way these associations are utilized in the construction of paired-associate lists.

CONNECTIVE LINKS

An entirely different approach to the study of mediation in paired-associate learning is found in studies where the mediator is a sentence or drawing representing a relation or interaction between the stimulus and response elements. In contrast to the previous studies no effort is made to require the child to learn the potential mediator. The sentence is read or the picture is presented, typically only on an initial trial, and the experimental session is devoted to the learning of a single list containing the stimuli and responses for which the connective links have been illustrated. One of the primary interests in studies using this method has been in investigating developmental changes in children's ability to utilize such connective links.

Reese (1965), for example, studied children at three age levels (mean ages of 44, 58, and 77 months). The stimulus elements were pictures of animals. The response elements were pictures of objects (e.g., UMBRELLA) or drawings of animals engaged in activities with the objects (e.g., CAT carrying an UMBRELLA). On the first trial the experimenter verbalized the responses or described the interactions between the animals and objects. Learning was more effective when the children saw, heard, or both saw and heard the relation described than when they merely saw the response elements and heard them named. The youngest children learned more slowly than the children at the two older age levels, but the lack of a significant interaction between age and condition indicated equivalent experimental effects at each age level. Similar results have been found by Davidson (1964) with sixth graders.

A developmental study by Jensen and Rohwer (1965) offers further insight into the role of verbal connectives as mediational devices. Whereas Reese (1965) provided the connective relation between stimulus and response, the children in this study were required to supply their own. The experiment began with a study trial in which the children were shown the members of the paired-associate list (pictures of common objects) they subsequently were to learn. Half of the children were asked to name each member. The other half were asked to construct a sentence containing the names of the stimulus and response elements. The children were asked to verbalize the names and sentences only on the study trial.

As can be seen in Figure 10-1, children who had named the pictures

Figure 10-1.   Mean number of trials to learn a 10-item list according to grade and experimental condition. (From A. R. Jensen and W. D. Rohwer, Jr., Syntactical mediation of serial and paired-associate learning as a function of age. *Child Development,* 1965, 36, 605. Copyright 1965 Society for Research in Child Development, Inc.)

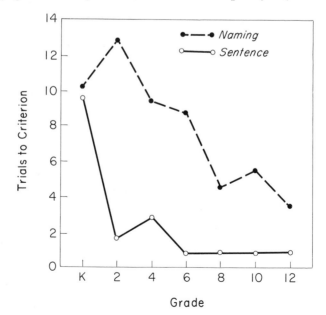

in the study trial showed a gradual improvement in performance on the paired-associate task with increasing age. A dramatic effect was obtained with the children who had constructed sentences; age differences in rate of paired-associate learning disappeared after age eight. Even the level of performance of the older children and adolescents was higher when they were asked to construct sentences, apparently because this induced them to mediate earlier in the experiment than otherwise would have been the case.

It is important to note that instructions to construct sentences had little effect on the performance of kindergarten children. Even though they were capable of forming sentences, they did not benefit greatly from the presence of a connecting link between stimulus and response. These results provide an interesting contrast with those discussed earlier. When instructed to supply their own connective relation between two words, kindergarten children appeared to be unable to use this relation as an effective mediator. Yet when the kindergarten children in other studies were forced to learn mediating associations or when the connective relation was supplied by the experimenter, their performance on the test trials was improved.

There are several possible reasons why five-year-olds may fail to mediate when the verbal mediators are not built into their training. Perhaps their linguistic structures are so tenuously established that without explicit training they are unable to integrate a third word into the association as an effective mediator; perhaps they fail to see the relation between making up a sentence and learning to associate two words; or perhaps they are unable to remember the sentence they have constructed to relate stimulus and response. Whatever the reason, this is one condition in which young children fail to show beneficial effects from verbal mediation in paired-associate learning.

In another developmental study with children from grades 1, 3, and 6 (Rohwer, Lynch, Suzuki, & Levin, 1967), the children were supplied various types of verbal and pictorial connectives. The three types of verbal connectives were conjunctions, prepositions, and verbs; there were three parallel types of pictorial connectives; coincidental, where the objects were placed side by side (e.g., rock, bottle); locational, where the objects were involved in situations implied by prepositions (e.g., rock in bottle); and actional, where the objects were involved in movements implied by verbs (e.g., rock hitting bottle). All materials were presented by means of movies. Learning in all conditions was remarkably rapid and in general learning was facilitated as greatly by verbal as by pictorial connectives. Among the verbal connectives, only a connective verb produced more rapid learning than occurred in a control group where the objects merely were named. Among the pictorial connectives, however, rate of learning was more rapid when actions rather than locational relations were depicted, and again when locational relations were depicted than when the objects merely appeared side by side. The lack of a significant interaction between age and condition indicated that the facilitative effects of the various types of connectives was as great in the first as in the sixth grade.

A companion study (Rohwer, Lynch, Levin, & Suzuki, 1967) contrasted the rate of learning when the objects were presented pictorially and when printed names of the objects were used. Learning was more rapid at both grades 3 and 6 with pictorial than with printed materials, and, confirming the earlier results, when the experimenter related the stimulus and response elements by a verb rather than by a preposition or a conjunction. Other studies (Rohwer, 1968; Rohwer & Lynch, 1966; Suzuki & Rohwer, 1968) add further evidence of the greater facilitating effects of verbs than of conjunctions or prepositions as connective links. Even in sentences containing the same words, a connective verb (e.g. The ROCK hit the BOTTLE and him) produced more effective learning than did a connective conjunction (e.g., The ROCK and the BOTTLE hit him).

What properties of verbs produce facilitation in paired-associate learning? It does not seem to be due to the fact that verbs exercise greater constraints on the number of possible words that can follow them than do prepositions or conjunctions (Rohwer & Lynch, 1967). Nor is it because verbs imply overt action, for learning does not differ when verbs do or do not imply overt activity (Rohwer & Levin, 1968). Other interpretations have been discussed, including the possibility that verbs evoke more effective visual imagery, but the basis for the effect remains unclear. [For an extensive discussion of the role of imagery in children's learning, see Reese, et al. (1970).]

The studies have produced remarkably consistent results. Connecting the stimulus and response elements by a verbal or pictorial mediating link facilitates children's paired-associate learning. As in studies with classical mediation paradigms, the degree of facilitation does not seem to differ greatly at different ages. We probably should not be surprised at this finding. It is not immediately obvious even to adults that an efficient strategy for learning would be to introduce some meaningful relation into the arbitrary associations by constructing mediating links. Supplying such a relation between stimulus and response, or requiring the child to supply his own, may transform the task from rote learning to one involving meaning. The one exception to this generalization occurs with five-year-olds. In this case, little benefit was derived from an instruction that required them to produce their own potential mediator. We cannot conclude that five-year-olds are incapable of using such connective links, however, for when the relation was supplied by the experimenter children at or below the age of five showed improved performance over that found when they merely named the stimulus and response elements.

NATURAL LANGUAGE

Daily language habits may influence the learning of paired associates in other ways than in their capacity as mediators. Words develop different degrees of associative strength as a function of relations established in everyday experience. When lists of paired associates are constructed so that the stimulus and response elements already have a high degree of associative strength, learning should be very rapid; as the degree of associative strength decreases, learning should become more and more difficult. In these studies, then, a meaningful relation already exists between the stimulus and response elements. We can study the effect of this relation on paired-associate learning by varying the associative strength of the two elements.

Associative Strength

How does one measure the associative strength between two words? Most investigators have relied on the results of word-association tests. A list of words is presented to a large number of children who are asked to look at the printed word and write down the first word they think of. To the word *cold*, for example, many children respond by writing *hot* or *warm;* relatively few children respond with such words as *shiver* or *water*. The primary response is defined as the one made by the greatest number of children; a response is considered to be idiosyncratic if it is made by only a few subjects in the normative group. If one wished to construct a list of paired associates with high associative strength, the stimulus element *cold* would be coupled with the response element *hot;* to construct a list with low associative strength, the response to *hot* might be *water*. [For a further discussion of these and other procedures used in studies of verbal learning with children, see Palermo (1963).]

An illustrative experiment is that of Castaneda, Fahel, and Odom (1961). After establishing the association value of a list of words for fifth and sixth graders, paired-associate lists were constructed by using strong or weak associates of the stimulus elements. Learning was significantly faster when the associative strength was high, a result that would be expected on the basis of common sense except for the fact that it is difficult to demonstrate with adults. The finding was replicated by McCullers (1961).

A more sensitive test of the effect of associative strength on learning was possible in a study by Wicklund, Palermo, and Jenkins (1964), who had extensive normative data concerning word-associations available for their use (Palermo & Jenkins, 1964). Lists of ten items were constructed so that the responses were primary associates to the stimulus words or were of medium or very low strength. For example, to the word *king*, 51% of the normative group responded *queen*; 4%, *man*; and 0.6%, *money*. The associative strength of the response elements was varied, therefore, by constructing lists containing one of these words as the response to the stimulus *king*. A second variable was the relative frequency with which the primary responses were made. For example, the primary response *queen* for *king* was a high frequency response, but the primary response *web* to the word *spider* was made by only 19% of the normative group. The latter is a primary response but one with low frequency. The ease with which fourth-grade children learned lists constructed in this manner varied directly with the strength of the associations, and primary responses were learned more rapidly when they were of high frequency. These results are in line with what we might expect. Linkages among words acquired in everyday life exert an active influence on children's learning of paired associates in the laboratory.

Figure 10-2.   Mean number of correct responses for the three groups of subjects, grades 1 and 4. (From N. N. Klinger and D. S. Palermo, Aural paired-associate learning in children as a function of free-associative strength. *Child Development*, 1967, 38, 1148-1149. Copyright 1967 Society for Research in Child Development, Inc.)

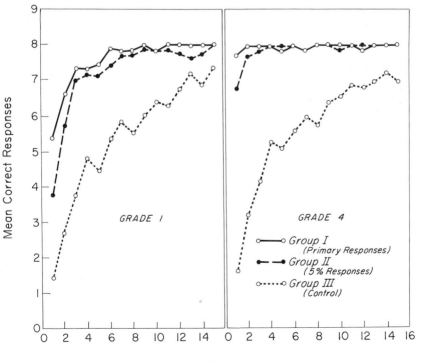

The same general procedure was used by Klinger and Palermo (1967) wtih six- and nine-year-olds, but the materials were presented aurally rather than visually. When stimulus-response elements had 0 associative strength (e.g., moon-book) performance was similar at the two age levels. Developmental differences did appear for the other two lists; the performance of the older children was perfect within a few trials, while that of the younger children was at a lower level, especially during the initial trials. As can be seen in Figure 10-2, the major effects were derived from the presence or absence, rather than the degree, of associative strength. Perhaps the most interesting aspect of these results is the great facilitation in learning that occurred even when associative strength between the stimulus-response elements was low.

The influence of associative strength on learning was investigated in a different manner by Shapiro (1965). If a response is paired with a stimulus that elicited it in free association, learning should be facilitated; but if the stimulus-response relations are rearranged in a list so that the response is paired with a stimulus different from that which elicited it in free association, learning should be impaired. Competitive and noncompetitive lists were prepared for visual presentation by combining stimulus-response elements containing primary or idiosyncratic associations. Rate of learning by fifth graders differed according to strength of association and type of list. These two variables interacted significantly, so that high association pairs were learned more rapidly than low association pairs in noncompetitive lists, but there was no difference in rate of learning the competitive lists according to strength of stimulus-response association. A third variable in this study is of special interest. It usually is assumed that data obtained from a normative sample provide a reliable index of the strength of associations for other groups of children of the same ages. Since Shapiro used the same children in the experimental and normative studies, she was able to select children whose associations tended to concur or to be discrepant with those made by the total group. Rate of learning differed in the two cases, but since there was no interaction with the other variables, one can assume that concordance with group norms is simply another index of the strength of the associations.

In all of the previous studies associative strength has been varied by selecting stimulus and response elements with different associative values. In a study by Palermo, Flamer, and Jenkins (1964), only the association values of the response elements was varied. This was achieved by using nonsense syllables with association values of 20%, 50% or 80% as the response elements, and high-frequency adjectives as the stimulus elements. The association value of a nonsense syllable is determined by the degree to which it elicits meaningful responses. For example, KAR would have a high association value, but the value for CXJ would be low. The association values of nonsense syllables for this study were taken from normative data previously obtained with college students. The association value, or meaningfulness, of the nonsense syllables significantly influenced the children's rates of learning; the level of performance achieved by the fifth-grade subjects varied directly with the association value of the response elements.

An entirely different approach was used by Ramiriz and Castaneda (1967). Association value of the stimulus elements was varied by selecting names of children who had received either high or low ranks in a prior sociometric study. It was assumed that the names of children who achieved high sociometric ranks were more meaningful, since children tend to be more familiar with the behavior of more popular peers. The rate with which the children learned to associate letters (consonants) with children's names was faster when the names were of children with high sociometric ranks. The results were not due to such factors as general association value of the names or pronounceability, for another group of children, unfamiliar with the names, learned the two lists with equal facility.

Finally, a study was reported by Paivio and Yuille (1966) in which materials were high-frequency concrete and abstract nouns. Learning was more efficient with concrete nouns, and the effect was stronger when the nouns functioned as stimulus elements than when they were the response elements. Concrete nouns may elicit a greater number of facilitating associations (i.e., are more meaningful) than abstract nouns, or concrete nouns may be more conducive to the development of relevant mental images of the stimuli.

These studies yield relatively low-order conclusions, for the results would be predicted from a wide variety of theoretical positions and from common sense. They are, of course, primarily studies of transfer, for they assess the degree to which children's learning is aided when the materials to be learned have some prior associative strength or are meaningful because of their relation to occurrences in the children's everyday lives. The value of the studies appears to lie in demonstrating experimentally that such transfer does occur, that even very modest degrees of prior familiarity may have strong effects on learning, and that older children who have had greater practice in using language are able to utilize previously acquired associations more effectively than are younger children.

Degree of Training

Associative strength between stimulus and response also may be varied by providing different amounts of training in the experimental situation. If a response is associated with a particular stimulus in an initial task and a new response must be associated with the stimulus in a subsequent task, the amount of training received in the first task should result in increasing interference in learning the new association. In other words, high degrees of training in learning one association should produce negative transfer in learning a new response to the old stimulus.

Spiker (1960) reported three experiments designed to assess whether this prediction would be upheld. Sixth graders received either 6 or 15 trials in learning four paired associates. They then were presented a new list of eight items in which the four stimuli from the first list were coupled with new responses and the other four pairs contained new words. The difference in rate of learning the two types of items was greater for the group that received the greater number of trials on the first list, apparently reflecting greater interference of response elements from the first list. At the same time, the extended training resulted in superior performance in learning the new pairs of items—a non-associative form of facilitation. Comparable effects were found when children were instructed to rehearse the associations of the first list or to use mnemonic devices (e.g., Imagine a *boat* made of *cake*).

A study by Spiker and Holton (1958) also found increasing degrees of negative transfer as the number of trials given in the initial task was increased. Since the interference appeared to be partly attributable to the fact that children failed to respond within the time limit allowed (two seconds), extending the time for response might reduce interference. White, Spiker, and Holton (1960) therefore repeated the previous study, allowing four seconds for response. Degree of training on the first task now failed to produce differences in associative interference as measured by frequency of correct response.

Extending the time for response also improved performance by preschool children (Price, 1963). The children performed more poorly with a two-second than with a six-second anticipation interval, but when, during the later stages of training, the interval was six seconds for all children, roughly equivalent levels of performance were attained. Since the level of performance of the two-second group improved rapidly when the time available for responding was extended, it appeared that the shorter time intervals had affected performance rather than learning. The children "knew" the correct response, but were unable to produce it with brief intervals between stimulus and response. The upshot of this research is that performance in learning new associations to an old stimulus is not impaired by extended practice on the first list if the child is given sufficient time to sort the correct response from the interfering associations.

MODE OF PRESENTATION

We have referred to studies that presented materials aurally and visually. Will mode of presentation have different effects, depending on the child's developmental level? Much of the verbal learning of the young child occurs through the spoken word, therefore learning might be more rapid if the items were presented by the aural than by the traditional visual mode. The effects might be different later in childhood when the child becomes skilled at reading. Two studies present some support for these expectations. Budoff and Quinlan (1964) found that seven- and eight-year-olds learned more rapidly with aural than with visual presentation of the paired associates, and Shapiro (1966) found the same effect with ten- and eleven-year-olds. With thirteen- and fourteen-year-olds, however, Shapiro found no significant difference between the two modes of presentation.

One must distinguish pictorial from verbal presentation of visual materials. Learning to read is a newly acquired skill for children, while looking at pictures is a familiar activity. What would happen if the visual materials were pictorial, rather than verbal representations of objects? Hill and Hecker (1966) found no differences in rate of learning by seven- and eight-year-olds when the materials were black and white drawings of objects compared to oral presentation of the names of the objects.

The most extensive investigation of the effects of mode of presentation on paired-associate learning was reported by Otto (1961), who selected children at grades 2, 4, and 6, who were good, average, and poor readers and had IQs between 95 and 110. The task involved learning to associate low-association value nonsense syllables with geometric forms. Three modes of presentation were used: (a) visual; (b) visual presentation of the form, plus reading of the nonsense syllable by the experimenter; and (c) a combination of the first two, plus the requirement that the child trace the nonsense syllable with his finger. Poor readers in grade 2 required approximately twice as long to learn the list as the good readers, but by grade 6 this difference had decreased. There was a significant interaction between grade and mode of presentation: the combined mode was most effective at grade 2, the visual mode at grade 4, and at grade 6 the different modes were of approximately equal effectiveness.

These studies provide only preliminary information about how children's rate of learning is influenced by the mode of presenting materials. For older subjects mode of presentation may have differential effects for different individuals, but group differences appear only with younger children. The modes that are effective are those in which children are well practiced: listening and looking for young children, reading for older children.

CONCLUSIONS

This is the last chapter dealing directly with the role of language in learning, but it is not the last time we will mention language. In contrast to our previous discussion of the relation of language to nonverbal learning, studies of paired-associate learning have produced impressively consistent findings. The studies offer many examples of what may be interpreted as the operation of verbal mediation. Whether the task involved classical mediation paradigms or used children's natural language as mediators, there was consistent evidence of children's utilizing extra-list associations in learning lists of paired associates. In line with the results predicted from mediation theory, facilitation or interference could be demonstrated, depending upon how the lists were constructed. Through all the studies there was a consistent finding that after the ages of four or five, the youngest ages studied, children seemed to be able to use and benefit from the presence of mediating associations and connective links between stimulus and response. Whether paired-associate learning is simply a more sensitive means of detecting the presence of mediational processes, or whether verbal mediation has a more direct influence in verbal than in nonverbal tasks is a matter for further investigation.

Studies of the relations between children's daily language habits and paired-associate learning also produced consistent results. The strength of pre-experimentally acquired associations strongly influenced the rate with which children learned lists of paired associates. When the stimulus and response elements had even low degrees of associative strength there were strong facilitating effects. Similarly, interference in learning new responses to old stimuli could be demonstrated by varying the relations between stimulus and response elements of different associative strengths.

Paired-associate learning is considered by some to be a tedious area of research. This may be true, but, as we shall see in later discussions, the learning of paired associates turns out to be one of the most sensitive and effective tasks for assessing children's learning abilities. The ease with which children learn lists of paired associates is closely related to their success in school and to other measures of long-term learning. As we come to understand how paired-associate learning may be improved we may gain useful insights into more effective techniques for teaching children materials of practical use.

Behavior Modification

We found in our discussion of infant learning that the frequency of head-turning, vocalization, and smiling were markedly increased if these responses led to interesting or beneficial consequences. That is, responses could be strengthened through the systematic application of reinforcement. The concept of reinforcement has played an important role in theoretical discussions of the learning process for the past sixty years. Thorndike, Watson, Hull, and Skinner—all have been reinforcement theorists. Currently, the best known reinforcement theorist is Skinner, for his work, more than that of any other psychologist, has influenced thinking about the utility of the concept of reinforcement in the interpretation of behavior.

When a variable is found to exert powerful effects on behavior in the laboratory, we might expect it to have equally strong effects on behavior in everyday life. Our expectations can be confirmed, however, only by leaving the highly controlled environment of the laboratory and venturing into the everyday world. This we will do in the present chapter. Thus far, we have discussed laboratory studies. In this chapter we turn our attention to experiments on behavior modification, where child psychologists have attempted to apply knowledge gained in the laboratory to problems encountered in the home, schoolroom, and clinic.

Behavior modification is based on a simple idea: If you wish to strengthen a response, reinforce it; if you wish to weaken a response, withdraw reinforcement. The nucleus of the idea is simple, but there are many complex ramifications. Success in behavior modification appears to be attributable not only to the systematic control of the outcomes of behavior but also to astute analyses of the effective conditions of reinforcement. Before reinforcement techniques can be applied successfully in modifying behavior the experimenter must answer a series of difficult questions. What shall be used as a reinforcer? At what rate should reinforcement be given? What if the response to be reinforced is not currently manifested by the child? When should punishment be used? Let us consider each of these questions briefly before discussing examples of how they have been answered in actual practice. (For extensive discussions of behavior modification with children, see Bandura, 1969; Krasner & Ullman, 1965, Lovaas, 1967, and Ullman & Krasner, 1965.)

REINFORCERS

As we saw in Chapter 3, the definition of what constitutes a reinforcer is an empirical problem. Any stimulus event that increases the strength of a response is considered to be a reinforcer. Reinforcers may be general or idiosyncratic. If a child is hungry, food is likely to be an effective reinforcer. Most children like candy, toys, to see interesting pictures, to be told they are doing well, and to initiate positive and supportive responses from adults. A long list of stimuli that have been found to have reinforcing value for children has been presented by Bijou and Sturges (1959). The experimenter cannot assume, however, that what is reinforcing for one child will be equally effective as a reinforcer for another child. Some children may be especially responsive to sea shells, french fried potatoes, or baseball cards, while for other children these objects are of little interest or value. Older children can tell us what they like. Selecting reinforcers for younger children may depend much more on trial and error.

Since children may become satiated for a particular reinforcer, especially if it is impossible to deprive them of this reinforcer outside the experimental setting, it often becomes necessary to vary the types of reinforcer used with a particular child. When there are extended experimental sessions, tokens often are substituted for direct forms of reinforcement, with the promise that the tokens may be exchanged for some valued object or event. In this case, it is helpful if the child is offered an array of choices and allowed to select what he wishes to "buy."

SCHEDULES

The effects of varying the rate at which reinforcers are presented should be mentioned, even though this variable has not been investigated directly in studies of behavior modification with children. Reinforcement can be presented according to a ratio or an interval schedule. The decision must be made whether to reinforce every response or every nth response (ratio schedule), or whether to present a reinforcer every minute or every nth minute (interval schedule). Further, the ratios or intervals may be fixed, as in the preceding examples, or variable. In variable schedules the ratio or interval changes in successive phases of the experiment. At first, every response may be reinforced, then every other response, with a continuously changing ratio so that in the end only every fifteenth or twentieth response is reinforced. Both intermittent and variable schedules reduce the chances of satiation and increase the resistance of responses to extinction. Because of this, continuous reinforcement of behavior usually is restricted to the early phases of the child's experience in the experimental setting. In practice, decisions about the schedule and changes in schedule of reinforcement are dependent upon the sensitivity of the experimenter in his observation of the child's behavior. As in most forms of intervention and treatment, behavior modification involves skilled observation as well as knowledge of scientific concepts.

BEHAVIORAL SHAPING

Attempting to develop new forms of behavior in a child often is a tedious task. To solve this problem, the experimenter relies on the method of successive approximations or behavioral shaping. The experimenter initially reinforces any response that is within the domain of the behavior he wishes to generate and fails to reinforce other responses. Merely being in the presence of the appropriate stimuli may be deemed sufficient for reinforcement in the early phases of the experiment. Step by step, closer and closer approximations to the desired response are required before reinforcement is provided. Through selective application of reinforcement and nonreinforcement the experimenter attempts to guide the child into making the desired responses in appropriate situations.

PUNISHMENT

Child psychologists have tended to avoid using physical punishment in their experiments for both ethical and humane reasons. Thus, our knowledge about the effects of punishment on children's behavior is relatively restricted. When punishment has been used it has consisted of mildly unpleasant events, such as withdrawal of the opportunity to work for reinforcers ("time-out"), or social disapproval. Since in most situations nonreinforcement of a response has been found to be as effective, or more effective than punishment in eliminating undesired behavior, direct forms of punishment are used infrequently in studies of behavior modification.

From what we do know, punishment seems to influence behavior in several ways. First, it tends to decrease the strength of the response it follows. In fact, punishment is defined within the framework of operant conditioning as a "reduction in the future probability of a specific response as a result of the immediate delivery of a stimulus for that response" (Azrin & Holz, 1966, p. 381). According to this interpretation, a stimulus is considered to be punishing if it reduces the strength of the response it follows.

On some occasions a desired behavior cannot be evoked because of the appearance of some other form of behavior that interferes with or interrupts the desired responses. Skillful application of relatively severe forms of punishment at such times may be effective in suppressing the appearance of the undesired responses. If the undesired responses can be suppressed, it then may be possible to evoke and reinforce more appropriate behavior. We are faced, however, with the fact that the cessation, reduction, or escape from punishment may be reinforcing. Whereas the application of punishment may lead to suppression of the responses that are punished, behavior that enables the child to reduce or escape from punishment may be strengthened. For this reason, punishment may have the undesired side-effect of increasing the subject's tendency to leave the experimental setting. When this occurs, the possibilities of instituting desired responses through reinforcement are decreased. As we shall see, experimenters have capitalized on this apparent disadvantage in developing certain types of behavior in children.

STRENGTHENING RESPONSES THROUGH REINFORCEMENT

We can clarify how reinforcement has been used in behavior modification by discussing four typical studies. Two are studies with normal nursery school children and two are with deviant groups, mentally retarded and psychotic children.

Increasing Social Interaction

Allen, Hart, Buell, Harris, and Wolf (1964) report the case of Ann, a normal four-year-old, who engaged in an excessive amount of isolate play in nursery school. It was hoped that Ann's social interaction with other children could be increased through systematic application of social reinforcement. Accordingly, the teachers were instructed to reinforce Ann's contacts with other children by smiling at her, talking to her (in a manner that would facilitate and not detract from social interaction with children), touching her, and offering her assistance. Simultaneously, they were to avoid providing reinforcement when Ann was playing by herself.

As can be seen in Figure 11-1, Ann rapidly began to spend more time in social interaction with other children when this interaction was reinforced by the teachers. Ann had spent only about 15% of her time in social interaction during the five baseline days preceding the introduction of social reinforcement. In the six subsequent days she was involved in social interaction approximately 60% of the time. Could this increase in social interaction be attributed to the introduction of social reinforcement? To determine whether the reinforcement had been responsible for the change in Ann's behavior, reinforcement of social interaction was withdrawn after Day 11 and the teachers reinforced Ann when she played alone. Interaction with other children abruptly decreased. Following this, the contingencies again were reversed, and Ann was reinforced for social interaction. The percentage of time spent in social interaction increased. At the end of the study Ann was reinforced for social interaction in a manner equivalent to that provided to the other children in the nursery school group. The earlier regimen of reinforcement had enduring effects, for in subsequent post-experimental checks the percentage of time spent in social interaction never dropped to the baseline level.

This study is a good example of the successful application of the techniques of behavior modification. Ann exhibited a type of behavior that most teachers do not consider conducive to appropriate social development. Why Ann did not interact with other children more frequently was not known, and, from the point of view of behavior modification, was irrelevant. The question was whether the frequency of social interaction with other children could be increased. Ann was responsive to adult interaction. Rather than using this gratifying form of response to perpetuate behaviors

Figure 11-1. Daily percentage of time spent in social interaction with children during each morning nursery school session. (From E. K. Allen, B. M. Hart, J. S. Buell, F. R. Harris, and M. M. Wolf, Effects of social reinforcement on isolate behavior of a nursery school child. *Child Development,* 1964, 35, 512. Copyright 1964 Society for Research in Child Development, Inc.)

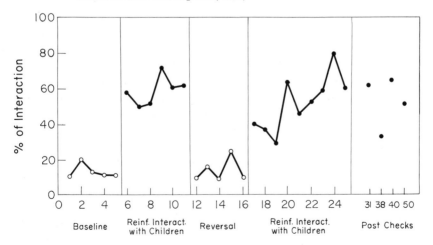

that interfered with Ann's interacting with other children, adult response was used to reinforce social interaction with other children. At first, interaction with other children was interpreted very liberally—Ann needed only to be in the presence of other children to obtain a positive response from her teachers. This form of reinforcement then became available only for more active social involvement. In the end, Ann was treated no differently from the other children in her group.

The study also illustrates how the design of studies of behavior modification typically involves rather radical departures from traditional experimental designs. There was only one subject—Ann. There is a risk, when a study includes only one subject, of being unable to determine whether the results are due to the experimental treatments or to other, unknown factors. To minimize the possibility of obtaining results that could be given alternative interpretations, the experimenters instituted a number of different experimental procedures. In addition to obtaining the baseline rate of response, conditioning, and extinction, the experimenters included a period of reconditioning and post-experimental checks of the durability of the effects. Even the most assiduous critic would find it difficult to attribute the variations in Ann's social interaction to factors other than the application and withdrawal of reinforcement.

Teaching Verbal Skills

A second example of the effects of reinforcement deals with behavior modification in a nursery school for underprivileged children (Risley, 1968). Many aspects of these children's behavior are impoverished; they are especially retarded in verbal skills. Their conversation and verbal behavior often lack the grace, clarity, and abstractness that characterise the verbalizations of middle-class children. Unless the child can verbalize social greetings, initiate conversations with adults, and use words to express more than immediate needs, his adjustment to the verbal world of the classroom will be relatively difficult. Would it be possible to increase the child's facility in using words through reinforcement procedures?

At the beginning of Risley's study only 20% of the four-year-olds in the nursery school greeted their teachers by saying "Good morning." It would be advantageous to the children in their later encounters with teachers and other adults if they could learn this trivial but ingratiating form of greeting. In an effort to activate this response the head teacher and her two assistants stood at the door, said "Good morning," and smiled at each child as he entered the nursery school. Within three months, 80% of the children responded to the teachers by saying "Good morning" in return. Once this level of response had been reached the teachers ceased saying "Good morning" and responding to the children's statements with smiles. After six days, the percentage of children saying "Good morning" dropped to 0. A reinstatement of the earlier procedure resulted in a rapid return to the 80% level. To determine whether the frequency could be increased still further, a more powerful reinforcer was introduced. Now the teachers reinforced each appropriate reply with candy. All of the children responded to the teachers' greetings appropriately within five days. Even when the teachers stopped initiating the response by saying "Good morning," around 95% of the children continued to respond. Reinforcement was manipulated further by having a single teacher, two teachers, or all three teachers reinforce the child with a piece of candy. The frequency with which the children greeted each teacher differed, depending upon the source of reinforcement.

One of the appealing aspects of behavior modification is that it fits in so easily with common sense. Why should not the frequency of "Good mornings" increase if they are initiated by a warm greeting and responded to with a pleasant smile or a piece of candy? Children *should* learn to speak effectively if they have good models and if their efforts lead to some meaningful consequence. Writers on behavior modification have emphasized such points and have illustrated how, in many situations, common sense expectations may be reasonable but unrealized. For example, in another aspect of his work with poverty families, Risley (1968) found that many of the mothers needed to be taught to be effective agents of social reinforcement. It is easy, in a busy and crowded home, to fail to respond to desirable behavior—but to respond vigorously to undesirable behavior. By training mothers to praise their children when they behaved appropriately and to withhold reinforcement for inappropriate behavior, Risley helped them apply what they all may have known but failed to do.

Improving Personal Appearance

Another example of how responses may be strengthened or modified through reinforcement is found in the Mimosa Cottage study reported by Lent (1968). Mimosa Cottage is one of the dormitories for retarded girls at the Parsons State Hospital and Training School in Kansas, a school that has become well known for its innovations in the training and management of the mentally retarded through the application of reinforcement techniques. An effort was made for a year in Mimosa Cottage to develop personal skills that would be useful to the girls as they moved from the training school back into the community. It is not difficult to spot a group of retarded girls on a field trip to a museum or shopping center. Typically, their clothing is in disarray, they walk with a stooped and heavy gait, their makeup is inappropriate, their facial expressions are dull, and their mouths gape.

The behaviors chosen for modification in this project were much more complex than those in the preceding studies. Furthermore, whereas reinforcement was used in the previous studies to modify performance, it was used in this study as a means of facilitating learning. Experimenters in the previous studies used reinforcement to strengthen the children's tendencies to perform what they already knew. In this study, an effort was made to teach the girls new skills. What should be the aims of training? These were decided by observing girls in the towns near the training school. The goals were to approximate as closely as possible the behavior and appearance of normal girls in the community.

Somewhat more sophisticated methods of reinforcement are required when the subjects are adolescent girls than when they are preschool children. Although the basic approach remained that of reinforcing desired behaviors, extensions of the reinforcement procedures were necessary. The reinforcers chosen for training were tokens that could be exchanged for objects and activities varying from food and cosmetics to movies and dances. The girls had to learn that the tokens had utility, just as other children must learn what a dime or quarter represents. In themselves, the tokens had little value, but they represented the means whereby the girls could gain many highly desired goals. To transform a token into an effective generalized reinforcer, it was coupled with primary forms of reinforcement, such as food.

Initially, the girls were rewarded for appropriate behavior with candy. Somewhat later, the token was given just before the candy, and a gradually increasing delay was introduced between the times the token was given and the candy could be "purchased." The possibility of saving tokens was revealed when the girls found that more desirable objects could be obtained in exchange for several tokens.

During the year various aspects of personal behavior were given attention, including dress, grooming, cleanliness, sitting, and walking. Each was divided into components; for example, walking was broken down into keeping head up, back straight, stomach in, toes forward, not shuffling, and walking lightly. Specific training programs were developed for each of the components, and when the children performed successfully they were reinforced. Training in walking proved to be particularly effective. The girls demonstrated significant improvement over the year in each component of this behavior. Unfortunately, the positive changes found in the training situation did not always produce equivalent changes in other settings. Girls who walked well in the setting where training was given lapsed back into their graceless shuffle when they walked around the grounds of the institution. In an effort to rectify this the girls were provided with partial cues that were common to the training and extra-training settings. For example, a metronome that had been used to establish the pace for walking during training was presented for short periods of time outside the training situation in an effort to elicit the appropriate patterns of walking.

The disintegration of behavior outside the experimental setting may place certain limitations on behavior modification. To have broad practical significance it is important that the behavior be manifested in situations other than those in which it was initially generated. When the cues are changed too drastically, the desired behavior may not occur. It is possible to develop methods for facilitating a smooth transition from training to other situations, but whether this is feasible in terms of time and effort remains to be seen. As of now we have little solid evidence about the efficiency with which this can be accomplished.

During the second year of the Mimosa project, training was shifted from personal skills to verbal and social ones. With the shift in emphasis, and the concomitant change in the pattern of reinforcement, verbal and social skills improved. But some of the personal skills deteriorated. For example, there was a significant decline in two of the six components of walking. Here is a potentially serious problem. The ultimate goal is the production and elaboration of responses without the use of external reinforcers. This goal is assumed to be attainable on the basis of acquired reinforcement. According to behavior theory, performance of an activity that has led to reinforcement on many occasions eventually should become reinforcing in itself. The self-produced stimuli arising from the activity should, because they have occurred in the presence of primary forms of reinforcement, acquire secondary reinforcing value. Many of us, for example, may have relied on the support and interest of others in learning how to skate, but eventually our source of gratification came from the pleasure produced by skating and not from a nod of approval given by some other person. A year of reinforcement apparently was not uniformly successful in producing this effect with the Mimosa girls. Would a longer period of reinforcement have led to a greater persistence of the skills? Or did the artificial milieu in which the girls lived lead them to look for their reinforcement from others, rather than developing their own standards and self-rewards for pleasant and appropriate appearances? Would the transition from external to internal sources of reinforcement have been more successful if the girls had been taught to reinforce each other? The problem of transforming an activity into a self-reinforcing system may turn out to be remediable by developing more effective procedures of reinforcement. Or it simply may be a limitation of this particular form of intervention.

Teaching Psychotic Children to Speak

Among the most compelling studies of behavior modification have been those dealing with severely disturbed children. Lovaas and his co-workers are among those who have chosen to work with some of the most intractable forms of behavior and with some of the most difficult types of children. One of the studies reported by this group (Lovaas, 1966) describes the methods used in teaching profoundly psychotic children to speak. The diagnosis of the children was childhood schizophrenia or autism. They either were mute or had grossly inadequate verbal repertoires in addition to other psychotic behavior which interferes with all forms of learning. As with the Mimosa project, the training procedure was broken down into small steps.

A variety of reinforcing agents was used, including bits of the child's meals, close physical contact, and warm social response. Since psychotic children frequently are inattentive, the child initially was reinforced merely for looking at the experimenter. After the child had learned to attend to the experimenter, he was reinforced for any type of vocalization. When the output of vocalizations reached one vocalization every five seconds, the next step was introduced. The experimenter now said a word every ten seconds and the child was reinforced only if he vocalized within six seconds after the adult's vocalization. After this contingency was learned, the next obvious step was to require the child to imitate what the adult said. At first, simple sounds, such as B, were selected, primarily because of their susceptibility to the use of prompts. A prompt is any stimulus that produces the correct response prior to training. For example, the prompt initially used to elicit the vocalization B was for the experimenter to move the child's lips so that the sound was produced as the child exhaled. The directness of the prompt was reduced slowly by touching the child's mouth, his cheek, and finally his jaw. The gradual removal of a prompt is known as *fading*.

Training in imitative vocalization continued with the introduction of a large variety of sounds, words, and phrases. But imitating sounds is not speaking. Teaching the child to speak involved a long and laborious set of steps. Employing the same general procedures, the child was taught to identify common objects, to use prepositions, pronouns, and terms involving time, and to use language in interactive speech. In identifying objects the experimenter showed the child an object, pronounced its name, and reinforced the child for repeating the name. The verbal prompt was faded. Instead of saying the whole word the experimenter said the first syllable, the first letter, and then the prompt was dropped and the child was reinforced only for spontaneously naming the object.

Of the eleven psychotic children studied, all had reached the point of being able to label objects without prompts. There were extraordinarily large individual differences in the rate with which the children reached this level of proficiency, varying from a small number of trials to several thousand. However, even after 1½ years of intensive training, children who previously had been mute were unable to reach the point in their training program where they were to be taught to use words denoting time. Their spontaneous speech was very restricted and consisted mainly of giving commands, generally in sentences of no more than five or six words. Greater success was attained with children who previously had been echolalic. Echolalia is an odd type of behavior wherein the person repeats everything said to him. When the tendency towards indiscriminate repetition was decreased through nonreinforcement, rapid progress often occurred, leading eventually to proficiency in conversational speech and acquisition of abstract words.

To the parent who has attempted to cope with a grunting, screeching psychotic child and who now hears the child making sensible comments about himself and his environment, behavior modification must seem to be nearly miraculous. Nevertheless, even after extraordinarily long and arduous involvement in the experimental procedures, the children still were psychologically disturbed, their language had a ritualistic quality, and they rarely conducted truly interesting conversations. These inadequacies do not constitute a serious criticism, but they do point out that even with carefully designed programs and systematically regulated reinforcement there are individual limitations in the degree to which behavior can be modified. [For extensive reviews of the literature concerning behavior modification with disturbed children, see Gelfand & Hartmann (1968) and Leff (1968).]

NONREINFORCEMENT AND "TIME-OUT"

The preceding studies have been concerned with modifying behavior through the introduction of reinforcement. A closely related set of studies deals with the question of whether a response already at high strength can be weakened through nonreinforcement. Presumably, the response has developed through prior reinforcement, and the problem for the experimenter is to ascertain what types of stimuli have been effective in reinforcing this response. Nonreinforcement may involve only the omission of reinforcement upon the appearance of the undesired response. A more active use of nonreinforcement is found in studies of "time-out," where the opportunity for reinforcement is withdrawn by removing the child or the relevant materials from the experimental situation. This is the "Johnny-go-to-your-room" technique. In this case, nonreinforcement takes on the characteristics of a mild form of punishment.

Self-destructive Behavior

In a hospital ward we are shown a child who exhibits self-destructive behavior. The right side of her head is bald and in the hairless areas are large scabrous sores. The child is reported to have pulled all the hair from the right side of her head and to hit her head on any hard object that is available—a wall, a desk, the back of the car seat. The wounds never heal; they become larger and deeper with each repeated blow. As the child engages in these self-destructive behaviors her facial expression is described as being oddly blank.

Obviously, the child's behavior is grossly deviant. Why does any human being behave in this fashion? From the point of view of behavior modification the question can be stated in a different form: What sources of reinforcement operate to maintain this form of behavior? It is not difficult to formulate a tentative answer. Most persons would be astonished by such behavior and would attempt to intercede by responding with sympathy and concern when the child behaved in this manner. In this concern may lie the source of reinforcement. Self-mutilating responses initially may have been strengthened and now may be maintained by the solicitous responses of persons observing the child. If this were the case, would withdrawal of reinforcement reduce the frequency of these responses? This possibility differs greatly from other interpretations of behavior that might emphasize guilt and self-punishment, but part of its attractiveness is that it is subject to experimental test.

Lovaas, Freitag, Gold and Kassorla (1965) sought to determine whether behavior modification was a useful approach to the treatment of self-destruction. Their subject was a nine-year-old girl who had engaged in this behavior since she was three years old. In addition to head-banging, she also banged her arms, slapped and pinched herself. It was necessary to demonstrate that the frequency of self-mutilation increased with reinforcement and decreased following the withdrawal of reinforcement. The experimental sessions lasted ten minutes a day, five times a week, for a total of 42 sessions. As a reinforcer, the experimenters chose the phrase, "I don't think you are bad." This phrase was chosen on the assumption that if the child engaged in self-destruction because of guilt, such a phrase might reduce her level of guilt. There were, then, two possible outcomes: a reduction in self-mutilation resulting from decreased guilt, or an increase in self-mutilation resulting from the reinforcing value of the verbal responses.

Sessions 1 through 15 were used to assess the baserate, or operant level of self-destructive behavior in the presence of a smiling and attentive adult. Verbal reinforcement was given on a continuous schedule (after every self-destructive response) in sessions 16 through 19, and the first extinction period began in session 20. Reconditioning was begun in session 24, but reinforcement now occurred on the average only after every fifth self-destructive response. The second extinction period began in session 27. During sessions 30 through 37 the experimenter did not smile and was inattentive to the child for the duration of the session following any self-destructive behavior. For two sessions, 33 and 38, the experimenter smiled and attended to the child while commenting, but at other times ignored the child.

The results are presented in Figure 11-2. There is a tendency for the incidence of self-destructive behavior to be higher when it was reinforced and to be lower when it was not reinforced or ignored. There was no notable tendency for the frequency of self-destructive responses to decrease more readily when the experimenter ignored the child after such responses than when the responses simply were not reinforced. The combination of social reinforcement (making the statement, smiling, and being attentive) of self-destructive responses and ignoring the behavior at other times seemed to produce the greatest increase in self-destructive behavior. Or did it? At this point, the deficiencies of the one-subject approach become apparent. To what should we attribute the large increase in self-mutilation between sessions 19 and 20? To the change from a fixed to a variable ratio schedule? Or to the cumulative effects of the preceding 33 reinforcements? And how shall we interpret the increase between sessions 32 and 33? Should we attribute this to an enhanced significance of the experimenter's statements after three days of ignoring the child? Or to the combination, within a session, of withdrawal of attention for non-mutilating behavior and reinforcement of mutilating behavior? So many different variables were operative across the 42 days that it is impossible to sort out their individual or interactive effects. We are forced to conclude that studies such as this must be regarded as demonstration studies, demonstrations that changes can be produced, and not as studies greatly extending our understanding of the bases for these changes. The primary contribution of such studies is to application rather than to the explication of this form of intervention.

Figure 11-2. Frequency of self-destructive behavior under the various experimental conditions. (From O. I. Lovaas, G. Freitag, V. J. Gold, I. C. Kassorla, Experimental studies in childhood schizophrenia: Analysis of self-destructive behavior. *Journal of Experimental Child Psychology*, 1966, 2, 77. © 1965 Academic Press.)

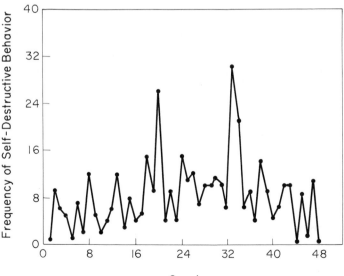

Thumbsucking

The "time-out" method is illustrated in a study by Baer (1962). Two preschool boys were selected for the study because of their high rates of thumbsucking. As with many children whose rate of thumbsucking is especially pronounced when they watch movies or television, these boys sucked their thumbs nearly continuously during the three 30-minute, baserate sessions in which they were allowed to view animated cartoons. The boys were seated side by side, separated by a small room divider. Two observers recorded their rate of thumbsucking by depressing a key whenever the subjects' thumbs were in their mouths. The keys were attached to cumulative recorders that automatically recorded a "unit" of thumbsucking each three seconds the keys were depressed.

The experimental treatment was introduced after the third session. Whenever one child, the experimental subject, inserted his thumb in his mouth the cartoons were stopped. When he removed his thumb the cartoons began again. This contingent withdrawal and presentation of the cartoons was alternated, in five-minute periods, with continuous presentation of the cartoons. The second boy was a yoked control. The designation, yoked control, means that this boy underwent the same experiences as the first boy but that the withdrawal and re-presentation of the cartoons was independent of any behavior he manifested. If changes in the first boy's behavior were produced by the experimental manipulations and no changes were observed in the second boy's behavior, it must be deduced that the differences were due to the influence of contingent versus noncontingent withdrawal and re-presentation of reinforcement. The two boys' roles were reversed on the second experimental day.

Figure 11-3. Cumulative curves of thumbsucking of the two subjects under alternating conditions of Control and Recovery. (From D. M. Baer, Laboratory control of thumbsucking by withdrawal and re-presentation of reinforcement. *Journal of the Experimental Analysis of Behavior,* 1962, 5, 527. Copyright 1962 by the Society for the Experimental Analysis of Behavior, Inc.)

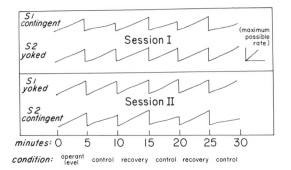

A careful look at Figure 11-3 reveals that the experimental operations were effective. On the first day the first subject's rate of thumbsucking was about maximal in all of the five-minute periods where there was continuous presentation of the movies ("recovery" periods), but decreased during the periods where the contingency between being able to watch the movies and thumbsucking was instituted ("control" periods). The second boy showed no decrease in rate of thumbsucking, even though he had been deprived of the opportunity to watch the films as frequently as the first boy. The random relation that existed for the second boy between thumbsucking and withdrawal of reinforcement did not influence this boy's behavior. The results were similar on the second day, except that the decreased rate of thumbsucking was shown by the second boy, the subject for whom a contingent relation now existed between thumbsucking and being able to watch movies.

The "time-out" procedure was effective in reducing thumbsucking, but the reduction occurred only during the periods in which the contingencies were operative. There was no suppression of thumbsucking during the recovery periods. More extensive training may have reduced the overall rate of thumbsucking, but for the present case we can conclude only that "time-out," acting as a mild form of punishment, was an effective, if transitory, means of suppressing behavior.

PUNISHMENT

Even though behavior modification relies primarily upon the presentation or withdrawal of reinforcement, relatively severe forms of punishment have been used. For example, Lovaas and his co-workers asked whether severe punishment for self-mutilation might not result in more rapid suppression of this behavior than occurred following withdrawal of social reinforcement. Some subjects therefore were given a strong electric shock following each self-mutilating response. When this was done, "The behaviors were suppressed within minutes, and remained suppressed for 11 months (Lovaas et al., 1966, p. 83)." In situations such as this, where the persistence of a response may endanger the child's existence or require that he live constantly immobilized by physical restraints, the use of a severe form of punishment may be a justifiable and effective means of suppressing behavior.

The use of punishment is not restricted to its capacity to suppress undesired behavior, for it also has been used as a means of generating additional sources of positive reinforcement. This may sound incongruous, but if we assume that any stimulus associated with pain reduction acquires positive reinforcing value, stimuli present at the termination of pain may emerge as positive, rather than negative reinforcers. Something like this occurs in everyday life in interactions between parents and children. Parents may become strong reinforcing agents for children, not only because they are sources of desired and necessary stimuli, but also because they are present to comfort and aid the child when he is in pain or distress.

Lovaas, Schaeffer, and Simmons (1966) have shown how punishment may be used to produce a desired response. In this case a painful and frightening electric shock was applied systematically with two autistic five-year-old boys in an effort to develop social responsiveness. Prior to the experiment the boys manifested no social responsiveness, speech, or appropriate play with objects. They typically spent from 70 to 80% of their time rocking and engaging in other stereotyped motor behavior.

The first goal was to penetrate the barrier that separated the boys from their environment by training them to come to the experimenter upon command. The boys were taken, one at a time, to an experimental room with a floor wired to form an electric grid. During two 20-minute pre-shock sessions neither boy responded to the experimenter's request, "Come to me." The experimenter repeated this request 100 times during each session. On the next three days a program of escape and avoidance conditioning was begun. Two experimenters faced each other, three feet apart, with the boy standing barefooted between them. It was possible for the boy to escape shock by approaching the experimenter upon command. To facilitate this response the experimenter beckoned and leaned toward the child. If the response did not appear in three seconds, the second experimenter pushed the child toward the beckoning adult. Self-initiated movement or being pushed terminated the shock. Later the child could avoid being shocked by moving toward the experimenter upon request. If this did not occur avoidance training devolved into escape training, for the child could no longer avoid shock but still could escape from it.

Gradually, the distance between the experimenters was increased and the additional cues provided by the experimenter were eliminated. By the end of these sessions the experimenters were standing at opposite ends of the room and gave only the verbal command. After the experimental sessions the boys were tested periodically without shock over the next eleven months. Two final periods of observation terminated the study. The procedure for these two sessions was the same as that for the preceding extinction series, except that upon re-entering the experimental situation the child was given one shock independent of any particular response.

The results appear in Figure 11-4. The introduction of shock on Day 3 resulted in extremely rapid increases in the proportion of the time the boys responded to the adults' commands. The boys' responsiveness remained high for nine months, but then dropped precipitously. Appropriate responding increased rapidly, however, with the administration of one noncontingent shock. Success also was reported in applying the same general experimental procedure to the production of more elaborate responses in the boys such as hugging and kissing the experimenter.

These studies leave little doubt that extreme forms of punishment may be effective in modifying behavior. Even so, one is very uneasy about methods that rely on severe physical punishment. We do not like to think of shocking children or subjecting them to painful experiences, even when they are as severely disturbed as those in the preceding study. We must realize, however, that shock was used as a last recourse after other approaches to helping the children proved futile. Autistic children are notoriously inaccessible, and it may be that only intense forms of stimulation can penetrate the barrier created by the encapsulation of the autistic child into his own asocial world. This may or may not be true, for although behavior modification was possible the research does little to reduce our ignorance about the basis of this strange disturbance. It is hard to think of a situation where severe punishment is an acceptable form of intervention with less disturbed children. Whatever advantages it may have in terms of efficiency and power may be offset by the manifold problems, humanitarian, ethical, and psychological, that accompany its use.

Figure 11-4.   Proportion of times the subjects responded to the experimenter's commands. (From O. I. Lovaas, B. Schaeffer, and J. Q. Simmons, Experimental studies in childhood schizophrenia: Building social behavior in autistic children by use of electric shock. *Journal of Experimental Research in Personality,* 1965, 1, 102, © 1965 Academic Press.)

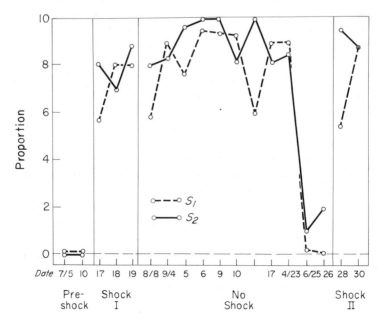

CONCLUSIONS

Research on behavior modification is a natural culmination of psychologists' long-term interest in the effects of reinforcement on learning. The central ideas behind modification are not new to psychology, nor is their application to the solution of practical problems. Over 40 years ago psychologists (Watson and Raynor, 1920; Jones, 1924a, 1924b) were publishing studies whose conceptualization is indistinguishable from many of the studies in behavior modification appearing today. What has been accomplished in recent years is the refinement and extension of these ideas and their application to a wide variety of problems in behavior management. Through vivid and sometimes dramatic examples, psychologists have demonstrated that behaviors can be created or suppressed, strengthened or weakened by carefully arranging the situation so that responses lead to systematic consequences.

The successes of behavior modification have led some adherents to convey the ebullience of a John B. Watson when they discuss the power of reinforcement in controlling and shaping human behavior. "Define the response, select the reinforcer, and then systematically reinforce." It sounds as if the primary task is to be vigilant in observing behavior and systematic in applying reinforcement. This may be true with animals. Animals can be guided into performing remarkable feats if the experimenter exerts judicious control in dispensing reinforcement. And it may be true of children living in situations where the experimenter is able to control important components of the child's environment. Even in cases where responses are defined and reinforcement is systematic, however, changes in behavior are not always readily produced. Problems become even more formidable when the experimenter cannot exert control over the child's everyday life.

By acknowledging the difficulties encountered in some efforts at behavior modification we are not asserting that the reinforcement theory on which it is based is necessarily impotent. The fact is that reinforcement of children's behavior is not an infallible mechanical process. Although behavior modification is not so superficial as some of its critics would assert, neither is it as simple as some of its proponents might wish.

Thus far, advances in behavior modification have been more of a technological than of a theoretical nature. The importance of a sophisticated technology cannot be underestimated, but technology cannot long develop without continuous expansion of its theoretical base. It is as demonstrations and not as experiments that studies of behavior modification have their greatest impact. We can gain a more comprehensive knowledge of the operation of reinforcement if we look at other studies with children in which the effects of reinforcement on learning have been investigated.

12

Influences on
Reinforcer Effectiveness

Reinforcement theorists recognize that the selection of effective reinforcers may prove to be difficult. Bijou and Baer, for example, have discussed the problem of selecting a reinforcer in the following manner:

In many instances we are able to make a good guess because of what we know about the culture that the child shares. For example, we know that in our culture saying "That's fine," when a child completes a performance will for *most* children strengthen the tendency to repeat that act under similar circumstances. However, we know, too, that it would be wrong to assume that saying, "That's fine," will strengthen the preceding behavior for *all* children, and indeed, we may know some "negativistic" children for whom "That's fine" seems to be a negative reinforcer (Bijou & Baer, 1961, p. 34).

This statement introduces the problem, but is it not even more complicated than these writers imply? Is it just that supportive comments will be effective as reinforcers for some children and ineffective for others? Consider such factors as who makes the statement, what conditions precede the delivery of the statement, how many times it has been repeated, and the child's expectations concerning supportive response. In other words, the context in which supportive statements are made may be critical in determining whether they will function as effective reinforcers. Reinforcement theorists do not avoid such problems, but in presenting their ideas they sometimes give the impression that such factors are not major issues for their position.

It will be profitable to pursue the discussion of social reinforcement throughout the present chapter, both because the literature on social reinforcement is interesting in itself and because it offers vivid illustrations of the problems encountered by proponents of reinforcement theory.

Admittedly, social reinforcement is one of the most complex forms of reinforcement. But research on this topic provides dramatic illustrations of the difficulties encountered when the experimenter tries to ascertain whether a stimulus will function effectively as a reinforcer. The decision to concentrate our attention on social reinforcement is dictated also by the fact that it has been one of the forms of reinforcement studied most extensively with children. That child psychologists should have been so interested in social reinforcement is not surprising. From early infancy the responses of parents and other significant adults form the referent by which the child decides whether his behavior is permissible, satisfactory, or commendable. Adult approval is more frequently—and more clearly—expressed by a nod, smile, or "That's fine," than by the dispensation of tangible reinforcement. Since adult approval is the most common means of effecting behavioral change in children, it is important that the operation of social reinforcement be understood. [For thorough reviews of this literature, see Horowitz (1967) and Stevenson (1965).]

ENVIRONMENTAL FACTORS

As we have said earlier, a typical means of increasing the effectiveness of a stimulus as a reinforcer is to place the subject in an environment where this class of stimuli is not readily available. Is this true for social stimuli? Anyone visiting an orphanage or institution for children would be likely to agree that it is. It takes little time before the visitor is surrounded by children, some clinging to his legs, others grasping his hands, and nearly everyone barraging him with questions. Many of the children seem to "feed" on social response. They are delighted by any indication of social approval and are insistent in their overtures if the response is not given spontaneously. Why do children behave in this way? An obvious explanation is that the children live in what may be called a state of social deprivation resulting from the limited opportunities in their environment to interact with interested, responsive adults. Such deprivation seems to enhance the effectiveness of social stimuli as sources of reinforcement. If these observations are valid, the effectiveness of social stimuli as reinforcing agents should be increased for children living in environments that offer minimal contact with adults, and decreased when the opportunities for supportive response from adults are great.

These suggestions have been tested in numerous studies. Some have been conducted in institutions and others in the laboratory. Children living in institutions should be more responsive to social reinforcement than those who live in ordinary environments. Similarly, children who have been deprived of social contacts in the laboratory should be more strongly influenced by social reinforcement than children who have not had this experience. The technique used to deprive children of social stimuli in the laboratory has been to isolate the child for brief periods, usually on the pretext that the experimenter must leave to prepare the equipment for the study.

Institutionalization

We will begin by discussing a study of eight-year-olds who lived in an orphanage and whose performance was compared with that of children living at home (Zigler, 1963). The children were tested in a social reinforcement or a neutral condition. In the social reinforcement condition, the experimenter frequently made positive comments about the child's performance, such as "That's fine," "Very good," or "You really know how to play this game," as he played a game called Marble-in-the-Hole. In the neutral condition, the experimenter was attentive but aloof; he remained unresponsive to the child throughout the experimental session. If the supportive comments were effective reinforcers, performance in the social reinforcement condition should be above that in the neutral condition. And if living in an orphanage produced social deprivation, the level of response should have been higher for the orphanage than for home children.

The Marble-in-the-Hole game was a simple, repetitive task with little inherent interest. There were orange marbles and blue marbles, in apparently endless supply. The orange marbles were to be dropped in one hole of a container and the blue ones in a second hole. The children could play the game as long as they wished and when they were through they were to tell the experimenter they wanted to stop. It was assumed that the supportive statements would strengthen the tendency to respond, thereby increasing the child's willingness to remain in the experimental situation. This task is typical of those used in studies of social reinforcement. The purpose in choosing such dull tasks is to maximize the influence of social reinforcement on the child's performance. Without some external source of reinforcement the child should quickly tire of such games and cease responding.

The results were in line with those expected. The orphanage children spent nearly twice as long in the game as the home children in both the social reinforcement (mean = 16.1 versus 8.4 minutes) and neutral conditions (mean = 10.6 versus 3.9 minutes). The supportive comments were effective reinforcers for both groups of children, for both groups spent significantly more time in the game when the adult praised their performance than when he remained silent. Merely performing in the presence of an attentive but unresponsive adult appeared to be a rewarding experience for the orphanage children. They spent nearly as long in the game in the neutral condition as the home children did in the social reinforcement condition. This study and many others indicate that the effectiveness of supportive comments as reinforcers is influenced by the availability of social stimuli in children's daily lives.

It is interesting to look at the variability as well as the average levels of performance. There were large individual differences within each group in the amount of time different children were willing to spend in the task. Many interpretations of these differences may be suggested, but at least for the orphanage children, differences in experience before entering the orphanage may have been an important determinant of their response to social reinforcement. Children who have experienced long periods of neglect and isolation generally may be more reactive to social reinforcement than those whose experiences prior to institutionalization were less unpleasant. The pre-institutional history of the children may be a variable worthy of consideration.

This was done in two studies using institutionalized mentally retarded children (Zigler, 1961; Zigler & Williams, 1963). Psychologists at the institution were asked to rate each of 60 children on a scale of pre-institutional social deprivation. In making these ratings such factors were considered as whether the child lived with a series of different families, was abused or neglected, or had a close relationship with his parents. The

Figure 12-1.   The mean time in seconds spent by children in the low and high deprivation groups during initial test and retest. (Data from E. F. Zigler and J. Williams, Institutionalization and the effectiveness of social reinforcement: A three-year follow-up study. *Journal of Abnormal and Social Psychology,* 1963, 66, 200.)

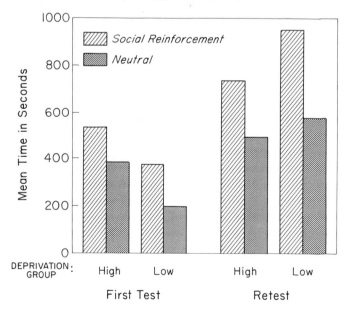

sample of children was dichotomized into high and low deprivation groups on the basis of these ratings. When first tested the children had spent an average of two years in the institution and had a mean age of ten years. Three years later, 49 of the children were tested again. In both cases testing was conducted in the same manner as in the previous study (Zigler, 1963).

The results are summarized in Figure 12-1. In all cases the children performed for longer periods when they were praised than when they were not. On the initial test, the children remained longer in the game in the high than in the low pre-institutional social deprivation group. Three years later the pattern was reversed: social reinforcement had a greater effect on the performance of children in the low than in the high deprivation group. Living in an institution for three additional years had the greater effect on children who entered the institution from the better home environments. Thus institutionalization does not have equivalent effects on all children. Its effects depend in part on the children's earlier environments and how long they have lived in the institution. The effects also may depend upon the type of institution in which the children live. Large differences have been found in the influence of different institutions on children's responsiveness to social reinforcement (Butterfield & Zigler, 1965).

These results fit in well with a deprivation hypothesis. Praise from an adult was more effective as a reinforcer when children had restricted opportunities for social interaction with adults in their everyday lives than when interaction was readily available. Does this relation also hold when children experience short-term deprivation of social stimuli in the laboratory?

Deprivation and Satiation

Much of the interest in laboratory studies of social deprivation can be traced to a study by Gewirtz and Baer (1958b). Normal preschool children were tested in a marble-sorting task following one of three pretraining conditions. Before performing the experimental task the children had experienced (a) 20 minutes of social isolation, or (b) 20 minutes of drawing and cutting in which the experimenter repeatedly told the children they were doing well, or (c) they were tested immediately after leaving the classroom. The first condition was designed to produce a state of social deprivation and the second, a state of satiation for social stimuli. The experimenter first observed the child in the marble-sorting task to determine his preferred response, in this case, the hole in which he inserted the greater number of marbles. For the remainder of the experimental period, the experimenter reinforced responses to the second, nonpreferred hole. Reinforcer effectiveness was measured by the relative increase in response to the nonpreferred hole. The results were clear:

social reinforcement was most effective following deprivation and least effective following satiation.

In a related study, Erickson (1962) attempted to condition children to select one class of nouns from successive pairs by reinforcing these choices with social or nonsocial (marbles) stimuli. Prior to the experimental task, the children were given a 15-minute period of (a) social deprivation (having no social stimuli available while solving puzzles) or (b) social satiation (receiving frequent praise from the adult while solving the puzzles). Children showed greater evidence of conditioning with social reinforcement after deprivation than after satiation, but there were no consistent differences in performance between the deprived and satiated children who received nonsocial reinforcement. The deprivation-satiation operations were effective and their influence was limited to the domain of stimuli represented in the pretraining experiences.

Can more precise relations be demonstrated between satiation and the later effectiveness of social stimuli as reinforcers? That is, is the power of social stimuli as reinforcers differentially influenced by different degrees of satiation? Exploration of these questions would give us a stronger test of the effects of satiation than occurs in comparisons of satiation and deprivation conditions. Gewirtz (1967) has reported several relevant studies. In a typical study five-year-old boys were asked by the experimenter to describe articles depicted in a series of drawings. As the boys did this, the experimenter responded "Good," 4, 12, 30, or 60 times. After this pretraining period the boys were asked to indicate which of two pictures they preferred in 90 pairs of pictures, each pair consisting of a picture of an animal and a plant. For the first 15 pairs each child's preferences were assessed and for the 75 remaining pairs the experimenter reinforced choices of the nonpreferred category by saying "Good," whenever the child chose a picture in this category.

Frequency of choices of the reinforced category decreased directly as a function of the number of times the reinforcing stimulus had been uttered by the experimenter in the pretraining period. Differences between 4 and 12 presentations and between 30 and 60 presentations were not statistically significant, however, and the data from these groups were pooled to produce Figure 12-2. A strong conditioning effect was evident for the boys who received the smaller number of supportive comments during pretraining, but there was little change in performance across the five blocks of 15 trials for the boys who received 30 or 60 reinforcements. "Good" had lost its effectiveness as a reinforcer after having been uttered by the experimenter so often and so repetitively. The results were replicated in additional studies, and in all cases the density of supportive comments during a pretraining period was inversely related to the subsequent effectiveness of these comments as reinforcing agents.

It might be concluded from these studies that social isolation has its major effects in increasing the later reinforcing value of social stimuli. On the basis of further investigation, however, it appears that this is an over-simplified conclusion. Children left alone in an empty room experience not only a withdrawal of social stimuli, but also minimal degrees of general sensory stimulation. Would the results be the same if the children were deprived of social stimuli, but were able to engage in other interesting activity during their period of isolation? To investigate this question Stevenson and Hill (1964) tested children after they had experienced one of three different conditions of isolation: the children remained alone in an empty room for ten minutes, the children remained alone but viewed an interesting abstract film, or the experimenter was the children's companion in viewing the film. The absence of only social stimuli had a less significant effect on performance in the marble-dropping task than the absence of both social and interesting visual stimuli. For boys, the results of the condition involving social deprivation were more similar to those of the nondeprivation condition than to those involving both social and sensory deprivation. The results for girls were less systematic. Isolation may have different effects on the subsequent influence of social reinforcers, and the degree of such differences is related to the sex of the child. Such results leave the stimulus-deprivation hypothesis in limbo.

Figure 12-2.   Mean number of correct choices in nonpreferred category by children receiving 4 or 12, or 30 or 60 prior reinforcements. (From J. L. Gewirtz, Deprivation and satiation of social stimuli as determinants of their reinforcing efficacy. In J. P. Hill (Ed.), *Minnesota Symposia on Child Psychology,* Vol. 1. Minneapolis: University of Minnesota Press, 1967, p. 20, © Copyright 1967, University of Minnesota.)

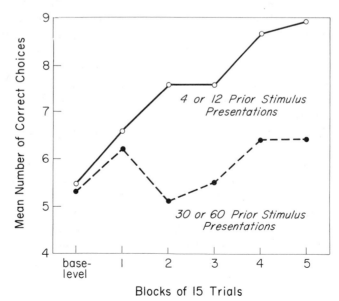

CHARACTERISTICS OF THE EXPERIMENTER

Little attention has been paid by psychologists to the characteristics of the adult chosen to act as experimenter. It usually is considered sufficient to describe the subject's characteristics in detail, leaving the experimenter as an assumed "standard" that has similar effects on all subjects. Recent work has shown that this assumption is often unjustified, for it has been demonstrated in many contexts that experimenters themselves may be important determinants of the outcome of their research (Rosenthal, 1966). It seems especially appropriate, therefore, to consider how the experimenter's characteristics may influence the child's behavior in studies of social reinforcement. Children have different types and amounts of experience with adults, who serve as models and as sources of emotional gratification for children.

Sex of the Experimenter

One of the first characteristics to be investigated was the sex of the experimenter in relation to that of the child. We need only look at the literature on personality development and at our own everyday experiences to suggest that praise from men and women may have different effects, depending upon whether the subject is a boy or a girl. There were hints that this might be the case in early studies of social reinforcement (e.g., Wolf, 1938), but Gewirtz and Baer (1958a) were the first to give explicit attention to this variable. The subjects in their study were four- to six-year-olds, and they were tested by a man or a woman. The marble-sorting game used in the study has been described earlier (Gewirtz & Baer, 1958b). As measured by the degree to which children's performance was influenced in the marble-sorting game, supportive comments made by men were more effective for girls than for boys and those made by women were more effective for boys than for girls. This cross-sex effect immediately leads one to think of the Oedipal theory of Freud. Regardless of whether we choose to follow this interpretation, the results pose an important restriction on our previous conclusions. Praise from adults may be maximally effective only if the adult and the child are of the opposite sex.

The next logical question is whether the cross-sex effect will be found at all ages. A study by Stevenson (1961) indicates that it is not. Children of ages three to five, six to eight, and nine to eleven years were used as subjects. A total of 504 children were included in the study. Such a large number of children was needed because a secondary purpose was to ascertain whether comparable effects would be found when different adults served as experimenters. If one wishes to make generalizations about the sex of the adult independent of other characteristics of the adult one cannot use only one man and one woman as experimenters. For example, it is possible that the effectiveness of a man and a woman may differ, not because of their sex but because of personal characteristics. By chance the man may be unappealing to most children and the woman may elicit warm, positive response. The differences in their influence on children's behavior may be due, therefore, not to the fact that they are a man and a woman, but because one is appealing and the other is not. This dilemma can be resolved by using a sample of men and women as experimenters. If the effect holds up across a sample of experimenters one can be more confident of its generality. Consequently, in the design of this study six men and six women acted as experimenters, each testing seven boys and seven girls at each of the three age levels.

The measure of performance was the increase in rate of response in a marble-dropping game following the introduction of social reinforcement. The baserate of response was determined during the initial minute of the game. After this the experimenter made supportive comments about the child's performance twice a minute for the next 5 minutes. The average difference score, derived by subtracting the number of responses made each minute in minutes 2 through 5 from that made in minute 1, is presented in Figure 12-3 for each age-of-child, sex-of-child, and sex-of-adult combination.

Figure 12-3. The average difference score obtained for each minute for each age group (CA) and sex of experimenter (E)—sex of child (S) combination. (From H. W. Stevenson, Social reinforcement with children as a function of CA, sex of E, and sex of S. *Journal of Abnormal and Social Psychology,* 1961, 149. Reprinted by permission of the American Psychological Association.)

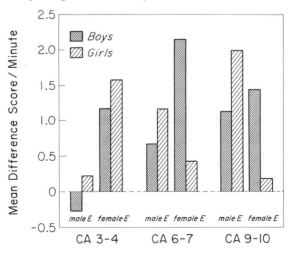

At ages three and four there was no evidence of a cross-sex effect. Instead, women tended to be more effective reinforcing agents than men for both boys and girls. Women are the primary caretakers of young children. Perhaps young children's close relationship with their mothers and other women makes women more effective as reinforcing agents. The cross-sex effect appeared at ages six and seven. Here, as in the study by Gewirtz and Baer, the effect was produced mainly by the markedly higher level of performance of boys than of girls tested by women. Why this should be the case is not clear. A cross-sex effect was suggested at ages nine and ten, but it was not statistically significant. Age of the child, therefore, is important in determining whether a cross-sex effect will be found.

A closer look indicates that the results are even more complicated. The different adults were not equally effective in reinforcing children's behavior; the average level of performance of the samples of children tested by the various experimenters differed significantly. Generally, the differences among adults in their effectiveness as reinforcing agents increased as the children got older. Nine- and ten-year-olds were more sensitive to the personal characteristics of the experimenter than were three- and four-year-olds. We can see why the cross-sex effect was not significant for the oldest group. These children were less influenced by the sex of the adult than they were by other factors. Differences among the experimenters, as reflected in the children's average levels of performance, were greater for women than for men and for girls than for boys.

The simplicity of any ideas we may have had about social reinforcement is shattered. We may train adults to respond to children in a standard manner, but the degree to which they will be able to influence the child will depend—at least—upon the kind of person the adult is, his sex, the child's sex, and the child's age.

Role of the Experimenter

If there are such profound differences among individuals in their effectiveness as reinforcing agents it should be possible to isolate some of these characteristics and train individuals to adopt them. Allen, Spear, and Johnson (1969) attempted to do this in a study with ten- and eleven-year-olds. The experimenters, four men and four women, were trained to portray "warm" and "cold" roles in their interaction with the children. These roles, representing extremes on the dimensions of involvement and reactivity to the child, were defined in the following way:

In the cold role, the experimenters used little eye contact and did not smile. They were trained to withdrawal physically by settling back in their chairs and to show minimal interest in the subject by gazing about the room. The instructions and reinforcements were delivered in a flat, lethargic manner. In the warm role, the experimenters were instructed to use frequent eye contact, to smile when appropriate, and to speak in a warm, interested manner. Each leaned forward and watched the subjects performance to convey the idea that he was involved in the game (Allen, Spear, & Johnson, 1969, p. 3).

The children were tested with a marble-sorting game in which they were instructed to insert marbles into the holes of a board matching the color of the marbles. Difference scores, representing the difference in number of marbles inserted in minute 1 (baserate period) and minutes 2 through 6 (reinforcement period) are presented in Figure 12-4. The results offer an unusual twist on the cross-sex effect. The role played by the experimenters had significant effects on children's performance—but only when the children were of the opposite sex from the adult. The training session apparently served to reduce differences among the different adults playing each role, for the cross-sex effect was significant in this study, whereas it was not for nine- and ten-year-olds in the study by Stevenson (1961).

Figure 12-4.   Mean difference score for each minute of the experimental task, according to sex of experimenter, sex of child, and condition. (From S. A. Allen, P. S. Spear, and J. Johnson, Experimenter role effects on children's task performance and perception. *Child Development,* 1969, 40, 6. Copyright 1969 Society for Research in Child Development, Inc.)

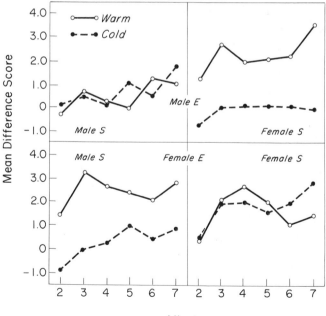

The role played by the experimenter in earlier interactions with children also may influence his effectiveness as a reinforcing agent. Children often are wary of adults with whom they are not familiar. Even though they generally may have had positive experiences with adults, children also are criticized by adults and have other kinds of unpleasant experiences with them. Strange adults may be less effective with children than adults whom children know to be nonpunitive or enjoyable. If, therefore, an adult were to establish himself as a tolerant, permissive person, or if he behaves very positively towards the children he may increase his effectiveness as a reinforcing agent. In other words, the child's acquired attitude toward the specific adult may determine his reaction to the adult's praise.

This suggestion was put to experimental test by McCoy and Zigler (1965). Six- and seven-year old boys played the marble-sorting game after neutral, positive, or no interaction with the experimenter. In the neutral condition the experimenter (a woman) took the boys in groups of six to a classroom where they were given attractive art materials with which to work. She attempted to be as neutral as possible, keeping busy at her desk and attempting not to elicit bids for social interaction. In the positive condition the boys again were allowed to work with the art materials, but the experimenter was diligent in her efforts to interact with each boy and tried to be complimentary, helpful, and responsive. Three sessions, held one week apart, were conducted in this manner. One week after the third session the boys were tested with the experimental task. When this task was given, the experimenter attempted to behave in the same manner to all groups, making supportive comments twice a minute for as long as the child played the game.

The boys for whom the adult was a stranger terminated the game after an average of 2.5 minutes, but boys in the other two conditions played much longer. When the experimenter had behaved in a neutral manner in the earlier sessions the boys remained in the task for an average of 9.6 minutes, and when she had interacted positively with the boys they remained for an average of 13.4 minutes. The experimenter was less effective when she was a stranger than when she was a familiar but neutral adult, and, in turn, she was less effective in this role than when she had been responsive to children in her earlier interactions with them.

These studies demonstrate that an adult can heighten his effectiveness as a reinforcing agent if he is enthusiastic, involved, and responsive to the child, either during the experimental session or in earlier interactions with the children. There is more to it than this, for children undoubtedly are sensitive to characteristics more subtle than those incorporated in these roles. Only through further research will we gain a more sophisticated understanding of the differences among adults that influence children during different periods of their lives.

The Agent of Reinforcement

Rather than attempt to create different roles for the experimenter we could use experimenters who have different natural relations with the child. For example, parents or peers could be used as reinforcing agents and we could contrast the effectiveness of fathers and mothers, popular and unpopular peers, parents and strangers. These comparisons have been made, and the results of these studies make us more aware than ever of how hard it is to fit the data on social reinforcement into any simple model.

Stevenson, Keen, and Knights (1963) invited the parents of preschool children to participate in their study and trained them to be experimenters. Trying to predict whether parents would be more effective than strangers from the data discussed this far is difficult. On the one hand, parents of middle-class preschool children, and especially mothers, have had years of predominantly supportive interactions with their children. From the McCoy and Zigler (1965) findings we might predict that the order of effectiveness would be mothers, fathers, and then strangers. On the other hand, the child has received more frequent supportive response from his parents than from strangers and may be relatively more satiated for parental reinforcement. If this were the case, mothers should be the least effective reinforcers, fathers next, and strangers, the most effective of all. The results were in line with neither prediction.

Of the various sex-of-parent, sex-of-child groups, the only one to show increments in response following the introduction of social reinforcement in the marble-sorting task were preschool girls tested by their mothers. Both boys and girls tested by their fathers showed marked decrements in performance and moderate decrements were found when boys were tested by their mothers. Praise from strange men had little effect on the performance of either boys or girls, but strange women were able to increase the rate of response significantly for both boys and girls. Were the children awed by their fathers' appearances in nursery school and increasingly reluctant to perform in the presence of their fathers? Were the boys embarrassed by their mothers' frequent praise? Were the girls more comfortable with their mothers and responsive to her evaluations of their proficiency? The study raises more questions than it answers. Even so, it is a baffling indication of how complicated the process of social reinforcement turns out to be.

It is not troublesome to train children as reinforcing agents. For example, Hartup (1964) trained four- and five-year-old preschool children to say "That's fine" to one light and "That's good" to another. The lights, visible only to the child acting as experimenter, became the cues for dispensing social reinforcement. The children were told that they would have to "read" the lights to tell another child how well he was doing and that they should remain quiet at other times. The investigator brought the subject to the experimental room, instructed him about the marble-sorting game, and obtained the base rate of response. He then introduced the child who would act as experimenter. During the next six minutes one of the lights was illuminated every 20 seconds, indicating that the experimenter was to make a supportive comment. To insure that the child serving as experimenter followed directions correctly, the investigator observed the sessions through a one-way vision screen. The selection of experimenters for this study was based on the findings of a prior sociometric analysis of the friendship status of the children in the classroom. Pairs of children were constituted so that the experimenter was either a liked or disliked peer of the subject.

Verbal approval was an effective reinforcer only for the five-year-olds tested by a disliked peer. In all other groups performance deteriorated during the six minutes in which the supportive comments were made. For four-year-olds, the decline was greater for children tested by a liked peer than by a disliked peer. Perhaps the children were less satiated for social reinforcement from the disliked peer. This is possible, but it may be less a matter of relative satiation than of the expectations of the subject about approval from a disliked peer. Reinforcement may have greater incentive value for the child when it is from an unexpected source. Additional data favoring such an interpretation are found in two more studies.

Ferguson (1964) worked with second and fifth graders. Instead of responding to a light, the children were trained to read the supportive statements as they were illuminated on a panel. Again, the marble-sorting task was used. Second grade subjects were less responsive to social reinforcement from other second graders than they were from fifth graders. A ready interpretation of this finding is that fifth graders had greater prestige in the eyes of the second graders. But fifth graders also were less responsive to reinforcement by their age-mates; performance was higher when they were tested by second graders than by fifth graders! In both cases, reinforcement had a greater effect when it came from an unexpected source.

In a third study, reported by Tiktin and Hartup (1965), the experimenters were elementary school children selected on the basis of their popularity in the peer group. When children were reinforced by popular peers their performance decreased across the six-minute reinforcement period in the marble-sorting task. When they were reinforced by unpopular peers there was a significant increase in performance.

The results with parents and peers are not compatible with those obtained when the relationship between the experimenter and the child was established during a short period before the study or when the experimenter behaved in different ways during the experimental period.

The data obtained following short-term interactions between experimenter and child do not help us in predicting the results found when the relationship between the experimenter and the child has developed over a long period of time. The data outstrip our theories. We cannot, at least for the present, organize this bewildering array of information into a coherent pattern.

CONCLUSIONS

The research on social reinforcement introduces us to the complexities that surround the concept of reinforcement as it is applied to children's learning and performance. Whether one responds to this research with dismay or excitement, it leads to an unavoidable conclusion: trying to determine whether a stimulus will function as an effective reinforcer is extraordinarily difficult. As these difficulties unfold, it becomes obvious that a simplistic interpretation of reinforcement is untenable. Reinforcement may be a powerful concept, but it is not a simple one. What these studies seem to say is that reinforcement is a relative process, based not on the absolute characteristics of the stimulus, but on its relation to the subject and his state at a particular time. We gain little assurance from these studies that a reinforcer, once isolated, will have general applicability. A stimulus capable of reinforcing one type of behavior will not necessarily be effective in reinforcing different types of behavior or the same behavior at a later time. The principles of reinforcement theory may be straightforward in themselves, but their application to the child in his everyday life proves to be excruciatingly complex.

There is no dearth of positive findings in studies of social reinforcement; the challenge is to bring them into some type of order. As each interpretation of the data begins to grow in strength, new variables appear that throw the interpretation into question. We could worry less about the results of this research if it were not for the fact that social reinforcement, to some degree, enters into practically every psychological study of children's learning. Whenever an experimenter defines a task that is to be mastered by the child the potentiality for supportive response exists.

13

Material Reinforcers

Let us go now from the intangible mode of social reinforcement to the tangible and look at the research on material forms of reinforcement. We will be interested in a series of questions about material reinforcers. When does the presentation of material reinforcers result in improved learning? Are certain types of material reinforcers more effective than others? Can conditions be arranged to increase the effectiveness of material reinforcers? Do delays in reinforcement hinder learning? Is children's learning influenced by secondary sources of reinforcement? Child psychologists have spent a great deal of time attempting to find answers to such questions.

FORM OF REINFORCEMENT

In most learning situations something happens in the course of the child's performance to tell him whether or not he is responding correctly. This information is often transmitted by the presentation of a material object of some value. Or the child may be informed when he is correct by the onset of a signal, such as a light or sound, or the appearance of a worthless token. We can determine whether material reinforcement improves learning by comparing the performance of children who receive material rewards with that of children who receive only a signal (i.e., knowledge of results).

Material Reinforcers versus Knowledge of Results

Nine-year-olds know the value of money. Should they not learn to discriminate between two stimuli more rapidly if they receive money after every correct choice than if they merely see a light flash? Would not the amount of money received be influential in determining their rate of learning? Miller and Estes (1961) have investigated these questions.

Nine-year-old boys were given the task of learning to tell twins apart. The only differentiating cue in the line drawings of the twins' faces was the height of the eyebrows. The face selected by each boy on the first trial was reinforced and was considered the correct stimulus throughout the task. The boys were divided into three groups. One group was informed of each correct response by the flash of a red light, thus their reinforcement consisted solely of the knowledge that their choice was right or wrong. In a second group, each correct response yielded a penny, and in a third group, fifty cents. The boys were required to forfeit either one cent or fifty cents, the same amount received for each correct response, when they made an incorrect choice. Since the criterion for learning was 16 consistently correct responses, boys in the fifty-cent group left the experiment with a minimum of $8.00!

In the "signal" group an average of 21 errors were made in reaching criterion. Those who received a penny made an average of 32 errors, and those receiving fifty cents for each correct response, 34 errors. Not only did a monetary reward fail to produce significantly faster learning than a signal, but a penny seemed to be just as effective as fifty cents.

How are such results to be interpreted? Common sense ideas about the effects of rewards are of little help, for the results fail to conform to common sense expectations. The best clues come from observing children. Most elementary school children have a high level of motivation to perform well. They may have some trepidation about the experimental situation, and indeed older children often appear to be very anxious about how well they will perform. Such concerns usually are readily dispelled. Thus when the experimenter enters the typical middle-class schoolroom he is faced with an eager and expectant child whose behavior is not easily controlled by material sources of reinforcement. Level of motivation to perform well is so high that the addition of material objects, even ones of high value, may add little to the reinforcement occurring from merely being correct. Furthermore, it is sometimes the case, and this appears to have occurred in the Miller and Estes study, that the appearance of material reinforcers is distracting. Miller and Estes point out that the children seemed to be preoccupied with the money, counting it and worrying about the possibility of losing it. It seems, then, that material reward may result in poor performance if it distracts the child, causing him to divide his attention between what he has earned and what he is to learn.

Terrell (1958) also has found that material reinforcers may not lead to the most efficient learning. Children between the ages of four and nine years received one of three forms of reinforcement: (a) a signal light, (b) a piece of candy, or (c) a bean, which they could transfer from one jar to another with the expectation that the beans could be traded for a bag of candy when they accumulated enough of them. (The signal light also followed correct responses in the last two groups.) Equivalent rates of learning were found with the three forms of reinforcement.

There was a fourth condition in this study. Here, children were promised a bag of candy after they had made the light go on enough times. Rate of learning in this condition was significantly slower than that in the other three conditions. Evidently, the vagueness of a promise with no accompanying indication of what constituted attainment interfered with learning. Or was it that the children in the "promise" group were prohibited from making meaningful manipulative responses, that, in themselves, may constitute a source of reinforcement? This possibility was studied by Terrell (1959), who told children to imagine they received a piece of candy after each correct response and to put the imaginary candy in a make-believe bag that later could be exchanged for a real bag of candy. Children between five and nine who engaged in the manipulation of imagined objects learned the two-choice size discrimination in fewer trials than children who were promised a bag of candy when they made the light go on enough times, or than children who were reinforced only with the light. Magical manipulation may be a more effective reinforcer than a signal light, even if fifty cents is not!

Social Class

The preceding studies were conducted with middle-class children. Would the results be comparable when the children were from lower socioeconomic groups? There are several arguments why they might not. Most middle-class children in the United States have abundant material possessions. Another trinket or another piece of candy may have less value for them than for lower-class children. Also, doing well in school-like tasks and being correct may be much more highly valued by striving middle-class children than by children from lower-class families.

A study by Terrell, Durken, and Wiesley (1959) included both middle- and lower-class children in an additional study of size discrimination. The children were reinforced with a signal light or a light and a piece of candy. As in the preceding studies, middle-class children learned the discrimination faster with only the signal light. Lower-class children learned more readily with the candy. This significant interaction between social class and form of reinforcement supports arguments that the effectiveness of reinforcers differs according to social class.

Conditions can be arranged, however, to produce results contrary to these arguments. Most experiments use dull tasks. Learning to discriminate between cones, balls, and cubes of different size ceases to be interesting after a while. Marshall (1969) has asked, therefore, whether different results would be obtained if the task had high intrinsic interest. A device was constructed so that as a marble traversed its course from a hole to a cup it passed a series of objects and shapes, some of which moved or sounded when struck by the marble. The series of events occurred only when the child inserted a marble into a hole bordered by the same color. There were marbles of three colors, and the criterion for learning the marble-hole discrimination was six consecutive correct responses. A companion task involved the same discrimination, but the mechanics of the device were covered so that the child saw nothing but the insertion of the marble and its later appearance in the cup. The children were tested under one of several reinforcement conditions, including one in which the experimenter said, "Yes, that is the hole for the _____ marble," and another in which the child gained a material reward for each correct response. An assortment of rewards was available, including candy, dolls, and small cars, and the child chose the one for which he wished to work. The subjects were middle- and lower-class kindergarten children.

Performance did not differ according to social class when material rewards were promised, but lower-class children did much more poorly than their middle-class counterparts when they were given only symbolic reward. These results seem to give some support to the assumption that lower-class children have not learned to value symbolic reward as highly as middle-class children. In a third condition, however, the experimenter commented about the correctness of the response immediately after the insertion of the marble, rather than at the termination of its excursion through the apparatus. Social class differences disappeared. But for lower-class children hearing the statement after a delay was less beneficial than when it was made immediately after response. The children may have needed immediate information to focus their attention on the task.

The results were broken down by type of task. Class status was not a significant variable when the task was interesting. With the dull task, however, children of lower social class did more poorly than middle-class children. Moreover, middle-class children actually learned more rapidly when the task was dull! Clearly, we cannot make generalizations about reinforcement effects and social class unless we specify the type of task that is being used.

We might have hoped that research on material reinforcement would be simpler than that on social reinforcement. But the external consequences of a response seem to be inextricably interrelated to the internal sources of reinforcement that come from being correct or doing a good job. Learning may be self-rewarding. Material rewards may exert an influence on learning, but their influence seems to be determined more by their symbolic value than by their price. Perhaps this is why research on reinforcement effects with children is so complex and why the results are so often discrepant with those obtained with lower animals.

Penalizing Errors

Any parent can suggest one way in which the value of material objects can be increased for a child: try to take something away from the child and its value suddenly increases. Sorting toys is a good example. The child may have abandoned some of his toys, but the possibility of their being given away seems to convert them into cherished treasures.

In most learning tasks the child has everything to gain by being correct and nothing to lose by being wrong. As more and more reinforcers are amassed, the value of each may decrease. This tendency may be changed by introducing a penalty for incorrect response. The usual penalty is to require the child to return a reward object each time he makes an error. Brackbill and O'Hara (1958), for example, gave kindergarten boys 15 pieces of candy and told some of them that each time they made a correct choice they would find another piece of candy, but that each time they made an error they would have to return a piece to the experimenter. Another group was not required to relinquish candy for in-

Figure 13-1.   Mean trials to criterion in discrimination learning as a function of grade, task, and reward condition. (Data from G. J. Whitehurst, Discrimination learning in children as a function of reinforcement condition, task complexity, and chronological age. *Journal of Experimental Child Psychology,* 1969, 7, 320.)

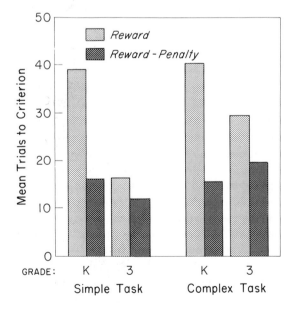

correct choices. Learning of a three-choice discrimination was faster when there was a penalty for errors.

Similar results were found by Stevenson, Weir, and Zigler (1959). In an effort to vary the amount of pre-experimental satiation for the reward objects five-year-olds were given either 5, 10, 20, or 40 colored stickers (pictures of animals and flowers) in the pre-experimental period. The children then received a sticker for each correct response in a discrimination task and half were required to relinquish a sticker following incorrect responses. Only those given the two smaller numbers of stickers and penalized for errors tended to learn the discrimination. The effects of introducing a penalty for incorrect response were dependent, therefore, upon the number of reward objects the child had available.

Penalizing children for errors may enhance the value of the reinforcer. It also may have other, more direct influences on behavior. Children seemed to be more cautious when they ran the risk of losing one of their prizes; they were more likely to look at the stimuli before making a response. Since the greatest obstacle to learning seemed to be due to failure to look carefully at the stimuli, any increase in attention should produce more effective learning.

The preceding results have been extended and reaffirmed by White-hurst (1969). Three variables were of concern: reinforcement conditions, complexity of the task, and age. Children of kindergarten age (five and six years) and third graders (eight and nine years) were presented a size discrimination. In the simple form of the task the position of the stimuli was an irrelevant dimension. That is, the children had to learn which of the stimuli was correct, ignoring the left-right position of the stimuli. In the complex form of the task, color, shape, and position of the stimuli were irrelevant dimensions. For every correct response the children were given a bead that could be used to purchase objects from the assortment that was available. For half of the children a bead was retrieved by the experimenter following incorrect response. As can be seen in Figure 13-1, learning was more rapid when there was a cost to the child for making errors.

These studies offer consistent evidence that introducing a penalty for incorrect response improves learning. An obvious interpretation is that the potentiality of loss increases the value of the reinforcing objects. An alternative, but not contradictory interpretation, is that penalty results in the child's paying closer attention to what he is doing.

Reward and Punishment

Penalizing children for errors is a mild form of punishment. Other forms of punishment also have been studied. Penney and Lupton (1961) reinforced some children with candy for each correct response, or coupled this positive form of reinforcement with a loud, unpleasant sound for incorrect responses. The level of performance in a difficult pattern discrimination was higher when children received both reward and punishment than when punishment was omitted. In fact, the group that received no punishment continued to perform at a chance level throughout the task. A third group, which received only punishment for incorrect responses, showed the highest level of performance.

In a related experiment, Spence and Segner (1967) found that children given candy for correct response and a raucous buzzer for incorrect response learned a series of object discriminations more effectively than did a group receiving only reward for correct response. No significant difference was found between the performance of the group given both candy and the buzzer and of a third group given only the buzzer. The study included complementary groups for whom the words "right" and "wrong" constituted the reinforcers. There were no significant differences among the verbal reinforcement groups. Of additional interest is the finding that there was no significant difference in the effectiveness of material and nonmaterial rewards for middle- and lower-class children, a further demonstration of the un-replicability of the Terrell et al. (1959) results.

Spence and Segner were careful to point out the information value of the presence or absence of reinforcement to their subjects; thus the children's set presumably was quite different from that of children in the other studies discussed. The interpretation favored by the authors for the poor performance of the candy-only group was that the delivery and accumulation of rewards distracted children's attention from the task and thereby interfered with their performance.

With good reason, child psychologists have not tended to use intense forms of punishment. An exception to this is a study by Nelson, Reid, and Travers (1965). Strong electric shock has been found to have strong effects on learning in lower animals. Would such a strong aversive stimulus result in similar effects with children? In a study that probably will not be repeated because of its ethical problems, children received either a tone, the words "right" or "wrong," or strong electric shock as feedback for correct and incorrect responses. The task required the child to learn which of two responses was associated with a series of words or with combinations of letters or numbers. Despite the fact that the shock was so strong that it produced tears in some children, no significant differences in rate of learning were found among the various conditions. For children, the information conveyed by the shock may be more important than its aversive properties in influencing response.

These studies indicate that material rewards do not necessarily facilitate learning. Because children are social organisms who are highly dependent upon the manner in which the adult structures the task, and who enter the experimental situation with preferences and great varieties of prior experiences, their interpretation of what is defined as a reward or a punishment and the way their performance is influenced by them may be very complex. As Spence and Segner (1967, p. 37) point out, "It is becoming increasingly apparent that reinforcers do not have a simple set of properties that affect performance in a uniform manner but may play a number of complex roles, depending on such variables as the characteristics of the subjects, the task, the nature of the reinforcers themselves, and the precise manner in which they are introduced into the situation."

DELAY OF REINFORCEMENT

Those who are content to translate the results of research with animals to the management of children are likely to state with some emphasis that reinforcement should be delivered immediately after the appropriate response has been made. What such persons fail to acknowledge is that children, in contrast to animals, have means of bridging the gap between the time of response and the delivery of the reward; most importantly, language. There is no consistent evidence that delay of reinforcement produces inferior learning by children. There are two exceptions: a delay of reinforcement may be disruptive or produce inefficient learning when (a) the child cannot readily verbalize the basis of response, as in certain motor tasks, or (b) the child learns responses in the presence of discriminative stimuli that interfere with later reproduction of the appropriate response.

Discrimination Learning Tasks

A child is presented several stimuli, one of which is correct. He makes his choice and is reinforced either immediately or after a delay. Will a delay in reinforcement retard the rate at which the child learns to discriminate among the objects? The majority of studies of discrimination learning in children have found that a delay of reinforcement produces negligible effects on the rate of learning. For example, in a summary of seven studies by Brackbill and her associates involving 14 comparisons, immediate reinforcement resulted in faster acquisition in only one case (Brackbill, Wagner, & Wilson, 1964). Renner (1964) found a similar trend in his review of research with older human subjects and with delays up to 30 seconds; the majority of the studies did not reveal poorer performance with delayed reinforcement.

Nevertheless, two studies have found significantly slower learning for groups receiving a seven-second delay than for those receiving immediate reinforcement in learning form and size discriminations (Terrell &

Ware, 1961; Ware & Terrell, 1961). These two studies offer clues as to why, in some cases, a delay of reinforcement may retard learning. Five- and six-year-olds were presented simultaneous form and size discriminations. The child might receive immediate reinforcement for the form discrimination and delayed reinforcement for the size discrimination. Stimuli differing in form appeared on some trials and those differing in size appeared on others. Children seemed to lose interest in the problem associated with delayed reinforcement; they tended to respond impulsively and to look away from the discriminative stimuli.

The possibility that the detrimental effect of delayed reinforcement may be attributable to inattention resulting from boredom has been investigated in several subsequent studies. Fagan and Witryol (1966) found that such effects could be eliminated if the children were instructed to look at the source of reinforcement during this period of delay. Maintaining attention to the source of reinforcement presumably made it less likely that interfering responses would be learned during the delay period. Other children receiving delayed reward but no instructions about what to do during the delay period performed more poorly than a group receiving immediate reinforcement. Erickson and Lipsitt (1960) also have found that delays of three to six seconds did not retard learning when children were instructed to pay attention to the reinforcing stimulus.

Children's learning may not be disrupted by a delay of reward, then, if children are able to maintain appropriate attention to the task during the period of delay. Another related factor may be children's ability to bridge the period of delay with forms of self-instruction. Terrell (1965) has noted a tendency for younger children to be more negatively affected by delay than older children, which may be related to the fact that spontaneous self-instruction is less likely to occur with younger than with older children.

Delayed Reinforcement and Retention

Brackbill and her associates have demonstrated that delay of reinforcement actually may produce secondary gains. In a series of studies they have found that delayed reinforcement facilitates retention. In a typical study (Brackbill, Wagner, & Wilson, 1964), eight-year-olds were given an 18-item discrimination learning task. The materials were English-French equivalents. Two cards were used on each trial; one contained the correct pair (e.g., *street-rue*) and the second, the English word and an incorrect associate (e.g., *street-cas*). Choices were indicated by pressing a lever below the card. Reinforcement occurred either immediately or after 10 seconds. If the response was correct, a light came on above the card, a buzzer sounded, and a marble was dispensed. The marbles could be traded for a prize at the end of the session. If the child was wrong, there was a click and the light above the correct card came on.

The mean number of trials required to learn the correct response for each pair of cards (with a criterion of three successive correct responses) was very similar for the immediate and delayed reinforcement groups (48 and 47 trials). The discriminations were relearned either a day or a week later. The mean number of trials required for relearning after a lapse of one day were 33 and 14 trials for the immediate and delayed groups respectively. The corresponding means for the groups who relearned the discriminations after a week were 26 and 11 trials. Delayed reinforcement facilitated relearning. Furthermore, delayed reinforcement was of greater value in relearning difficult than easy items. Rate of relearning the three most difficult items, assessed by the number of trials required in original learning, was compared to that for relearning the three easiest items. While children who had received immediate reinforcement took 10 times as long to relearn the difficult compared to the easy items, those in the delayed reinforcement group relearned each type of item with equal speed. Comparable results have been found for oral presentation of the materials, thus the conclusions are not restricted to the visual mode (Lintz, 1968).

Despite the consistency of the beneficial effects of delayed reinforcement on retention, its explication awaits additional research. One of the most likely interpretations is that a delay in reinforcement enables children to rehearse. One of the few studies indicating better original learning with delayed reinforcement was reported by Wright and Smothergill (1967). Here, delayed reinforcement was more effective in learning a discrimination than immediate reinforcement if children actively compared the discriminative stimuli during the delay period. (The stimuli, line drawings, were blurred unless the child manipulated a device to bring them into clear view.)

Motor Tasks

The preceding conclusions have been based on discrimination learning tasks. Will they be the same for other forms of learning? There are several studies of the effects of delayed reinforcement on the performance of instrumental motor responses, such as simple lever-pulling. The child is told to place his hand on a starting point and at the onset of a signal light to pull a lever through its full excursion to terminate the signal or to receive a reward. The measure of response is the time it takes to move the lever across its pathway.

A study by Rieber (1961a) is illustrative of this type of research. Children were told to pull a lever to obtain reward. The excursion of the lever terminated in either immediate or a 12-second delay in reinforcement. The initiating signal (a light) remained visible during the delay period for half of the children and terminated with the child's response for the other half. The speeds with which kindergarten children moved the lever did not differ between immediate and delayed reinforcement when the signal was not visible during the delay period. When the signal remained on during the delay, speeds were significantly slower. Similar results have been found in other studies (Penney, 1967; Rabinowitz, 1966; Rieber, 1961b; Rieber & Johnson, 1964).

A parsimonious interpretation of these results is that competing responses, presumably conditioned to the signal, were learned during the delay period, thus producing slower rates of response. A study by Harris (1967), however, dampens one's enthusiasm about this interpretation. Harris tested children with an apparatus surrounded by large panels. In one condition the panels were covered with a large variety of interesting toys; in the second condition, the panels were bare. The enriched environment did not produce significantly slower response than did the stimulus-poor environment, even though the opportunities for developing interfering responses seemingly would be greater when there were so many interesting things for the child to view.

Whatever interpretation eventually proves to be appropriate, the findings suggest that one of the reasons immediate reinforcement may be effective is that it terminates response. If a delay in reinforcement enables the child to rehearse the correct solution or if the child is capable of maintaining relevant observing responses during the delay, a delay in reinforcement will have little, if any, effect on children's learning. If, however, the child learns competing responses during the period of delay, learning will be impaired.

SECONDARY REINFORCEMENT

The concept of secondary or learned reinforcement is an important one in behavioristic theories of learning. Through this concept behaviorists attempt to explain the apparent strengthening of responses by what seem to be neutral stimuli. The use of tokens is a common example. The token may be a useless piece of cardboard. Just before a primary reinforcer is dispensed the child is given a token. It is assumed that the token becomes a secondary reinforcer because of its repeated presentation prior to the child's attaining a stimulus that already is an effective reinforcer. Secondary reinforcement occurs, therefore, when a stimulus, through its association with a reinforcer, acquires the capacity to influence behavior in a manner similar to that of the original reinforcer. The strength of the secondary reinforcer is assessed in extinction trials, where the secondary reinforcer appears but is never followed by the primary reinforcer. If the number of responses made under such conditions exceeds that found when neither reinforcing stimulus is present, secondary reinforcement has been demonstrated.

In looking at the research we get the impression that secondary reinforcement is an elusive process that is not readily demonstrated with children. In fact, Longstreth (1966, p. 26) concluded his review of the literature with the statement: "It becomes reasonable to argue that the phenomenon has not yet been clearly demonstrated with human subjects," and cites methodological and interpretive problems in many of the studies that seem to have yielded evidence for its occurrence. The child presses a lever to receive candy, and a light flashes before the candy appears. How do we know that the light, when presented alone, does not elicit subsequent pressing, rather than strengthen the preceding pressing behavior? How do we know that the omission of the primary reinforcer does not lead to frustration, which may have the effect of strengthening subsequent behavior? Do we know that the primary reinforcer was effective in strengthening behavior in the first place? If not, where does the secondary reinforcer gain its strength? These are the types of questions that may be asked of many of the studies purportedly demonstrating secondary reinforcement effects.

A study by Sidowski, Kass, and Wilson (1965) illustrates some of these points. Their goal was to separate the eliciting and reinforcing functions of the neutral stimulus. The apparatus was a simulated slot machine. Kindergarten children received a penny each time they pulled down the handle of the machine during ten training trials. The neutral stimulus, a red light, appeared (a) 0.5 seconds before and during the delivery of the reinforcer, (b) during both the time of response and the delivery of the reinforcer, and (c) before and during response. During extinction, the light appeared for only half of the subjects. The greatest numbers of responses were made during extinction when the light and penny were paired during the training trials, the result predicted from a secondary reinforcement position. Somewhat dismaying, however, was the fact that there was no significant difference in the number of responses made when the light was present and when it was absent during the extinction trials.

The elusive nature of secondary reinforcement also is evident in a study by Kass, Beardshall, and Wilson (1966), where the apparatus and general procedure were the same as those of the preceding study. A secondary reinforcement effect was not obtained. In a second nonconfirmatory study Kass and Wilson (1966) found no indication that pairing a light with the delivery of a primary reinforcer had any significant effect on performance during extinction.

Longstreth (1966) has presented results that are opposite from those predicted from a secondary reinforcement hypothesis. For example, children were tested in a situation in which either a bright or a dim light led to reward and the other did not. Three stimulus conditions were operative during extinction: (a) the positive cue and the sound that accompanied the delivery of reward during training, (b) the positive cue alone, and (c) the negative cue alone. Extinction was fastest in the first condition, despite the fact that the cues present during extinction in this condition most closely approximated those operative during the training trials.

We are left with clarity on only one point: secondary reinforcement effects are not easily demonstrated with children. We have conflicting evidence concerning the possibility that a neutral stimulus, solely from its prior association with a reinforcing stimulus, gains the ability to strengthen or maintain responses learned under primary reinforcement. We have no evidence that a secondary reinforcer is capable of strengthening new responses. Studies have demonstrated that pairing a neutral cue with reward may change a child's responses to the neutral cue—he may look at it longer, describe it more favorably, and have greater expectations that it will lead to reward (e.g., Nunnally, Knott, & Duchnowski, 1967)—but these studies have not been concerned with the reinforcing properties of the neutral cue. As of now, secondary reinforcement may at times be a useful concept in discussing children's learning, but only through additional, carefully conducted research can we assess its viability.

PARTIAL REINFORCEMENT

We often are told to be consistent in our responses to children, to reward behaviors that are desirable and to omit reward when the behavior is unacceptable. If by chance or in desperation reward is not withheld for undesirable behavior, the behavior will tend to recur many more times. What is being said is that a schedule of partial reinforcement prolongs the time of extinction. This is true with babies, as we have seen, and it is true with children.

In contrast to other effects discussed in this chapter, the partial reinforcement effect is not difficult to demonstrate. Several large parametric studies give us a good idea of how percentage of reward during training is related to number of responses made during extinction. Kass (1962) showed children of ages four, six, eight, and ten years how to operate a simulated slot machine. They were given 30 trials in which they could win pennies to purchase a prize. During these trials they received one of six percentages of reinforcement: 0%, 16⅔%, 33⅓%, 60%, 80%, or 100%. Extinction trials began immediately after the 30 training trials and continued until the children wanted to stop or until they had made 370 responses. The results, as seen in Figure 13-2, indicate that as the percentage of reinforcement received during training increased, the number of responses made during extinction decreased. Although four-year-olds made a significantly smaller number of responses during the extinction trials than the three older groups, the form of the curve was equivalent at the four age levels.

A second study (Kass & Wilson, 1966) used the same general procedure, but varied both the number of training trials and the percentage of reinforcement. Six- and seven-year-olds were given from 3 to 60 training trials with 33⅓% or 100% reinforcement. The number of responses made during extinction decreased significantly as the number of training trials increased and was uniformly higher following partial than following continuous reinforcement. The degree to which children persisted in the task is seen in the fact that after only three training trials with partial reinforcement they made an average of nearly 240 responses during extinction.

Several interpretations of the partial reinforcement effect have been offered. Children may have difficulty in discriminating when extinction trials begin after they have been trained under a schedule of partial reinforcement. Certainly, the onset of the extinction trials would be more readily discernible if the child previously had received consistent reinforcement of every response than if reinforcement occurred only after a series of nonreinforced trials. This leads to a second interpretation. What should we consider the unit of response—a single pull of the lever or the series of pulls that occurred prior to reinforcement? If one were to conceive of the unit as consisting of a series of responses, the number of trials

Figure 13-2. Mean log responses to extinction as a function of percentage of reinforcement during training trials. (From N. Kass, Resistance to extinction as a function of age and schedules of reinforcement. *Journal of Experimental Psychology*, 1962, 64, 251. Reprinted by permission of the American Psychological Association.)

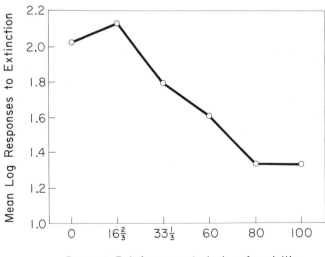

made in extinction would necessarily be greater than if the unit were a single response. It also is possible that during training children develop expectancies concerning their likelihood of being reinforced. If a child has learned not to expect a reward for every response he should persist in responding for a longer time during the extinction period than if he has come to expect continuous reinforcement. The issues related to these various interpretations are still being investigated and as of now we have little basis for deciding among them.

CONCLUSIONS

Most children are highly motivated to learn. This motivation does not appear to be strongly dependent upon a desire to obtain material rewards. In fact, it is difficult to produce differences in performance by manipulating external reinforcement, except when children have been subjected to conditions of deprivation. This is not to say that the consequences of response do not have important effects on learning. Rather, the most important consequence appears to be knowledge of the correctness or appropriateness of response. After infancy, pleasing the experimenter, and later, pleasing themselves seems to be the most important incentive for children's learning. In the few cases where punishment has been used, its effectiveness appears to be due to its increasing the child's attentiveness to the task.

Delay of reward does not appear to have strong effects on children's learning, even though it may have profoundly deleterious effects on the learning of lower animals. Children can do with ease what animals can do only with great difficulty or not at all: they can control both their physical and cognitive orientation to the task and can bridge the delay between response and reward with words. At present, secondary reinforcement appears to be of limited relevance to the discussion of children's behavior, primarily because studies have not yet offered convincing demonstrations of its occurrence. On the other hand, providing information to the child on only a portion of the acquisition trials seems to affect their performance in a manner comparable to that found with lower animals: it increases the number of responses made in extinction trials. The most favorable evidence for a reinforcement theorist comes from the last finding. We will see how it fares in the next chapter, where we will discuss a closely related topic, probability learning.

CHAPTER
14

Probability Learning

I have prepared a pack of cards for a study in probability learning. Among the 100 cards in the pack, 70 are red and 30 are black. I have shuffled the pack several times so that the cards are in a random order. My six-year-old subject enters the room and, after he is seated, I begin my instructions: "Let me tell you about this game. Here is a pack of cards and in it are red cards and black cards. You are to try to guess the color of the top card. After you have guessed, I will turn the card over so that you can see what color the card is. Now, what color do you think this top card will be?" The child makes his guess, I turn the card over, and we proceed, card by card, through the deck.

This is an unusual task for most children. Whatever the child does and whatever he may learn, he can achieve no more than partial success (partial reinforcement). There is only one way in which he can make the maximum frequency of correct responses—by saying "red" every time. This would be the rational thing to do. If all children did this, studies of probability learning would be of only slight interest. But they do not. Further, if children performed in the manner characteristic of many adults by predicting the more frequently recurring event with a probability equal to the probability with which the event occurs (i.e., saying "red" 70% of the time), studies with children would add little to the body of information available from research with adults. But, again, they do not.

What makes this problem so intriguing is that by using partial rather than continuous reinforcement, we have completely transformed the task. Since no solution leads to consistently correct responses, children must function as prediction makers to a greater degree than in many learning problems. Prediction makers? It sounds as if we are about to abandon the vocabulary of the stimulus-response psychologist. This we must do. In discussing probability learning it is very natural to talk about strategies, hypotheses, and expectancies, rather than about habits. This transition from an associative to a cognitive orientation is not difficult to make. In fact, it would be cumbersome if we tried to describe children's behavior in these tasks without recourse to terms implying cognitive activity. Children will tell us, or we can find out for ourselves if we look carefully at their behavior, that reinforcement and nonreinforcement, rather than strengthening or weakening particular stimulus-response relations, seem to be the basis for maintaining or discarding strategies.

DEVELOPMENTAL STUDIES

The first step for a developmental psychologist is to determine whether performance changes with increasing age. Then he must attempt to understand the processes underlying such changes. Unless an effort is made to take the second, more difficult step, the data constitute little more than another normative description of behavior. Fortunately, probability learning has been studied extensively enough so that we not only know what happens with increasing age, but also have some understanding of why it happens. (For a detailed review of the research on probability learning in children, see Goulet and Goodwin, 1970).

One of the first studies to demonstrate differences in performance in probability learning as a function of age was reported by Jones and Liverant (1960). The task was very similar to the one described in our earlier example. The children saw a clown's face rather than a pack of cards. On the collar of the clown's costume were two buttons. One button was programmed to yield reinforcement (a poker chip) with a probability of .70 and the other with a probability of .30. The subjects were preschoolers between the ages of four and six and elementary school children of ages nine to eleven. The preschoolers chose the .70 button more frequently throughout all trials than did the elementary school children. By the last 20 of the 100 trials, the preschoolers chose the .70 button approximately 85% of the time. Elementary school children, on the other hand, distributed their choices in accordance with the probabilities of occurrence of reinforcement. From trial 60 through 100 they selected the .70 button approximately 70% of the time. Similar effects were found with other children when the probabilities of reinforcement were split in a 90:10 fashion.

The results have been replicated by Derks and Paclisanu (1967), who used a two-choice problem involving an 85:15 split. The proportion of choices of the more frequently reinforcing event was consistently higher for nursery school children than for children in grades 1, 2, 3, 5, and 7. We have the beginning of an interesting effect, for in most studies of learning young children do not perform more effectively than older children.

The Three-choice Problem

It would be useful to follow developmental changes in probability learning that have been found in other studies. Before we can do this, however, we must describe a different type of task, for most of the developmental studies of probability learning have used a three-choice spatial problem. The child is seated in front of a panel containing three knobs. Above the knobs is a signal light, and below the knobs is a hole through which marbles are delivered into an enclosed plastic container. The child is told that when the signal light goes on he is to press one of the knobs. If he presses the correct knob a marble will drop into the box. Only one knob is to be pressed at a time, and the goal is to get as many marbles as possible. Choices of one position are partially reinforced; choices of the other two positions never are reinforced. Since the schedule of reinforcement is random, there is no way for the child to predict when he will be reinforced. When he presses the "correct" knob he will get a marble on some trials and on other trials he will get nothing.

Weir (1964) consolidated the data from a number of studies to produce a picture of the changes that occur in performance on this task

Figure 14-1.   Percent correct responses during last 20 trials as a function of age and reinforcement schedule. (From M. W. Weir, Developmental changes in problem-solving strategies. *Psychological Review,* 1964, 71, 476. Reprinted by permission of the American Psychological Association.)

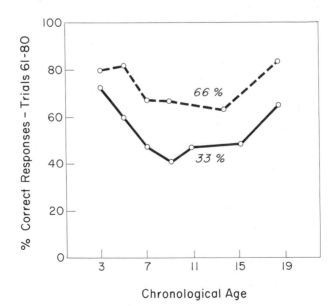

between the ages of 3 and 19 years. All of the subjects had been tested under comparable experimental conditions on the three-choice task. The relation between age and performance that emerged from these studies is presented in Figure 14-1, which depicts the percentage of correct responses at each age level for trials 61 to 80, the last 20 trials of the task. At age three a high percentage of the responses was to the knob yielding reinforcement. Then, instead of an improvement in performance we see a decline. Nine-year-olds did more poorly than three-year-olds and performance remained at a low level until age nineteen. With both 33% and 66% reinforcement, performance of the youngest and the oldest subjects exceeded that of children in the middle years of childhood. Although the terminal levels of response for the preschool and college-age subjects were similar, the rates at which these levels were approached differed markedly—a rapid settling on the reinforcing knob by the preschoolers and slow, continuous improvement in performance by the oldest subjects.

Modes and Strategies of Response

We can do more than tabulate frequencies of correct response. If we were to follow each subject's performance through the course of the 80 trials we would obtain some insight into the ways children of different ages cope with this type of problem. First, we might ask about the effects of reinforcement and nonreinforcement on children's tendencies to repeat a response. Weir (1964) has given us this information. When the percentage of response repetition after reinforced and nonreinforced trials was plotted by age, a U-shaped relation was obtained. Both the youngest and oldest subjects tended to repeat the response after both reinforcement and nonreinforcement. These subjects adopted a win-stay, lose-stay strategy; regardless of the consequence of their response, they tended to repeat it. Children of intermediate ages demonstrated a win-shift, lose-shift strategy. In contrast to the extreme age groups, they were likely to shift their response, whatever its outcome.

A common, but relatively primitive strategy was to search for the correct response by moving back and forth across the knobs with a left-middle-right or right-middle-left sequence of responses. This is not an efficient approach, for it will inevitably yield a low frequency of reinforcement. The relation, as plotted on a graph, between the number of these patterns and age was that of an inverted U. This strategy was more characteristic of children between the ages of five and nine than it was for younger or older children. (See Figure 14-2).

It would be possible, although difficult, to discern some of the more complex strategies by perusing subject's data sheets. A more direct approach was used by Stevenson and Weir (1963), who required their subjects (12-, 15-, and 18-year-olds) to verbalize during the course of their performance. The three-choice task was used and the responses to one of the knobs were reinforced 33% of the time. To insure that the subjects would produce information about the bases of their responses, they were tested in pairs, where they were instructed to reach a common decision about each response they would make, or alone, where they had to tell an observer why they were making each response. Verbalizing in this manner did not affect the overall levels of performance of these subjects, for the frequency of choice of the reinforcing knob did not differ from that of other subjects who were tested alone and not required to verbalize.

Nearly three-quarters of all verbalizations fell into two categories. In the first, subjects stated they were responding on the assumption that correct response was dependent upon learning some pattern or sequence of responses (e.g., "Well, the point is to get as many marbles as we can. So there has to be a pattern back there somewhere. So let's just press and try to find the pattern. Just press the different ones until we find the sequence they go in. They've got to have some kind of order"). In the second category, subjects stated that the experimenter was changing the reinforcement schedule, was changing the reinforcing stimulus, or was not loading the apparatus (e.g., "I'm sure that the marble comes out of that one, but I'm still afraid he might change it"). Thus the most common assumptions were that reinforcement was contingent upon some pattern of response or upon some whim of the experimenter.

Figure 14-2. Mean number of patterned responses (left-middle-right or right-middle-left), according to chronological age. (From M. W. Weir, Developmental changes in problem-solving strategies. *Psychological Review*, 1964, 71, 473. Reprinted by permission of the American Psychological Association.)

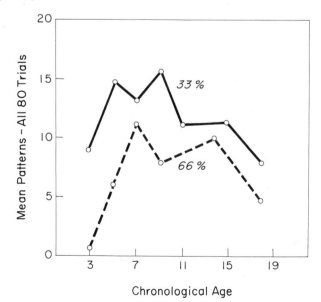

The remaining verbalizations were divided among five other categories. The verbalizations indicated that response was determined by prior choices (e.g., "I'll push this one because I haven't pushed it for a while"); by a feeling that a particular knob would be correct (e.g., "I just have a feeling it will be there. There isn't any other reason"); by some irrelevant aspect of the situation (e.g., "Let's push No. 2 because there are two of us"); by guessing (e.g., "We're just jumping around until we find out how it works"); or by chance (e.g., "I don't have any reason for pushing this one").

Some patterns and sequences were unbelievably complex. Some subjects developed and memorized strings of ten or more responses, reviewing to themselves the sequence and where in the sequence they currently were. Interestingly, only 1 of the 234 subjects included in this study was able to state the appropriate strategy for maximizing reinforcement and only 8 subjects (or pairs of subjects) maximized their reinforcement by consistently choosing the correct knob during the terminal 20 trials. Generally, the 18-year-olds were more frequently successful than the 12-year-olds.

Other Studies

There are other ways in which developmental changes in children's approaches to probability learning may be studied. We might, for example, change the probabilities of reinforcement during the experimental trials and observe children's abilities to adapt to the modified schedules. Kessen and Kessen (1961) did this in a study with children of median ages 3½ and 4½ years. The children performed in a two-choice problem where the probabilities of reinforcement changed in the middle of the experiment (e.g., from 50:50 to 50:70). The younger group was reluctant to give up a response once it was established. When the new schedule was introduced, they continued to respond on the basis of the earlier schedule of reinforcement. The older children, however, were able to modify their behavior so that their responses corresponded more closely to the changed probabilities of reinforcement.

A related effect was found by Odom and Coon (1966), who made a radical change in the probability of reinforcement by following acquisition trials with 20 extinction trials. During the acquisition trials pattern responses (left-middle-right or right-middle-left) in the three-choice task were reinforced. Reasonably, 19-year-olds developed such patterns more readily than did children of 6 and 11 years. The subjects who did develop such patterns (45%, 60%, and 85% at ages 6, 11, and 19 years), were placed on extinction. When the patterns were no longer reinforced, there was a rapid drop in the number of pattern responses made by the two oldest groups. There was no evidence of extinction for the six-year-olds. They were unable to give up the pattern response when it was no longer reinforced. One important change that occurs with increasing age seems to be a heightened sensitivity to the relations between response and reinforcement. Young children readily learn initial response-reinforcement relations in a probability learning task. However, when this relation is changed in the course of an otherwise unchanged situation, young children are less able than older children to modify their behavior in an appropriate manner.

Could a situation be devised that would produce more than one indication of children's ability to adapt to a probabilistic task? We could then determine whether children can apply their strategies or preferred modes of response in more than one context. To answer this question, Stevenson and Odom (1964) presented the probability learning task as a game of hide-and-seek. The procedure was as follows. The child and the experimenter were seated on opposite sides of a table and in front of each was a row of three boxes. The experimenter hid objects (plastic trinkets) so that the child, in looking in the experimenter's boxes, would find a trinket in one box three-fourths of the time, in another box one-fourth of the time, and would never find a trinket in the third box. In other words, the experimenter's hiding followed a 75:25:0% schedule. On alternate trials the child hid trinkets. The experimenter's seeking, as well as his hiding, followed a prearranged schedule. For half of the children the experimenter looked in the child's boxes according to a random schedule, and for the other half, he followed a fixed schedule of looking in one of the child's boxes three-fourths of the time, in a second box one-fourth of the time, and never looking in the third box. Had the children adopted the optimal strategies for gaining and retaining trinkets, they would have looked only in the box the experimenter baited 75% of the time and would have hidden their trinkets only in the box the experimenter never chose. However, there was no correlation between these two behaviors for children of ages 3 to 5, 7 to 8, and 10 to 12 years. Their strategies of response differed according to their roles as hiders and seekers. As was found in the earlier studies, however, the children tended with increasing age to be more variable in their seeking behavior, to change their responses more frequently after both reinforcement and nonreinforcement, to adopt patterned responses more frequently, and to utilize positional responses less frequently.

Comments

At first, many of these results seem paradoxical. We usually do not find three-year-olds surpassing the performance of much older children. The innocence—or the inability—of the very young pays off in probability learning tasks. Reinforcement increases their tendency to repeat the response, and the tendency is somewhat greater following reinforcement than following nonreinforcement. This is not the case for older children. They impose their own expectations on the task. In spite of their ineffectual efforts they act as if they believed they eventually would be able to solve the problem and achieve consistent reinforcement. In maintaining this belief they are forced to move away from the reinforcing stimulus and try other alternatives, thereby reducing further their possibility of obtaining reinforcement. At later ages, the subjects still try to solve the problem through complex strategies. In contrast to the middle-aged children, however, they are able to abandon the strategies when they prove to be unsuccessful.

With other than very young children can we ever say that the major effect of reinforcement is other than a source of information, used by the child to confirm or change his expectations and to develop new and tentative solutions. Such a view does not necessarily diminish the importance of the concept of reinforcement—if we are willing to talk about reinforcement of expectancies rather than reinforcement of habits. Behavior theorists place a greater emphasis on the reactive aspects of the child's behavior than upon its active, information-seeking properties. For them, the environment is something independent of the child, and they often fail to consider the active role the child plays in the construction and organization of his environment through his interactions with it.

EXPECTANCIES FOR REINFORCEMENT

We have assumed that children's performance in a probability learning task is defined in part by their expectancies for reinforcement. Is there any evidence that this is more than a post hoc interpretation of the developmental changes that have been observed? There are at least two ways in which such evidence can be obtained. We could select children whose everyday experience might lead them to develop different expectancies for reinforcement. For example, children living in a normal, responsive environment should develop higher expectancies for reinforcement than children who have spent many years in an institution. This type of study would permit only an indirect test of our assumption, for we never could be sure that differences in performance might not be attributable to other factors that differentiated such groups of children. More direct evidence could be obtained if we attempted to alter children's expectancies for success within the experimental setting. This might be accomplished by pretraining children with different frequencies of reinforcement. If children are assigned to the pretraining conditions randomly and if their later performance in the probability learning task differs, we may be more willing to accept the results as evidence that performance was influenced by the children's prior histories of reinforcement.

Both approaches were used in two studies by Stevenson and Zigler (1958). In the first study, the subjects were institutionalized retarded children and normal children living at home. The children were matched on mental age (approximately 6 years) and tested on the three-choice task with reinforcement schedules of either 0:0:33% or 0:0:66% for the three alternative choices. As predicted, the performance of the institutionalized children was above that for the home children with both schedules of reinforcement. The institutionalized children appeared to be more willing to accept a solution that led to less than consistent reinforcement than children living in normal homes, presumably because children living in an institution have learned from everyday experience that their efforts do not always lead to a high incidence of success.

A more convincing test of the hypothesis was obtained in the second study. An effort was made to establish different expectancies for reinforcement by varying the level of success the children achieved while playing three pretraining games. The subjects were normal five-year-olds. Before performing in the probability learning task, they played the three games either with consistent or partial success. In a picture game, for example, they were given 12 cards, each bearing a rectangle of a different color. They were told they would see 12 pictures of animals and were to decide which color went with each animal. The experimenter informed half of the children that each of their choices was correct, and the other half that their responses were correct on only four of the 12 choices. The same 100% or 33% schedule of reinforcement was operative for the other two games. After the children had played these three games, the experimenter introduced the three-choice probability learning task with a 0:0:66 % schedule of reinforcement. Success in the pretraining games led to poorer performance on the probability learning task than did prior lack of success. Children who had been reinforced inconsistently during the pretraining games, and presumably had learned to expect less than consistent reinforcement, chose the correct knob more frequently than did those who previously had experienced consistent reinforcement.

Additional evidence related to this hypothesis was obtained in a study by Gruen and Zigler (1968), who repeated the preceding study with middle- and lower-class six-year-olds. It was assumed that middle-class children have backgrounds of more frequent reinforcement than lower-class children. If this assumption is appropriate, middle-class children, expecting to find a solution yielding consistent reinforcement, should vary their responses more widely than the lower-class children and thereby show a lower frequency of response to the correct stimulus. Performance of the two groups of children differed significantly, and in the predicted direction. As in the preceding study, three pretraining games were presented before the probability learning task, with subjects receiving either high or low frequencies of reinforcement. Type of pretraining experience had no overall effect on performance, but a difference did appear when the analyses were made separately by social class. For middle-class children, pretraining with low frequencies of reinforcement increased the incidence of choices of the reinforcing stimulus over that found following pretraining with high degrees of success—the results obtained by Stevenson and Zigler (1958). Lower-class children's performance was not influenced by pretraining. Apparently, the short-term manipulation of success was insufficient to overcome the expectancies of lower-class children regarding their potential for success.

Similar results were obtained for middle- and lower-class children of ages five, six, and ten years by Odom (1967). Frequency of correct response decreased with increasing age in both social classes, but at every age the lower-class children made a greater number of responses to the correct stimulus than did the middle-class children. Could these results be due to differences in intelligence? This seems unlikely, for neither in this nor in the Gruen and Zigler study were any of the within-group correlations between IQ and frequency of correct response significant. Would it be possible, then, to obtain more direct evidence that the differences in performance of middle- and lower-class children are related to differences in their everyday success?

Several studies by Zigler and his associates are related to the question. Kier and Zigler (1970), for example, asked teachers to rate lower- and middle-class children on the basis of their achievement in school. The children selected for the study were in the top and bottom quartiles of the distributions of these ratings. Four groups of children were included in the study. All had comparable mental ages (mean = seven years), but they differed in social class and school achievement. If the social class differences reported in the previous studies are related to the child's history of reinforcement, one might expect that lower-class children who had experienced success in school would behave more like middle-class children than would those whose school experiences had been less successful. All children were presented the three-choice task with 66% reinforcement of one knob. For middle-class children, there was no difference in performance between those in the top and bottom quartiles of school achievement. Among the lower-class children, however, success in school was a significant variable; children in the bottom quartile made a significantly greater number of responses to the correct knob than did those in the top quartile (means = 63 and 50 responses, respectively). Lower-class children who experienced success in school apparently were less willing to accept a mode of response that yielded inconsistent reinforcement than were those whose efforts at learning had been less successful. It is unclear why the differences for the middle-class children were not significant.

A second measure was obtained for approximately half of the subjects. This measure was derived from the children's estimates of their likelihood of success in a card-sorting task. The correlation between the children's estimates of success and the number of correct responses made to the reinforcing stimulus in the probability learning task was —.39. Thus the degree to which children expressed high expectancies for success was inversely related to the frequency with which they chose the reinforcing stimulus in the probability learning task.

In a subsequent study, Gruen, Ottinger, and Zigler (1970) related children's level of aspiration to their performance in the three-choice probability learning task. Level of aspiration was assessed by determining the discrepancies between estimated and actual success in throwing a bean bag at a target. The subjects were lower- and middle-class children with mental ages of either seven or ten years. It was predicted that the higher the level of aspiration, the less likely the children would be to settle for a solution that yielded only partial success. Children with high levels of aspiration should perform more poorly on the probability learning task than those with lower levels of aspiration. This is what was found. Level of aspiration scores were separated into three categories— high, middle, and low. Children in the high level-of-aspiration group chose the reinforcing stimulus an average of 78 times on the 120 trials presented, while the averages for the middle and low level-of-aspiration groups were 92 and 89, respectively. Although the main effect of social class was not significant, there was a significant interaction between social class and level of aspiration. The three groups of lower-class children performed at approximately the same level, thus the overall differences in performance according to level of aspiration were derived primarily from the performance of the middle-class children.

Paradoxically, there were no general differences in the level of performance of lower- and middle-class children in this or the Kier and Zigler study. However, these and the other studies dealing with social class were conducted in different parts of the country. It is not unreasonable to assume that the experiences of lower- and middle-class children vary greatly, depending upon whether the children live in small towns or large cities, in slums or suburbs. Until the characteristics of social class membership are more clearly understood, social class remains an interesting but imprecise variable.

In general, the studies dealing with motivational variables seem to point to the importance of expectancy for reinforcement as an important determinant of children's performance in probability learning. Expectancy for reinforcement is difficult to manipulate and measure, but the interpretation of these studies in terms of what children expect rather than what they obtain seems to be as effective as any alternative interpretation of the results that can be considered.

EFFECTS OF INSTRUCTIONS

Why attempt to establish expectancies in children when you can tell them about the level of reinforcement that is attainable in this type of task? If the preceding arguments are correct, and children typically enter the probability learning task with different expectancies for reinforcement, it should be possible to produce different levels of performance by either confirming or disavowing such expectations through instructions. Weir (1962) investigated this possibility by instructing children at ages five, seven, and nine years that there was no way they could obtain a reward on every trial. The children were told:

> Now let me tell you something about this game. It's impossible for *anybody* to get a marble on every single push. But let's just see how you do. Remember, just push one knob each time the light comes on, and also remember that there is *no* way you can get a marble on every single push (Weir, 1962, p. 731).

Other children were told that a solution was possible, that there was a way they could get a marble on every single push. No instructions were given to a third group of children. The different instructions failed to influence performance at any age level.

Perhaps the children were too young to use the instructions appropriately. Gruen and Weir (1964) therefore repeated the study with a broader sampling of ages, including subjects of ages 7 to 8, 12 to 14, and college students. The instructional conditions were the same as those of the previous study. Again, instructions had no overall effects on performance. There was a significant interaction between experimental condition and age, such that college students performed in the manner predicted by selecting the correct knob more frequently when they were told that no solution was possible. For the youngest children, however, the effects of instructions were opposite from those predicted.

Apparently, it is very difficult to disengage children through instructions from the sets with which they approach this task. That this should be the case with young children is no surprise, but it is more difficult to understand why 12- to 14-year-olds were unable to modify their performance when they were told, in effect, that no solution was possible. However, these results are not discordant with the fact that a very high percentage of older children are able, upon questioning, to indicate the response that led to reinforcement. Although they can identify the knob that yielded a marble and acknowledge that the other two knobs never paid off, they are unable to translate this information into an efficient strategy of response.

TYPE OF REINFORCER

In discrimination learning tasks, differences in performance as a function of type of reinforcer are difficult to obtain. In probability learning tasks, differences are easy to find but difficult to interpret. Generally, we might expect that any effects found in probability learning tasks using no material reinforcers or ones of low value would be magnified if the reinforcers are highly desired by the child. This has been found to be true in some cases, but not in others. What makes these studies so interesting is that the effects are replicable even though they are hard to understand.

The Three-choice Task

In our previous discussion of the three-choice task it was assumed that children learn rather quickly that the reinforcing stimulus does not pay off 100% of the time. If the child accepts this frequency of reinforcement, he should choose the reinforcing stimulus with a high degree of consistency. If this frequency of reinforcement is not acceptable, the child should attempt to find a solution that will increase the frequency with which he is reinforced. This attempt would lead to variable behavior, with the result that the frequency of choice of the reinforcing stimulus would be lower than that occurring if such an attempt is not made. It is assumed that the object or event used as a reinforcer affects performance by determining the degree to which the child attempts to find such a solution and that if the reinforcer is of high value the child will be more likely to seek a solution yielding consistent reinforcement than if the reinforcer is of low value. In the end, the higher the child's desire for the reinforcing object, the lower his frequency of reinforcement will be.

Stevenson and Weir (1959) tested these predictions with five-year-olds on the three-choice task. For half of the children, responses were reinforced with small plastic trinkets, and for half with marbles. Previous experience indicated that trinkets were more attractive and desirable to children than marbles. Responses to one of the three knobs were reinforced either 100%, 66%, or 33% of the time. Type of reinforcer did not influence rate of learning when reinforcement was consistent. The children rapidly learned to select the correct knob with both types of reinforcer. When responses to the correct knob were reinforced only 66% or 33% of the time, however, children who received trinkets chose the correct knob less frequently than did children who received marbles. After the first few trials, level of performance was higher when the children were reinforced with the less desirable objects. Similar results were found by Das and Panda (1963).

Would the same effects be found with other than five-year-olds? Stevenson and Hoving (1964) replicated the conditions of the previous study with 4-, 9-, 14-, and 20-year-olds. Responses were reinforced with nickels or metal washers. To avoid having the younger children return to the classroom with possibly large amounts of money, they were allowed to "purchase" prizes from the experimenter. The previous results were replicated with the four-year-olds. Children who received nickels made fewer responses to the reinforcing knob than did children receiving washers. For the two intermediate ages, the level of response of the "nickel" groups was above that of the "washer" groups. Type of reinforcer did not differentiate the performance of the oldest subjects. It appeared, therefore, that the youngest children were performing in line with an expectancy theory, but that the performance of the older subjects could be predicted more satisfactorily from a utility theory. According to a utility theory, individuals should strive to maximize their possible gain to the degree that the consequences of their efforts are desirable. This theory, and many common sense ideas about reward, predict that level of performance will vary directly with the value of the reinforcer. Several studies offer support for such a prediction.

The Two-choice Task

Practically all of the studies supporting a utility theory have been conducted with a two-choice task. Brackbill, Kappy, and Starr (1967), for example, showed eight-year-olds a deck of 200 cards that contained pictures of cats and dogs. The child's task was to predict whether a cat or a dog would be revealed as he turned over each card in the deck. One animal was represented on 75% of the cards and the other animal on 25% of the cards. Each correct guess yielded either simply the knowledge that the guess was correct, or one, three, or five marbles that later could be turned in for a prize. The greatest difference in level of responding was attributable to the presence or absence of reward, but a decreasing hierarchy of "correct" responses was found as the magnitude of the reward decreased.

Several other studies obtained similar results. For example, Siegel and Andrews (1962) found lower levels of response by preschool children when the rewards were of low value than when they were of high value. Lewis, Wall, and Aronfreed (1963) found with seven-year-olds, but not with eleven-year-olds, that the addition of supportive comments from the experimenter resulted in a significantly higher level of correct responding than occurred when the children were given only information about the outcome of their previous guesses. Six- and seven-year-olds in a study by Walters and Foote (1962) were more likely to make the correct response when they were given tokens that could be exchanged for a prize than when they were rewarded only with tokens.

Rosenhan (1966) investigated the relation between type of reinforcer and social class in probability learning. Six-year-olds were praised for response to the more frequently reinforcing stimulus in a 70:30 two-choice problem or were given statements of disapproval following responses to the less frequently reinforced stimulus. It was assumed that lower-class children are more sensitive to the responses of an adult than are middle-class children. The prediction that performance would be more strongly facilitated by praise in the lower-class than in the middle-class children was supported, as was the prediction that the performance of lower-class children would be more disrupted by disapproval.

The procedures used in all of the preceding studies omitted one important step. Differences in the value of the reinforcers for the individual child were not established empirically, but on the basis of the experimenter's judgment or from general preferences children demonstrated in pretests. Bissett and Rieber (1966) attempted to remedy this defect in a study of six- through seven- and ten- through eleven-year-olds. Each child's preferences for a large variety of objects were assessed by a paired-comparison procedure. Each child then was reinforced in a 33:0 two-choice task with an object that, for him, was selected with the greatest or the least frequency in the paired-comparisons. The results replicated those of the previous studies. A higher level of performance was found at both age levels for children who were reinforced with objects of high value.

Comparison of Two-choice and Three-choice Tasks

There is an obvious need to reconcile the results from the studies varying the levels of reinforcer. Why should some studies lend support to an expectancy theory and others to a utility theory? Could the basis of the discrepancies lie in the type of problem used? Weir and Gruen (1965) investigated the possible effects of the number of choices and type of problem. The prototypes for the problems were the two-choice problem of Siegel and Andrews (1962), in which children guessed which of two toy milk bottles contained a prize, and the three-choice spatial problem. The conditions of the Siegel and Andrews study were replicated and extended to include three choices. The three-choice problem was presented both as it had been in previous studies and was modified so that only two choices were available. When there were two choices the ratio of reinforcement was 75:25, and when there were three choices the ratio was 75:12.5:12.5. In all cases the subjects were preschool children and the reinforcers were prizes or knowledge of results. Children given the prizes with the Siegel and Andrews two-choice problem performed at a higher level than children receiving knowledge of results, thus replicating the findings of Siegel and Andrews. When the task was extended to include three choices, no differences in performance according to level of incentive were found. Furthermore, with the standard three-choice spatial problem, children performed at a lower level when they were given prizes than when they were provided only with knowledge of results, thereby replicating earlier findings with this problem. When only two alternatives were allowed in the spatial problem, however, the differences in performance between the two reinforcement conditions were minimal.

Here the problem rests. The effects can be repeated, but for some reason, still unknown, the type of reinforcer will have different effects, depending upon the manner in which the probability task is constructed.

CONCLUSIONS

Results of studies of probability learning would be a source of less distress for the reinforcement theorist if they were derived from an idiosyncratic situation that is encountered rarely in everyday life. Actually, however, the schedule of partial reinforcement inherent in these tasks more closely approximates what exists in everyday situations than does the typical task involving consistent reinforcement. Probability learning has been considered to be a form of problem solving (Weir, 1964). If this designation is appropriate, and if the application of partial reinforcement creates a situation in which children actively strive to solve a problem rather than to learn a particular response, the question again may be raised whether any but the most primitive types of learning can be discussed in terms of the stimulus-response-reinforcement model.

There seems to be little question that after the ages of four or five children direct their responses in a probability learning task on the basis of hypotheses and expectations whose operation can be detected by asking children about the basis of their response or by varying the situation so that the effects of their hypotheses and expectations are exaggerated. Developmental studies of probability learning have proved to be especially revealing. The more readily children can develop complex hypotheses, the less likely they are to maximize their frequency of reinforcement. Only after the individual is capable of evaluating the effectiveness of his hypotheses and of modifying them so that they are more closely in accord with the objective situation does performance reach the level characteristic of the preschool child. Predictions about children's performance based on their expectancies for reinforcement, rather than on the level of reinforcement that is attainable, are relatively consistently supported, whether the estimates are derived from the child's everyday life, pretraining experiences, or performance on other tasks. As with so many learning problems, the results prove to be increasingly complex as the experimental designs become more elaborate. It seems apparent from these studies, however, that little progress will be made in clarifying these effects until we have a better understanding of the types of hypotheses the child is capable of developing, the influence of his expectations on the formation of these hypotheses, and his ability to modify his approach when his efforts prove to be ineffective.

15

Nonreinforcement

Our emphasis thus far has been on the effects of reinforcement on learning, and, except in the discussion of extinction, we have given little direct attention to nonreinforcement and its effects. There is a simple reason for this. In contrast to the extensive literature on the effects of reinforcement on children's learning, relatively few studies of nonreinforcement have been reported, and among these the range of problems is quite restricted. We know from the studies that have been done that nonreinforcement may have strong effects on learning and performance. This is nothing new, of course, for any teacher can point to the long-lasting effects of failure on children's ability to learn. What is new about these studies is that they demonstrate the particular kinds of effects that occur when the consequences of response are unpredictable or completely violate the expectancies of the child.

Defining what is meant by nonreinforcement is as difficult as defining reinforcement. We can never be sure that all potential sources of reinforcement are absent from any particular situation. The problem can be simplified, however, if the discussion is restricted to situations where there is no external or tangible form of reinforcement. The term, nonreinforcement, will be used, therefore, to describe the condition that exists when children's responses produce no external or tangible consequence, such as the approval of the experimenter or the delivery of a trinket.

Responses of infants to nonreinforcement were discussed in an earlier chapter. Omitting reinforcement during extinction trials produced fussing, crying, and withdrawal. Similar forms of behavior may be observed in older children. Omission of the reinforcement of a previously correct response often causes children to become perplexed, exasperated, or upset. They may vacillate between response and withdrawal. If there is a continuing cessation of reinforcement they may become irritated. Their behavior resembles that which typically follows frustration.

When we say that the effects of nonreinforcement or nonreward resemble those derived from frustration, we are suggesting, in part, that nonreinforcement alters the motivational status of the child. Perhaps the most systematic discussion of the motivational effects of nonreinforcement is that of Amsel (1958, 1962), and much of the relevant research with children has been conducted to evaluate his ideas. [A comprehensive review of this research has been published by Ryan and Watson (1968).]

A motivational or drive interpretation assumes that frustration will occur when the subject experiences a conflict between his expectations concerning reinforcement and the frequency or type of reinforcement he actually receives. The emotional arousal accompanying frustration is assumed to produce a temporary increase in the subject's level of drive. What effects this increase will have on performance depends upon the type of task in which the subject is performing. If the task involves a simple, well-learned response, an increase in drive should strengthen the tendency to respond. Following nonreinforcement, response should be more vigorous and rapid. If the task is one in which the correct response is relatively weak, an increase in drive may have a disruptive effect on performance through the indiscriminate strengthening of all responses, including incorrect ones.

Most of the relevant research with children has been conducted with extremely simple tasks. The child is told that when a signal light comes on he is to press a button or move a lever. At the termination of response, the child receives a reward or nothing. Since even young children can press buttons and move levers with ease, performance is evaluated, not in terms of the frequency with which the response occurs, but in terms of its forcefulness or speed. In most studies a comparison is made between rate of response in a condition involving continuous reinforcement with that found in a condition involving partial reinforcement. It is predicted from a drive theory that rate of response will be faster when some of the trials lead to nonreinforcement than when each response terminates in reward.

In general, the results from studies involving simple performance tasks have supported these predictions. They provide equally strong support for another interpretation of the effects of nonreinforcement on performance. Children may have learned from everyday experience that they should try harder when they are not consistently successful. When lever-pulling leads to little or no success, they may apply this knowledge and increase their efforts, if the only way that is available to them is to respond faster or more vigorously. Seeing that their current mode of response is no longer successful, children try harder. From the evidence that is available from this limited experimental design, it is impossible to know which of these two alternative interpretations is more appropriate.

SPEED OF RESPONSE

Tasks used in studies of lever-pulling with children were adapted directly from those developed for use with rats. One of the first studies was reported by Penney (1960). There were two levers. The children, five-year-olds, were required to pull the first lever through its excursion before they could pull the second lever. The speed with which the second lever was pulled through its pathway was faster when the response was partially reinforced than when it was consistently reinforced. (Movement of the second lever always resulted in reinforcement.)

Penney's results were replicated and extended by Ryan (1965). Speed of response differed significantly between groups receiving consistent and partial reinforcement. However, when a trial by trial analysis of performance was made, there was no indication that movement of the second lever was faster on trials following nonreinforcement than on those following reinforcement of the first lever-pull. Although an intertrial interval of 45 seconds was allowed, there may have been insufficient time for the effects of frustration to dissipate. Ryan and Moffitt (1966) evaluated this possibility by administering only one trial per day. A trial by trial effect was found. Movement speeds on lever 2 (which always led to reinforcement) were faster following nonreinforcement than following reinforcement of lever 1. Following reinforcement on lever 1, however,

Figure 15-1.   Speed of response as a function of percentage of reinforcement. (Data from T. J. Ryan, Instrumental performance as related to several reward schedules. *Journal of Experimental Child Psychology,* 1966, 3, 402.)

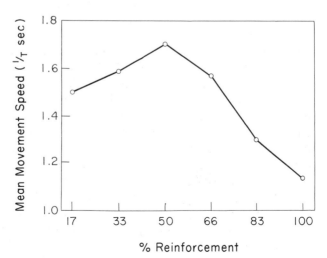

speeds were comparable to those children who were reinforced consistently on lever 1.

Single lever-pulling tasks also have been used (Bruning, 1964; Ryan & Cantor, 1962; Ryan & Moffitt, 1966). In all cases, movement speeds were faster with 50% than with 100% reinforcement. Broader ranges of percentages of reinforcement were used by Ryan (1966). Five- and six-year-olds were tested with six schedules, varying between 17% and 100%. As can be seen in Figure 15-1, speeds of response decreased in an orderly fashion as percentage of reinforcement increased from 50% to 100%. Speeds of response increased, however, as the percentage of reinforcement increased from 17% to 50%. An inverted U-shaped relation between speed of response and percentage of reinforcement is suggested by these findings. Facilitation of response with partial reinforcement begins to diminish as the likelihood of nonreinforcement exceeds that of reinforcement. The effect has been replicated by Ryan and Voorhoeve (1966).

The results of these studies all point to the same conclusions. Partial reinforcement results in faster responding than does consistent reinforcement. The relation between probability of reinforcement and rate of response is not linear, however, for as the probability of reinforcement drops below .50, rates of response begin to decrease. This may indicate that the effect is maximized when each event has an equal probability of occurrence and the conflict between expectancies for reinforcement and for nonreinforcement is greatest.

VICARIOUS EFFECTS

Nonreinforcement may influence the performance of an observer as well as a participant in the experimental task. Studies of the vicarious effects of nonreinforcement have dealt with simple forms of behavior, lever-pulling and button-pressing. When such responses are made by another person and not reinforced, the rates of response for the observers are increased, just as they are for the participants. Expectations may be built up, therefore, not only on the basis of the consequences of the child's own responses, but also through his observing the consequences produced by the responses of other persons.

Procedures used in studies of the vicarious effects of nonreinforcement are relatively complicated; thus they will be discussed in some detail. We will begin by looking at a study by Bruning (1965), who investigated the effects of a change in the magnitude of reward on lever-pulling. Children were given two sets of 30 trials. On the first 30 trials, lever-pulls were reinforced consistently for half of the children with one piece of candy, and for the other half with five pieces. On the second 30 trials, reward was maintained at the original level or shifted to the alternative level.

The five-year-old subjects performed alone, or observed another child for half of the trials and then performed themselves. Response was faster during the first 30 trials when the reward was one piece of candy than when it was five pieces. Speed of response changed markedly when the reward objects were changed, increasing when the magnitude of reward decreased and decreasing when the magnitude of reward increased. The effects were the same, whether the children performed during the first 30 trials or merely observed the performance of another child. It seems, therefore, that children were frustrated when they received only one piece of candy after being accustomed to receiving five pieces. Conversely, the introduction of the larger amount of candy apparently decreased the children's motivation to respond. The value of reward, or more directly its influence on performance, may depend on its relation to the reward the child received earlier or observed another child receive.

Percentage, rather than magnitude of reinforcement was varied by Rosenbaum and Bruning (1966). First graders were given 30 trials in which lever-pulls were reinforced 50% or 100% of the time. Children performed themselves or observed the performance of another child of the same sex. In 30 subsequent trials none of the responses was reinforced. During the second set of 30 trials, the child continued to perform, or replaced the child he had observed.

Speed of response during the acquisition trials was faster with 50% than with 100% reinforcement when the subjects were boys. Neither percentage of reinforcement nor training condition significantly affected the performance of girls. Boys whose performance was observed by another boy had slower speeds of response than boys who performed alone. There was no evidence of extinction. In fact, children who had been reinforced consistently responded more rapidly during the 30 nonreinforced trials than during the earlier, reinforced trials. This unusual result may have been due to the fact that the child could not get out of the situation and had no choice of response. In this study, as in the preceding ones, each trial was initiated by the onset of a signal light. Children were required to perform, even when it became apparent that no reinforcement could be obtained. This probably was very irritating and the children expressed this irritation by increasing the speeds of their response.

The essential features of the preceding study were repeated, with some modifications, by Ryan and Strawbridge (1969). The modifications involved the time of participation by the observer and the set with which the children approached the task. Both participants and observers performed for 40 trials. Half of the observers performed on alternate trials with the participant ("active" observers) and half performed only after the participant had completed all 40 trials ("passive" observers). Further, half of the children were instructed that receiving or failing to receive a reward was determined by the experimenter ("other-blame"), and half, that they were responsible themselves for the outcome of their efforts ("self-blame"). All responses made by the observers were reinforced, but the participants received either 50% or 100% reinforcement.

The three experimental treatments had significant effects on the participants' performance; speeds were faster with 50% reinforcement, when the children performed in the presence of an active observer, and when they received self-blame instructions. Alternating trials with an active observer apparently created a competitive situation. The effect was due, however, to the performance of boys. Boys, but not girls who acted as participants responded faster in the presence of an active observer than when the observer was inactive. Faster response resulting from self-blame instructions apparently reflected the children's greater frustration or determination to succeed when they felt that they, rather than an erratic and unpredictable experimenter, were responsible for their failure to achieve consistent reward.

Looking now at the observers' performance, the most important finding was the interaction between schedule of reward and sex. Boys who had observed their partners receive 50% reinforcement had faster speeds of response than boys whose partners received 100% reinforcement. The difference for the girls was not significant. Furthermore, a significant interaction between type of participation and sex indicates that being an active observer had a greater effect on the performance of boys than of girls.

This was an elaborate and productive study. Even the reinforcement of children's lever-pulling turns out to be a multiply determined process. Variables such as the sex of the child, the set with which he approaches the task, his assessment of the situation as a competitive or noncompetitive one, and the source to which he attributes his failure may have significant effects on his performance. Interactions involving sex of the child are especially interesting, for they point to the possibility, usually unrevealed because of a failure to analyze for sex effects, that boys may respond differently to partial reinforcement of their behavior than do girls. Other studies support such a suggestion. Kass (1964), for example, found that in a simulated gambling situation boys were more likely to take risks by selecting slot machines with high but inconsistent levels of reinforcement than were girls, who were more likely to select a machine that yielded a low but consistent level of reinforcement.

Kobasigawa (1965) approached the investigation of the vicarious effects of reinforcement and nonreinforcement somewhat differently. The performer was an adult who was told his task was to place marbles in a narrow trough until it was full. He was allowed to complete the defined goal or his performance was interrupted when he had inserted only one-fifth or nine-tenths of the marbles. A buzzer signalled the end of a trial and the child was told that he was to push a button that turned off the buzzer, thereby allowing the performer an opportunity to begin the next trial. Preventing the performer from reaching the goal should have been frustrating, and this frustration should have been greater the closer the performer was to completing the task when he was interrupted. If the frustration was shared by the child observing this activity, the child's speed of button-pushing should have been slowest when the performer was able to insert all the marbles and fastest when the performer was interrupted near the goal. This is what was found. Speed of button-pushing by the subjects, first-grade boys, was greater when the performer was blocked near the goal than when he was allowed to succeed or was far from success.

The vicarious effects of partial reinforcement may be interpreted equally well by a drive or a learning view. According to the first, we assume that children may share the participant's apparent frustration at receiving inconsistent reward. As a consequence, their level of drive and speed of response are increased. On the other hand, children may see that the participant's efforts are yielding only partial success, and may try to create a more optimal outcome by doing what they have learned in similar situations in the past—working harder.

EFFECTS OF BLOCKING CHILDREN'S PERFORMANCE

The study of Kobasigawa revealed the effects of blocking another person's progress on the performance of an observer. A study by Holton (1961) demonstrated the same effects on the performance of the participant. Preschool children were given boards with holes into which marbles could be placed. When all the holes were filled with marbles, the child could trade the board for a prize. Marbles were obtained by pressing a panel. For some of the children, reinforcement ceased before the child had filled the board. Half of these children needed only a few more marbles, but the other half needed a larger number. Still other children were reinforced for only a small number of trials, but needed a small number of marbles when nonreinforcement began. The amount of force exerted on the panel increased in all groups following the introduction of nonreinforcement. The increase was greater when nonreinforcement occurred near the goal and followed a large number of reinforced trials than when nonreinforcement occurred further from the goal. Nonreinforcement seemed, therefore, to be more frustrating after long experience with reinforcement and when the child had nearly completed the task. It should be noted, however, that Endsley (1966), in a much more complex situation, did not obtain this effect. When the task is not rigidly structured, children may develop avoidance responses that interfere with performance.

NONREINFORCEMENT IN DISCRIMINATION LEARNING

We have been discussing the effects of nonreinforcement in simple performance tasks where the response has been acquired by the child in previous situations. The conclusions take on a somewhat different emphasis when children must establish the response through experience in the experimental situation. Results from studies of the effects of nonreinforcement in discrimination learning indicate that learning may be more strongly influenced by the child's being able to find out what is incorrect rather than what is correct, by his desire to avoid being wrong rather than his hope of being right.

Ratio of Reinforcement and Nonreinforcement

The prototype of this research is a study conducted by Cantor and Spiker (1954). A game was played with two toy cars. The child was to choose one of the cars and roll it down an incline. If he had chosen the "correct" car, a marble was released. The child was free to choose a car only on some of the trials. The rest were forced-choice trials in which the child was told which car he must use. The experimenter could create different ratios of reinforcement and nonreinforcement for the child by varying the relative frequency with which he required the child to use each car. The question is whether these ratios had differential effects on the ease with which the child was able to select the correct car on the free-choice trials. Preschool children were given the correct car two times and the incorrect car two times, or the correct car two times and the incorrect car one time in each block of forced-choice trials. In this way the frequency of reinforcement was constant, but the frequency of nonreinforcement differed. Learning was more rapid with the greater number of nonreinforcements.

Evans and Endsley (1966) used the same experimental task with a different schedule of forced-choice trials. All children were given four sets of six forced trials, which were alternated with four sets of four free trials. In each set of six forced-choice trials the children received one, three, or five reinforcements. Five nonreinforced trials were more effective than five reinforced trials in leading the children to choose the correct car on their free trials. An intermediate level of learning occurred when the number of reinforced and nonreinforced forced-choice trials was equal.

Later, Endsley (1968) extended the range of reinforced and nonreinforced trials so that the children had from none to six nonreinforced trials in each block of six forced-choice trials. The results are presented in Figure 15-2. The relation is systematic. As the number of reinforcements received during the forced-choice trials increased, the number of correct responses on the 16 free trials declined.

Several interpretations of this effect have been advanced. A theory such as Spence's proposes that learning is a function of the differential strength of approach and avoidance responses to the discriminative stimuli. In the context of this theory it may be assumed that the avoidance of nonreward has a more powerful influence on learning than the approach to reward. It follows, then, that as the amount of nonrewarded experience with a stimulus increases, the greater the likelihood the child will avoid the nonreinforced stimulus in his free choices. A second interpretation emphasizes the role of nonreinforcement in directing the child's attention to the discriminative stimuli. This position proposes that there is less utility in observing the characteristics of a stimulus that leads to reward than of a stimulus associated with nonreward. A final interpretation is that nonreinforcement produces a state of deprivation. For example, the value of a reinforcer may be greater for children who have received 36 nonreinforced forced-choice trials than for children who have been rein-

Figure 15-2. Mean number of correct responses in 16 free-choice trials, according to each ratio of nonreinforced to reinforced forced-choices. (From R. C. Endsley, Effects of differential prior exposure on preschool children's subsequent choice of novel stimuli. *Journal of Experimental Child Psychology,* 1968, 6, 566, © 1968 Academic Press.)

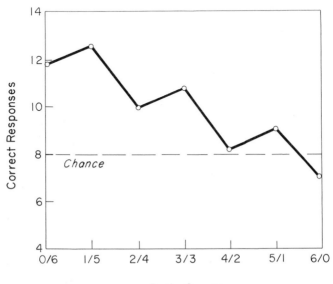

Ratio Groups

forced on each of these trials. None of the studies provides a critical test of these hypotheses.

Nondifferential Nonreinforcement

In the preceding studies nonreinforcement was applied in a differential fashion during the forced-choice trials. That is, choices of the to-be correct stimulus were reinforced and choices of the to-be incorrect stimulus were not. Learning was increasingly facilitated as the number of nonreinforced forced-choice responses to the incorrect stimulus was increased. Nonreinforcement could be applied nondifferentially. Children could be presented the discriminative stimuli during a pretraining period in which all responses are reinforced, for example, 0%, 50%, or 100% of the time. Will nonreinforcement or partial reinforcement applied in such a nondifferential fashion influence the child's rate of learning to discriminate among the stimuli?

A study by Stevenson and Pirojnikoff (1958) dealt with this question. Preschool children were shown three blocks (circle, triangle, and square) and some stickers (colored pictures of flowers, birds, and animals). The experimenter told the child he was going to hide a sticker and the child was to try to find it. During 20 pretraining trials every choice made by the child was reinforced, half of the choices were reinforced, or none of the choices was reinforced. Without comment, the experimenter then changed the task so that only choices of one of the blocks yielded a sticker. The rate of learning this discrimination was significantly influenced by the pretraining experiences. Children who had received no consistent reinforcement during pretraining responded in a random fashion, but three-fourths of the children who previously had been reinforced consistently learned the discrimination. The mean numbers of correct responses made in 40 training trials were 15.8, 19.1, and 26.2 for the 0%, 50%, and 100% pretraining groups, respectively. Children who had no pretraining experience made an average of 23.8 correct responses. Thus later learning was not greatly improved by 20 trials of nondifferential reinforcement, but nondifferential nonreinforcement had a deleterious effect.

These results are in line with an associative interpretation of the effects of nonreinforcement. According to the argument that nonreinforcement has a greater effect on the development of avoidance responses than reinforcement does on the development of approach responses, it would be predicted that learning would be impaired to a greater degree in the two conditions involving nonreinforcement than it would be facilitated in the condition involving reinforcement. Further, rate of extinction of incorrect responses during the training trials should be slower following 50% reinforcement than following 100% reinforcement, thereby producing more rapid learning in the 100% group. The interpretation favored by the writers, however, was one involving frustration. The children seemed to find nonreinforcement during the pretraining trials very frustrating. They became restless and upset. They grabbed the blocks and slammed them down when they continued to find no stickers. The emotional response of frustration seemed to interfere with the children's ability to respond appropriately in the discrimination learning task.

Is there any way in which one could demonstrate that the poorer learning following nonreinforcement or partial reinforcement may be due to frustration rather than to the prior acquisition of specific response tendencies to the discriminative stimuli? One way in which this could be done would be to use different stimuli in the pretraining and in the discrimination learning tasks. In this case any interference with learning that might occur could not be due to the child's having developed specific responses to the discriminative stimuli during the pretraining period.

Steigman and Stevenson (1960) reported the results of a study using this procedure. Preschool children played three games during the pretraining period. The games were constructed so that the experimenter could reinforce or fail to reinforce children's responses arbitrarily. For half of the children only 2 of 12 responses made in each game were deemed to be incorrect, while for the other half the children were informed that they were incorrect on 10 of each 12 responses. The children then were tested on a three-choice size discrimination task. A high frequency of prior nonreinforcement on unrelated tasks resulted in significantly poorer learning. The mean number of correct responses made in 40 training trials was 26.5 for the children who had experienced infrequent nonreinforcement, and 17.5 for those who had experienced frequent nonreinforcement. One of the ways in which nonreinforcement disturbed later learning was found in the tendency of children to develop stereotyped patterns of response. For example, children who had infrequent success in pretraining displayed a greater tendency to repeat responses to size and to position, regardless of whether they were correct or incorrect, than did children who had experienced high degrees of success. Deleterious effects of nonreinforcement are found even when novel stimuli are used in the learning task.

We can conclude that although nonreinforcement may facilitate performance in simple performance tasks, it may interfere with learning in more complex problems. If nonreinforcement is applied only to incorrect responses, rate of learning may be improved; but if nonreinforcement is applied nondifferentially to what later will be both correct and incorrect responses, learning will be retarded. These findings have important practical applications. We may be able to improve children's learning if we give them extensive experience in seeing what they are doing wrong, but if this experience leads to a general sense of failure we may create a condition that will interfere with efficient learning.

CONCLUSIONS

The facts emerging from studies of nonreinforcement are relatively consistent. Their interpretation is not. Perhaps the failure of this research to provide definitive support for a particular interpretation is because different children respond differently to nonreinforcement, some being frustrated and others challenged. In a highly structured task children work harder or respond faster when they fail to achieve consistent reinforcement. May not some children accept nonreinforcement as a cue that they should increase their efforts, and others respond with frustration and distress at not being able to accomplish their goals? Why were some children able to learn the form and size discrimination after extensive nonreinforcement, while other children were not? A more thorough exploration of individual differences in children's responses to nonreinforcement would prove to be highly productive, both from practical and theoretical points of view.

One of the most interesting contributions of this literature appears in the studies indicating that nonreinforcement may affect the performance of observers, as well as of participants. It is not immediately obvious that children's performance would be so strongly influenced by the consequences of another child's efforts to attain reward. Another informative set of studies are those in which the number of nonreinforced trials was found to be an important determinant of children's rate of learning. Most research on reinforcement variables concentrates on the production and reinforcement of correct responses. The studies on nonreinforcement challenge this emphasis by pointing out that the benefits derived from knowing what not to do may exceed those gained from knowing what should be done.

16

Incidental Learning

Usually, our goal is to determine how well the child can learn what we want him to learn. Most of the studies we have discussed have been of this type. In such "intentional" learning tasks we instruct the child about what he is to do, or call his attention to what is to be learned by presenting the materials in certain ways and reinforcing only relevant responses. The experimenter displays a set of blocks or a list of nonsense syllables and the child is instructed to find which block is correct or which associate is to be produced. The child is rewarded only when he makes the correct response.

Another category of learning is incidental learning. Incidental learning occurs when the child acquires responses or information that are irrelevant to the central task as defined by the experimenter. We do not tell the child he should attend to such materials and there is no apparent utility in his doing so. In fact, by attending to irrelevant stimuli he may progress more slowly in learning what he is supposed to learn. In reading, for example, the child must attend to the relevant aspects of words and disregard their irrelevant features, such as their color or size. Children who are capable of ignoring such irrelevant aspects of the stimuli should be able to concentrate their attention more fully on the task at hand. There is some evidence that this is the case, for children who are better readers turn out to have lower scores on tests of incidental learning (Siegel, 1968).

Procedures for investigating incidental learning have been categorized into two types (Postman, 1964). In the first type, the child is exposed to certain stimuli but is given no instructions to learn. After this experience, his retention of the stimulus materials is tested unexpectedly. For example, the experimenter may show the child a long list of nouns and ask the child to indicate which refer to animate and which refer to inanimate objects. The child is given no indication that he should remember the nouns, but after the list is presented he is asked to recall as many of them as possible.

In the second type, the child is given a learning task, but in the course of his experience he is exposed to stimuli that are not referred to in the instructions he has received. The amount of incidental learning is assessed by testing the child's retention of those stimuli that are not relevant to the central task. For example, the child may be shown a set of cards that depict common objects printed in different colors. He is instructed to learn the order in which the objects appear in the set and no mention is made of the fact that each object is drawn with a different color. After several trials in which he attempts to remember the order of the objects, he is asked to recall the order of the colors. Both procedures have been used in studies with children, but most of the studies have relied on some variant of the second type.

The study of incidental learning is important for many reasons. A major contribution of this research is the information it provides about the relation between perception and learning. What do we mean by an effective stimulus? Until now we have considered a stimulus to be no more than what the experimenter has decided is the stimulus. This clearly is an inadequate definition, for children do not always direct their attention to the cues that constitute what the experimenter considers to be relevant. The experimenter who is speaking about the circle the child sees projected before him and the child who is looking at the lint on the screen is a typical example of the discrepancy between what the adult and the child deem an appropriate stimulus.

Research on incidental learning is directed at other important questions. How common is incidental learning? Is its frequency influenced by the developmental level of the child? Does the child learn more effectively when he is instructed to learn or when he merely is given experience with the materials? Do instructions to learn have equivalent effects at all ages? Can conditions be arranged so that children are more likely to learn something about the irrelevant features of their environments? Conversely, is it possible to direct children's attention more effectively to the relevant cues so that there is minimal learning related to the irrelevant aspects of the situation?

Other studies are concerned with incidental learning that occurs in social situations. A great deal of what children learn in their everyday social experiences appears to be of an incidental nature. Indeed, many aspects of what is called identification may be a product of incidental learning. Children may learn certain modes of response, mannerisms, preferences, and goals, not because of explicit teaching or instructions, but because they observe them in their interactions with their parents, teachers, and peers. They may become like these peers and adults in behavior and appearance because they adopt incidental as well as salient characteristics of such models. What variables related to the child and to the situation influence the learning of incidental features of the behavior of other persons?

DEVELOPMENTAL STUDIES

We will address ourselves first to the question of whether incidental learning varies with the chronological age of the child. Developmental studies of incidental learning have covered a broad range of ages. The youngest children were the three- to seven-year-olds included in a study by Stevenson (1954). The children played a game in which they could unlock boxes and find prizes. At each end of a life-sized Y-maze were two boxes, one locked with a padlock. The child was told to go to the open box, find a key, and open the lock of the second box to find a prize. In each open box was an assortment of objects, including on one side a small white purse, and on the other side a matchbox. Depending on the experimental condition, the key was on, under, or in the purse and the matchbox. After an equal number of experiences with each pair of boxes, the child was asked to find the purse or matchbox. Since neither object had been mentioned by the experimenter and since there was no necessity for the child to learn their location, the child's ability to locate the object was assumed to be the result of incidental learning.

Success in finding the incidental object was dependent upon the child's age and the relation between the object and the sequence of actions necessary to attain the prizes. Incidental learning was significantly better when the child had to manipulate the test object actively than in the other two conditions, where the object was present in the child's visual field but bore little relation to the task he was performing, and where the object formed a barrier that could be pushed aside in a haphazard fashion. The number of children displaying the correct response increased gradually with increasing age in all three conditions. All but the three-year-olds performed significantly above chance in the condition involving active manipulation of the test object, while in the other two conditions only the performance of the six-year-olds was significantly above chance.

Would the tendency to acquire irrelevant information continue to increase at still older ages? There is reason to believe it would not. At some point in development this tendency should decrease, for if the mature individual were responsive to the vast arrays of irrelevant stimuli that are continually available, he would be flooded with momentarily useless information. Efficient and effective behavior usually requires the individual to become selective in his attention.

Maccoby and Hagen (1965) have provided data relevant to this point.

They assumed that young children are handicapped in focussing their attention selectively because of their inexperience in separating task-relevant and task-irrelevant aspects of a situation. While the child learns to categorize, code, and label objects, incidental learning may increase, but at a later stage of development, it should be possible for the child to direct his attention selectively. It was predicted, therefore, that a curvilinear relation would be found between age and incidental learning.

To test this prediction, a set of cards bearing different colors and different pictures was shown to children in grades 1, 3, 5, and 7. The cards were turned face down and the children were asked to point to the card bearing a particular color. After the children had learned to remember the positions of the cards by their color, incidental recall was tested by asking the children to locate cards bearing particular pictures. Whereas recall on the first intentional learning task improved with age, incidental recall tended to be related to age in a curvilinear manner. There was a slight but nonsignificant increase in the number of correct responses between grades 1 and 5, but between grades 5 and 7, children's recall of the locations of particular pictures declined significantly. The main findings of this study have been replicated with different materials by Hagen (1967).

A curvilinear relation between incidental learning and chronological age also was found by Siegel and Stevenson (1966). The procedure for this study was divided into three parts. First, the children learned a standard three-choice successive discrimination problem. This was followed by 12 presentations of each discriminative stimulus (e.g., truck) imbedded in a stimulus complex (e.g., truck, fish, rooster, star). The response button that had been correct for each discriminative stimulus remained correct for the stimulus complex in which it later appeared. Incidental learning was tested by presenting the surrounding objects of the stimulus complex separately. Would children make the responses to the incidental objects that had been associated earlier with the discriminative stimuli?

Frequency of correct response increased significantly between ages 7 and 11 and decreased significantly between ages 11 and 14. The point of decline occurred, as it had in the Maccoby and Hagen study, around the ages of 11 to 12 years. Neither in this nor in the Maccoby and Hagen study was there a significant relation between the measures of intentional and incidental learning. Evidence for the independence of these two processes also has been presented by Druker and Hagen (1969), Hagen (1967), Hagen and Sabo (1967), Hetherington and Banta (1962), and Siegel (1968).

A closely related study by Crane and Ross (1967) assessed the ability of eight- and eleven-year-olds to profit from the presentation of information that was irrelevant at one stage of their performance, but later became relevant. If eleven-year-olds are able to attend selectively, they should profit less from prior experience with irrelevant cues than eight-year-olds. The children were required to learn a two-choice discrimination problem with either color or form as the relevant dimension. If color was relevant, form was irrelevant, and vice versa. After this discrimination was learned, the irrelevant cues were made completely redundant in that each irrelevant cue was paired consistently with a relevant cue (e.g., blue circle; yellow X). In a final test stage, the children were required to learn a two-choice problem in which the irrelevant cues became the relevant cues. The cue that had been associated consistently with reward (e.g., circle) was correct for half of the children and the cue that had been paired with nonreward (e.g., X) was correct for the other half.

Younger children learned the final problem more rapidly when the previously "positive" irrelevant cue was correct than when the previously "negative" irrelevant cue was correct. The irrelevant cues had acquired functional significance for these children. The older children, however, appeared to have concentrated their attention more completely on the relevant aspects of the stimuli, for their rate of learning did not differ between the two conditions.

In the three previous studies, the incidental stimuli were presented in the context of tasks involving intentional learning of other materials. The question arises whether a curvilinear relation would be found in naturalistic situations where there is no compelling reason for any specific type of learning to occur. If the developmental trend in incidental learning were curvilinear, additional evidence would be provided for the assumption that older children develop an ability to disregard aspects of the environment that are not essential for the conduct of ongoing behavior. Hale, Miller, and Stevenson (1968) therefore attempted to simulate a naturalistic situation by presenting the materials in a filmed skit. The skit contained a simple plot with unfolding action, which allowed elaboration in incidental aspects of its dialogue, background actions, costuming, and setting.

The skit was shown, presumably for the children's pleasure, in grades 3 through 7. At its conclusion, booklets were handed out that contained 30 multiple choice and true-false questions. The questions tapped aspects of the verbal and visual content of the film that were incidental to the central plot. The results, summarized in Figure 16-1, reveal a curvilinear relation between age and correct response to questions dealing with incidental material. The drop in performance between grades 6 and 7 appears to be related to the development of an ability to disregard nonessential features of a situation. The most reasonable interpretation of this finding is that the seventh graders were attending to the central plot of the film and paid relatively less attention than did younger children to the specific manner in which the information was presented. The performance of girls was uniformly above that of boys. Significant sex differences have not been found in other studies of incidental learning, and in this study girls may have been more attentive than boys to the social content of the film.

Here, then, is a series of studies using different tasks and different measures of incidental learning, all of which yielded an increase in incidental learning until around the ages of 11 or 12, and then a decline. A curvilinear relation has been found in still other studies (Druker & Hagen, 1969; Hagen, 1967; Hagen & Sabo, 1967). What are the mechanisms whereby incidental learning increases during the early years? They undoubtedly have something to do with the improvement in children's ability to discriminate between relevant and irrelevant stimuli and, as Maccoby and Hagen (1965) proposed, to use mediational and other cognitive processes involving coding, labeling, and categorizing the contents of their environments. More basic, however, is the possibility that the range of perceptual activity increases up to a point with increasing age.

Piaget, among others, has made such a proposition, and it has been tested recently by Vurpillot (1968). Using photographic recording of eye movements, Vurpillot found developmental changes in the manner in which children scanned pairs of complex stimuli prior to making

Figure 16-1.   Mean number of correct responses as a function of grade and sex. (From G. H. Hale, L. K. Miller, and H. W. Stevenson, Incidental learning of film content. *Child Development,* 1968, 39, 73. Copyright 1968 Society for Research in Child Development, Inc.)

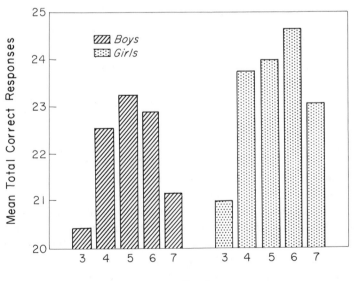

same-different judgments. Vurpillot reported that children younger than six never took into account the whole of a stimulus, but restricted their scanning to limited areas and made their judgments on the basis of a mere sample of the available information. The improvement between the ages of six and nine in children's ability to judge similarities and differences seemed to be due to a more systematic use of the information that was available. Older children scanned the features of the stimuli more broadly before making a judgment. Improvement in incidental learning may be derived, then, from developmental changes in the range of perceptual activity employed by children.

How can one account for the decline in incidental learning after the elementary school years? For the present, the results seem to reflect the emergence of an ability to direct attention selectively, wherein the child subordinates or suppresses response to incidental features of his environment and concentrates on those that are relevant to his immediate goals. Evidence bearing directly upon this interpretation has been supplied by Druker and Hagen (1969). At the conclusion of their study, they asked their subjects several questions, such as where the child looked first when he saw the row of cards and whether the child said anything to himself while he was looking at the cards. As can be seen in Figure 16-2, children's tendencies to scan only the relevant features of the stimuli increased across grades, while there was a decrease in their tendencies to scan both the relevant and irrelevant features. A similar pattern appeared in the manner in which children labeled the stimuli. The older children had a greater tendency to label relevant aspects of the stimuli, but the tendency to label both the relevant and irrelevant aspects decreased with age. The decrease in incidental learning may represent an active attempt by the child to disregard the aspects of the situation that he has discovered to be irrelevant in his pursuit of a particular goal. He may demonstrate this disregard by failing to look at or label the irrelevant stimuli, but may use these techniques with relevant stimuli in an effort to improve his performance.

Additional evidence that the decline in incidental learning is a product of older children's tendencies to disregard irrelevant cues comes from a study by Siegel (1968). On the assumption that it should be easier to disregard irrelevant cues if they remain constant across trials than if they are continuously changing, Siegel varied the manner in which the irrelevant cues were paired with the discriminative stimuli in a Siegel and Stevenson (1966) type of task. Three irrelevant cues were associated with each discriminative stimulus. Irrelevant cues were presented as a group (e.g., truck, *star, fish, rooster*) either four or twelve times, or singly (e.g., truck-*star*, truck-*fish*, truck-*rooster*) four times each. As predicted, incidental learning was greater when the cues differed on successive trials than when the same groups of cues were seen repeatedly. There was no

difference in amount of incidental learning after four or twelve presentations of the grouped stimuli, thus the tendency to disregard the irrelevant
cues appears to have occurred rather rapidly.

Further, if the poor incidental learning of older, but not of younger
children is due primarily to their disregard of incidental cues, instructions
to attend to these cues should produce a dramatic improvement in the
performance of older, but not of younger children. Siegel and Corsini
(1969) repeated the essential details of the Siegel and Stevenson (1966)
study with 8- and 14-year-olds. Half of the subjects were instructed to
attend to the irrelevant cues and half were not. When 14-year-olds were
instructed to attend to the incidental cues which were unrelated objects,
they performed at a significantly higher level than 8-year-olds. When no
instructions were given the two age groups performed at comparable
levels. The design of both this and the preceding study are more complex

Figure 16-2.   (a) Percent of subjects at grades 4, 6, and 8 who
stated they had attended to both relevant and irrelevant items and
who stated they had attended only to relevant items, and (b) who labeled only relevant items and who labeled irrelevant items. (From
J. F. Drucker and J. W. Hagen, Developmental trends in the processing of task-relevant and task-irrelevant information. *Child Development,* 1969, 40, 379–380. Copyright 1969 by the Society for Research
in Child Development, Inc.)

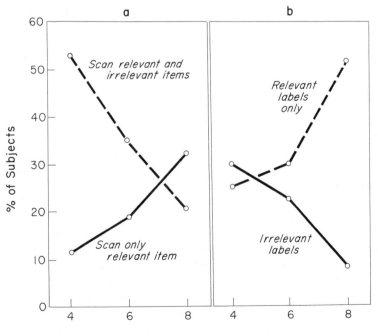

than have been indicated, but it seems appropriate to conclude that the results offer support for the assumption that the ability to attend selectively improves with increasing age.

VARIABLES RELATED TO INCIDENTAL LEARNING

Attempts have been made in other studies to influence the occurrence of incidental learning by introducing certain experimental variables. Among the variables investigated thus far are level of incentive, type of instructions, and the spatial relation between irrelevant and relevant cues.

Incentive Effects

In some studies with adults an increase in motivation has been found to result in poorer incidental learning. Heightened motivation was assumed to restrict the subjects' range of perceptual activity, thereby decreasing their attention to irrelevant aspects of the situation.

Kausler, Laughlin, and Trapp (1963) tested seventh and eighth graders to determine whether similar effects would be found with children. A 14-item serial learning list was used in which each of seven forms appeared with two of seven colors. After learning the list on the basis of form, incidental learning was measured by determining the number of correct form-color pairings that could be recognized. Half of the subjects had been told they could win money, and half simply were asked for their cooperation. Incidental learning was greater when the subjects were offered money, both for the subjects who later stated they had tried to learn the color-form combinations and for those who stated they did not.

A study by Wray (1968) used a very similar procedure, but found no significant difference in incidental learning by seventh graders who were promised fifty cents for satisfactory performance on the intentional learning task and those who were offered no external incentive. The question of whether children's response to incidental cues is influenced by their level of motivation is an interesting one, but as of now we have little idea what the answer might be.

Instructions

In three studies an attempt was made to influence children's incidental learning by verbal instructions. In no case did instructions have their expected effect. Stevenson and Siegel (1969) gave children in grades 3 through 7 one of three types of instructions before they viewed an eight-minute film—the same film used by Hale, Miller, and Stevenson (1968).

The children were told, "When the movie is over, we are going to ask you some questions about what you have *heard*. So be sure you *listen* to everything in the movie carefully." Others were instructed to be attentive to everything they saw in the film, and still others, to be attentive to everything they saw and heard. As in the earlier study, the children then were asked a series of multiple choice and true-false questions about incidental aspects of the visual and auditory content of the film.

The mean numbers of correct responses were remarkably similar for the three instructional conditions at all grade levels. No support was obtained for the prediction that instructions to attend to a particular category of stimulus would produce an increase in the frequency of correct response to questions pertaining to that category of stimuli. Instead, the number of correct responses increased consistently across grades for the questions related to the visual content of the film, but decreased significantly between grades 5 and 7 for questions related to audio portions of the film. The means were consistently greater for audio than for visual questions. The primary effect of the instructions seemed to be that of alerting the children to the fact that they would be asked questions about the film, rather than directing their attention to particular aspects of the film's content.

Instructions also were used by Hagen and Sabo (1967) in an effort to increase the selectivity of children's attention. The children were given a booklet, whose pages contained four to seven rows of pairs of drawings. In each pair was a household object and an animal. The members of each pair were the same on each page and each pair retained a specific

Figure 16-3.   Mean number of items recalled in clustered and non-clustered lists under conditions of intentional and incidental learning. (Data from M. E. Vaughan, Clustering, age, and incidental learning. *Journal of Experimental Child Psychology,* 1968, 6, 328.)

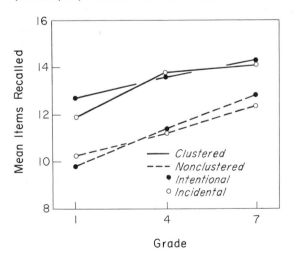

position on all ten pages of the booklet. Blank cards were interspersed among the pairs of stimuli when there were not seven pairs on a page. The subjects were instructed (a) to remember the exact pairing of each animal with each household object, (b) to remember the exact order of the drawings in the row, or (c) to remember both the pairings and the order. Instructions to attend to the order of the pictures had no significant effect on performance. Following such instructions, recall of the order of the drawings was not significantly better than recall of the pairings at any of the four grade levels (grades 3, 5, 7, and 9) included in the study. More in line with what was expected were the results for the group instructed to attend to specific pairings. Recall of the pairs was better than recall of positions, and performance on both improved with increasing age. A grade-by-grade analysis indicated, however, that this instruction had a significant effect only at grades 7 and 9. Only at these grades was recall of pairs better than recall of positions. When told to remember both characteristics, the children showed better recall of pairs than of positions, but there was no improvement in performance across grades. Generally, therefore, there was only slight evidence that children were able to direct their attention selectively on the basis of instructions.

Vaughan (1968) used an entirely different procedure. Children in grades 1, 4, and 7 were shown 16 pictures of common objects. The pictures included four examples each of four categories of objects (e.g., animals, clothing, furniture). The four examples of each category appeared in sequence (i.e., were "clustered") for half of the subjects, and for the other half they appeared randomly through the list (i.e., were "nonclustered"). The children were to make up a sentence about each object. Half also were told they should try to remember as many of the pictures as possible, for they would be asked to name them later. As can be seen in Figure 16-3, recall by children who received no explicit instructions to remember the names of the objects was as good as that by children who knew they were going to be asked to reproduce the list. Clustering had a significant effect, for in both the intentional and incidental learning conditions a greater number of pictures was recalled when the pictures appeared in a clustered list.

These results reaffirm what we have found in previous discussions. Modifying children's learning by verbal instructions is difficult. Children apparently find it hard to abandon preferred modes of response or to adopt new approaches to learning merely because they are told they should do so.

Spatial Relation between Central and Incidental Stimuli

If incidental learning is negatively related to the child's ability to direct his attention selectively, any condition that enhances selective attention should diminish incidental learning. In previous studies the incidental stimuli were contiguous to or incorporated in the central stimulus materials. Perhaps it would be easier for children to direct their attention selectively if the stimuli were not so close together. Druker and Hagen (1969) therefore presented their stimuli (pairs of drawings, each containing a household object and an animal) so that the drawings within each pair were contiguous or spatially separated. The central task involved the recall of the spatial position of household objects and the test for incidental learning required the child to match household objects and animals. The number of correct responses was significantly lower at all grades (grades 4, 6, and 8) when the drawings were spatially separated than when they were contiguous, thus supporting the hypothesis that an increase in the discriminability of central and incidental stimuli results in poorer incidental learning.

INCIDENTAL LEARNING IN SOCIAL SITUATIONS

It is not difficult to demonstrate children's imitative learning of incidental features of an adult's behavior. Wilson (1958), for example, had children play a game with an adult in which they sought a prize in one of two identical boxes. The adult and the child took turns in seeking the prize, with the adult always preceding the child. Children gradually began to imitate the adult's choices, since such choices invariably led to reward for both the adult and the child. When imitative responding was established, two containers differing in color and shape were introduced. The model consistently chose one of the containers. After eight trials the adult was called from the room and the game continued with the child. Even though they had not been instructed to do so, the children had learned the nature of the critical cues while imitating the model's choices. Their rate of learning to select the correct container was much more rapid than that of children who had been given the task as a standard discrimination learning problem.

More interesting, perhaps, is information about the characteristics of the child and the situation that foster such learning. One obvious possibility is the type of relation that exists between the child and the adult. It is reasonable to assume that children will be more likely to imitate an adult's behavior if they have a close relation with the adult than if their prior interactions with the adult have been impersonal and remote. Bandura and Huston (1961) tested this assumption. Half of the subjects, preschool children, were exposed to a model who behaved in a very nurturant manner. The adult attempted, in two 15-minute sessions, to create a warm and rewarding relation with the child. For the other half of the children, the adult was nonresponsive and disinterested.

The child then was introduced to the experimental task. There were two identical boxes, one of which contained a reward. The adult responded first, followed by the child. During the course of her responses, the adult exhibited verbal, motor, and aggressive responses that were irrelevant to the selection of a box. These incidental behaviors were imitated with a high frequency; for example, 90% of the children imitated the model's aggressive response (knocking a doll off one of the boxes) and 45% marched toward the boxes in the manner performed by the model. The frequency of imitation of incidental responses was greater following the nurturant than following the non-nurturant interactions, but these conditions did not influence the frequency with which the children imitated the model's choice of a box. There was some evidence that dependent children were more likely to show imitative behavior. Dependency, as rated from observations made in nursery school, was positively related to imitative verbal behavior.

The same task was used by Bandura, Ross, and Ross (1963) to study the effects on imitative learning of the role adopted by the model. Two adults served as models and an attempt was made to establish a different role for each adult. One adult was the controller and dispenser of resources. In this case the resources were of a physical nature; the adult "owned" the toys and dispensed cookies and juice. The second adult assumed the role of consumer and was the recipient of the first adult's favors. In a second situation, the children were the recipients and the other adult was ignored by the controller. Each adult exhibited a different set of novel, irrelevant verbal and motor responses while making his choice of a particular reward-box. Children displayed a greater tendency to imitate the model who had been the controller of resources, regardless of who had been the recipient of his favors, than to imitate the adult who had been the passive consumer.

The influence of parental nurturance on children's imitation of incidental features of parental behavior was studied by Mussen and Parker (1965). The subjects were five- and six-year-old girls whose mothers had been categorized as nurturant or non-nurturant. Several weeks before the study, the experimenter administered the Porteus mazes, a set of printed mazes of increasing difficulty. The same mazes were used in the experimental sessions. The mother traced the pathway through each maze, and then the daughter, who had observed the mother's performance, was given her turn. The mothers had been coached to make irrelevant verbalizations, irrelevant marks on the mazes, and to choose particular crayons. Maze performance did not differ between girls with nurturant and non-nurturant mothers, but girls with nurturant mothers showed a significantly greater tendency to imitate incidental features of their mothers' behavior than did the girls with non-nurturant mothers. Thus, whether the model is the child's mother or another adult, the frequency of imitation of incidental behavior is influenced by the closeness or warmth of the relation between the model and the child.

There was a hint in the Bandura and Huston (1961) study that dependency and incidental learning are positively related. This point was elaborated by Ross (1966). Ross taught children how to run a post office. Specifically, this involved teaching them seven types of responses, such as collecting money and giving change, regulations for letters, and how to dial the telephone. In demonstrating these responses, the adult displayed many irrelevant forms of behavior, such as putting one foot on a chair while dialing the telephone, making irrelevant verbalizations, and taking a circuitous route to the mail box. When the children took over the post office, careful observations were made of the frequency with which they demonstrated both central and incidental features of the adult's responses.

The subjects were children in the upper and lower quartiles of a sample of 101 preschool children who had been rated for dependent behavior by their teachers. It was predicted that incidental learning would be greater for the high- than for the low-dependent children. That is what was found. Low-dependent children appeared to be selective in what they attended to, as evidenced by their greater ability to reproduce the relevant aspects of the adult's behavior, while the high-dependent children tended to pay equal attention to all aspects of the model's behavior. The ratio of intentional to incidental responses reproduced was 3.4 to 1 for low-dependent children and 1.2 to 1 for high-dependent children. Low-dependent children appeared to perceive the situation as one involving achievement, while the high-dependent children responded to it as one for broad social play. It may be that one component of independent behavior is the tendency to select and respond to the aspects of a situation that are most likely to pay off in reward for achievement.

A final example is a study by Hartup and Coates (1967), who demonstrated that incidental features of another child's behavior may also be imitated by children. On the assumption that models who are rewarding to the child are more likely to be imitated than nonrewarding models, children were paired on the basis of the reinforcement received from other children in their everyday interactions in nursery school. The subjects were separated into those who received either a high or a low frequency of reinforcement from their peers. The model was a child of the same sex who had been observed to reward the subject frequently or a child who never rewarded the subject. A maze-tracing task was used. The models were coached about the form their responses should take. They were to make certain irrelevant comments, select particular pencils, and engage in other forms of irrelevant behavior. Significant effects were found only in the tendency of the subjects to imitate the incidental verbalizations of the models. Among children generally receiving a high frequency of reward from their peers, those who played the game with a rewarding model imitated incidental verbalizations nearly four times as frequently as children who played with a nonrewarding model. On the other hand, among children who were infrequently reinforced by their peers in daily play, the difference in imitation related to type of model was slight.

A consistent theme in these studies is that the acquisition of the incidental features of the behavior of other persons is influenced by the type of relation that exists between the model and the subject. The probability that incidental aspects of a model's behavior will be imitated is greater if the model is nurturant in the sense of being warm and supportive, if he controls objects or events that are valued by the child, or if he frequently behaves in a positive manner toward the child in everyday life. Characteristics of the subject also influence his tendency to imitate the behavior of others. If the child generally is dependent upon others for guidance and support, he will be likely to imitate a model's behavior in a broad manner and will fail to attend selectively to those aspects of the model's behavior that are central to the task in which he is participating. These situational and personality characteristics were studied in the context of incidental learning, but there is no reason to assume they would not have strong effects on other types of learning as well.

CONCLUSIONS

Preschool children seem to have difficulty in discriminating between the relevant and irrelevant aspects of a situation, and attend to both in a restricted fashion. As the child grows older, he appears to sample the stimuli in his environment more broadly, and in the process continues to acquire information about both their relevant and irrelevant features. From what we know at present, the ability to focus attention selectively is readily accomplished only after the ages of 11 or 12. The ability is dependent, however, on the nature of the situation. There is an interaction between the capacity of the subject to process information and the nature of the situation in which he finds himself. Young children can attend well to salient stimuli and adults may remember certain distinctive but irrelevant stimuli, even while concentrating on the relevant task.

Learning seems to be influenced by several perceptual processes: the child's ability to sample broadly from the stimuli in his environment, to discriminate relevant from irrelevant stimuli, and finally, to respond selectively to those that are of current relevance. In general, the mature individual behaves in an adaptive fashion by actively disregarding some aspects of his environment. He ignores irrelevant stimuli in an effort to respond effectively to others.

Instructing children to direct their attention to particular features of their environments does not necessarily insure that they will be able to follow such instructions. Only in the later years of childhood are children apparently able to use instructions effectively to control their attention. It is no surprise, therefore, that so much time is spent by elementary school teachers in attempting to get children to attend to their school work. Children's attention may be more susceptible to control by the materials and the manner in which they are presented than by the teacher's exhortations.

Much of children's everyday learning appears to be incidental, rather than intentional. This was seen clearly in studies of the imitation of incidental aspects of social behavior. Children readily imitate the behavior of peers and adults, especially if the other person is one who has a close and supportive relation to the child, or possesses characteristics or resources the child values. Although experience may not always be the best teacher, young children do seem to learn a great deal through casual observation of persons and situations encountered in their daily lives.

17

Attention and
Discrimination Learning

Although for many years attention was dismissed by psychologists—especially the hard-line behaviorists—as an unacceptable mentalistic construct, it recently has come to play a central role in many conceptualizations of the learning process. This has been especially true in discussions of discrimination learning, where successful performance obviously is dependent upon the child's ability to isolate the properties that differentiate the stimuli. Unless the child attends to the stimuli he will be unable to determine what these properties are. This is not a subtle point, and even behaviorists have found it necessary to speak of orienting or observing responses. In their most primitive form, orienting or observing responses are those in which the subject places himself so that he is capable of observing the relevant stimuli. In other versions (e.g., Zeaman & House, 1963), the observing response is considered to involve a response to the relevant dimensions of the stimuli, rather than simply to their spatial locus. Western psychologists have not been alone in introducing a form of attention into their theories, for Soviet psychologists such as Sokolov (1963) also have given the orienting response a central role in their discussions of learning and perception.

This is not the first time attention has been mentioned in the context of discrimination learning. In reversal and nonreversal shifts, for example, the salience or attention-getting properties of the stimuli were found to determine the ease of initial learning and the type of shift that would be made. In studies of reinforcement variables, the appearance of material reinforcers seemed to distract children's attention from the discriminative stimuli, and the introduction of a penalty for incorrect responses appeared to make children more attentive to the stimuli. Verbal labels were assumed to facilitate learning partly because they increased the child's attention to the relevant cues. In these cases, however, the concept of attention was used in post facto interpretations, for the experiments were not designed originally to study the relations between attention and learning. We wish now to extend this discussion and deal in some detail with studies whose primary purpose has been to investigate how learning is influenced by attention to the relevant features of the stimuli.

EMPHASIZING THE RELEVANT CUE

Superficially, most discrimination learning problems appear to be quite simple. All that is asked of the child is that he select the correct stimulus from an array of two or more stimuli. Each time he chooses the stimulus deemed to be correct by the experimenter he discovers a prize or some other indication he has been correct. Eventually, he begins to choose the correct stimulus consistently. The apparent simplicity of such problems is deceptive, for children often find discrimination learning tasks quite difficult. Their difficulties arise from many potential sources, and among these is a failure to recognize the basis on which the discriminative stimuli differ. If such differences are emphasized, rate of learning may be increased.

Perhaps the simplest way to highlight the characteristics of the positive cue is to present it initially in isolation. The fading-in technique used by Cole, Dent, Eguchi, Fujii, and Johnson (1964) in their study of transposition illustrates this approach. The positive stimulus, a square, was presented in full form, while the negative stimulus was represented initially by a thin line. The negative stimulus emerged gradually, so that by the later trials it, too, was fully represented as a square. By making the positive cue strongly dominant, errorless learning was possible.

The fading-in technique also was used by Caron (1968) in a study where correct response depended upon discriminating between rounded and angular figures. Since many pairs of figures were used, the child had to learn and use the concepts of angularity and roundedness in order to respond appropriately. Training trials were constructed so that during the early trials the outlines of the figures were barely perceptible. As the trials continued the figures were faded in through a series of five steps so that they eventually appeared in full outline. To emphasize the critical dimension, a corner of each angular figure and its counterpart on the rounded figure were darkened in black ink. Thus during the early trials only the critical features of the figures were readily discernible. Following this type of training, three-year-olds were capable of utilizing the concepts appropriately in the solution of two-choice discrimination learning problems.

The preceding studies demonstrate that learning is more effective if, during the early trials of the task, differences between the relevant attributes of the stimuli are highlighted. Spiker (1959) used a different technique to demonstrate this point. In 24 preliminary trials, a bright light (3000 ft.-candles) was the positive cue and a dim light (15 ft.-candles) was the negative cue in a two-choice task. For the next 24 trials a medium-bright light (500 ft.-candles) was substituted for the dim light as the negative cue. A second group of preschool children received all 48 trials with the bright and medium-bright lights. Children given early experience with the exaggerated difference in brightness learned the initial discrimination very rapidly and maintained a high level of correct response when the negative stimulus was replaced after 24 trials. On the other hand, children trained with the two similar stimuli on all 48 trials never attained a level of performance significantly above chance. Superior learning following early experience with exaggerated differences between the cues also occurred in a second study. For the first 24 trials the procedure was identical to that of the first study, and then the positive and negative cues were reversed. Children who had been trained initially with the extreme stimuli learned to select the medium-bright light more rapidly than did the children who had viewed the more similar stimuli on all 48 trials. In both studies, therefore, learning to attend to differences in brightness was facilitated when extreme differences in brightness were present during early phases of training.

A final example is found in a study by Bijou (Bijou & Baer, 1963), who was able to train children between the ages of three and six to perform complex matching-to-sample tasks with remarkable effectiveness. Several techniques were used to increase children's attention to the relevant attributes of the stimuli. In the first problem, for example, the children saw a circle, below which were a circle, square, and rectangle. The use of simple geometric forms emphasized the identity of the sample and the correct alternative. The sample and the alternatives gradually became more complex in form and the number of choices increased from three to five. Eventually, the children were able to make complex matches involving mirror images, but this occurred only after they had had extensive experience in which their attention was directed to the relevant cues.

These studies all point to the same conclusion. Children can learn surprisingly difficult discriminations if they are given appropriate experience in learning to attend to the relevant cues. This experience can be provided in several ways. The positive cue can be presented initially in isolation, the difference between the positive and negative cues can be exaggerated, or the characteristics of the problem can be emphasized by using easy examples. With such assistance, children rapidly learn to attend to the relevant features of the stimuli and can apply what they have learned to other, even more difficult tasks.

SPATIAL DIMENSIONALITY

It is obvious that we can select stimuli embodying physical characteristics so salient that attention to these characteristics is assured. Subtle
differences among stimuli, such as differences in their spatial dimensionality, also may influence the child's attention to their relevant characteristics.

The possible influence of the spatial dimensions of stimuli on children's
learning was demonstrated in three studies, all with three-year-olds. The
children were faced with the problem of learning to discriminate between
two squares differing in size. This would appear to be easy enough, but
Kuenne's (1946) subjects required an average of 335.8 trials to learn the
problem. When Alberts and Ehrenfreund (1951) repeated the study,
however, the discrimination was learned in an average of 54.8 trials, and
in a later study by Stevenson and Langford (1957) the mean number of
trials was 13.6. Although the experimental procedures differed in several
ways, the critical difference appeared to be the manner in which the
squares were represented. In the first study, they were painted on the
doors of the boxes containing the incentives. In the second, they constituted the doors to the incentive boxes; and in the third, they appeared as
blocks which the child lifted to reveal the incentive.

To determine whether, indeed, differences in rates of learning could be
attributed to differences in dimensionality of the stimuli, rather than to
other factors, Stevenson and McBee (1958) presented four- and six-year-
olds with a three-choice size discrimination in which the stimuli were
black cubes, plaques cut from quarter-inch masonite, or squares painted
on white cardboard. For different subjects, the small, medium-sized, or
large stimulus was correct. Children trained with cubes or plaques showed
rapid improvement over the 40 training trials, but there was practically
no increase in the tendency to select the correct stimulus by children
trained with patterns. Comparable results have been found by Dornbush
and Winnick (1966) when form, rather than size, was the relevant cue.

Why does the addition of the third dimension increase the ease of
learning? Part of the basis could be due to the fact that three-dimensional
objects differ not only in their visual properties, but also in their tactual
and kinesthetic qualities. Differences in size may be accentuated by the
presence of these additional, correlated cues. Falk (1968) investigated
this possibility by allowing half of her subjects to use only visual cues and
half to use all possible cues. The procedure was the same as that of Stevenson and McBee for half of the subjects. For the second half, three clear
plastic shields were interposed between the child and the stimuli, and the
child could displace a stimulus from its position over a reward-well by
pushing the shield in front of it. The weights of the stimuli were altered

in this condition so that an equivalent amount of force was required to displace each stimulus in a set. The stimuli were cubes, square plaques, or squares drawn on cardboard. When all cues were available, more correct responses were made with the cubes than with the other two types of stimuli. When only visual cues were available, there was no significant difference in performance according to the dimensionality of the stimuli. The added visual cues of depth provided by the cubes did not help to produce faster learning, but the tactual and kinesthetic cues derived from handling the stimuli were of significant benefit.

We conclude, therefore, that learning can be improved substantially if stimuli are represented in three dimensions. The additional tactual and kinesthetic cues provided by three-dimensional objects appear to enhance differences among stimuli, thereby increasing the likelihood that children will attend to these differences. The only qualification to this conclusion is derived from a study by Kerpelman (1967), where children learned to discriminate among irregular pentagons more rapidly when they were planometric than when they were stereometric. The additional cues provided by the third dimension may be confusing rather than helpful if the figures are complex.

SPATIAL RELATIONS

Nowhere have we considered the effects on learning of the spatial relations among stimulus, response, and reward. Such relations may have an influence on learning by determining where the child will direct his attention. If the hand guides the eye and children look where they touch, attention to stimuli should be greater if the stimuli are near the locus of response than if stimulus and response are spatially remote. As a consequence, discrimination of differences among stimuli should occur more rapidly when stimulus and response are adjacent than when they are spatially separated.

In an initial study, Murphy and Miller (1959) presented ten-year-olds with a two-choice pattern discrimination. The child had to look at the discriminative stimuli and then lift one of two blocks that covered the reward-wells. The stimuli were immediately above the reward-wells or were separated from the wells by six inches. Learning was more rapid when the cue and the locus of response and reward were contiguous than when they were separated.

A more elaborate study was conducted with preschool children by Jeffrey and Cohen (1964). Learning was rapid when stimulus, response, and reward were contiguous (the child lifted a stimulus block to find the reward). There was little change in performance across 60 training trials, however, when all three components were separated spatially, or when there was contiguity of stimulus and reward, or of response and reward with separation of the third component. (An example will help to clarify what occurred in the last three conditions. When all three components were separated spatially the stimulus blocks were in one position, the blocks to which the child responded were in front of and separated from the stimulus blocks, and the reward was retrieved by the child's lifting a block located at still a third position). Since a high level of learning occurred in a condition where the stimulus and response were contiguous but the locus of reward was separated, the most important combination appeared to be contiguity of stimulus and response.

The same experimental conditions were used in a study with nine-year-olds by Wunderlich, Nazzaro, and Youniss (1968). In addition to varying the spatial relations of stimulus, response, and reward, the location of the discriminative cue on the stimulus-block was varied. The cue (a color) was located around the border or was centered on the block. Since children typically grasp blocks by edges, it was assumed that placing the discriminative cues around the border would increase the likelihood the children would notice them. Two significant effects were found. Conditions involving stimulus-response contiguity produced faster learning than those involving spatial separation of stimulus and response— the findings reported by Jeffrey and Cohen for younger children. Learning also was more rapid when the cues were on the borders than when they were centered on the stimulus-blocks.

Spatial organization of a task seems to be a potent variable in determining rate of learning. When stimulus and response are spatially separated, learning is impaired, but it does not seem to make much difference if either the stimulus or the response are separated spatially from the reward. More generally, the results point to the importance of placing stimuli where they are most likely to capture the child's attention.

IRRELEVANT CUES

In preceding studies the stimuli differed in only one relevant property. Sometimes, however, stimuli may contain information that is irrelevant to the solution of the problem. If the child ignores such information, it should not interfere with his acquisition of the correct response. If, however, the irrelevant information is distracting or confusing, learning will be impaired. There is little doubt that the presence of irrelevant information interferes with children's learning, especially when children are young.

A direct test of this effect was reported by Lubker (1967). Three groups of eight- to ten-year-old children were presented a two-choice discrimination. Blocks, varying in form, brightness, and size, were combined in different fashions to constitute three series of pairs of blocks that differed in the number of irrelevant dimensions present. The relevant dimension for all subjects was form. For one group of subjects, each pair of stimuli differed only in form, and different pairs of stimuli were used on different trials. The relevant dimension was constant, but on different trials the stimuli differed in size and brightness (e.g., large white *square* versus large white *circle*; small black *square* versus small black *circle*). For a second group of subjects, each pair of stimuli differed in form and brightness (e.g., small *black square* versus small *white circle*); and for a third, each pair differed in form, brightness, and size (e.g., *small black square* versus *large white circle*). Again, different pairs of stimuli were used on different trials, but on each trial the number of within-pair irrelevant dimensions was the same—one for the second group and none for the third group. Learning was significantly slower when either one or two irrelevant dimensions were present within each pair of stimuli than when there were no irrelevant dimensions.

The same result was found in a very similar study by Osler and Kofsky (1965) with four-, six-, and eight-year-olds, where the stimuli varied in form, size, and color. Developmental changes were found in the tendency to respond to irrelevant cues. An analysis of the sequences of the children's

Figure 17-1.   Mean number of correct responses for problems with no within- or between-trial irrelevant stimulus dimensions (0-0), one or two between-trial irrelevant stimulus dimensions, and one or two within-trial irrelevant stimulus dimensions. (From B. J. Lubker, The role of between- and within-setting irrelevant dimensions in children's simultaneous discrimination learning. *Child Development,* 1969, 40, 963. Copyright 1969 Society for Research in Child Development, Inc.)

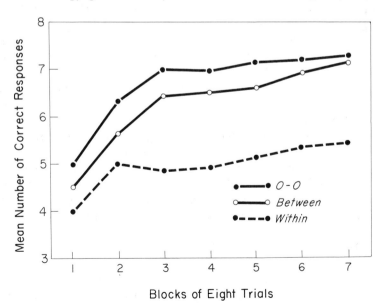

responses revealed that the four- and six-year-olds responded more frequently to the irrelevant dimensions than did the eight-year-olds.

It should be noted that in Lubker's (1967) study the number of between-pair irrelevant dimensions was inversely related to the number of within-pair irrelevant dimensions. For example, when the stimuli differed on one within-pair relevant dimension (form) there were two between-pair irrelevant dimensions (brightness and size); when there were three within-pair relevant dimensions (form, brightness, and size) there were no between-pair irrelevant dimensions. The independent contribution of within- and between-pair irrelevant dimensions was evaluated in a second study (Lubker, 1969). The results were clear. The presence of irrelevant dimensions within a pair of stimuli impairs learning. As can be seen in Figure 17-1, rate of learning was relatively rapid when there were no irrelevant dimensions represented within or between pairs of stimuli. Learning was only slightly slower when there were one or two between-pair irrelevant dimensions (and no within-pair irrelevant dimensions), but it was markedly slower when there were one or two within-pair irrelevant dimensions (and no between-pair irrelevant dimensions).

The degree to which learning is retarded by the presence of irrelevant information is one index of how information is used by children in guiding their response. Another index is the degree to which learning is facilitated when the superfluous information is redundant rather than irrelevant. Eimas (1965) gave kindergarten children a series of two-trial problems in which the cues varied in a systematic manner between the first and second trials. Performance improved in an orderly manner on trial two as the number of redundant cues increased. Even though the second problem could be responded to correctly on the basis of one of the components (e.g., color), learning was more efficient when compound cues were available (e.g., color and form).

The conclusions from these studies are straightforward. We can make learning easier for children, especially for young children, by eliminating irrelevant information, for they have a hard time doing this for themselves. We also can be helpful if we heighten the differences among stimuli by having them differ consistently in more than one aspect. The beginning reader, for example, might be confused less often by letters such as "b" and "d" if, in his first encounters with the letters, they differed in color or size as well as in direction. When irrelevant information is redundant it may be helpful; otherwise it is a hindrance.

VARYING CUES

The preceding studies give us some idea of what happens to learning when we modify stimuli by adding information that is irrelevant to the solution of a problem. What would happen if we introduced a more extreme modification by changing the stimuli from trial to trial? Learning would be impossible, of course, unless the changes conformed to some rule or the changes were made in only one of the stimuli at a time.

In a study by White (1965) the cues were ever-changing. For example, if on a particular trial one of two stimuli included a small square superimposed on a large square, only the small square along with two vertical lines functioned as this stimulus on the subsequent trial. When the child responded correctly on this trial, the stimulus was transformed into one vertical line with a second line attached to a circle. On the next trial, the stimulus appeared as a circle embedded in dots, and so on through multiple changes, with each new stimulus retaining only a portion of the attributes of its immediate predecessor. Ten- and eleven-year-olds were able to track such variations when they occurred for the positive stimulus, and although they seemingly paid little attention to such changes in the negative stimulus, three-fourths of the children subsequently were capable of learning a problem in which changes were made in both the positive and negative stimuli.

A less complex, but related design was used by Walk and Saltz (1965) in a two-choice discrimination learning task. Different numbers of geometrical figures were used as positive and negative cues. For some children the positive cue was a constant single figure, while two or three different figures were used as the negative cue. For other children, only one figure was used as the negative cue and two or three as positive cues. Eight- and nine-year-olds performed better when there was a single positive cue than when there was a single negative cue. For example, 83% of the children given a single positive cue and two negative cues learned the discrimination, but only 25% of the children given a single negative cue and two positive cues were able to do so. For five- and six-year-olds, there were no significant differences according to number of figures used as positive and negative cues; in no case did more than one-third of the children learn the discrimination.

A related study was reported by White (1966), who compared the performance of children on a two-choice object discrimination task where there were single positive and negative cues (the standard type of discrimination learning task), varying negative cues, or varying positive cues. 20 different cues (pictures of birds) were used in the latter two conditions. The greatest differences in rate of learning these three types of problems appeared for preschool children; by the ages of nine and ten the differences had disappeared. Thus when all children are trained to criterion, younger children are more strongly distracted by the presence of varying cues than are older children.

Brown (1969) used the same types of stimuli as White had used, but before the new cues were introduced the children were brought to criterion in learning to discriminate between pictures of two birds. In the test trials the children were shifted to a problem in which there was either (a) a new negative stimulus, (b) a new positive stimulus, (c) a series of 20 new negative stimuli, or (d) a series of 20 new positive stimuli. In all cases the stimuli were pictures of birds. The introduction of a single new stimulus, positive or negative, did not greatly alter the performance of four- or seven-year-olds. However, when a series of positive or negative cues was introduced, performance of four-year-olds, but not of seven-year-olds, was markedly disrupted.

The performance of older children seems to be guided much more by what they think than by what they see. For them, stimuli seem to function as sources of information, rather than as cues that elicit differential tendencies to respond. Even radical changes in the stimuli do not necessarily mean that older children will fail to attend to the characteristics that provide a basis for continuance of correct response. With younger children it is a different matter. When stimuli are presented in such a fashion that distraction might occur, young children's performance begins to deteriorate.

Young children appear to be less able to cope with changes in their environment by themselves. They may be misled in the face of changing cues, even though the changes are orderly and systematic. Maintaining the attention of young children to relevant cues is, as every parent and teacher knows, a difficult and sometimes exhausting task.

STIMULUS FAMILIARIZATION

We know that children prefer what is novel to what is familiar—as long as the novelty is not so great as to be frightening. Such a conclusion is supported both from everyday observation and from research. Under a wide variety of circumstances and from infancy throughout childhood, novel stimuli are more effective than familiar stimuli in attracting children's attention and in leading to positive response. Let us look at a number of examples.

If children are shown a set of forms and then asked to rate both the familiar forms and some new ones on a scale varying from "strongly dislike" to "strongly like," the novel forms are rated more positively (Cantor, 1968). If children have listened to tones or viewed colored lights during one period, they will work harder in a second period to produce the stimuli they had not experienced earlier (Odom, 1964). Or if they have heard one tone and then are free to produce this or a new tone, they prefer the new one (Gullickson, 1966). Children spend more time looking at figures they have not seen before than those they already have viewed, and the effects are roughly the same, whether the test trials are conducted five minutes, two days, or even a week later (Cantor & Cantor, 1964). Further, children look longer at the more novel or more incongruous of two figures (Faw & Nunnally, 1968). If children are allowed to play with one set of toys for varying amounts of time, they later tend to choose novel toys and the strength of this tendency depends upon how long they played with the first toys (Endsley, 1967). Moreover, when free to choose from among several sets of toys, their tendency to choose a set of toys is greater, the more unfamiliar toys there are in a set (Mendel, 1965). There are qualifications to these generalizations, of course. In the last study, for example, novel toys were preferred more by boys than by girls, by older than by younger preschool children, and by children with low rather than with high levels of anxiety. In general, however, the studies lead us to conclude that children are less likely to attend to what is familiar than to what is new.

In the context of studies of learning, it has been suggested many times that the effectiveness of a stimulus in eliciting response decreases as the subject becomes increasingly familiar with it. If this is true, we are faced with a rather ironic state of affairs. The repetition of a stimulus is a necessary component for learning, but by repeating it we may be reducing the readiness with which it will elicit the child's attention.

A number of studies have been conducted with children to explore the validity and implications of this suggestion. In a typical study (Cantor & Cantor, 1964), kindergarteners heard a buzzer or saw a light for 40 two-second exposures before they were introduced to a lever-pulling task. Both the light and buzzer served as signals for response. Speed of reaction was markedly faster for the novel than for the familiar stimulus. As the children became more and more familiar with each type of stimulus during the test trials, reaction times to both stimuli decreased.

In a second study (Cantor & Cantor, 1965), preschool children were given 40 three-second exposures to a red or green light. After this, they were required to press a button of a color corresponding to that of the light. Again, response speeds were faster for the novel than for the familiar stimulus. The magnitude of the effect seemed to depend, however, on whether the preceding trial involved a familiar stimulus. When the data were analyzed trial by trial, speeds were fastest when a novel stimulus followed a familiar stimulus and speeds were slowest when a familiar stimulus followed itself. The Cantors termed this a *change effect*, and assumed that their results might be due to a heightened motivation resulting from the "surprisingness" of a novel stimulus.

The stimulus familiarization effect has been found in numerous other studies (see Cantor, 1969a, 1969b), but what is the underlying mechanism? Several interpretations have been offered. First, novelty may be surprising and may produce an increased level of drive or heightened orientation that facilitates the execution of the motor response. Or, a prolonged attention response may be conditioned during the familiarization trials that interferes with rapid responding in the lever-pulling task. Although studies exploring the various hypotheses have not been exhaustive, the most satisfactory explanatory mechanism seems to be one invoking habituation. Familiarization trials may induce habituation, thereby reducing the effectiveness of the stimulus in eliciting attending responses.

Two studies by Bogartz and Witte (1966) are especially relevant for the evaluation of these hypotheses. In the first study, kindergarteners were required to remove their finger from the response-button at the onset of the stimulus during both the preliminary familiarization and later test trials. Requiring the same response in both sets of trials should decrease the possibility that responses would be learned during the familiarization trials that later would compete with the execution of the motor response. Again, however, the children showed faster speeds of response to the novel than to the familiar stimulus.

Evidence against a surprise interpretation also was obtained. The authors noted that the sequence of trials in the Cantor and Cantor (1965) study had been constructed, inadvertently, so that on 75% of the trials the stimulus was different from that presented on the previous trial. Such a sequence would be likely to produce an alternation pattern of response, and reaction times should be faster when the trials conformed to this pattern (i.e., involved alternation) than when they did not. Schedules therefore were constructed for a second study so that they contained equal numbers of trials with the novel and familiar stimuli, but the trials were organized in such a fashion that they involved 75% alternation-25% repetition or 75% repetition-25% alternation of stimuli. The stimulus familiarization effect was found. More importantly, however, the children tested with the first schedule (75% alternation-25% repetition) responded faster on changed than on unchanged trials, whereas those tested with the second schedule (75% repetition-25% alternation) responded faster on unchanged than on changed trials. Rate of response was more rapid, therefore, when the event corresponded to the pattern of events the child had learned to expect, whether the pattern was one of alternation or repetition. Rapid response to the change of stimuli seems to be due to the structure of the schedules rather than to novelty.

Only the habituation hypothesis has not been discredited. This hypothesis has considerable strength, for it not only accounts for a drop in reaction time across trials, but also predicts that the drop will be faster for stimuli to which the child has been exposed in pre-experimental trials than for novel stimuli. Unfortunately, the stimulus familiarization effect has been investigated only with lever-pulling and button-pressing tasks; thus we are unable to evaluate its significance for other types of learning.

REPETITION WITH REWARD

Does experience with a stimulus always lead to diminished effectiveness in eliciting response? Not necessarily. In studies of stimulus familiarization the stimulus was presented in a neutral context; it never was followed by reward or any form of positive evaluation. The results may be quite different if the child's experience with materials leads to some significant consequence.

A major body of information comes from a series of studies by Nunnally and his associates, who have isolated some of the effects of pairing reward and punishment with neutral stimuli. The design of these studies is similar to those used in studying secondary reinforcement, but rather than being concerned with the influences of rewards in modifying the effectiveness of the stimuli as secondary reinforcers, the primary interest is in how such experiences alter the child's reactions to the stimuli.

The apparatus used in some of the studies was a spin-wheel. When the pointer stopped on a particular nonsense syllable, a penny was delivered; when it stopped on the others, the children had to give back a penny or nothing happened. In two studies (Nunnally, Duchnowski, & Parker, 1965; Nunnally, Stevens, & Hall, 1965) children described the nonsense syllable associated with reward in more favorable terms than the others; they more often expected it to be associated with reward in another game; and they looked at it longer in a "looking box" than at other nonsense syllables.

In a similar study, Hall (1967) had second- and third-grade boys perform for 12 days with a simulated slot machine. When one geometric form appeared in the aperture of the machine, a penny was delivered. Nondelivery of a penny was preceded by the appearance of a second form. Subsequently, there were seven days in which no pennies were delivered. After each session with the slot machine the children were asked to pick from among the positive, negative, and a neutral form the one they thought was "best," "nice," "awful," and so on. The form that had been associated with payoff was evaluated more positively than the neutral form in all 19 sessions (12 training, 7 extinction); the neutral form, in turn, was evaluated more positively than the form associated with nonreward.

The basic approach was repeated within the context of a study of discrimination learning (Nunnally & Faw, 1968). The purpose was to determine whether the affective and attentional value of a stimulus is altered by prior experiences of reward or punishment. Third graders were shown three lids on which the names of three nonsense syllables were printed. When the child turned over the lid, he found written on the underside, "Earn 2¢," "Pay 2¢," or the underside was blank. The lids were used in a standard two-choice discrimination learning task. All combinations of pairs of lids were presented and the trials were continued until the child chose the correct (rewarding) lid and/or avoided the "penalty" lid six times in a row.

The children returned four days later and were given three tasks. Verbal evaluation of the forms was assessed by showing the children three stick figures to which the names of the nonsense syllables were attached. Five positive, five neutral, and five negative statements were read and the children were asked to identify the stick figure that best corresponded to these statements. Selective attention was measured with a "looking box" in which the child could depress a button that allowed him to look at the nonsense syllable as long as he wished. Finally, expectancy for reward was tested on a spin-wheel game. The children were asked to anticipate whether they would win or lose candy, or whether nothing would happen, depending on the nonsense syllable on which the pointer landed. Around the circumference of the wheel the three nonsense syllables were printed repeatedly, thus providing a potential basis for such expectations. The nonsense syllable associated with reward was evaluated more positively, looked at longer, and associated with a greater expectancy of success than were the negative and neutral nonsense syllables. Results for the latter two nonsense syllables did not differ from each other.

We conclude from these studies that more is acquired during the course of learning than the particular verbal or motor responses in which the experimenter or teacher are interested. The child's reactions to stimuli seem to be altered by the experiences he has with them. Depending on whether the experiences are satisfying or unproductive, the child is likely to evaluate the stimulus differently, to have different expectations about its general rewarding properties, and to spend different amounts of time looking at it. While mere repetition of a stimulus may lead to habituation, we might expect that if the child has had pleasant experiences with stimuli before encountering them in a learning task, they will be more likely to attract his attention, and thereby produce more rapid learning.

PREFERENCES

From the preceding discussion we might deduce that children use all aspects of the stimulus situation with equal effectiveness in learning a discrimination problem. That they do not is illustrated in studies in which the relevant cue coincides with or is discordant with the child's preferences. This was found to be the case in studies of discrimination-shift problems discussed earlier, and is true in other studies as well. For example, after the fourth year children generally prefer form over color, even though below that age they tend to prefer color over form as a means of classifying stimuli. Suchman and Trabasso (1966) have demonstrated with ten-year-olds that children who showed a preference for form over color in pretests later learned to sort cards faster by form than by color, with the opposite effect occurring for children who preferred color over form. In a related experiment, Wolff (1966) found that some seven-year-old children preferred height and some preferred brightness as a means of classifying stimuli. When the children later were presented a two-choice discrimination using stimuli that differed both in height and brightness, those who had preferred brightness learned a brightness discrimination more rapidly than a height discrimination and those who had preferred height learned the height discrimination more rapidly.

Another example of how the choice of stimuli may affect learning is found in a study by Shepp (1963), where pieces of candy were used both as discriminative stimuli and as reinforcers. More rapid learning occurred when the reward was candy of the same form and color as the positive cue than when it was dissimilar to both the positive and negative cues, or when it was identical to the negative cue. The tendency to select a stimulus was greater when it was identical to the one functioning as the reinforcer.

Perhaps the most extensive investigation relating stimulus preferences and discrimination learning has been reported by Gliner, Pick, Pick, and Hales (1969). A series of parallel experiments were conducted in which children were required to discriminate haptically (by touch) and visually between objects differing in shape and texture. The significance of the research is enhanced by the fact that careful psychophysical studies were conducted so that values of shape and texture could be used that were comparable in their discriminability. Texture was varied by covering different stimuli with sandpaper of 15 different degrees of courseness. Variations in shape were created by changing the ratio of the axes of an ellipse to produce 15 shapes ranging from a circle to an elongated ellipse. The subjects were from kindergarten and the third grade.

Children were presented a two-choice, haptic discrimination task with stimuli that differed in both shape and texture. Would they consistently use one or the other of the dimensions to solve the problem when both were available and equal in a psychophysical sense? Test trials were conducted in which the relations between shape and texture present during the original learning trials were reversed. If the child had been trained to choose a rough, elongated object rather than a smooth, round object, test trials were conducted with a rough, round object and a smooth, elongated object. If the child chose the rough object on the test trials, he was assumed to have responded during the training trials to differences in texture, and if he chose the elongated object he was assumed to have responded earlier to differences in shape. On the first test trial, 64% of the kindergarteners responded on the basis of texture, and 67% of the third graders responded on the basis of shape. Evidence was found, therefore, both for dimensional preferences and a change in these preferences with age. When the study was repeated with visual discrimination of the two stimuli, both kindergarteners and third graders responded overwhelmingly on the basis of shape (95% and 88%, respectively).

An effort was made to determine whether preferences can be modified by varying the discriminability of the stimuli. Stimuli were selected so that their difference in the nonpreferred dimension was more readily discriminable than that in the preferred dimension. The stimuli differed more markedly in shape (nonpreferred dimension) than in texture for the kindergarten children, and for third graders the differences in texture (nonpreferred dimension) were greater than the differences in shape. Under these conditions, it was found that the basis of response in haptic discrimination could be shifted for kindergarteners, but third graders continued to respond on the basis of their preferred dimension. Visual preferences were even less subject to modification. Both kindergarteners and third graders continued to respond on the basis of shape, their preferred dimension, even when the difference between the two shapes was slight and the difference between the two textures was large.

Does this necessarily mean that attention is directed so selectively that children learn nothing about differences that exist between the stimuli in the nonpreferred dimension? In visual discriminations, children appear to attend primarily to differences in shape, but while doing this they also may be acquiring information about differences in texture. If this were the case, experience in discriminating between objects differing in both shape and texture should facilitate learning of a problem in which the objects no longer differ in shape, but the original differences in texture are preserved. Negative results were obtained. Children at neither age appeared to have learned enough about the differences in texture to improve their performance in the second problem.

Why children have strong preferences for different attributes of stimuli remains unclear. Differences in texture may have more value for the development of touch than for the development of vision. Form may convey more useful information than color or texture for the visual experiences of older children. Whatever the explanation, such preferences are present at an early age and seem to become more strongly entrenched as the child grows older. The moral that may be derived from these studies is that one should capitalize on such preferences whenever possible, and devise other means of capturing the child's attention when the problem requires response to a nonpreferred dimension.

RESPONSE BIASES

Before leaving this discussion, we should consider how preferences for particular types of response also may influence children's rates of learning.

Let us take the situation to its extreme. We will show the child two identical objects and reinforce whichever choice the child makes. In such a two-choice task with undiscriminable stimuli and nondifferential reward, three-year-olds tend to persevere in responding to the same position whereas four-year-olds tend to alternate their choices between the positions (Jeffrey & Cohen, 1965). Greene (1964) reported similar results for four- and five-year olds. On trial 2 of a two-choice color discrimination problem, nearly 70% of the children shifted their response to the stimulus that was not chosen on trial 1.

The tendency for young children to alternate responses is not restricted to the artificial situations used in these studies, for children also alternate their choices when they are allowed to choose candy of two different colors (Strain, Unikel, & Adams, 1969) or when they are allowed to choose one of two toys, such as toy locomotives, cars, or crayons (Harris, 1965).

Schusterman (1963) reported effects similar to those found by Jeffrey and Cohen for three- and five-year-olds, but ten-year-olds displayed neither response pattern. Rieber (1966) repeated the Jeffrey and Cohen study with seven- and nine-year-old children. Nearly three-fourths of the children showed alternating behavior when either response was consistently reinforced, but the number of alternations dropped significantly when response to each stimulus received only partial reinforcement. Considering these studies, it appears that a preference for alternation is present at age four, persists through age eight, and drops out by age ten.

There are several possible interpretations of this effect. Children may switch their response to a new stimulus out of curiosity to discover what would happen if it were chosen; they may have learned to expect that adults are unlikely to reinforce a particular choice consistently; or they may wish to be "fair" and give each alternative an equal chance of being selected. Whatever the ultimate explanation, learning may be impaired when the requirements of the task fail to coincide with the tendency to alternate responses. The difficulties encountered in trying to train young children in discrimination learning tasks often can be traced to the operation of such biases. Stimulus factors lose their potency if the child settles for a reward on every two or three trials and persists in demonstrating response biases that are independent of the stimuli with which he is confronted.

CONCLUSIONS

Studies of attention and discrimination learning reveal how a problem can be made easy or difficult for children, depending upon how we represent the relevant cues and display the stimuli. The importance of such factors has been appreciated only recently, for earlier investigators were more concerned with mechanisms relating stimulus and response than with the role of attention in learning.

The simplest way in which the child's attention can be directed to the relevant features of the discriminative stimuli is by emphasizing or highlighting differences between the stimuli. Children can learn relatively difficult discriminations if they have had previous experience with simple discriminations in which the difference between the positive and negative cues is exaggerated, or if the positive cue is dominant during the early phases of their training.

The amount of relevant information conveyed by stimuli exerts an important influence on learning. If stimuli are three-dimensional, or if they differ from each other in more than one visual property, children learn a discrimination rapidly. If, on the other hand, the additional information is irrelevant to solution of the problem, that information interferes with learning. Interference is especially marked when children are young, for young children are less able to isolate relevant and disregard irrelevant information than are older children. The introduction of new positive or negative cues also disrupts the performance of young children; new cues seem to distract and confuse them and their performance falters for long periods of time. Older children, however, display a remarkable ability to maintain correct response in such problems.

Spatial relations between stimulus and response influence rate of learning through their effect on attention. Learning is more rapid when stimulus and response are spatially adjacent than when they are remote from each other, apparently because children attend more closely to where they are responding than to other regions of the experimental situation. Attention also is influenced by the relative novelty of a stimulus. Novel stimuli elicit attention, but frequent repetition of a stimulus leads to habituation, with an accompanying diminution in attention. The negative influence of habituation can be counterbalanced to some degree, however, if the stimulus is associated repeatedly with reward. Stimuli associated with reward are attended to later for longer periods of time, are evaluated more positively, and are expected to lead to reward in other situations. Children evidence strong preferences for attending to particular attributes of stimuli, and learning is rapid when the demands of the task coincide with these preferences. Otherwise, children's tendencies to direct their attention to certain features of the stimuli in preference to others may interfere with effective learning.

By now it is obvious that analysis of the learning process will be incomplete, and necessarily inadequate, until the roles of attention and perception are better understood. We are faced with two general questions, the first of which has been considered in the present chapter. How can we gain better control of children's attention, and how can we be assured that the child's perception of the stimulus will correspond to the requirements of the task? Psychologists generally have been more interested in how perceptual processes are learned than in relating perception to other forms of learning. This relation was important to Gestalt psychologists, who defined learning as a perceptual reorganization of the field, but following the decline of Gestalt psychology, perception and learning have for the most part gone their separate ways. During the past decade, however, there has been a reawakening of interest in the role of attention, and perception has been reunited with learning in studies of perceptual learning. With the introductory information of the present chapter in mind, we will proceed to consider these topics more thoroughly in the next two chapters.

18

Attention and Transfer

The development and use of language makes it possible for the child to relate one situation to another in terms of common words or phrases. Similarly, a child who has learned to attend to a particular dimension of the stimuli, such as size, subsequently may discriminate among stimuli on the basis of size more readily than a child who has not had the earlier experience. Thus an alternative to verbal mediation is mediation that occurs through the activation of attending or observing responses acquired through earlier experience in similar situations. There has been controversy about the relative merits of these two forms of mediation, and the controversy has stemmed in part from the fact that the two hypotheses frequently yield equivalent predictions. Before being able to assess their relative merits, however, we must look at the literature on the relation of attention and transfer.

We will deal with transfer as it exists in three general types of problems: stimulus generalization, discrimination learning, and cross-modal transfer. While the research in each case will be discussed in some detail, the major purpose behind these discussions will be to relate the phenomena to the topic of attention.

STIMULUS GENERALIZATION

Learning ordinarily is not totally stimulus-specific. If there were no transfer of information gained in one context to other contexts, learning would have to be vastly more extensive and reiterative. At the same time, if generalization is too extensive, responses may be made to situations that are so dissimilar to the one in which the response originally was learned that behavior may turn out to be inappropriate.

The concept of stimulus generalization was used first in studies of conditioning with animals. Stimuli similar to the conditioned stimulus were found to be capable of eliciting the conditioned response in a somewhat diminished form, and the more dissimilar the test stimuli were to the conditioned stimulus, the smaller the amount of generalization. Studies with children usually have dealt with spatial generalization. The child is seated before an array of lights located on a horizontal arc. The light immediately in front of the child is turned on and the child is trained to depress or release a key at the moment of the onset of the light. After a series of training trials conducted in this manner, peripheral lights are illuminated, one by one. Will the child respond to the peripheral lights and will the frequency of his response depend upon the spatial remoteness of these lights from the central light?

Developmental Studies

From a developmental point of view, mature individuals might be expected to show more restricted gradients of stimulus generalization than younger children. At least this is what casual observation of children might lead us to expect. The four-month-old, for example, may respond to other adults in the same way he responds to his mother. Later, only the mother or familiar adults may elicit behavior such as the social smile.

Several studies have supported the conclusion that stimulus generaliza-

Figure 18-1. Gradients of stimulus generalization as a function of mental age. (From V. J. Tempone, Stimulus generalization as a function of mental age. *Child Development,* 1965, 36, 232. Copyright 1965 Society for Research in Child Development, Inc.)

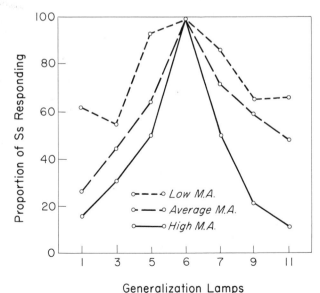

tion decreases as the child grows older. Mednick and Lehtinen (1957) used seven- to nine- and ten- to twelve-year olds on the spatial generalization task. The stimulus generalization gradient, as assessed by frequency of response to peripheral lights, was flatter for the younger children. Tempone (1965) found a similar effect when mental rather than chronological age was varied. The children were all eight years old, but had mean mental ages of 6.6, 8.8, and 10.9 years. As may be seen in Figure 18-1, the slope of the generalization gradient became steeper with increasing mental age.

What do such findings mean? Do they reflect some fundamental process, or are they the product of other factors? In most studies of stimulus generalization the subjects are told to respond as rapidly as possible and not to be concerned if they make errors. Reinforcement for correct response in these studies is verbal encouragement, a form of reinforcement that may be less effective with younger than with older children. It is possible, therefore, that the greater generalization of younger children may reflect lack of interest, or lack of attention to the task.

To test this possibility, Jeffrey and Skager (1962) made an effort to increase children's motivation to attend closely to the stimuli during the training trials. Each correct response was rewarded with a poker chip and the children were penalized for incorrect response by being required to relinquish a chip. The chips could be cashed in at the end of the game to see a movie. The procedure was identical for a control group, except that no poker chips were used. The proportion of six- to seven-year-olds showing generalization to peripheral lights was significantly smaller with the added incentive than without it. There was no significant difference in performance between the two conditions for nine- to twelve-year-olds. Furthermore, when material rewards were present, differences in stimulus generalization between the two age groups disappeared. It seems that if children are highly motivated to attend to the training stimulus, they are more likely to differentiate it from other stimuli during the test trials.

The amount of experience children have with the training stimulus also may influence stimulus generalization differentially at different ages. According to a theory such as Spence's, the strength of the generalized tendency to respond to other stimuli is dependent upon the strength of the response acquired in training. An increase in the number of training trials should produce greater stimulus generalization. This line of reasoning should be applicable to the performance of young children. With older children, however, the opposite effect might be expected. Older children presumably respond on the basis of some form of mediation. With increasing amounts of training, the cues defining the effective stimulus should become increasingly redundant, thereby making it more likely that a specific and relevant mediating response would be developed. Such a mediator should operate to restrict the degree of stimulus generalization. Tempone

(1966) investigated these predictions. Two groups of children, 6½ to 7½ and 10½ to 12 years old, were presented 15, 30, or 45 training trials in the spatial generalization task. As predicted, the mean number of responses to the generalization lights increased for the younger children, but decreased for the older children with increasing amounts of training.

These studies leave the status of developmental changes in stimulus generalization unclear. They set forth the possibility that differences in stimulus generalization found according to chronological and mental age may be influenced by the child's motivation to attend to the stimuli and the application of mediating responses. If this is true, developmental changes in stimulus generalization represent a secondary rather than a primary effect.

Other Variables

Several studies have investigated the effects of variables other than developmental status. A series of studies with preschool children, all of which used lever-pressing as the response and lights varying in hue or brightness as the stimuli, have been reported by Spiker and White.

Generalization may be increased if children are trained with multiple rather than single stimuli. White and Spiker (1960), assuming that training with several different stimuli would encourage children to generalize, trained an experimental group with three stimuli differing in hue and brightness. Responses to all three stimuli were reinforced. The control group was trained with only one of the stimuli. A significantly greater number of generalized responses was made when training had been conducted with multiple stimuli. In a related study, White (1958) investigated the hypothesis that a test stimulus differing from the training stimulus on only one dimension will elicit more generalized responses than will a test stimulus differing on two dimensions. The test stimuli differed from the training stimuli in brightness, hue, or brightness and hue. Thus dissimilarity between training and test stimuli was created by varying the number of different attributes rather than the values of one attribute. As predicted, test stimuli that differed from the training stimulus on two attributes elicited fewer generalized responses than did stimuli differing on only one attribute.

A study by Tempone (1968) with older children is especially illuminating. Tempone trained six- and seven-year-olds under one of four conditions. Lever-pulls in the presence of a ten-inch black square always were reinforced. Differences among training conditions were created by varying the stimulus in whose presence lever-pulls were not reinforced. For different groups, the negative stimulus was a nine-inch black triangle, a four-inch gray square, a white screen, or a black screen. In the first two cases the positive and negative stimuli could be compared on the basis of differences in their contours, while in the latter two cases such comparisons were impossible. It was hypothesized that contour would become more salient and would be attended to more closely when the positive and negative stimuli differed on this attribute than when they did not. As a consequence, children should discriminate differences between the training and test stimuli more readily in the former than in the latter case.

As can be seen in Figure 18-2, tests for generalization with black squares of ten, six, and four square inches revealed no gradient of stimulus generalization when training was conducted with a negative stimulus that possessed no contour. Children responded to the test stimuli at as high a level as they had to the training stimulus. When the negative stimulus did possess contour, a typical gradient of stimulus generalization was found. Thus when the discrimination between the positive and negative cues could be made only on the basis of the presence or absence of a form, the children responded to the novel forms in a nondifferential fashion. When they were required to attend to form as a means of discrimination between the positive and negative cues, they were less likely to respond to the novel stimuli in the way they had to the training stimulus.

Figure 18-2.   Mean number of responses made to training and test stimuli when there was a comparison stimulus with contours and when no comparison stimulus was present. (From V. J. Tempone, The nature of the stimulus in primary stimulus generalization. *Canadian Journal of Psychology,* 1968, 22, 247, © 1968 *Canadian Journal of Psychology.*)

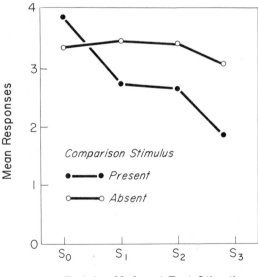

Training (S_0) and Test Stimuli

Results such as these call the concept of stimulus generalization into question. The frequency of generalization could not be derived from the absolute properties of the positive stimulus, for the positive stimulus was the same in all conditions. Rather, the frequency was determined by the characteristics of the negative stimulus. More generally, these findings support the view that the perceptual properties of a stimulus are not dependent upon the absolute characteristics of the stimulus itself, but gain meaning only as the stimulus is compared and contrasted with other stimuli.

Stimulus generalization is dependent then on the child's ability to discriminate between the training and test stimuli. (Other research related to this conclusion may be found in Prokasy and Hall, 1963.) Discrimination between the training and test stimuli occurs more readily, and stimulus generalization thereby is reduced, when the child is highly motivated to attend to the positive and negative stimuli during training, when the differences among stimuli are emphasized by conducting the training with several different stimuli, and when the differences between the training and test stimuli differ on more than a single dimension. Whether a previously learned response will be made to novel stimuli appears to depend upon how well the child has isolated and attended to the distinctive characteristics of the positive stimulus. If he fails to do this, response is indiscriminate. If he does do this, he quickly ceases to make the previously learned response.

DISCRIMINATION LEARNING

Most learning curves portray learning as a negatively accelerating function in which performance improves less and less rapidly as the number of trials increases. Plotting average numbers of correct responses in this manner does not always present a representative picture of the performance by individual subjects. Although average level of performance within a given block of trials may reflect an intermediate value, some children may be performing quite effectively while others are responding at a chance level. Perhaps a more useful approach to summarizing performance would be to plot what is called a backward learning curve. We could look first at the block of trials where each child reached the criterion for learning and plot changes in his performance backward from this point. When this is done, the curves often reveal a sharp increase in frequency of correct response in the vicinity of the criterial trials, preceded by a plateau of varying duration in which there is little evidence of progress. When viewed in this way learning does not appear to be a continuous process, but may be considered to involve two stages. During the first stage the child may be learning to attend to the appropriate stimulus dimensions and during the second stage, to associate the defined response with the correct stimulus (Mackintosh, 1965; Zeaman & House, 1963). According to this view, slow learning is attributed to the child's failure to attend to the appropriate stimulus dimension. Once attention is directed to the relevant dimension rapid improvement in performance would be expected.

Transfer is handled by assuming that the attentional response learned during the solution of the original problem may be elicited by the new set of stimuli. If this happens, attention is directed immediately to the relevant dimension, and the child has only to learn which of the stimuli now is correct. This is, therefore, a two-process theory. The mediator is an attentional response and the two processes consist of (a) discriminating and attending to the relevant dimension, and (b) attaching the choice-response to one of the cues.

It is assumed by attentional theorists that discrimination is mediated at all ages. By making this assumption they place this model in direct conflict with those positing that mediation occurs through verbal means and is dependent upon the child's level of linguistic development. This does not necessarily mean that there are no developmental changes in attentional mediation. Young children still may not mediate, even though they have the ability to do so. According to this view, the greater superiority in learning that occurs with increasing age is considered to be a result of the greater capability of the older child in detecting relevant stimulus dimensions, presumably because of greater prior experience with such dimensions. Slow learning is attributed to the child's failure to attend to the appropriate stimulus dimension. Once attention is directed to the relevant dimension, rapid improvement in performance is expected. It should be possible, therefore, to increase mediation by giving the child experience that increases the salience of the relevant cues, or by using cues that already are salient for the child. [For a discussion of the historical background of the verbal and attentional mediation models, see Tighe and Tighe (1966).]

Discrimination-Shifts

The attentional model is immediately applicable to the discussion of intra- and extradimensional shifts. According to this model, the two types of shift will be learned at different rates. Intradimensional (reversal) shifts will be learned rapidly, for the attentional response developed during original discrimination training is applicable to the new problem. Relieved of the necessity of developing a new attentional response, the child merely needs to ascertain which of the values on the relevant dimension is correct. Extradimensional shifts, on the other hand, should be learned more slowly.

The previously acquired attentional response is inappropriate and the child must acquire a new attentional response to the currently relevant dimension. Until a new mediating response is acquired, the child cannot proceed to the next step of learning which choice is correct.

Arguments can be summoned from a number of studies to support the contention that the salience of the cues is a determining variable in children's performance on discrimination-shift problems. It will be recalled, for example, that in both the Mumbauer and Odom (1967) and Smiley and Weir (1966) studies, training with dominant or salient dimensions was associated with rapid learning of the original discrimination and frequent or rapid reversal shifts. When the nondominant dimension was relevant in the original problem (and the dominant dimension was relevant in the second problem) the original discrimination was learned slowly and there was rapid acquisition of extradimensional shifts. Mumbauer and Odom also found that labeling was effective in increasing reversal shifts only when the nondominant dimension was relevant; when the dominant dimension was relevant, reversal shifts occurred no more rapidly for children who labeled the stimuli than for those who did not. Although the results of studies such as these are in line with predictions from an attentional model, it is possible to interpret the effects equally well by a verbal mediation model. This lack of definitiveness exists, in part, because the children in these studies were at least five years old, and children of this age are capable of verbal mediation. To preclude, or at least greatly reduce the possibility that children would use verbal mediators, it is necessary to study younger children.

One such study is that of Caron (1969), who investigated the learning of discrimination-shifts by three-year-olds, a group that is unlikely to be capable of spontaneous verbal mediation. The stimuli varied in brightness and height. Before beginning the experiment, tests were conducted to determine which dimension was dominant for each child. On the basis of this information, the children were assigned to one of three groups: (a) dominant dimension relevant, (b) nondominant dimension relevant, or (c) nondominant dimension relevant following pre-experimental games. For the third group, an effort was made to increase the salience of the nondominant dimension by having children play a matching game in which they were required to attend brightness or height, whichever was their nondominant dimension. No effort was made to assess the dimensional preferences of children serving in a control group.

After learning the original discrimination, half of the children were presented a reversal shift, and half, an extradimensional (nonreversal) shift. The results are summarized in Figure 18-3. The extradimensional shift was more difficult than the reversal shift, except when the shift was from the nondominant to the dominant dimension. Children for whom the relevant dimension was dominant, or whose salience was increased by pretraining games, demonstrated faster learning on the original problem, faster learning on the reversal problem, and slower learning on the extra-dimensional shifts than did children who were trained originally with the dimension which for them was not dominant. In view of the generally demonstrated deficiencies of three-year-olds in verbal mediation, the attentional hypothesis appears to account for the results at this age level more rapidly than can a hypothesis invoking verbal mediation.

What would happen if young children's attention were directed to an attribute of the stimuli that was not in concordance with their verbaliza-tions about the stimuli? To answer this question McConnell (1964) at-tempted to pit verbal and attentional mediators against each other. Again, the subjects were three-year-olds, and the stimuli differed in brightness and height. Rather than assessing the relative dominance of the two dimensions for the subjects, an effort was made to increase the perceptual salience of height or brightness by varying the manner in which the stim-uli were displayed. A tray contained 40 cylinders, 10 each of tall black, short black, tall white, and short white cylinders. All of the tall cylinders were placed on one side of the tray and all of the short cylinders were placed on the opposite side, or the cylinders were divided in a similar

Figure 18-3.   Mean trials to criterion on reversal and extradimen-sional shifts for groups trained originally with dimensions that were dominant, nondominant, or whose salience was increased by pretrain-ing. (Data from A. J. Caron, Discrimination shifts in three-year-olds as a function of dimensional salience. *Developmental Psychology,* 1969, 1, 337.)

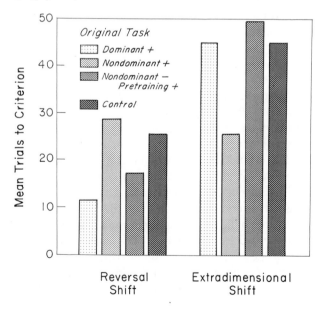

fashion according to brightness. The cylinders appeared in a random array for the control subjects.

In commencing each trial, the experimenter selected a tall black and a small white cylinder from the tray. Choices of one of the stimuli were consistently correct. Children who viewed the objects arranged by height were required to verbalize the basis of each choice by brightness; those viewing the objects arranged by brightness were required to verbalize on the basis of height. After this discrimination was learned, the response-reward contingencies were reversed. In addition, trials were interspersed in which a short black and a tall white cylinder were presented. Height was the relevant dimension for both pairs of stimuli on the second problem. Verbalization was no longer required and the stimuli appeared in a random arrangement on the tray.

Arrangement by height (and verbalization by brightness) produced a slight facilitating effect on performance in the second task, but arrangement by brightness (and verbalization by height) had a marked interfering effect. Relevant verbalization was not sufficient to overcome the effects of the arrangement in which the child had viewed the stimuli. The results for groups of eight-year-olds were quite different. For them, relevant verbalization was helpful, for they learned the second discrimination more readily after they had verbalized by height than did eight-year-old control subjects. The three-year-olds apparently developed an attentional mediator during the first task that transferred to the second task, and this attentional mediator had a stronger directing effect on their performance than did their previous verbalizations.

These studies are with young children. There are others, too, such as that of Trabasso, Stave, and Eichberg (1969) with four-year-olds, that add support to the hypothesis that the salience of cues is a determining factor in producing faster original learning and more frequent reversal shifts. Taken together, these results and those discussed in Chapter 9 lead one to consider seriously the final conclusion reached by Wolff (1967) in his extensive review of discrimination-shift studies that "the principal factors operating in the shift process *in general* are probably attentional in nature." Although attentional and verbal mediation models can account equally well for the results of studies with older children, the attentional hypothesis is the more effective hypothesis for understanding the results obtained with children under five.

Transfer of Concepts

Young children have great diffiuclty in learning problems in which they must respond to classes of stimuli rather than to a specific stimulus. According to the verbal mediation hypothesis, this difficulty is a result of their inability to produce and use verbal labels. If, for example, the young child is required to choose only stimuli that are white, regardless of their form or size, transfer from one set of stimuli to another should occur only if the child has had extensive training in labeling the relevant attribute. In contrast, an attentional model predicts that, independent of verbal ability, transfer will occur if the child is provided experience through which the salience of the relevant feature is enhanced. As was the case with shift problems, the attentional model can be assessed most meaningfully if "preverbal" children are used as subjects.

Caron (1968) offers convincing evidence that young children, incapable of using or responding appropriately to the relevant verbal labels, can solve problems involving multiple examples of a particular concept. The stimuli were pairs of drawings representing angular and curved figures, and the child's task was to learn to choose one of these two types of figures in a series of problems. Before beginning the study the children were screened to insure that they were unable to use or respond correctly to labels such as "pointy" or "round." Efforts then were made to increase the salience of the relevant dimension through several training procedures. The assumption was that by increasing the probability children would attend to the relevant dimension, the task of sorting out the correct and incorrect examples could be done with relative ease.

Among the methods used in pretraining was a fading-in procedure in which the critical feature appeared fiirst in isolation and then, through a series of steps, was completely incorporated into the fully formed figure. A fitting-in procedure required the child to find figures that contained a part that would fit into a V cut out of a board. To do this they had to select the angular forms and reject the rounded forms. In later stages they merely pointed to the stimulus that fitted the V. The third procedure directed the child's attention to the relevant cue by requiring him to place his finger on one of the tips, rather than on the body of the figure. Appropriate control groups were given experience in inserting full figures into a box-like receptacle or in viewing fully formed figures. After completing the training programs the children were given discrimination learning trials with the fully formed figures, generalization trials with new pairs of figures, and two forms of post-test. In the post-tests the child was shown a toy train and told that one form in each pair would make the train go and one would make the train stop. He was to find out how he could make the proper choices. This phase was continued with new stimuli and the child was asked to say whether they would make the train go or stop.

The training procedures were highly successful. The degree to which performance was aided by these procedures is seen in the fact that when stimulus pairs two through five were presented on the first discrimination problems, 25 of the 52 children made no errors, while only 2 of the 28 control subjects did so. Similar results were found on the generalization and other test trials. Generally, the most effective procedure for facilitating later learning was one that combined the child's fitting the figures into the V and pointing to one of the corners of the figures.

At the conclusion of the study an effort was made to determine whether the subjects were able to verbalize the principle for solution. Only four children, two in the experimental and two in the control groups, were able to describe the basis for their choices. It seems very unlikely, therefore, that the children were responding through verbal mediation. The study demonstrates that careful training in increasing the salience of the relevant dimension enables preschool children to respond correctly to multiple examples of abstract concepts about which they are incapable of verbalizing.

Comments

Which is the more powerful explanatory concept: verbal or attentional mediation? For older children, we do not know and probably cannot define a method for determining the answer. Older children are capable of mediating verbally and attending selectively. It may be that the two hypotheses are closely interrelated. Verbalization may have a directing effect on attention, and conversely, the appearance of salient cues may be conducive to verbalization about these cues. With younger children, the story is different. As seen in the preceding studies and in many others that have been discussed, three-year-olds have difficulty in labeling and producing relevant verbalizations. Nevertheless, when appropriate conditions are constructed to increase the salience of the cues, something like attentional mediation occurs. Having responded to one stimulus dimension in an initial problem, subsequent problems whose solution is dependent upon response to this dimension are easy for the young child. If the salient dimension is incorrect, performance suffers from interference.

Perhaps both the verbal and attentional mediation hypotheses are valid, but their applicability may depend on the age of the child. The young child's mediating responses may be strongly determined by the perceptual characteristics of the stimuli, while those of older children may be more dependent upon the child's ability to transform his perceptions into words. Such a developmental progression is not a novel proposal, for Piaget has given many examples of how the perceptual control of the behavior of the young child is relinquished to verbal control as the child grows older. What both Piaget and these studies seem to be saying is that for the young child, behavior is strongly influenced by action and perception; for the older child, behavior is more commonly a product of language and thought. Whatever the resolution of this argument, it seems appropriate to conclude that we may accomplish more in leading young children to effective learning by capturing their attention than by plying them with words. A similar argument has been made by Jeffrey (1968) in a discussion of the relation of attention to early cognitive development.

CROSS-MODAL TRANSFER

A third form of transfer now will be considered. In both stimulus generalization and discrimination learning, transfer was within a single sensory modality. We have seen, for example, that certain types of experience in learning a visual discrimination may be of benefit in learning other problems that also involve visual discrimination. Might not transfer also occur across sensory modalities? That is, might not information gained through the use of one modality, such as vision, be of assistance in solving subsequent problems involving the same stimuli, but requiring the use of a second modality, such as touch?

The attentional model discussed in the preceding section would have some difficulty in interpreting positive results, for no mechanism is proposed whereby the mediating attentional responses that control visual perception could be transferred, for example, to the movements of the hand required in tactual discrimination. A verbal mediation hypothesis would not encounter such difficulties. For example, if the child has verbalized that "circle" is correct on the basis of visual experience, he could use this mediating response when faced with a tactual discrimination.

Recognition

Before discussing research on cross-modal transfer it could be helpful to review several developmental studies of intra- and cross-modal recognition; that is, studies of children's ability to recognize objects after encountering the objects with the same or a different sensory modality. A typical example is a study by Zinchencko and Ruzskaya with three- through six-

Table 18-1.   Percentage visual recognition errors after various forms of exploratory activity

Exploratory Activity	Chronological Age			
	3	4	5	6
Visual	50.0	28.5	0	2.5
Tactual	47.7	42.3	25.0	23.1
Visual + Tactical	30.8	21.0	11.5	1.9
Practical Manipulation	15.4	10.5	0	0

Data from A. V. Zaporozhets, The development of perception in the preschool child. In P. H. Mussen (Ed.), *European research in cognitive development. Monographs of the Society for Research in Child Development*, 1965, 30, 89.

year-olds reported by Zaporozhets (1965, p. 89). Children were tested for
visual recognition of abstract forms after one of four types of exploratory
experience: visual, tactual, visual and tactual, or "practical manipulation"
(i.e., experience in inserting the forms into corresponding holes in a
board). As can be seen in Table 18-1, both intra- and cross-modal recognition improved rapidly by the sixth year. Visual recognition was as difficult for three-year-olds after visual as after tactual exploration, but at the
other ages tactual exploration resulted in poorer visual recognition than
did visual exploration. Combined visual and tactual exploration was more
effective at practically all ages than exploration with either mode alone.
The most effective exploratory activity was practical manipulation, for at
all ages the percentage of errors was low. Fitting the objects into a form-
board presumably required the children to attend closely to the characteristics defining each object.

Abravanel (1968a) investigated cross-modal recognition of spatial dimensions and found developmental changes comparable to those of the
preceding study. Rapid developmental changes in recognition during
early childhood also have been found by Blank and Bridger (1964). Children were presented objects (e.g., cylinder, triangle) for tactual exploration and were required to identify the object visually from a pair of objects. Only 68% of the responses were correct for three-year-olds, but 95%
of the five-year-olds' responses were correct. Further evidence of important developments in perceptual recognition around the age of five was
reported in a second study by Abravanel (1968b). For example, children
allowed to explore a V or an inverted V tactually were asked to identify
the corresponding object from two that were presented visually. Fewer
than one-third of the three-year-olds were able to make correct identifi-
cations, while six-year-olds consistently were correct.

Cross-modal recognition does occur and there are striking developments in this ability during the late preschool years. What are the bases
of this improvement? Why are six-year-olds so much more effective in
cross-modal, as well as intra-modal recognition than three-year-olds? An
answer is found in observations made of children of different ages while
they explore objects. As shown by Vurpillot (1968), there are developmental changes in the effectiveness with which children scan stimuli visually. Ginevskaya (reported by Zaporozhets, 1965) discovered similar
changes in haptic exploration. When given an object to identify by touch,
3- to 4½-year-olds grasped the object and tried to manipulate it; 6- to 7½-
year-olds, however, traced the outlines of the objects, spanned the object
to discover its dimensions, and felt the surface to determine its solidity
and construction. Such observations are interpreted by Soviet psychologists as supporting a motor-copy theory of perception. According to this
view, the function of exploratory perceptual activity is to develop a mental likeness, an image, of the objects. Visual and tactual images become

more accurate and correspond more closely to the features of the objects because of the more effective exploration of these objects by older children. Zaporozhets (1965, p. 82) has stated the point this way: "more and more experimental data are being accumulated testifying to the fact that sensory processes become more complicated gradually, as a result of which perceptual images, appearing at different ontogenetic ages . . . reflect the environments more fully and more adequately."

If the consequences of orienting and attending are to develop a mental image of the object, this image may function as a mediator between various sensory modalities. Cross-modal recognition and transfer would be dependent, then, upon the accuracy of the image developed by the child during his initial experience with the objects. Before the age of five, cross-modal transfer should be poor because of the imprecise image that is produced by the young child's inadequate exploratory activity. Thus this position makes the same predictions for young children as are derived from a verbal mediation model. However, when experiences force more adequate exploration of objects, cross-modal transfer by young children would be predicted from the motor-copy theory.

Transfer

Studies of cross-modal transfer have used variants of standard discrimination learning tasks. During the training trials a set of stimuli is presented and the child is required to learn which member of the set is correct. Cross-modal transfer is assessed by requiring the child to learn a second discrimination using a different sensory modality. [For a more thorough discussion of various approaches to the study of perceptual integration in children, see Pick, Pick, and Klein (1967).]

A typical study is that of Blank, Altman, and Bridger (1968). The subjects were four-year-olds who were unable, both at the beginning and the end of the study, to label the stimuli. The training task required the children to discriminate between two three-dimensional forms (a rectangular and a bridge-like shape) either visually or tactually. In the transfer task the same stimulus remained correct or the second member became correct. The training problem was learned more rapidly with tactual than with visual discrimination. Cross-modal transfer from the visual to the tactual mode was obtained; on the average, the children learned the second discrimination with less than one error when the same stimulus remained correct and with few errors in the reversal task. There was no evidence of cross-modal transfer from the tactual to the visual mode.

The same stimuli were used in tests for intra-modal transfer in a second study (Blank & Altman, 1968). As was the case in the first study, the tactual discrimination was learned more rapidly during both training and reversal trials than was the visual discrimination. Both within and across modalities, therefore, transfer was greater when the second discrimination was learned tactually than when it was learned visually. The authors suggest that children are forced to explore the characteristics of the stimuli more thoroughly when they are presented tactually than when they are presented visually, with the consequence that tactual discriminations are learned more rapidly than visual discriminations.

A study by Bloom and Moore (1969) revealed essentially the same results for 12- and 13-year-olds. The stimuli varied in form (circle, square) and size (large, small). Both intra- and cross-modal transfer was assessed in reversal and nonreversal shifts. The subjects learned the reversal problem more rapidly when the stimuli were presented tactually than when they were presented visually, regardless of whether the original problem had been learned visually or tactually. For nonreversal shifts, the opposite effect was found, especially for those shifted from a visual to a tactual discrimination. It apparently was more difficult to isolate a second dimension with tactual than with visual exploration.

These studies demonstrate the operation of cross-modal transfer, especially when the transfer is from visual to tactual discriminations. Tactual exploration in the absence of vision appears to place greater demands upon the children than visual exploration, and in order to make appropriate choices the children explore the stimuli more carefully. Since cross-modal transfer was demonstrated in the Blank, Altman, and Bridger (1968) study with children who were unable to label the stimuli, it may be assumed that verbal mediation is unnecessary for such transfer to occur. Only when the problem involves cross-modal response to a concept does cross-modal transfer appear to depend upon the child's ability to verbalize (Blank & Bridger, 1944; Houck, Gardner, & Ruhl, 1965).

The approach taken by Pick, Pick, and Thomas (1966) to the study of cross-modal transfer was different from those that have been discussed. Children were given training in making visual discriminations and tested for transfer in the tactual modality, or training was given tactually and transfer was tested visually. The stimuli were letter-like forms. Standard forms (three for visual discrimination, one for tactual discrimination) were presented during the training trials and the children (six-year-olds) were required to judge whether each of six comparison stimuli was the same or different from the standard form. The forms used for making these comparisons included two copies of the standard form and four transformations produced by changing such features as the linearity, orientation and size of the standard form. Training trials continued until the children were able to make consistently correct responses in one trial. The stimuli then were presented in the second modality. In Group A, the same standard was presented but different transformations were used during the training and test trials. In Group B, a different standard was used, but the types of transformations were the same as those used during original training.

If cross-modal transfer is dependent upon developing a mental image of the standard form, transfer should be greater when the same standard was used in training and test trials than when the standard was different (Group A). On the other hand, if transfer depends on learning the dimensions of difference ("distinctive features") that are critical for distinguishing between the relevant forms, performance should be more effective when a different standard was used in tests for transfer (Group B). Only children in Group B showed savings in errors on the visual task after training in the tactual task and in the tactual task after training in the visual task. The results point to the importance of learning the dimensions on which stimuli differ, rather than on developing a mental image of the standard form. The "distinctive features" and the imagery hypotheses will prove to play important roles in our discussion of perceptual learning in the next chapter.

CONCLUSIONS

Stimulus generalization, often considered to be a fundamental psychological process, has been found to be greater for the young and dull than for the old and bright. Developmental changes in stimulus generalization vanish, however, when the level of motivation is made equivalent for children of different ages. The more restricted generalization found for older children seems to be derived partly from their readiness to attach labels to stimuli. When this occurs and other stimuli do not share these labels, stimulus generalization decreases. If training is conducted with no comparison stimulus present, later tests show indiscriminate generalization. If, however, conditions are arranged so that the child isolates the distinctive properties of the training stimulus, stimulus generalization all but disappears. Stimulus generalization appears to be derived in part from the child's failure to attend closely to differences between the training and test stimuli.

One of the possible influences of attention on discrimination learning is made explicit in a two-process model postulating (a) the initial development of attending responses to the relevant dimensions of the stimuli, followed by (b) the attaching of the choice-response to one of the cues. This model competes successfully with the verbal mediation model in predicting the relative ease of learning reversal and extradimensional shifts and gains additional strength from the results of studies with "preverbal" children. When dimensions are dominant ones for the child or the salience of the dimension is increased through appropriate pretraining, reversal shifts are learned rapidly, and, depending upon the dimension of the stimuli that is relevant, extradimensional shifts may be learned with ease or with great difficulty. Attentional processes also play an important role in concept learning. If the salience of the cues defining the concept is increased through pretraining, children are able to demonstrate mastery of a concept they are unable to verbalize.

Studies of cross-modal transfer have extended the categories of task for which an attentional model is appropriate. When stimuli are presented cross-modally, recognition and positive transfer of training do occur. To account for these findings, Soviet psychologists have proposed that the product of attentional, exploratory responses is a mental image of the stimulus. This position has been contrasted with one that assumes that attention to stimuli leads to the acquisition of information about the distinctive features of stimuli and that transfer is dependent upon the use of this information.

Complex psychological research is not necessary to convince anyone that attention plays an important role in learning. But what are the means through which this takes place? Several alternative interpretations have been considered in this chapter. Does the effect lie in the child's tendency to verbalize about cues to which he is attending? Although such verbalizations may be helpful, they are not necessary for rapid learning and efficient transfer. Is it, then, that learning and transfer are dependent upon the acquisition of attentional responses? Or is it more complicated than this? Does attending to stimuli produce a mental image of the characteristics of the stimuli, or does it lead to the acquisition of information about the distinctive properties of the stimuli? It is not obvious how the attentional model can be stretched to encompass the research discussed thus far. At the same time, this research gives us only a portion of the evidence related to the "distinctive features"–mental image controversy. We can gain further insight into these questions if we turn to a discussion of perceptual learning.

Perceptual Learning

Perceptual learning is a new treatment of the mechanisms of learning that has been undertaken by psychologists whose backgrounds were in the study of perception. We approach the discussion of this form of learning through the theory proposed by Eleanor Gibson in her book, *Principles of Perceptual Learning and Development* (Gibson, 1969). This is the first systematic discussion of the relation of perceptual learning and development, and as far as child psychology is concerned, most of the work that has been done in perceptual learning has had its impetus in this theory. It will take some time for the full impact of this important book to be felt in psychology, for much of what Mrs. Gibson has to say departs radically from many of the traditional tenets that have guided research in child psychology.

We can get some sense of what the theory is about by looking at how perceptual learning is defined. According to Mrs. Gibson, perceptual learning "refers to an increase in the ability to extract information from the environment, as a result of experience and practice with stimulation coming from it." It is "self-regulating, in the sense that modification occurs without the necessity of external reinforcement. It is stimulus-oriented, with a goal of extracting and reducing the information in stimulation. Discovery of distinctive features and structure in the world is fundamental in the achievement of this goal" (Gibson, 1969, p. 3, 4).

Here, then, is a fundamental break with what many psychologists have had to say about how children learn. The child does not respond, he actively investigates. His behavior is not dependent upon external reinforcement, for obtaining a clearer sense of the structure of objects and events about him is its own reward. The child seeks information, the resolution of uncertainty, rather than a return to some optimal biological or psychological state. Stimuli are not predefined, but emerge as their distinctive characteristics are isolated through experience.

The product of experience is not the acquisition of new responses but an increased sensitivity to the ways in which stimuli are alike and how they are different. The basic mechanism of learning is differentiation, the abstraction of distinctive characteristics, not association of stimulus and response. Behavior becomes more complex, not because the child has learned more responses but because the environment has become more differentiated. The child sees more and hears more because he has learned to discriminate more.

WHAT IS LEARNED

We can gain a better understanding of what is implied in the preceding summary if we consider in somewhat greater detail what Gibson believes is learned in perceptual learning. Perceptual learning produces a greater degree of specificity of perception, whereby the perception of the object comes to be in greater correspondence with all of the attributes possessed by the object. The child is able to discriminate and differentiate an object more accurately after he has had experience in comparing and contrasting this object with others of varying degrees of difference. He is able to detect properties, patterns, and distinctive features of the object to which he previously did not respond. An early experiment of the Gibsons will illustrate these points (Gibson & Gibson, 1955).

The experiment was a study of scribbles. There was one standard, four-coil scribble. 18 variations of this scribble were drawn by altering it along three dimensions: number of coils, orientation (left-right), and compression. The variations were constructed so that they would be relatively undistinguishable from the standard scribble when they were first viewed. In addition, 12 other drawings differed from the standard along many dimensions (e.g., cloud-like form, concentric circles, horizontal scratches). These 30 drawings were assembled into a pack that also contained four replicas of the standard.

The child was shown the standard and asked to go through the pack of cards and say which drawings were the same as the standard. The child went through the pack, never being told whether his judgments were correct or incorrect. The procedure was repeated; that is, the standard was presented and the child was asked to go through the pack again, until all 34 judgments were made without error. At least this is what was planned. Only two of the ten younger children (six to eight years) tested were able to reach this criterion. These children made an average of 13.4 errors on their first trial. After they had gone through the pack six times their errors had been reduced to an average of 3.9. Older children (8½ to 11 years) performed more effectively. They made an average of only 7.9 errors on the first trial and were able to respond correctly to all items after an average of 4.7 trials. When errors were made, they were not random. The ability to differentiate the comparison and the standard stimuli became progressively more difficult as the number of dimensions on which they differed became smaller. Few, if any errors were made for the dissimilar drawings. Variations that differed from the standard on all three dimenions were judged with great accuracy by the older children, and only 28% of the responses of the younger children to these drawings were in error. When the standard and the variations differed on only one dimension, however, 53% of the responses of the younger children and 27% of the responses of the older children were incorrect.

The children demonstrated perceptual learning. Independent of any external reinforcement, they had learned to differentiate the characteristics of the standard scribble that distinguished it from the variations and the other drawings. Young children were able to do this less well than older children, but at both ages the number of undifferentiated items decreased with increasing practice. Discriminations became more specific, presumably because the children had learned the features or properties of the standard scribble that were distinctive and the ways in which the comparison stimuli differed from the standard.

This is one example of perceptual learning. During the remainder of the chapter we will discuss others that will help clarify further what perceptual learning is all about, and how it differs from other viewpoints. Research on perceptual learning is divided into two general types, studies of the detection of distinctive features and studies of the predifferentiation of stimuli. In the first, an effort is made to design experiments that place predictions from the distinctive features hypothesis in direct opposition to those derived from an image or schema hypothesis. In the second, the child is given preliminary experience with an array of stimuli and the question is whether nonreinforced experience in differentiating the dimensions on which stimuli differ will be of later utility in discrimination learning.

DISTINCTIVE FEATURES

The attentional models of discrimination learning discussed in the preceding chapter were two-process models of learning, positing first the development of an attentional response and then the attachment of a choice-response to the stimulus leading to reward. Zeaman and House (1963) assumed further that the attentional response is directed at the relevant dimensions of the stimuli, but gave little effort to delineating the characteristics of this response or the basis on which it is made. Much of Mrs. Gibson's interest has centered on this problem. While departing from the stimulus-response position of attentional theorists, she, too, has maintained that being able to attend to relevant dimensions is of primary importance in discrimination learning. It is not, she proposes, a matter of learning a *response* to the relevant dimension, but of isolating distinctive features, dimensions of difference, that distinguish one object from another. What appears to emerge from Gibson's view is a three-process model: the child must attend to the stimuli, isolate the distinctive features that differentiate the stimuli, and then make some arbitrary discriminative response. The distinctive features hypothesis is less a contradiction than a supplementation and reinterpretation of what attentional theorists have had to say.

Similarly, a contrast between the distinctive features hypothesis and the image hypothesis discussed earlier cannot be drawn with great clarity. According to the latter view, repeated experience results in the development of an image (schema) of the objects, which is stored in memory and against which sensory data are compared. If the data "match" the image, the objects are considered to be the same, otherwise they are judged to be different. It is possible, as Caldwell and Hall (1970, p. 7) have suggested, that images or schemata "are composed of distinctive features and that when many distinctive features have been stored, one has a 'refined' schemata." We are, however, getting ahead of our story, for at one time Gibson believed the two positions to be in greater opposition than now seems to be the case. Some of the first work on the distinctive features hypothesis was conducted to show how predictions from this hypothesis were more accurate than those made by imagery theorists.

Feature versus Image

A study designed to test predictions from either the distinctive features or image hypotheses must meet certain restrictions. If the abstraction of distinctive features or the development of an image are to be a result of experience in the experimental setting, the stimuli must be novel and the subject must not have had extensive experience in isolating the properties by which they differ.

A study by Pick (1965) appears to have been successful in meeting these requirements. The subjects were naive five-year-olds and the stimuli were unfamiliar letter-like forms. There were six standard forms and six transformations of each standard, involving changes in such dimensions as size, perspective, orientation, and curvature (see Figure 19-1). The child was shown three of the standard forms and 15 cards, which included three transformations and two copies of each standard.

The task was to judge whether each card was the same or different from the standards. Errors were corrected and the procedure was repeated until consistently correct judgments were made. The same procedure was followed in a transfer task, except that only one uncorrected judgment was made for each form. For a control group, the transfer task included new standards and new transformations. The same standard but different transformations were used for Group A in training and transfer trials, and in Group B, a different standard was used, but the types of transformations were the same as those used during training. [This design parallels that of Pick, Pick, and Thomas (1966) in their study of cross-modal transfer.]

Support for the distinctive features hypothesis would be found if fewer errors were made during transfer for Group B, where the transformations differed on the same dimensions in both training and transfer. If, on the other hand, fewer errors were made in Group A, where the standards remained the same but the transformations varied, evidence would be found for the image hypothesis. An average of 5 errors was made by the control group, 3.9 by Group A and 1.9 by Group B. Evidence was in the direction indicated by the distinctive features hypothesis.

The generality of these findings was tested by repeating the experiment

Figure 19-1.   Standards and transformations used in Pick's study of distinctive features. (From A. D. Pick, Improvement in visual and tactual form discrimination. *Journal of Experimental Psychology*, 1965, 69, 33. Reprinted by permission of the American Psychological Association.)

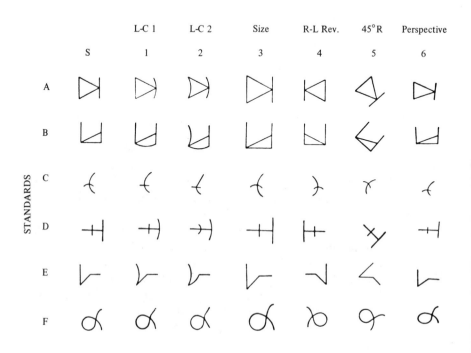

with tactual stimuli. Because tactual discrimination requires more time, only one standard and five transformations were used. Positive, but equivalent transfer was found when the standards remained the same during training and test and when the dimensions of transformation were unchanged. The results for vision were not confirmed for touch. Could the discrepant findings be due to differences in the manner in which the stimuli were compared? Simultaneous comparison of the visual stimuli was possible, but tactual exploration occurred successively; that is, the children used only one hand, exploring first the standard and then the comparison stimulus. Since memory of the standard stimulus was necessary to make a judgment, the procedure may have forced the children to develop an image of the standard stimulus.

If this interpretation is correct, simultaneous tactual comparison of the stimuli should produce different results. The procedure of the second study was repeated, but the child was allowed to use both hands in simultaneous comparison of the stimuli. The mean number of errors made in transfer by the control group was 1.9, the same value obtained when the standard was unchanged in training and transfer. An average of only .4 errors was made when the standard differed but the dimensions of transformation were the same. Again, the distinctive features hypothesis was supported.

The results do less to reveal weaknesses in the image hypothesis than to demonstrate the strengths of the distinctive features hypothesis. Detection of the dimensions on which stimuli differ may be sufficient for discrimination in most situations. Images or some mental representation of stimuli are necessary, however, when judgments or other responses must be made in the absence of a stimulus. Under such conditions the child may actively attempt to develop some form of image or schema.

A Re-examination

Pick's study appears to be well controlled and appropriately designed. The children were young and the stimuli were unfamiliar. The design was counterbalanced so that different combinations of standards and transformations were used with different children. For example, referring to Figure 19-1, some children in Group B were trained with standards ABC and transformations 123, and tested with standards DEF and transformations 123. Others were trained with standards DEF and transformations 456 and tested with standards ABC and transformations 456. The combinations of standards and transformations were reversed for the other half of the subjects. Further, subjects in Group A were trained with standards ABC and transformations 456, and tested with standards ABC and transformations 123. Combinations of standards and transformations were counterbalanced for other subjects.

Consider this situation more carefully. In Group B (distinctive features group), where the dimensions of transformation were the same in training and test, the children were able to learn during the training trials, for example, that a left-right reversal of the standard was considered to be "different" from the standard. This information was denied to the subjects in Group A (image group), where a size transformation may have been present during training but a reversal transformation appeared on the transfer trials. If the attributes of a stimulus are the "same" but its spatial orientation is "different," which decision is to be made? If the child has learned through earlier experience that the experimenter considers a reversal to be "different," tests with this transformation should involve no conflict in decision. If the child has not had this experience, the basis for decision during the test trials may be unclear.

Using the above rationale, Caldwell and Hall (1970) proposed that Pick's design inadvertently biased the results in favor of the distinctive features hypothesis. The definition of "same" and "different" may not be firmly established in five-year-olds, and they may be dependent upon information from the experimenter about how these judgments are defined. A study therefore was designed to determine whether such information would be helpful.

The conditions of the Pick experiment were repeated for a portion of the subjects (again, five-year-olds). In addition, two conditions were created in an effort to provide children in both the distinctive features and image groups with information about the experimenter's conceptions of "same" and "different." Pick's design also was followed in both of these conditions, but for one group of subjects the transformations were presented in the form of overlays the child could superimpose upon the standards. The child was informed that if the two figures did not line up perfectly, without rotation or displacement, they were to be judged different. For another group of subjects, the transformations were rearranged into the two combinations 134 and 256. These particular combinations of transformations should make it possible for all children to learn that line-to-curve, size, and rotation transformations were defined by the experimenter as being different from the standard.

Pick's results were obtained in one of the two samples included in the replication groups. When the transformations were in the form of overlays, differences between the distinctive features and image groups vanished. In comparison to the performance of the replication groups, overlays produced significant improvement for subjects tested with the same standards but different transformations, but not for subjects who were tested with different standards but the same transformations. Re-arrangement of the combinations of transformations also removed any difference in performance between the distinctive features and image groups. For some reason, errors generally were markedly below those found in Pick's study.

Where does this leave us? The proposition that children learn to discriminate among stimuli by abstracting their distinctive features seems to be plausible. Placing the distinctive features hypothesis in opposition to an image or schema hypothesis is, in the end, probably a hollow effort. If anything, the two hypotheses are complementary. Mental representations of stimuli are necessary when the requirements of the task preclude simultaneous comparison of the stimuli. In any case, there must be a long-term residual following extensive experience at abstracting distinctive features. Whether we wish to say this consists of the retention of a set of distinctive features or the combination of these features into some form of mental image or schema seems to be unimportant, and efforts to contrast the two hypotheses place us in what is probably an irresolvable dilemma.

PREDIFFERENTIATION OF STIMULI

The point was made earlier that discrimination learning is easier when a salient cue is relevant than when it is not. Cues provided by stimuli are not always salient, however, and the child must learn to differentiate the cues during the course of his experience in the experimental task. What type of experience is necessary for differentiation to occur?

We turn now to a series of studies by Tighe and Tighe. Some of these studies have been discussed briefly in previous chapters, but we wish to look at their research more closely in relation to the theoretical background from which it emerged. In line with Gibson's theory, Tighe and Tighe assume that "the abstraction of distinguishing features (dimensions) of stimulation is primarily a matter of learning through perceptual experience" (Tighe & Tighe, 1969, p. 367). Early in an experiment, children may respond to stimuli as undifferentiated wholes or in an absolute manner, identifying each stimulus according to its absolute properties. As the child has more and more experience, he comes to realize that the properties of each stimulus are not unique, but are shared by other stimuli. As these invariant characteristics are isolated, the child becomes able to classify stimuli according to their dimensions of difference, rather than their absolute properties. Since stimuli typically differ on more than a single dimension, the abstraction of these dimensions may require extensive experience.

Number of Stimulus Values

Children obviously cannot abstract a dimension when only one value of the dimension is represented in the stimuli. A dimension, as opposed to an absolute property, emerges only when comparisons can be made among stimuli possessing different values of this property. Height emerges as a dimension when stimuli differ in height. How many different values of height are sufficient, then, for the child to abstract height as a dimension?

Information comes from a study by Tighe and Tighe (1968) in which children were given experience during pretraining with two, three, or four values of each of two dimensions. For example, 16 stimuli were constructed to include four values of height and four values of brightness. The children were asked to judge whether these comparison stimuli were the same as or different from a standard stimulus. Eight experiences, two with each of four different standard stimuli, were provided with each comparison stimulus. To make the task meaningful, replicas of the standard were interspersed among presentations of the comparison stimuli. When each of the two dimensions differed on three values, nine comparison stimuli were constructed, and when the stimuli differed on only two values, four comparison stimuli were used. All judgments were accepted without correction; thus pretraining was of a nonassociative, nonreinforced nature.

Two pairs of the comparison stimuli were selected for the training task (e.g., tall white versus short black; tall black versus short white). One value of one dimension was deemed to be correct (e.g., tall) and training was continued until the child chose the tall stimulus of each pair nine out of ten times. (Each value of each dimension was correct, however, for an equal number of children.) The test phase consisted of a reversal shift. Whereas the tall stimuli had been correct, responses to the short stimuli now were reinforced. Reversal trials continued until the criterion of nine correct out of ten responses was met.

The effects of pretraining were evaluated by comparing the performance of children who had made same-different judgments with that of children who had spent equivalent amounts of time assembling puzzles and arranging pictures. The children in this, and in all of the other Tighes' studies were first graders.

Experience in predifferentiating the stimuli did not aid the children in learning the original discrimination. The Tighes attributed this to the fact that during the training task the children were learning the "rules of the game." It was assumed that predifferentiation facilitates learning only after these rules are learned. (It should be relatively easy to determine the validity of this argument. Children given experience with another discrimination learning problem, as well as pretraining in making same-different judgments should learn the training problem with great rapidity.)

Pretraining in making same-different judgments with two values of each dimension was of no apparent benefit to the children on the test problem. A reversal shift was learned as slowly after pretraining with only two values of each dimension as after experience with unrelated stimuli (means = 20.6 versus 20.4 trials). Apparently, the children had failed to abstract height and brightness as independent dimensions during pretraining. Reversal learning was rapid, however, following judgments of stimuli that varied on three or four values of each dimension. The reversal was learned in fewer than half the trials required by the control group. This finding has been replicated in several other studies (Tighe, 1965; Tighe & Tighe, 1968; Tighe & Tighe, 1969). It is interesting, but perplexing why three but not two values were required to define a dimension.

Number of Trials

It is unlikely, at least with young children, that much could be learned in only one exposure to the comparison stimuli. The question, therefore, is how many exposures are necessary for perceptual learning of the type studied by the Tighes to occur. To answer this question, children were given 4, 8, or 12 experiences with each comparison stimulus during pretraining (Tighe & Tighe, 1968). In addition, half of the children were told when their judgments were correct and half were not. As in the first study, pretraining had no significant effect on learning the original discrimination.

Informing children about the accuracy of their judgments had no significant effect on reversal learning. Nor were 12 exposures to the stimuli more useful than 8; approximately 6 trials on the average were required in both cases to learn the reversal. When only 4 experiences with the stimuli were allowed, an average of approximately 22 trials was needed to reach criterion for reversal learning. This number did not differ significantly from that of children who received no pre-experimental experience with the stimuli. We conclude from this and the previous study that differentiation of dimensions of difference among stimuli requires repeated experience with multiple examples of the ways in which the stimuli differ.

Observing versus Judging

Is it necessary for children actively to compare and contrast stimuli in order to abstract their common dimensions? Would the dimensions not become apparent simply through observation? Tighe and Tighe (1968) therefore pretrained children with four values each of height and brightness and required the children either to make same-different judgments or merely to observe the stimuli as they were presented. The mean number of trials necessary to learn the reversal shift was 5.4 when judgments were made during pretraining, but an average of 23 trials was required when pretraining consisted only of observation.

Perceptual learning is not a passive process. Children must explore and judge the similarity and differences among stimuli if pretraining is to be of value. But that which is necessary may not be sufficient. Other children, pretrained in making judgments of stimuli differing in only two values of height and brightness, learned the reversal shift no more rapidly than children who had no prior experience with the stimuli, nor than children who had spent the pretraining period in passive observation.

Irrelevant Dimensions

We know from Lubker's (1969) study that in the absence of pretraining the addition of irrelevant dimensions greatly increases the difficulty of discrimination learning. If, however, the dimensions are predifferentiated, children should be able to handle the presence of irrelevant dimensions with relative ease. In fact, the beneficial influence of predifferentiation should become increasingly apparent as the number of irrelevant dimensions is increased. Having differentiated the stimuli according to height, brightness, and form, for example, it should be relatively easy to ascertain which of the dimensions is relevant and which value of this dimension is correct.

Tighe and Tighe (1969) set about testing this prediction by presenting

Figure 19-2.   Mean number of trials to criterion for pretrained and control groups as a function of the number of irrelevant dimensions represented in the discriminative stimuli. (Data from L. S. Tighe and T. J. Tighe, Transfer from perceptual pretraining as a function of number of task dimensions. *Journal of Experimental Child Psychology*, 1969, 8, 498.)

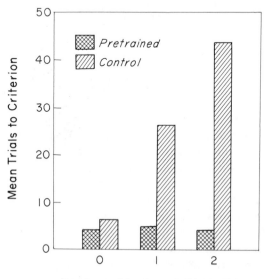

Number of Irrelevant Dimensions

children with training and test problems in which there were either zero, one, or two irrelevant dimensions. When the number of irrelevant dimensions (excluding the spatial arrangement of the stimuli) is increased, there must be an increase in the number of pairs of discriminative stimuli. With one relevant and no irrelevant dimension, only one pair is necessary to represent variation in the relevant dimension. With one relevant and one irrelevant dimension, two pairs of stimuli are necessary. If there are one relevant and two irrelevant dimensions, four pairs of stimuli must be used to represent two values of each of the dimensions. An increase in the number of dimensions also requires an increase in the numbers of stimuli used during pretraining. To represent three values on one dimension, three comparison stimuli are needed. To represent three values on two dimensions, 9 stimuli are needed, and when there are three values of three dimensions, the number of pretraining stimuli must be increased to 27.

The average number of trials required to reach criterion for reversal learning is presented for the various groups in Figure 19-2. When there were no irrelevant dimensions, the problem was learned as rapidly without predifferentiation of the stimuli as when pretraining had been given. The levels of performance diverged as the number of irrelevant dimension increased. Children who had made same-different judgments prior to the experimental task were able to learn the reversal shift as easily when there were two irrelevant dimensions (and four pairs of stimuli) as when there were no irrelevant dimensions (and one pair of stimuli). This was not true for children who had spent comparable amounts of time during pretraining assembling puzzles or arranging pictures. For these children, learning a reversal shift with two irrelevant dimensions was extremely difficult.

Labeling and Perceiving

The argument has been made that verbalization may be helpful, but is unnecessary for discrimination learning. What is required is that the child be capable of isolating and attending to the dimensions represented in the stimuli. Tighe and Tighe (1969) have offered further evidence for this point. During predifferentiation trials children compared stimuli embodying four values of height and of brightness with four different standards. Half made same-different judgments and half were required to supply labels indicating the basis of the difference (e.g., taller, shorter). Further, half were tested on a reversal shift, and half on a test of transposition one step removed from the training stimuli.

The addition of labels had no significant effect in learning the reversal or in transposing. Children who had labeled the stimuli were no more effective than those who had made same-different judgments. Both groups, however, learned the reversal more rapidly and transposed more frequently than did children whose prior experience had been with unrelated stimuli. Differentiating the stimuli was helpful, but attaching labels to the stimuli added nothing to this process.

Comments

There are many routes to the goal of getting children to differentiate the attributes of a stimulus. Differentation can occur if children are given enough experience with enough different examples of the attributes, even in the absence of external reinforcement and without verbalization about the attributes. The experience must, however, involve active response; passive observation is of no help. Even the Tighes would not conclude, however, that verbalization and reinforcement are of no potential use. Their purpose in these studies was not to attack the verbal mediation hypothesis or reinforcement theory, but to demonstrate the central significance of differentiating the critical features of the discriminative stimuli. This they have done. A lingering question is why predifferentiation had no effect in any of the studies on original learning. This is an important one for differentiation theorists to answer.

CONCLUSIONS

With the appearance of perceptual learning, the stimulus attains its rightful status as a central variable in discussions of the learning process. Rather than viewing the stimulus as a given, perceptual theorists consider the stimulus to be defined with greater and greater precision through learning. Its definition is in terms of distinctive features, those aspects of a stimulus that distinguish it from all others. The child, as must all organisms, discovers these attributes only with repeated experience and multiple examples. The isolation of distinctive features depends on the child's ability to abstract the dimensions on which stimuli vary. Since children differ in their backgrounds of experience, there are individual differences in the rate and degree to which differentiation can take place. Similarly, there are developmental changes in the specificity with which the attributes can be defined. Older children and adults have vast experience in differentiating objects and events in their everyday lives and are able to isolate distinctive features more rapidly and extensively than the less experienced younger child.

The residual effect of differentiating stimuli is some form of mental representation of the stimulus, either a set of defining dimensions or a mental image or prototype. The isolation of distinctive features occurs through perception, but perception is guided by cognitive processes. Distinctive features are isolated and abstracted, not merely observed. Labeling stimuli may direct attention to certain attributes, and, at times, be of assistance. External reinforcement is but one source of information. It may be immediate and direct, but it is not a prerequisite for differentiation. Obviously, differentiation cannot occur unless the child attends to the stimuli, but perceptual learning produces an increased sensitivity to the stimuli, and not simply a strengthening of attentional responses.

These are the conclusions we may reach from Gibson's view of perceptual learning and the studies done in support of it. The studies offer persuasive evidence that differentiation of the stimulus is an important aspect of learning. As for the theory, it may be a turning point, a point at which learning is considered less a product of the acquisition and elaboration of responses than of perception and thought.

Observational Learning

If we were to observe a child during his first days at nursery school, we would find that he spends a good deal of time observing the behavior of other children. He sits by the Junglegym, intently watching other children play. He observes carefully as they build towers of blocks and as they paint at the easel. During snack time, he watches others before drinking his juice and eating his crackers. By observing other children, the child is learning how to behave in nursery school. He is finding out what behaviors are appropriate, how materials can be used, what the teacher does, and so on. He is learning by watching others, as well as by trying out things for himself and by following instructions.

Nearly all our previous discussions have involved situations where the child must learn through action, rather than through observation. A vast amount of learning occurs, however, in social situations where the child remains inactive but is able to view the efforts and effects of adults and peers as they engage in activities with each other. Observational learning of irrelevant features of various activities occurring in social contexts was discussed in Chapter 16. We turn our attention in this chapter to studies of observational learning dealing with the central or relevant, rather than the irrelevant features of the experimental situation.

Although the problems of analyzing performance in learning tasks become much more complex when all the variables that operate in a social context must be considered, many of the ideas discussed in preceding chapters are relevant. Observational learning is not a passive process. The child must look and listen, rather than merely see or hear, if what he experiences is to influence his later behavior. Observational learning is selective. Children do not incorporate all information that is available in a social situation. Characteristics such as the salience of the observed behavior, its outcome, the ease with which the information can be coded and stored, the motivation of the child, and the relation between the child and the person observed are among the many variables that influence the degree to which observational learning will occur.

It is impossible to present a comprehensive picture of all the ramifications of research on observational learning in one chapter, for the research is closely related to studies of imitation, modeling, social influence, vicarious reinforcement, and many other topics. This broad area of research has been discussed by Aronfreed (1969) and Bandura (1969). We will begin our discussion with illustrative studies and then review in somewhat greater detail the research on two topics, aggression and syntactic constructions in speech.

ILLUSTRATIVE STUDIES

The basic requirement in a study of observational learning is that the child be present while another person learns a particular task or participates in some type of activity. After this experience, a test is made by presenting the child the same task or permitting him to participate in the activity he observed. To ensure that the child's performance is not a result of what he has learned in other situations, the tasks and activities must be new to the child or consist of unusual combinations of previously learned responses.

We can use a study by Rosenbaum (1967) to illustrate many of the features of studies of observational learning. An observer and a performer were present in each experimental session. The performers solved 20 four-choice position discriminations in which one of each four positions was correct. They responded by inserting a stylus into holes of an 80 hole matrix (20 rows, 4 columns), and were required to locate the correct hole before proceeding to the next row. Both performers and observers then were given a printed duplicate of the matrix and asked to mark the position that was correct in each row. The subjects were from grades one through six.

As can be seen in Figure 20-1, retention scores obtained by observers were above the chance level of 5.0 correct responses at all grade levels. Observers demonstrated a significant degree of learning, even though their experience had been limited to viewing another person's efforts and the consequence of his response. Their scores not only were above chance, they exceeded those obtained by the performers themselves! Spared the chores faced by the performers of following directions, inserting the stylus at the correct times, remembering which holes had and had not been tried, the observers apparently were able to stand back and view the performers' efforts in a casual, but effective manner.

The study included other groups of subjects. Each hole was numbered from 1 to 80, and for other pairs of subjects the performer was asked to call out the number of the correct hole in each row, and for still other pairs, the observer was instructed to call out the number when he saw that the performer was correct (a green light went on). Hearing someone else verbalize the number of the correct hole was more helpful for both performers and observers than no verbalization or having to verbalize themselves. Hearing what was correct was more useful than seeing what was correct or saying what was correct. As can be seen in Figure 20-1, retention was better at all ages and in all conditions for observers than for performers.

Once we have read the results of this study we can think of many situations where observation is more effective than direct participation in learning how to do something. A kibitzer in a game or an onlooker during the assembly or repair of some object may offer suggestions that are more

Figure 20-1.   Mean number of correct responses made by performers and observers according to grade in conditions of (1) no verbalization of the correct response, (2) verbalization of the correct response by the second member of the pair ("passive" verbalization), and (3) verbalization of the correct response by the performer or the observer (active verbalization). (Data from M. E. Rosenbaum, The effect of verbalization of correct responses by performers and observers on retention. *Child Development*, 1967, 38, 619.)

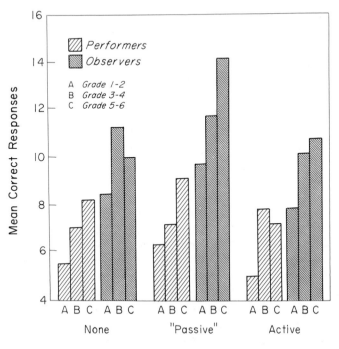

constructive than those apparent to the fumbling participant. An uninvolved observer may have a better perspective of the requirements of the task and of the steps necessary for solution than the person who is engrossed in the requirements of the task. These results were obtained in a task that was new for both the performer and the observer. More typically, the performer is skilled and the observer is a novice. To what degree does observational learning occur in this type of situation?

Coates and Hartup (1969) investigated this problem, using a procedure that parallels that of Rosenbaum in several ways. The subjects, four- and seven-year-olds, viewed a short movie of a man performing a series of novel acts. Before seeing the movie they were told they would be asked later to show what the man in the movie had done. 20 critical behaviors were displayed. As is the case in many studies of observational learning, responses were selected which had a low probability of occurrence for children who had not seen the film. Because of the desire to select types of behavior the child would not demonstrate spontaneously, the responses involved in studies of observational learning often appear to be odd, if not somewhat bizarre. In this case, the performer in the film did such things as build a tower of blocks in a unique way, put a toy on top of the tower, and walk backward four steps from the tower. When the film was over, the experimenter took the child to another room and asked him to demonstrate what the man in the movie had done.

Four-year-olds did not learn a great deal from their observation of the film. They were able to reproduce an average of only 6 of the model's responses. Seven-year-olds, however, were able to reproduce an average of 14 of the 20 responses they had seen.

Would verbalization of the content of the film assist children in reproducing the responses? Two additional groups of children were tested. For one, the experimenter verbalized each act and asked the child to repeat his descriptions. For the second, the children were asked to tell the experimenter all the things the model was doing. Previous discussions would lead us to expect that four-year-olds would not tend to make implicit verbalizations of the content of the film. They should demonstrate better retention, therefore, when the content was verbalized than when it was not. The results were in line with this expectation. Whereas an average of only six responses were reproduced by the four-year-olds with no verbalization, they were able to reproduce 10 responses when they verbalized the acts themselves, and 12 when they repeated the descriptions made by the experimenter.

Seven-year-olds, who presumably are capable of spontaneous verbal mediation, did no better after repeating the verbalizations of the experimenter than when they viewed the film silently. When they were required to make overt translations of the behavior into words, they did significantly worse than they did in the other two conditions. Being forced to

construct their own overt verbalizations interfered with later performance.

We see from both studies that observational learning improves with
age. After the age of seven or eight, children do remarkably well in reproducing a series of responses they have observed to be correct or that
have been demonstrated by an adult model. Retention of what has been
observed is facilitated if observation is accompanied by relevant verbalization by another person. It is interesting to note, however, that being
forced to produce their own verbal descriptions was not as helpful as
hearing another person's descriptions. The effort required to translate a
series of acts into words interfered with the retention of what was observed for the performer as well as the observer. This is not in accord
with the usual finding that verbalization aids learning. However, in the
research that has been discussed, verbalization was of a single concept or
a particular response, rather than of a series of unrelated acts. Thus these
studies provide evidence that there are exceptions to the maxims that the
child learns best by doing and that verbalization facilitates performance.

Attentiveness

Characteristics of the model influence the degree to which observational
learning will occur. This was the case in the observational learning of irrelevant features of the model's behavior (Chapter 16), and it is the case
when relevant aspects of the model's behavior are to be reproduced. Two
characteristics, attentiveness of the performer to the child before the experiment and sex of the performer, were studied by Rosenblith (1959).
Before the study, kindergarteners were given the Porteus Maze test.
When they returned for the experimental sessions, children of each sex
were assigned to adult models of each sex. For the first ten minutes the
model either maintained attentive interaction with the child or terminated
this interaction after five minutes and spent the next five minutes reading
a book. At the end of this period a maze the child previously had failed
was presented to the model, who traced it slowly and correctly. Then the
child, who had observed this behavior, was given the maze. This procedure was followed for several different mazes.

Observation was more effective in improving performance than having
additional trials with mazes, and prior attention from the performer resulted in greater improvement than did withdrawal of attention. Girls
were less sensitive to the experimental manipulations than boys, for differences between the conditions were smaller for girls than for boys.
Overall, a male was more effective as a model than a female, but since
there was only one adult of each sex it is difficult to determine whether
the effect was dependent upon the sex or other characteristics of the models. Furthermore, these general statements must be qualified by the pres-

ence of significant interactions among the variables. For example, with-drawal of attention by a male model produced greater improvement in performance by boys than did continued nurturance. What is important, however, is that the children learned more through observation than they did through continued participation by themselves, and that generally they were more likely to attend to and reproduce the behaviors of a model who proved to be supportive than of one whose responses to the child were less predictable.

Characteristics of Children

Explorations of the characteristics of children who differ in their ability to learn through observation are limited, but some information is available from two recent studies (Friedrichs, et al., 1970; Stevenson, Williams, & Coleman, 1971). The procedure for the two studies was identical; they differed only in the type of children tested. The subjects for one were middle-class preschoolers, while those in the other were pre-school-age children attending day care centers in lower-class neighborhoods.

Observational learning was measured by the speed with which the children assembled puzzles after observing them being assembled. The puzzles were constructed so that five irregularly shaped pieces fit inside a wooden frame in one specific spatial arrangement. They were so complex that even adults had difficulty in learning to assemble the puzzles by themselves. The experimenter told the child to observe carefully, then removed the pieces from the board and placed each piece on the table adjacent to its previous position in the form. The pieces were returned slowly to the board in the order in which they were removed, and the experimenter verbalized this order to the child. The child was allowed two 2-minute trials in which to assemble each of the two puzzles.

Eight other tasks also were presented. The tasks were constructed to assess types of behavior that might be related to the effectiveness of observational learning: social imitation, persistence, time spent in observing different pictures, impulsivity, variability of behavior, carrying out instructions, attention, and level of aspiration.

In the social imitation task the experimenter made a series of irrelevant comments and actions while pursuing a particular goal. The correlations between performance in this task and in the observational learning task were insignificant (r's $= .12$ and $.10$), thus the ability to reproduce relevant and irrelevant features of an adult's behavior were unrelated. This is in line with other findings in which no relation was found between retention of central and incidental content of learning tasks.

The ability to carry out instructions and to pay attention were positively related to observational learning. In following instructions the children were asked to carry out seven sets of instructions with toy animals and objects, varying from ones that were simple to some that were quite complicated. Thus both in observational learning and in this task the child was required to perform a series of acts, in one case those he had heard described and in the other, those he had observed. The significant correlations obtained for the attention task are not surprising, for one of the requirements for effective observational learning is that the child attend closely to what the performer is doing. The only other task for which significant correlations were obtained was level of aspiration. Children with high levels of aspiration did not do well in observational learning. These children may have been eager to perform on their own and found it difficult to observe the behavior of another person as carefully as was necessary for assembling the puzzles.

It appears, therefore, that observational learning can be improved if the performer has a close, supportive relation to the child, if the child does not have an unusually high level of aspiration, and if the child has the ability to pay attention and follow instructions. Other variables have been isolated and, for the most part, they have appeared in studies of the observational learning of aggressive responses.

AGGRESSION

If children learn by observing the behavior of others, then what about the violence and aggression they see while watching television and movies? Could this have an influence on their everyday behavior? Many people believe that it does, and their position is strengthened by the results of a number of studies of the learning of aggressive responses through observation.

One of the first investigations was reported by Bandura, Ross, and Ross (1961). Since this is a prototype for many later studies, it is useful to describe the procedure in detail. The study was conducted in three phases: exposure to real-life aggression, instigation of mild frustration, and opportunity to display aggression. During the initial phase, the experimenter seated the child at a table and told him he could play with some stickers and make some prints. The model was seated at another table, where there were tinker toys, a mallet, and a large inflated Bobo doll. For ten minutes the model behaved in either an aggressive or a nonaggressive fashion. After spending a minute playing with the tinker toys, the model began to pommel the Bobo doll, hit it with the mallet, sit on it, and engage in other forms of physical and verbal aggression. When playing the nonaggressive role, the model continued to play with the tinker toys. The model for half of the boys and girls was a male, and for half, a female. Children in a control group were not given the opportunity to observe a model.

To produce mild frustration, the experimenter allowed the child to play with a variety of attractive toys, and once the child had become engrossed in play, abruptly told him he no longer could play with these toys but could play with some in an adjacent room. Children's aggression was measured by determining the numbers and types of responses they made while they were in the experimental room. This room contained the toys used by the model in displaying aggression, as well as other aggressive and nonaggressive toys. The children remained in the room for a 20-minute period.

Observation of adult aggression not only produced an increase in the frequency with which children displayed aggression in the absence of the model, but also played an important role in shaping the form in which the aggression was expressed. Children in the control group and those who had observed a nonaggressive model displayed little imitative aggression; 70% of these children had scores of zero. Children exposed to an aggressive model displayed a significantly greater amount of aggression than occurred in either of the other two conditions. For example, girls exposed to a female model made an average of 5.5 imitative responses involving physical aggression, and 7.2 when exposed to a male model. The comparable means for boys were 12.4 and 25.8. Overall, boys showed significantly more physical aggression than did girls, but there was no difference between the sexes in the incidence of verbal aggression. Imitative physical aggression was greater with a male model for boys than for girls, but imitative verbal aggression with a female model was greater for girls than for boys. Boys tended to reproduce what an adult male did, while girls tended to repeat what a female model said.

Although our main interest is in the reproduction of the forms of aggression displayed by a model, it should be pointed out that observation of aggression had more far-reaching effects on the children's behavior. Since there were plenty of toys in the experimental room, the children were not forced to choose those that had been used by the model in order to occupy their time. They did spend large amounts of their time with these toys, but other forms of play also were influenced significantly by the manner in which the model had behaved. Children who had observed a nonaggressive model spent more time in nonaggressive play, such as playing with dolls and sitting quietly, than did children who had observed the aggressive adult. Furthermore, nonimitative aggression also was less frequent than it was for children who had observed an aggressive model. After viewing a nonaggressive model, children behaved less aggressively with the other toys in the room and were less likely to initiate new modes of aggression with the mallet and Bobo doll. Thus observation of aggression had generalized as well as specific effects. It had a strong determining influence on the type of aggressive responses that were displayed and, of equal importance, it served to activate aggression in general.

Filmed Aggression

In the preceding study, children observed real-life aggression. Would similar effects be obtained if they observed aggression portrayed in a film? Three different means of portraying aggression were used in a subsequent study (Bandura, Ross, & Ross, 1963a). Some children again saw the real-life display of aggression. Others saw the same behaviors demonstrated by an adult in a film. For a third group, the aggressive model was an adult dressed in the costume of a cartoon animal. Other than the change in the means by which the child viewed the aggressive model, the procedure was the same as that of the preceding study.

All three experimental groups displayed more imitative physical and verbal aggression than did children who had not seen the film. While imitative aggression was greater following exposure to a real-life model than to a cartoon character, the incidence of imitative aggression did not differ between children who had been exposed to aggressive adults in person and in film. Boys again displayed more imitative and nonimitative aggressive responses than did girls. For nonimitative aggression, scores were higher for children who had observed the films than for those in the control group.

The potential power of films and television in increasing aggression in children is clearly demonstrated in this study. Viewing aggression is not a cathartic experience. It does not decrease the child's need to display aggression. Rather, it offers the child examples of the specific forms that aggression can take and serves to heighten his general tendency to be aggressive.

The Consequences of Aggression

A typical scenario for a movie or television Western depicts a good guy and a bad guy, both of whom display aggression, with the good guy ending up the winner and the bad guy vanquished. It is not unreasonable to assume that children will be more likely to reproduce the aggressive behavior of the good guy than of the bad guy. That is, the consequences of a model's aggression may influence the child's tendency to reproduce the model's aggressive acts.

In a third study by Bandura, Ross, and Ross (1963b), preschool children were allowed to watch one of three 5-minute programs on a television set. The central characters were two men, Rocky and Johnny. Rocky approached Johnny, who was playing with some attractive toys, and asked if he could play. Johnny refused. Rocky then exhibited a series of aggressive responses directed at the toys and at Johnny. In one film Rocky emerged the victor and departed with Johnny's toys. In a second film Johnny was victorious and Rocky fled to a corner of the room. In a third, control film the two adults engaged in vigorous but nonaggressive play.

Children displayed more imitative aggression after they had seen an aggressive model rewarded for his aggression than when the model was punished. The frequency of imitative aggression also was higher when the aggressive model was rewarded than when the children viewed the nonaggressive film or had not seen a film. Interestingly, however, seeing a model punished did not decrease the children's tendency to display imitative aggression below that found in the control group. In a postexperimental interview, the children described Rocky as "mean," "wicked," "rough and bossy," but at the same time chose him three times as often as their preferred character when he had been successful than when he had not.

Do these results mean that the children learned less through observation when they saw the aggressive model defeated than when he was successful? This is unlikely, for the consequences of aggression were not evident until after the aggression had been displayed. The consequences to the model must influence the child's willingness to display what he has learned, rather the amount he has learned.

It would be relatively easy to demonstrate that this is the case. Instituting direct rewards to the child for displaying imitative aggression should increase his motivation to translate what he knows into action. New films, therefore, were made in which the model performed four novel aggressive responses to the Bobo doll, each accompanied by a distinctive verbalization (Bandura, 1965). The sequence was repeated twice, after which the model was seen to be rewarded lavishly for his aggression. In an alternative ending the model was admonished, described as a bully, and told to quit acting aggressively. Other children saw the film with the endings deleted. After ten minutes in the experimental room where the child was free to perform aggressive acts spontaneously, the experimenter asked the child to "Show me what Rocky did in the TV program" and promised a reward for each response demonstrated.

Differences among the three conditions were eliminated when the child was rewarded for reproducing the model's aggression. The children had learned equivalent amounts from viewing the three films, even though they had shown less spontaneous imitative aggression after seeing the model punished than after seeing him rewarded. Sex differences in imitative aggression also were weakened when the children were rewarded for displaying aggression. There is no reason to believe that boys learn more from observing aggression than do girls; one need only assume that they are more willing, even without direct reward, to display the aggression they have observed.

We have evidence then, for a contiguity theory of observational learning. Observation seems sufficient for learning to occur. Seeing a model rewarded may increase the likelihood the observer will display what he has seen and heard, but the observed response need not be rewarded for observational learning to take place. Spontaneous performance represents what the child is willing to display, rather than what he knows. When inhibitions for the expression of aggression are removed by rewarding such acts, we obtain a more accurate representation of what has been learned. Sex differences in imitative aggression also disappear under the influence of direct reward. Girls, who ordinarily show less aggression than boys, prove to be no less capable than boys in reproducing the aggressive content of what they have observed when recall is approved of and rewarded by the experimenter.

Figure 20-2.   Mean number of imitative aggressive responses made by boys and girls in experimental groups immediately after observing an aggressive model and during a retest six months later, and by a control group that had not viewed an aggressive model. (Data from D. J. Hicks, Imitation and retention of film-mediated aggressive peer and adult models. *Journal of Personality and Social Psychology,* 1965, 2, 99.)

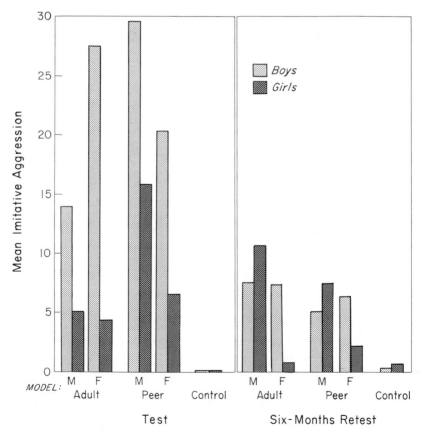

Retention

A critic of these studies might complain that they have demonstrated only short term effects and that the influence of observing aggressive models may disappear over longer periods of time. Hicks (1965) anticipated this criticism by testing children six months after they had observed aggression displayed in a film. The procedure was the same as that of Bandura (1965), except that the aggressive models were peers as well as adults. Six months after viewing the films, the children were brought back to the experimental room for a second 20-minute testing period.

On the initial test all four types of model were found to be highly effective in shaping the children's aggressive responses. As can be seen in Figure 20-2, children who had viewed a male peer as the model showed the highest frequency of imitative aggression. Six months later, the amount of imitative aggression had decreased, but it still was markedly above that found for children who had not seen the films. Now, the highest frequency of aggression was found for children who had viewed an adult male model. As was the case in Bandura's study, children retained more than they performed. In the six-months retest, the promise of a reward resulted in the recall of more aggressive acts than children displayed spontaneously in their free play.

Effects of observing aggression do dissipate over time, but they do not disappear. After viewing an eight-minute film six months earlier, children were able to recall an impressively large number of the aggressive acts they had observed. Learning through observation is not a flimsy, transient form of learning.

Other Variables

It is commonly believed that children are more likely to imitate the behavior of familiar adults than of strangers, to display aggression if the adult is permissive about the expression of aggression, and if they have experienced a prior period of frustration. These variables were investigated in three additional studies.

Madsen (1968) prepared two films, one in which the aggressive model was a male teacher with whom the children had interacted in nursery school for the preceding six weeks, and another in which the aggressive model was a strange male. The relative familiarity of the model did not influence the amount of imitative aggression for girls, but boys displayed three times as much imitative aggression when the model was a familiar adult than when he was not. It is not clear whether viewing the different male models had a primary effect in influencing what the boys observed or what they were willing to display. In any case, it appears that the boys' imitative aggression is increased when the aggressor is a potential object of identification.

There is a difference between sanctioning aggressive behavior and reinforcing it. In previous studies, the object of reward and punishment for aggression was the model. In a study by Hicks (1968), approval or disapproval of aggression displayed in a film was directed at the child who served as the subject. While watching the film, a male adult made such statements as "He sure is a tough guy" and "That's really something," or, for other children, "That's wrong" and "That's awful." The adult accompanied the experimenter and half of the children to the experimental room, but remained behind for the other half.

Boys made an average of 53.9 imitative aggressive responses when the adult who had shown approval and delight at the expression of aggression was present; girls made an average of 17.0 responses. When the children performed in the presence of the adult who had displayed disapproval of aggression, the comparable means were 9.1 and 4.1. Both boys and girls, therefore, were more likely to express aggression in the presence of an adult who had approved of aggression than in the presence of an adult who had disapproved of it. When the adult was absent, scores were lower for the children who had been with an adult who approved of aggression and higher for children who had been with an adult who disapproved of aggression. The trend, then, was for aggression to be displayed to a greater degree when an approving adult was present and when a disapproving adult was absent. This is in line with common sense, for children generally are wary about behaving in a manner they know will violate the attitudes held by a supervising adult.

Kuhn, Madsen, and Becker (1967) sought to determine whether frustration indeed does produce increased imitative aggression. For some of their subjects, the experimenter attempted to induce frustration after they had viewed an aggressive model in a film. "I'm sorry," said the experimenter, "but you did not pay attention to the movie and I am not going to give you your candy. You will have to wait until later for it." Following this statement, children showed less aggression in their free play than when the experimenter had not scolded them and broken his promise. This is not what would be predicted from a hypothesis proposing that aggression will increase following frustration, but is in line with the prediction that a high degree of arousal interferes with retention.

These are interesting studies but, like many of the others dealing with imitative aggression, they do not tell us the complete story. We would like to know, for example, whether the same results would have been obtained if a number of different adults had served as models and if there had been more frequent use of female models. Since sex differences in performance may be dependent upon the sex of the adult, we do not know whether there are differences in the effects of adult attitudes and of strange and familiar adults on the performance of imitative aggression by boys and girls or whether the results were due to the fact that girls were observing the aggression of men rather than of women. We will have this information only with additional research. For the present, we know that variables controlling aggression in other types of situations may not always have the same effects on the display of aggression that has been learned through observation.

MODIFICATION OF SYNTACTIC CONSTRUCTIONS

It will be recalled that in the preceding studies the model displayed verbal as well as physical aggression. The verbal component of the model's behavior was reproduced less readily by children than were the various forms of physical aggression. Verbal behavior appears, therefore, to be somewhat resistant to modification through observational learning. But we must remember that the period of observation used in these studies was limited. Five- to eight-minute exposures to a model's verbal output may not provide sufficient time for imitative responses to develop.

Models obviously do influence the verbal behavior of children. How else, for example, does the child acquire grammar and syntax? Parents usually do not make direct attempts to teach the child directly how to put words together to form intelligible sentences, but most children do this properly and easily by the age of three or four. This level of mastery is reached because the child hears language, uses it, and has his constructions reinforced, corrected, and elaborated by other persons. Although children may have an innate propensity to structure their linguistic output in certain ways, as psycholinguists sometimes have proposed, it is through hearing language used that this propensity is actualized. Because the child appears to deduce the rules by which sentences are organized rather than memorizing examples in which the rules are applied, his speech is not restricted to the mimicry of adults but represents the use of rules to generate his own novel sentences. Reinforcement of intelligible utterances may be direct in that other persons consciously attempt to reward the child's efforts, or incidental in that such utterances are more likely to produce a change in the environment and accomplish the purposes of the speaker.

Experimental Studies

Several attempts have been made to isolate variables that control children's imitation of the forms of adult speech. The first was reported by Bandura and Harris (1967). The syntactical constructions chosen for this study were the prepositional phrase and the passive voice. Increasing the output of prepositional phrases should be relatively easy, for this is a well rehearsed construction for children. Passive constructions are used less frequently in daily language, and it should be more difficult to increase the frequency with which they are used.

Three variables were studied singly and in combination: exposure to an adult who used the two constructions with high frequency, reinforcement for utterances of the model and child that followed the two syntactical constructions, and instructions to the child to pay close attention to the kind of sentence that was reinforced. The children were second graders.

The experiment was explained as an exploration of how people make up sentences. The child was given 20 cards, each bearing a common noun, and was asked to make up a sentence using each word. This served to provide a base rate for the use of each construction. The model then had his turn. After he had made up 13 sentences, the child was allowed to make up 5 more sentences. Model and child alternated in blocks of 5 trials until the child exhausted a second set of 20 cards. The entire procedure was repeated for the alternate construction.

Passives were used first by the model for half of the children and prepositional phrases were used first for the other half. Three-fourths of the sentences spoken by the model contained one of the appropriate constructions. Relevant constructions were not used consistently so that there would be a contrast between "correct" and "incorrect" responses. Reinforcement of passive constructions in the absence of a model did not increase the use of passive constructions. Nor was mere observation sufficient to produce an increase in the use of passive constructions. A significant increase in their use occurred only when there was a model, reinforcement, and a set to discern the governing rule.

Prepositional phrases were used more frequently than passives by children during the base rate period and changes in their frequency of use were accomplished more easily than was the case for passives. Reinforcement plus an attentional set of these two variables combined with the presence of a model were effective in producing a significant increase in the production of sentences incorporating prepositional phrases. Neither for prepositional phrases nor passives did children duplicate the model's sentences; they used the rules to generate new but relevant ones of their own.

Thus syntactic style can be modified within a relatively brief period, but the ease with which this occurs depends on the frequency with which the construction is used in everyday speech. We should be surprised, perhaps, that the experimental treatments were effective, for the 21 sentences produced by the model is an impoverished sample in comparison to the rush of language experienced by the child over days, weeks, and months.

Odom, Liebert, and Hill (1968) replicated and extended the Bandura and Harris findings, again with second graders. Whereas the earlier study investigated the influence of observational learning on the use of constructions already known to the children, this study sought to determine whether new constructions could be acquired. The adult model generated two types of sentences: ones that included prepositional phrases that were grammatically correct (e.g., "The goat was at the door") and modified prepositional phrases that reversed the ordinary order (e.g., "The goat was the door at"). The combination of modeling, reward, and attentional set had the same effect on the production of grammatically correct sentences found by Bandura and Harris. Hearing grammatically incorrect prepositional phrases failed to produce an increase in the production of such constructions. Paradoxically, children in this condition did show a significant increase in their output of grammatically *correct* prepositional phrases. Rather than adopting the new rule, they adapted the model's output to conform to a rule they already knew.

Analyses of the children's phrases indicated that they were able to abstract not only the rule of incorporating prepositional phrases into their sentences, but also the specific case of using three-word phrases, the type used by the model. As in the Bandura and Harris study, the sentences rarely were in exact mimicry of the model's sentences.

The results cannot be due to inattention on the part of the child. In a repetition of the study, where children were required to repeat verbatim the model's sentences, there was no more than a negligible increase in the use of grammatically incorrect prepositional phrases.

The same procedure and experimental conditions were applied again with 5-, 8-, and 14-year-olds (Liebert, Odom, Hill, & Huff, 1969). If second graders were unable to abstract the new syntactical rule, perhaps older children would be able to do so. The number of sentences embodying the new grammatical rule did increase significantly for the 14-year-olds, but not for the younger children. It is possible, therefore, to demonstrate the acquisition of a new grammatical rule through observational learning and reinforcement, but only when children are old enough to abandon a more familiar rule and abstract a new conflicting one that generates irregular constructions.

Children are not insensitive to the manner in which a model organizes his verbal output. Through a combination of observation, reinforcement, and an attentional set, significant increases in the use of various grammatical constructions can be produced. Persons who have minimized the influence of learning in their discussions of the acquisition of language have tended to ignore the fact that learning may consist of the abstraction and application of rules, rather than parrot-like repetitions of what has been heard. To say that a child learns language is not to underestimate the importance of innate, biological factors, but it does serve to emphasize the fact that without adequate experience in hearing language and in receiving reinforcement concerning his own utterances, the child is unable to realize the potential that lies within him.

CONCLUSIONS

Active participation by the child is of great importance in producing many types of behavioral change; a baby cannot learn to walk and a child cannot learn to play baseball without performing the necessary acts himself. Nevertheless, we know from the research discussed in this chapter that learning also can occur through observation of the behavior of other persons. An important part of children's learning takes place as they observe peers and adults interacting with other people and objects in their environment.

Observational learning does not occur with equal ease for all types of behavior. For example, physical aggression is more readily imitated by young children than is verbal aggression. A syntactical construction that is used commonly in everyday speech can be increased more readily through observation than one that is used more rarely. Differences in the speed of observational learning probably are related to the fact that well learned components of behavior are more easily re-organized and directed at new goals than are those which the child performs less frequently in everyday life. However, new behaviors can be produced through observational learning. Children may learn more rapidly by observing the performance of another person as he acquires a new set of responses or solves a problem than by performing the responses themselves. The addition of verbal labels facilitates such learning, but the effects are greater when the verbalization is made by another person.

It is important in discussing observational learning to distinguish between what the child knows about a model's performance and what he is willing to perform. Reinforcement is effective in mobilizing knowledge into action, but how does this occur in everyday life? Children do not demonstrate every act they observe. What factors control this selective display of what has been learned? More basic is the question of the factors that control what the child observes in the first place, for the child cannot attend to all of the behaviors that are displayed in his environment.

A valid criticism of the studies of observational learning is that the procedures often appear contrived. What does the child think as he sits quietly making potato prints and a nearby adult, with no provocation, suddenly begins a weird display of aggressive responses to a Bobo doll? And what does the child imagine is happening when a seemingly reasonable adult persists repeatedly in inverting the order of prepositions and objects? We would like to know more about the observational learning of ordinary forms of behavior.

This is the last chapter dealing with stimulus factors in learning. In contrast to our previous discussions, where stimuli have been objects in the environment, the stimuli with which we have been concerned here arise from the behavior of other people. We have talked about the perception of objects and the observation of people. We do not *know* whether the same processes are operative in observational learning and in perceptual learning, but there is every reason to think they are. Observation, whether of objects, people, or events, provides the opportunity for the child to obtain information. Someday we will understand more thoroughly how the child processes this information and the ways in which this processing can be facilitated.

21

Learning Set

In the next two chapters we will explore what is known about how children learn concepts or rules of response. This is not our first encounter with the learning of concepts, but the concepts we have discussed earlier were those directly dependent upon particular dimensions of the stimuli. Learning "It is the black one," for example, is useful only when stimuli differ in brightness, and the rule "It is the small one" is applicable only when stimuli differ in size. Our interest now turns to problems where the concepts transcend the characteristics of any particular set of stimuli; where the concepts are abstractions derived from experience with stimuli differing on many different dimensions.

The first concepts we will discuss are found in research on learning set. This research was stimulated by the well-known studies of Harry F. Harlow. Although his work was with lower primates, his own curiosity about its application to the realm of childhood was important in promoting research in this area.

Learning set can be defined through a simple example. The child is presented two objects; choices of one are consistently correct. After this pair of objects has been responded to for a limited number of trials, a new pair is introduced. The second pair does not necessarily share any of the features of the first pair. The first pair may have consisted of a spool and a small tin plate; the objects in the second pair are a bead and a plastic leaf. Many pairs of such stimuli are available, all consisting of "junk" items gathered from a wide variety of sources. Every pair is presented according to the same procedure: the child makes a constant number of choices and the pair is replaced. There is no clue within each pair to guide the child's response, thus his first choice always must be made at random. However, if he repeats a choice that led to reward, he will discover a reward again. If he is unsuccessful on his first choice, he can make a correct response on the next trial by shifting from the first to the second member of the pair. Success on his second choice is insured if the child learns and applies the concepts of win-stay, lose-shift.

If the child does learn when to stay and when to shift, we say he has developed a learning set. He has learned the rules on which the problems are based. Having learned these rules, he is able to respond correctly on his first or second choice in each problem, regardless of the characteristics of the stimuli he encounters. Learning set is, of course, a special case of transfer of training. It is the type of transfer that occurs when there are multiple problems, all of the same class.

Many factors may contribute to the kind of improvement that occurs in studies of learning set, such as elimination of stimulus preferences and response biases, development of appropriate observing responses and attention to relevant cues, modification of expectancies concerning the difficulty of the problem and the likelihood of reinforcement, and acquisition of strategies for maximizing the information gained from each response. What we are proposing, then, is that while learning each successive problem, the child also learns something about the general characteristics and constraints of the class of problem with which he is faced.

The first studies of learning set with children were aimed at determining whether they could form learning sets (they could) and whether brighter children could form learning sets more rapidly than duller children (they did). Knowing this, investigators then attempted to explore the limits of children's learning abilities by making the problems more difficult. Rather than using a series of simple two-choice discrimination learning tasks in which one of two objects in each pair is consistently correct, oddity and conditional oddity problems were introduced. In an oddity problem the child is required to choose the odd object from among a set. Three or more objects are presented on each trial; one of the objects is dissimilar to the others. Since different sets of objects are used on successive trials, the child must abstract the quality of "oddity" as the relevant basis for response.

An even more difficult problem, the conditional oddity problem, can be constructed if additional cues are provided to indicate the dimension of oddity relevant on a particular trial. For example, the discriminative stimuli may differ in color and form. If they are presented in the presence of one cue (e.g., a wooden tray), oddity in color is the relevant dimension and in the presence of a second cue (e.g., a metal tray), oddity in form is the relevant dimension.

Our discussion will center on the results of studies employing these three types of task: two-choice discriminations, oddity, and conditional oddity problems. From this discussion we will obtain additional information about what children are capable of learning and the factor that lead to the most rapid success in developing learning sets. [See Reese (1963) for a detailed review of the literature on the first of these types of task.]

TWO-CHOICE TASKS

The two variables that have received the most attention in studies with two-choice tasks are age and intelligence. The purpose in including these variables has been to do more than provide normative data; an effort has been made to investigate the bases for differences in performance.

Developmental Changes

A good example of a developmental study of learning set was reported by Levinson and Reese (1967). Among the subjects tested were 53 preschool and 53 fifth-grade children. (Data also were obtained from college students and the aged, but they will not be discussed here.) The stimuli were "junk" objects, paired at random. Each pair was presented for four trials. To insure discrimination on the basis of object rather than position, the left-right position of the objects was varied randomly from trial to trial. New pairs of objects (i.e., new problems) were introduced until the child

Figure 21-1. Cumulative percentage of preschool and fifth-grade children reaching criterion on each block of ten problems. (From B. Levinson and H. W. Reese, Patterns of discrimination learning set in preschool children, fifth graders, college freshmen, and the aged. *Monographs of the Society for Research in Child Development,* 1967, 32, 64. Copyright 1967 Society for Research in Child Development, Inc.)

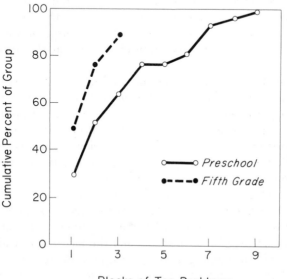

Blocks of Ten Problems

met the criterion for learning set; i.e., made no more than one error on Trials 2, 3, and 4 of five successive problems. The preschool children were presented 10 problems a day, with a maximum of 90 problems. The fifth graders were tested in one session with a maximum of 30 problems.

The rate at which learning sets were developed can be seen in Figure 21-1, where the cumulative percentage of children reaching criterion is plotted for each block of 10 problems. The older children demonstrated a more rapid rate of acquisition. At both ages, however, the curves follow the negatively accelerated form of a typical learning curve. Performance improved more rapidly during the early than during the later blocks of problems.

Another method of depicting the data is found in Figure 21-2, where backward learning curves are plotted separately for the preschool children according to the day on which criterion was reached. (Backward learning curves for the fifth graders were of the same form.) Some children learned very rapidly and for others the process was slow. Regardless of the number of problems required, performance can be separated into two phases, an initial phase where there was little improvement followed by a short phase in which criterion was attained quite rapidly.

Figure 21-2.   Learning set curves of preschool children who reached criterion on various days of testing (combined Trials 2, 3, 4). (The data for 6 children who reached criterion on Days 6, 8, or 9 are not plotted.) (From B. Levinson and H. W. Reese, Patterns of discrimination learning set in preschool children, fifth graders, college freshmen, and the aged. *Monographs of the Society for Research in Child Development,* 1967, 32, 13. Copyright 1967 Society for Research in Child Development, Inc.)

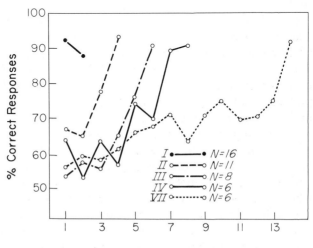

Blocks of Five Problems

Learning sets appeared to develop with a sudden understanding, or insight, into the requirements of the task, rather than through a slow, incremental process.

Errors were not random. From the beginning the children's responses were patterned, indicating the application of systematic approaches, or strategies, to the solution of the problem. For preschoolers, strategies related to position were dominant over those related to objects. For fifth graders, the inverse was true.

A lose-shift strategy was applied more rapidly than a win-stay strategy by children at both ages. That is, the children readily learned to change their responses after nonreward, but were slower to learn that they should repeat a response that led to reward. Nonreinforcement thus seemed to have a stronger effect than reinforcement. The younger children reached criterion when the win-stay strategy related to objects replaced the win-stay strategy related to position. The rapid formation of learning sets by older children was primarily a result of the greater speed with which they adopted the appropriate win-stay strategy.

Information directly related to developmental changes in the adoption of win-stay, lose-shift strategies is found in a study by Berman, Rane, and Bahow (1970). Four-, six-, eight-, and ten-year-olds were presented 144 two-trial problems in six daily sessions. A single object appeared on Trial 1 of each problem and on Trial 2 it was paired with a second object. On 12 of the 24 daily problems the object appearing on Trial 1 concealed a reward; on the other 12 it did not. Different "junk" objects were used in each problem. A win-stay strategy was relevant for solution on "reward" problems; i.e., problems in which the same object yielded reward on Trials 1 and 2. In "nonreward" problems. a choice of the new object was rewarded on Trial 2, thereby requiring the application of a lose-shift strategy.

Lose-shift was learned more rapidly than win-stay, for level of performance was higher at all ages on "nonreward" than on "reward" problems. Children learned to shift from the object that had not yielded reward on Trial 1 more rapidly than to repeat their choice of the object that had been associated with reward on Trial 1. Ten-year-olds found both types of problems quite easy; nearly all of their choices were correct by the end of the second day. Children below ten fared less well. Although their performance improved across the six days of testing, less than 18% reached criterion on both problems. Ability to verbalize the two strategies was not closely related to performance. Some children who were able to respond without error could not verbalize the basis of their response, and some who verbalized the rules early in training persisted in making errors.

It is not clear why children below ten find it so difficult to learn to repeat a response after reinforcement in this type of task. The novelty of choosing a new stimulus may be more attractive than repeating a response. Whether or not this is the case, learning sets are acquired more slowly by young children because they find it difficult to adopt and adhere to the rule that they should repeat a response after reward.

Further insight into the mechanisms underlying the formation of learning set comes from a study by White and Plumb (1964), in which eye movements were photographed during the period in which the discriminative stimuli were displayed. The children were from 3½ to 5 years old. Eight two-choice problems were presented and each problem was learned to a criterion of five correct out of six responses. Stimuli for "easy" problems were pictures of birds, and those for "hard" problems were stick figures differing in the angular orientation of the arms. Learning set was acquired more rapidly by children tested with the "easy" problems. As in the previous study, performance was divided into two phases: a first in which correct response was at or below a level of chance, and a second in which there was a rapid increase in frequency of correct response. Eye-movements were plotted for the last 12 trials of each problem. As the onset of criterion approached there was an increase in the frequency of these movements, with a subsequent decline. It appeared, therefore, that the children became more attentive to the stimuli just before they solved each problem.

These results are typical of those found in many other studies. For the most part, learning sets are formed very rapidly by children, although within an age group there are individual differences in the number of problems required for success. Performance lingers at a plateau for varying lengths of time, but improves rapidly when the child adopts win-stay, lose-shift strategies related to the characteristics of the objects, rather than to their position. Just before these strategies are acquired, children become increasingly attentive to the stimulus objects. At all ages studied, children's performance appears to be guided by the successive application of strategies, rather than by trial and error.

Intelligence

One obvious basis for individual differences in rate of forming learning sets in the child's level of intelligence. Significant correlations between these two variables have been found in many studies. For example, Koch and Meyer (1959) obtained a correlation of -0.59 between mental age and number of problems necessary to reach criterion of learning set for children between the ages of 20 and 66 months.

Two extensive studies of the relation of intelligence and the development of learning sets have been reported by Harter (1965; 1967). Level of intelligence as revealed by mental age and rate of intellectual development as revealed by IQ were varied. The first study included children at three levels of MA (5, 7, 9) at each of three levels of IQ (70, 100, 130). To constitute these groups it was necessary to select children of various chronological ages. The youngest children were 3½ and the oldest, 13. Ten four-trial problems with "junk" objects were presented a day until criterion was reached (90% correct response on five successive problems).

The correlation between number of problems to criterion and MA was -0.47, and for IQ it was -0.57. Age, independent of intelligence, was not a significant determinant of performance ($r = 0.04$). Developmental changes in rate of forming learning sets are derived, therefore, from differences in mental, rather than chronological age. An analysis of variance of these data revealed significant differences associated with MA, IQ, and the interaction of MA and IQ. There were greater differences in performance among the MA groups at IQ 70 than at the higher IQ levels; or, looking at it another way, there were greater differences in performance between IQ groups at MA 5 than at MAs 7 and 9. It appears that a ceiling effect was operating. These relatively simple problems were more effective in separating children at lower than at higher levels of intelligence.

Once performance began to improve, criterion was attained rapidly by all groups. Backward learning curves uniformly were of the type found in previous studies. What differentiated the performance of the brighter children from that of others was the relative briefness of the early plateau in performance.

Interestingly, only 34% of the children were able to verbalize how they solved the problems. The percentage increased with increasing MA, with 11, 30, and 48% of the children being able to verbalize appropriately at MAs 5, 7, and 9, respectively. As has been the case in many other situations, words may have been helpful, but they were unnecessary for the formation of learning sets.

In the second study, Harter included two levels of MA, 5½ and 8½, and three levels of IQ, 65, 100, and 130. The findings were similar to those of the first study, indicating more rapid development of learning set at the higher levels of MA and IQ. In precriterion performance, children with the lower MAs employed response-set strategies, evident in position preferences and position alternations, while those with higher MAs employed strategies contingent on the outcome of the prior response.

Half of the children were tested under a standard, neutral condition and half were praised for correct response. The performance of children with the higher MAs was not significantly influenced by these two conditions, but that of children with lower MAs was higher in the praise condition. There may, therefore, be motivational differences associated with intellectual level that have a determining effect upon the child's performance.

Intelligence tests are presumed to assess the child's ability to form abstract concepts. The results of these studies are consistent with this assumption. Both level of intelligence and rate of intellectual development are positively related to the ease with which children form learning sets. The correlations are moderately high, but a large portion of the variability in rate of forming learning sets is due to factors other than intelligence. What these factors might be is a problem for future studies.

ODDITY PROBLEMS

Success in oddity learning is dependent upon the child's ability to abstract the concept of oddity from his experience with successive problems. In most studies of oddity learning only one trial is allowed with each problem. Since a new combination of three or more stimuli appears on each trial, there can be no direct transfer of responses related to objects. Win-stay, lose-shift strategies related to objects are not relevant, and, in fact, may lead to errors if they are applied when a limited number of different stimuli are used. For example, the first trial may include the three stimuli, ABB, and by chance the combination on the second problem may be BFF. Obviously, neither win-stay nor lose-shift strategies can lead to success unless they are applied in conjunction with the concept of oddity. If response to the odd stimulus is rewarded on the first trial, the child should stay with the odd stimulus, otherwise he should shift to the odd member of the new set.

Developmental Changes

On the Stanford-Binet test of intelligence, children are asked at age 4½ to identify an object that is different from several others. The child is shown drawings of geometric forms: "See these crosses that are just alike? Here's one that is *not* like the others." He is asked to put his finger on the form that is not the same as the others. Six arrays of drawings are presented and the child passes the item if he is successful in finding the odd object in three of the arrays. The placement of this item suggests that oddity problems would not be learned readily by young children.

Developmental trends in oddity learning are evident in a study by Gollin and Shirk (1966). Red, blue, and green lights were combined into all possible sets of three, with one odd stimulus in each set (e.g., RRB, RBB, RGG). Children from ages four to seven were told to push a button under the light they thought was correct. Criterion for learning was six successive responses based on oddity. The percentage of children who were able to meet this criterion within the maximum of 54 trials increased from 42% at age four to 88% at age six. The percentages differ slightly in other studies (e.g., Lipsitt & Serunian, 1963), but the major development in oddity learning occurs in all studies after the age of four.

Children below the age of four rarely are successful in oddity learning.

Of 12 three-year-olds tested by Strong (1966), only two were able to learn an oddity problem and they required an average of 720 trials to reach criterion. Saravo and Gollin (1969) actually allowed children to observe the experimenter place the reward under the odd object on the first trial. Still, 62% of the three-year-olds were unable to learn the three-choice problem. Thus before the age of four children do very poorly. They begin to improve between the ages of four and six, and by age seven few are incapable of learning to apply the concept of oddity.

Relation to Intelligence

Brown (1970a) has studied the relation of mental age and IQ to oddity learning. Mental age was held constant (MA = 6) for children with average IQs of 70, 100, and 140, and IQ was held constant (IQ = 100) for children with average MAs of 4, 6, and 8. Two types of oddity problems were presented to all children, one using geometric forms, and the other, silhouettes of objects. On Day 1, 36 trials were given with one set, and the procedure was repeated on Day 2 with the second set.

The percentage of children reaching criterion (six successive correct responses) on each day is presented in Figure 21-3. The percentage was

Figure 21-3.   The percentage of children reaching criterion on each day of testing as a function of IQ and MA. (Data from A. L. Brown, Subject and experimental variables in the oddity learning of normal and retarded children. *American Journal of Mental Deficiency,* 1970.)

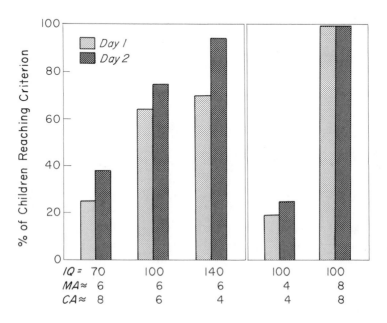

directly related to both IQ and MA. The most striking difference in performance occurred for the four-year-olds of average and above-average IQ. In oddity learning, as in two-choice tasks, both rate and level of intellectual development are significant determinants of performance.

Improving Oddity Learning

It should be possible to improve children's oddity learning. Although we may be unable to help three-year-olds short of direct tutoring, it should be possible to arrange conditions so that oddity learning by older children is facilitated. The results of a number of studies indicate this can be done.

Enhancing the Salience of the Odd Stimulus.   Discriminating the presence of something different should be easier if we increase the number of alternatives that are identical. For example, a blue light should be more salient when it appears in the context of four red lights than when it differs from only two red alternatives. Gollin, Saravo, and Salten (1967) have confirmed this assumption. Small windows were illuminated by sets of lights (red, blue, green). Five windows, four of which were illuminated by the same color (e.g., RBRRR), were used for either one or two blocks of 18 trials. The number of windows then was reduced to three, for a total of 72 trials. Other children were tested with three windows throughout all 72 trials (e.g., RBB).

When there were only three lights, five-year-olds made an average of eleven errors on the first block of 18 trials. Those tested with five lights made an average of three or fewer errors. Experience with five windows transferred to the three-window condition, for by the third block of 18 trials, an average of no more than one error was made in any of the groups. (An increased number of lights was of no benefit to eight-year-olds, all of whom learned the problem in all conditions, nor to preschoolers, who were unable to learn the problem in any of the conditions.) Verbalization was not highly related to performance. Of the children who learned the problem, only 20% at age five and 70% at age eight were able to verbalize the basis of solution. The effects have been replicated by Brown (1970a).

Stimulus Predifferentiation.   Schroth (1968) pretrained second graders in one of two ways. Half were told they were going to play a game to see how well children could tell differences between pictures (line drawings of forms), and half were told the experimenters were interested in the effects of looking at pictures and were instructed to look closely at the drawings. No feedback was given during pretraining. Later, when the children were tested in an oddity learning task with the drawings, those who had been instructed to notice differences among the pictures learned more rapidly than those who were told merely to attend to the pictures.

Both groups learned the oddity problem more rapidly than did children who were given no pretraining.

Stimulus Preferences. Stimulus preferences are a powerful determinant of performance, for rate of oddity learning is rapid when the odd stimulus is from a dimension that is dominant for the child (Brown, 1970*b*). For example, first grade children who preferred form to color (or color to form) learned an oddity problem more rapidly when the stimuli differed on their preferred dimension. Children who preferred form generally were more proficient in oddity learning than those who preferred color, when both were assigned to their preferred dimension.

Type of Concept. Rate of oddity learning may differ, depending upon the concept selected for the task. In a study by Lee (1965), solution depended upon the discovery of oddity in color, size, number, form, sex-type (e.g., iron, bracelet, pipe), or what was termed an analytic concept (e.g., tractor with four wheels, van with four wheels, fire engine with three wheels). Each child (ages four to six) was tested with five examples of each of the six concepts. To make the problems more difficult, each set of three objects differed on an irrelevant as well as a relevant dimension. For example, when color was the relevant concept, the three objects each were of a different size. Oddity in color and size were the easiest concepts to learn, and oddity in sex-type and analytic concepts were the most difficult.

Irrelevant Dimensions. The absence of irrelevant cues is helpful in oddity learning, as it is in other learning tasks. Third and fourth graders were tested by Lubker and Small (1969) with a four-choice oddity task with stimuli that differed in color, form, size, and thickness. Each stimulus within each set of four was of a different color. In addition, there was one relevant and either 0 (excluding color), 1, or 2 irrelevant dimensions. Children tested with one or two irrelevant dimensions performed only slightly above chance by the end of training (48 trials). When no irrelevant dimensions were present, over 90% of the children's responses were correct.

Distraction. The presence of irrelevant dimensions constitutes a source of distraction internal to the problem. Turnure (1970) investigated the effects of external distractors on oddity learning. Two sources of distraction were introduced: a mirror placed directly in front of the child or a phonograph playing records of children's songs and stories. Performance of children at 5½, 6½, and 7½ was impaired by the interfering sounds. The mirror functioned as a significant source of distraction only for the younger group.

We see from these studies that rate of oddity learning depends upon the conditions under which the child is tested. Oddity learning occurs more rapidly, at least at certain critical ages, if the stimuli are salient, are pre-differentiated by the child, differ on a preferred dimension, represent common concepts, possess no irrelevant cues, and if there are limited external sources of distraction.

Oddity and Identity

Is it necessarily the case that children will learn to choose a stimulus that is the same as another stimulus as readily as they can learn to choose a stimulus that is different? Brown and Scott (1970) have answered this question by constructing problems of the following type. A standard stimulus was presented, and then a pair of stimuli, one identical to the standard and one that was different. Half of the children (four-year-olds) were rewarded for choices based on identity, and half, for those based on difference. Different pictures of common objects were used on each problem, and only one choice was allowed with each set of pictures. Testing continued until the child reached a criterion of nine successive correct responses, or a maximum of 20 problems.

Nearly all children who were required to respond on the basis of identity, but fewer than half of those required to respond on the basis of difference were able to reach criterion. It was much easier, therefore, for children to learn to match a standard than to select a non-match.

Perhaps learning to select a matching object is more rapid because this choice is more reinforcing for young children. Such an interpretation follows from a study by Parten and Fouts (1969). Four- and five-year-olds, given the opportunity to turn on a light that was the same or different from a standard, showed strong tendencies to produce a matching stimulus. Part of young children's difficulty in learning oddity problems may be due to their reluctance to select the odd stimulus in a set, rather than to a failure to detect oddity.

Oddity and Conservation

One would not expect to find Piaget's concept of conservation discussed in relation to oddity learning. However, this is not as unusual as it first appears. We should review what is meant by conservation. Piaget's well-known task used in studies of conservation of volume can be used as an example. The child is shown two identical beakers filled with equivalent amounts of liquid. After the child has judged the amounts to be the same, the liquid in one of the beakers is poured into a third beaker that differs from the first two. The child is asked whether the beakers now contain the same amounts of liquid. Young children typically say they do not. Why? Because the water level differs in the two beakers. Piaget has attributed children's nonconservation (i.e., failure to recognize that there was no alteration in the quantity of liquid) to their inadequate cognitive development.

Gelman (1969) has offered a different interpretation. She has proposed that children may fail on tests of conservation because of their inattention to the relevant attributes of the situation. From the experimenter's point of view, only the amount of liquid is relevant. But the beakers may differ in size, shape, height, and width. On the test trial the beakers differ on all these irrelevant attributes. The child's judgment may be based on responses to the irrelevant attributes rather than to the relevant attribute of quantity.

Might it be possible, then, to teach children to attend to quantitative relations and ignore irrelevant features of the situation? This is what Gelman attempted. Standard tests of conservation of length, number, liquid, and mass were given to five-year-olds. Only those who failed to demonstrate conservation were retained for the study. For training, children were given various sorts of experience with oddity problems. Since oddity learning requires the child to isolate the qualities of sameness and difference and to ignore other features of the stimuli, this training may produce positive transfer in tests of conservation.

All children were given 32 oddity problems, six trials with each problem. They were asked to point to the objects that were the same or to the one that was different. New sets of stimuli were used for each problem. For one-third of the children, the stimuli were small toys. For the others, they were objects differing in length and number. Since children often judge number in terms of length, this procedure forced the child to discriminate when each dimension was relevant. On successive problems, stimuli also differed in color, size, and shape. Within each problem, the three stimuli were arranged in different ways. For example, if the stimuli were three or five dots, the dots spanned different lengths and appeared in different linear arrangements (e.g., below each other; in non-overlapping vertical arrays). Half of the children tested with these problems were given feedback about the correctness of their responses and half were not.

When toys were used as stimuli, oddity learning occurred very rapidly. The mean number of errors was 1.5, indicating that the children had entered training with well developed concepts of same and different. Despite the complexity of the problems used with the remaining children, those who received information about the correctness of their responses also learned rapidly, exceeding 90% correct responses by the tenth problem. The performance of children who were exposed to the stimuli but received no feedback concerning their responses showed no improvement across the 32 problems.

When retested for conservation of length, 80% of the children trained with toys failed to respond correctly; however, those trained with stimuli differing in length and number showed nearly perfect scores on tests of conservation of both length and number. Of the children who received no feedback about their responses, 60% showed evidence of positive transfer.

The "feedback" subjects also showed improvement in tests of conservation of liquid and mass (55% and 58% of their responses were correct). There was both specific and generalized transfer from oddity learning.

This is a complicated study, but it is an important one. We conclude from the results that conservation tasks are as much tests of the child's ability to deploy attention as of his understanding of concepts. The rapidity with which oddity problems were learned indicates that even five-year-olds have reasonably well developed concepts of quantity and length. When informed that these dimensions were relevant, they learned to respond to these dimensions very rapidly. And when they had experience with many different instances of quantitative equalities and differences, they were able to respond effectively in tests of conservation.

CONDITIONAL ODDITY

The conditional oddity problem is, by far, the most difficult of the problems related to learning set. The stimulus that is correct depends on the value of the background cue present on a particular trial. For example, there may be three stimuli, AAB, on a particular problem. The only basis for determining whether an A or B is correct is to attend to the background cue. The first choice on each problem must be a guess, but all subsequent choices can be correct. If the background cue is X and the child chooses an A and is rewarded, it should be obvious that oddity is not correct in the presence of X. It rapidly should become clear that oddity is correct in the presence of background cue, Y. The major interest in these problems has been in identifying the age at which they can be solved and in determining whether rate of learning can be improved.

A comparison of the relative difficulty of conditional oddity learning, oddity learning, and two-choice object discrimination was made by Hill (1965a) with one-, four-, six-, and twelve-year-olds. Half of the one-year-olds could learn to discriminate between a small green triangle and a tall red cylinder. This problem was easy for four-year-olds. On the oddity task the child had to learn to select the odd member of a set on the basis of shape or color. Few of the four-year-olds, half of the six-year-olds, and all of the twelve-year-olds solved this problem. The same stimuli were used in the conditional oddity problem, except that choices of the odd stimulus were rewarded when the objects were presented on a yellow tray, and of a non-odd stimulus when the objects were presented on a blue tray. The conditional oddity problem was learned by only 10% of the six-year-olds, but by 80% of the twelve-year-olds. Learning tended to occur rapidly or not at all; 75% of the children who reached criterion did so within 40 trials.

In a second study, Hill (1965b) attempted to improve conditional oddity learning by introducing prior training on an oddity problem. The odd stimulus occupied either an end position or all three positions (left, middle, right) of the stimulus array. After 40 trials, the conditional oddity problem was presented for a maximum of 100 trials. Twelve-year-olds, but not nine-year-olds, made significantly fewer errors in the conditional oddity problem after experience with the two- than with the three-position oddity task.

The difficulty of learning a conditional oddity problem is in contrast with the fact that conditional discrimination tasks not depending upon oddity can be learned by children as young as five (Gollin, 1966). Conditional discrimination tasks do not involve the concept of oddity; the child simply must learn to choose one stimulus of a pair in the presence of one background cue and the second stimulus in the presence of a second background cue.

Conditional discrimination problems can be learned rapidly. Routh and Wischner (1970), for example, found that children quickly developed a conditional discrimination learning set if they previously had learned to associate a different and distinctive nonsense syllable with each background cue and had learned the first problem to criterion. The combination of detecting the concept of oddity and of learning the contingency between response and background cue is vastly more difficult than learning either type of problem alone.

CONCLUSIONS

Learning sets of three types have been discussed in this chapter, those developed in two-choice discrimination, oddity, and conditional oddity problems. Although the difficulty of these problems differs greatly so that learning sets are developed readily by four-year-olds with two-choice discriminations, seven-year-olds with oddity problems, and twelve-year-olds with conditional oddity problems, learning in each case shares certain common features.

Children do not appear to form learning sets through trial and error. Their initial responses in each problem are random, as they must be, but subsequent responses reflect the operation of various strategies. Young children tend to apply primitive and ineffective strategies based on position and stimulus. Somewhat older children apply a lose-shift strategy, and then combine this with a win-stay strategy to form learning sets on two-choice tasks. Oddity problems require abstraction of the concept of oddity, and conditional oddity problems require both this and attention to background cues.

The transition from a chance level of response to nearly errorless performance occurs abruptly in each type of problem. Children suddenly "catch on." The point at which this occurs depends, in part, on the type of problem, the age of the child, his level of intelligence, and the manner in which the stimuli are presented.

The formation of learning sets is not highly dependent upon language. Children who have developed a learning set may be unable to explain the basis of their response, while others may verbalize appropriately but continue to make errors. Oddity learning can be hastened by manipulating certain characteristics of the stimuli, such as their salience, the type of concept they represent, their relation to the child's preferences, and the number of stimulus dimensions they embody. Prior experience with oddity problems aids children in learning conditional oddity problems. Information acquired during oddity learning may transfer to other tasks, such as those used in testing the concept of conservation. Both oddity learning and conservation appear to be strongly influenced by the child's ability to ignore irrelevant characteristics and attend primarily to those features of the situation that are relevant to the problem that is being presented.

Studies of learning set challenge the assumption that children of the same mental age but different IQs have comparable learning ability. Children with higher IQs form learning sets more rapidly than do those with lower IQs, even though the children have obtained the same mental ages on intelligence tests. Thus both level (mental age) and rate (IQ) of intellectual development are significantly related to the ease with which learning sets are formed. Chronological age predicts rate of learning only through its positive correlation with mental age.

Children can learn how to learn. When they have varied experience with problems involving a wide array of materials, they are able to abstract common rules for solution and apply those rules in solving new problems.

The ultimate goal in any type of learning cannot be the retention of large amounts of specific information. For the most part, this information will be forgotten. What can be retained are techniques for acquiring new information, learning how to attend to relevant cues and ignore irrelevant cues, how to apply hypotheses and strategies and relinquish them when they are unsuccessful. Teaching children how to learn may prove to be a more lasting contribution to their education than continuously requiring them to concentrate their efforts on the accumulation of facts.

22

Concept Learning

One might think that the literature of child psychology would offer abundant information about concept learning. This is not the case. We know a great deal about *when* children manifest certain concepts but have only a limited understanding of *how* concepts are learned. This unsatisfying state of affairs exists, in part, because psychologists studying higher thought processes have tended to be disinterested in the learning process, and learning psychologists generally have failed to explore complex forms of behavior.

Early child psychologists published numerous normative studies delineating the ages when children use concepts such as form, size, color, and number. [See Sigel (1964) for a review of this research.] The results opened our eyes to the fact that such concepts can be learned even by very young children, but these normative studies remained relatively isolated until Piaget appeared on the scene in the late 1920s. Piaget sought to construct a developmental theory of cognition, and his efforts led him to investigate the emergence of concepts such as causality, probability, and conservation. By constructing ingenious tasks and using developmental data in innovative ways, Piaget made this type of research much more lively and interesting, and for the past forty years psychologists, often in support of or in reaction to Piaget, have applied themselves diligently to the task of describing the development of the child's conceptual life.

However, by restricting their approach to the description of concepts the child may have learned through uncontrolled everyday experience, much of the work on the formation of concepts has failed to tell us much about the particular kinds of experiences that are necessary for the learning of such concepts. Learning psychologists during this period have continued to design well controlled laboratory studies but have been reluctant to venture into the study of how complex concepts are learned. While their research goes beyond the descriptive level, it has little to say about the explanation of more than the most simple forms of concept learning.

There is some hope this will change. The urgency of an important social problem may provide the impetus necessary for psychologists of all persuasions to investigate concept learning more thoroughly. During the past few years psychologists have been asked to assist in developing curricula for disadvantaged preschool children. Since these children have been deprived of many everyday experiences necessary for learning certain concepts, techniques must be devised for developing these concepts within the preschool setting. As of now, the approaches have been broad gauge efforts at stimulating general cognitive development. If psychologists are to be helpful in developing more precise methods, those interested in cognition must pay closer attention to the process of concept acquisition and those interested in learning must begin to study more complex forms of behavior.

Several different types of studies will be reviewed. First, there are the attempts that have been made in training concept formation of the types studied by Piaget. The purpose of these studies has been to determine whether concepts said by Piaget to be a product of the interaction of learning and maturation can be produced by experience alone. Then there are the more traditional studies of the relation of concept learning to age and intelligence. These studies are of special interest because they have defined some of the bases for the improved performance by older and brighter children. Finally, there is a group of studies aimed at obtaining information about children's generation of hypotheses. These data give us a clearer picture of how children go about learning simple concepts and why their performance is so often best described by an all-or-none model.

TRAINING IN CONCEPT FORMATION

Some attempts have been made to hasten concept formation through training. These studies are somewhat unusual, for they are among the few efforts of those interested in Piaget's ideas to go beyond description into the manipulation of variables. To understand the significance of these studies, a brief discussion of the characteristics of Piaget's theory will be helpful.

Piaget is an interactionist and a stage theorist. Neither experience nor maturation alone is posited to be sufficient for cognitive development; true development is a product of their interaction. In attaining mature, adult-like thinking, the child must pass through a series of stages, each of which is characterised by different processes or operations. According to Piaget, the infant is incapable of thought. His behavior is dependent upon the elicitation of reflexes, the acquisition of habits, the process of imitation, and the combination of habits in novel ways. Symbolic life develops during the preschool period, and the symbols are acquired through interaction with the world. The formation of symbols is aided by, but is not dependent upon language. At a third stage, occurring during elementary school years, the child can solve complex problems, but their solution occurs through action rather than thought, through concrete rather than abstract operations. Finally, during early adolescence, flexible and effective thought develops; the child distinguishes the real from the possible; thought appears; hypotheses are developed and deductions are made from these hypotheses. For the first time, true propositional thinking is possible.

Piaget has sought to ascertain the origin and development of cognitive structures, rather than the means by which concepts are developed. This lack of interest in the process of acquisition has been rationalized in the following way:

Piaget distinguishes between learning in the narrow sense and learning in the wider sense. The former involves the mere acquisition of specific responses to particular situations. Such learning is superficial: it is unstable, impermanent, and unlikely to generalize. Learning in the wider sense is based on development. It occurs when the child has available the cognitive structures necessary for assimilating new information. (Ginsberg & Opper, 1969, p. 177)

Attempting to hasten concept formation through training has been of little interest to Piaget, for he would predict from the start that the training would be ineffective. The evaluation of this prediction has been left to others. To the degree that positive results are obtained, Piaget's theory is weakened. Gelman's (1969) study discussed in the preceding chapter is one example of successful effort to accelerate concept formation. The effectiveness of her training procedures is rare, however, for the results in most of the other studies are negative. Of course, negative results do not necessarily mean that Piaget's predictions have been supported, but the large number of studies that have yielded negative or inconclusive results indicates that if concept formation is to be accelerated it must be accomplished by laborious or less than obvious methods.

A study by Wohlwill and Lowe (1962) is illustrative of the approaches that have been used. An effort was made to increase children's understanding of the conservation of number; i.e., to recognize the principle that a particular dimension (e.g., number) is invariant under changes in other, irrelevant aspects of the situation (e.g., spatial arrangement). Is failure to show conservation due to a lack of experience in counting the numbers of objects in different spatial arrangements, to a failure to differentiate number from length, or to a lack of experience in seeing that the addition and subtraction of elements changes the numerical value of a set? Training experiences attempted to evaluate these possibilities by having different groups of kindergarteners (a) count sets of elements before and after their spatial arrangement was changed, (b) observe that the same number of elements can occupy different spatial arrangements, and (c) see that addition and subtraction influences the number of elements present. A control group had no intervening experience between the pre- and post-tests for conservation of number. There was improvement in the performance of all groups on the second testing, but the improvement was as great in the control as in the experimental groups.

This is not an isolated example of the failure of children to improve their performance after various types of training procedures. Flavell, after reviewing all of the available training studies has summarized his conclusions in the following way:

Probably the most certain conclusion is that it can be a surprisingly difficult undertaking to manufacture Piagetian concepts in the laboratory. Almost all the training methods reported impress one as sound and reasonable and well-suited to the educative job at hand. And yet most of them have had remarkably little success in producing cognitive change. It is not easy to convey the sense of disbelief that creeps over one in reading these experiments. It can be hard enough to believe that children systematically elect nonconservation in the first place; it is more difficult still to believe that trial after trial of carefully planned training is incapable of budging them from this aberrant position (Flavell, 1963, p. 377).

The intransigence of "Piagetian" concepts in the face of a wide variety of training procedures is not in accord with what we would expect from a learning point of view. Could it be that the right techniques have not been applied, and that the learning-set approach taken by Gelman is more pertinent? Perhaps the training sessions have been too brief, but even in extending training sessions, all children do not profit from the experience (Smedslund, 1961). Obviously, more research must be done. It is unfortunate but true that concepts most relevant for education are the ones that are least explored and least understood.

DEVELOPMENTAL CHANGES

Concept learning is, for the most part, much more effective after age six or seven. This "critical" period has been discussed in earlier chapters, and is, as we have seen, a period when children become more proficient in their use of language. As has been pointed out, however, the development of language cannot be the sole basis for improved performance. This period seems, rather, to be one in which certain important cognitive skills first become effective. Among these is the ability to form internal representations of stimuli. It is a time when the child develops "the ability to string together internal representations of stimulus-response-consequence into sequences which, projected into the future, allow planning and, projected into the past, allow inference" (White, 1965, p. 210). The young child may be ineffective in concept learning because he is, to a much greater degree than the older child, dependent on the here and now and must operate without the concurrent mental representation of his long series of prior experiences.

We can give two types of examples of developmental changes in concept learning that occur around the ages of five and six. The first are from studies on concept identification, and the second are from studies of inference.

Concept Identification

Odom and Coon (1966) studied changes in concept identification between the ages of five and fourteen. Problems similar to reversal shifts were constructed with pictures of the heads and bodies of animals. During training, the heads of four animals and the bodies of four others were presented in pairs, with reinforcement following choices of heads. (Each category was reinforced for half of the children, but for simplicity only one of the sequences will be described.) The part of the animal not present during training was used in the transfer trials. During the transfer trials, the previously relevant category continued to be relevant for half of the children, and the other category became relevant for the others. Thus in the first case "heads" remained relevant but was represented by new instances, and in the second case "bodies" became relevant, but the bodies were those of the animals whose heads had been correct in the training period.

Five-year-olds required four times as many trials to reach criterion on the training problem as fourteen-year-olds. When the transfer trials consisted of a reversal of the original discrimination, there were no age differences in rate of learning. The youngest children apparently had labeled the stimuli during the training trials and used the labels to direct their performance in the transfer trials. When, however, the transfer trials required the children to continue to respond by category rather than by instance, the five-year-olds made many errors. Even though the five-year-olds may have responded mediationally, they did not organize the stimuli by conceptual categories. They had little difficulty, for example, in learning that the body of the tiger was correct after having learned that the head of the tiger was correct. Rather than responding to the head of a new animal, however, they continued to respond to the bodies of the animals that had been correct during training. Older children learned the problems very rapidly.

If it is postulated that young children do not organize stimuli according to classes, but are responding to independent instances, younger children should be more strongly influenced by the number of instances present in a task than by the number of categories or dimensions on which the stimuli vary. The converse should hold for older children. Their learning should be more strongly influenced by the number of categories than by the number of instances. Osler and Kofsky (1966) evaluated these possibilities in the following way.

Five-, eight-, and eleven-year-olds were tested with one of three sets of stimuli (drawings of geometric forms). In one set there were one relevant and three irrelevant dimensions, each represented by two values; in the second set, one relevant dimension represented by two values and one irrelevant dimension represented by eight values; and in the third set, one

Figure 22-1.   Mean number of errors to criterion for Set A (16 stimuli, four binary dimensions), Set B (16 stimuli, one binary, one eight-valued dimension), and Set C (4 stimuli, two binary). (From S. F. Osler and E. Kofsky, Structure and strategy in concept learning. *Journal of Experimental Child Psychology,* 1966, 4, 202, © 1966 Academic Press.)

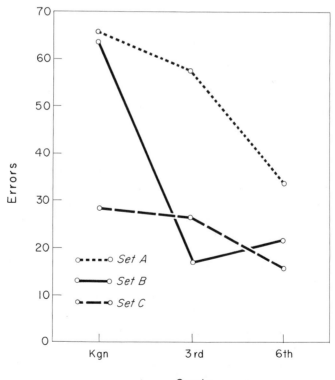

relevant and one irrelevant dimension, each represented by two values. Thus there were sixteen different stimuli in the first two sets and four in the third. The dimensions on which the stimuli differed were form, color, size, and/or number.

If the preceding reasoning is correct, the five-year-olds should perform similarly with the first two sets (since they contained the same number of stimuli), but older children should find the second set as easy as the third (since they contained the same number of dimensions). As can be seen in Figure 22-1, the results supported these considerations. The crucial factor for the youngest children was size of the set of stimuli, and for older children, the number of independent dimensions represented in the sets. Five-year-olds made large and equivalent numbers of errors on the first two sets (A and B), but with the third set (C) they learned nearly as rapidly as the older children. The older children learned the second and third sets with equal ease, but the eight-year-olds, and to some degree the eleven-year-olds, found the first set quite difficult.

In a subsequent study, Kofsky and Osler (1967) found that irrelevant information may thwart successful performance by five-year-olds because of their difficulty in shifting criteria for categorizing stimuli. Children at ages five, eight, and eleven years were asked to categorize stimuli such as those used in the previous study. At all ages the children showed preferences in the order with which they categorized the stimuli by form, color, size, and number, but only at age five did these preferences have a restrictive effect on their ability to make additional sortings. In concept learning, then, young children may perform well if the initial basis for classifying the stimuli is in accord with their preferences, but if it is not they may make many errors before they discern other bases by which the stimuli can be grouped into classes.

The associative nature of young children's performance also has been revealed in a study by Suppes and Ginsberg (1962). Efforts were made to teach five- and six-year-olds two values in a binary system. Three symbolic representations for the numerals 4 and 5 were used, with each representation following the form 100 (4) and 101 (5). The data conformed more closely to a model postulating paired-associate learning than one assuming concept formation. That is, the children appeared to have learned the numeral associated with each of the three representations, rather than the conceptual basis by which these or additional representations could be generated.

A common theme runs through these studies. The young child is viewed as a relatively rigid rote learner whose performance in a concept learning task is determined by the number of relations to be learned and who appears to label or respond to stimuli as isolated instances. Older children are seen to be flexible and capable of abstracting the classes represented by the stimuli, and to use these abilities in successive attempts to isolate the class or attribute of stimuli that is relevant for response.

Inference

The Kendlers (1967) have explored the performance of five-year-olds on a different type of problem, one requiring inference. Knowing a single if-then relation may be sufficient in solving many problems, but others require the integration of two or more sets of such relations. The Kendlers have asked whether young children are capable of integrating segments of behavior that previously have been learned but were not contiguously associated.

The task developed for studying this question required the child to learn three separate sets of relations during a series of training trials: response X leads to object Y, response A leads to object B, and object B leads to G, the goal. Concretely, they learned to press a lever or push a button to obtain Y and B (marble and steel ball, respectively), and to drop B in a hole to produce a prize. On the test trial, the children were told to try to win a prize (i.e., to reach G). To do this it was necessary to push the button that led to B, then to drop B in the hole. Very few five-year-olds were capable of giving a direct, inferential solution to this problem. By the third grade, however, approximately half of the children made a direct, correct integration. The kindergarteners had learned each component necessary for solution, but were unable to select in succession the two components that were necessary to reach the goal.

The study was repeated (Kendler, Kendler, & Carrick, 1966), but half of the children were required to label the two objects, Y and B. It was assumed that the label would provide a common stimulus element, linking the A-B and B-G segments. Kindergarteners who did not label the objects performed as poorly as they had in the first study, but when a common label had been learned in conjunction with learning segments A-B and B-G, they performed only slightly more poorly than third graders. Integration of information requires more than the ability to relate stimuli by means of a common label, but children who ordinarily do not tend to apply such labels may benefit from instructions to do so.

ROLE OF INTELLIGENCE

It is of little interest to recite further examples of how brighter children learn concepts more rapidly than duller children. What is needed is clarification of why this is the case. Fortunately, Osler and her associates have conducted a series of studies that give us some strong hints about how differences in intelligence may produce different rates of concept learning. All of the studies have used six-, ten-, and fourteen-year-olds, half above average (mean IQ of 121) and half of average IQ (mean IQ of 101).

In an initial study (Osler & Fivel, 1961) the correct response in a two-choice discrimination depended upon the utilization of the concept of bird, animal, or living thing. These classes of stimuli were assumed to represent increasingly difficult concepts. The older children and the brighter children at each age learned the concepts more rapidly, but there were no differences in the rate with which the three concepts were learned. To determine whether the concepts were learned rapidly or gradually, performance on the ten trials preceding criterion were analysed for each subject. Those whose percentage of correct response fell below the median on these two trials were classed as sudden learners, and above the median, as gradual learners. The incidence of sudden learners was a function of IQ, but not of age or concept, leading the writers to infer that the brighter children were better able to develop hypotheses than were the average children.

If bright children do develop hypotheses readily, their performance should be impaired when the stimuli are ones that elicit a wide variety of irrelevant hypotheses. The concept "two" was studied by Osler and Trautman (1961) with samples of children of the age and IQ levels used in the first study. The concept was represented either by pictures of common objects or by dots. It was assumed that the irrelevant cues contained in the pictures would facilitate the formation of a large number of hypotheses. Correct response required that the child select the member in each of a large number of pairs that contained two elements and reject the member that contained one or more than two elements. There was significant improvement with increasing age, and IQ interacted significantly with method of representation. Bright children had more difficulty in learning the discrimination when the stimuli were objects than when they were dots, but average children learned each with equal ease.

It also is possible that the superior performance of bright children lies in their greater capabilities in defining problems, rather than in their being more effective learners. Nonspecific instructions had been used in the Osler and Fivel (1961) study (i.e., "If you look at these pictures before pushing the handle, you will be able to get many marbles.") Could the greater effectiveness of the bright children be traced to their discerning more readily the problem that was to be solved? To investigate this question, Osler and Weiss (1962) repeated the earlier study, but added a condition in which the children were given the explicit instruction, "If you look at the pictures carefully you will see that there is something in the pictures like an idea that will tell you which one to choose to get a marble every time." The earlier results were replicated with nonspecific instructions but differences in the performance of bright and average children disappeared when the instructions explicitly defined what the child was to do. As expected, type of instructions facilitated the performance of the average children and had no differential effect on the performance of the bright children.

In a final study, Osler and Shapiro (1964) tested bright and average children with continuous and partial reinforcement. The task involved discriminating between two and three circles appearing in different spatial arrangements. The bright children were significantly superior to the average children when continuous reinforcement was available. With partial reinforcement, performance did not differ according to level of IQ. Support thus was obtained for the prediction that the performance of bright children would be disrupted to a greater degree than would that of average children when efforts at generating hypotheses met with only partial success.

These studies point to several factors that distinguish the concept learning of bright children. They appear to be able to define problems more readily and to produce more hypotheses than children of average intelligence. When the formulation of many hypotheses is of assistance in producing the correct response and when there is consistent affirmation of the utility of a particular hypothesis, bright children perform at a higher level than their age-mates of average intelligence. When the stimuli elicit few hypotheses and when the problem is clearly defined, IQ, at the levels tested, is not a critical variable in concept learning.

Intelligence and Social Class

Does social class membership influence concept learning when intelligence is held constant? Because of their assumed cultural deprivation, lower class children may perform less well in concept learning tasks than their more broadly experienced middle-class age-mates. This possibility was evaluated in a study by Scholnick, Osler, and Katzenellenbogen (1968). Middle- and lower-class children with mean IQs of approximately 90 (range from 75 to 101) were selected at ages five and eight. The experimental task required the isolation of one value of one dimension from among stimuli that differed on two values of three dimensions (color, form, and size). The problem was made more complex for the older children by including a fourth dimension, number.

Half of the children received pretraining on discrimination learning problems in which the stimuli varied on one dimension, but the dimensions were those represented in the concept learning task (e.g., large red circle versus small red circle; large blue triangle versus large red triangle). Twice as many lower- than middle-class children were unable to learn these discriminations, and among those who did reach criterion, rate of learning was slower for lower-class children. Thus pretraining in discrimination learning significantly improved the children's ability to isolate the relevant dimension on the concept learning task, but there were no differences according to social class in rate of concept learning.

Somewhat paradoxically, then, lower-class children did more poorly than middle-class children on simple discrimination learning tasks, but were not inferior in concept learning. Everyday experience apparently offered neither group information that was useful in concept identification, but middle-class children had learned enough in other contexts to be able to master the rules underlying the discrimination learning tasks relatively rapidly.

A later study (Osler & Scholnick, 1968) included only five-year-old, lower-class children with average IQs of approximately 90. Since in the previous study the stimuli represented the same dimensions in both the discrimination and concept learning tasks, it was impossible to evaluate the independent contribution of familiarization with dimensions and practice in interpreting feedback. Four experimental conditions therefore were constructed in which children were (a) shown the stimuli in the discrimination learning tasks and told which stimulus to select; (b) solved discrimination learning problems without the experimenter's assistance, but the dimensions of the stimuli differed from those used in the concept learning task; (c) solved the problems by themselves with reward for correct response, and the dimensions were the same as those used in the concept learning task; or (d) solved the problems as in (b) but were rewarded for correct response and penalized for errors.

The mean errors made in concept learning by children in the first two pretraining conditions did not differ from those obtained by a control group that received no pretraining. Thus neither familiarization with the dimensions nor experience in discrimination learning was sufficient to improve concept learning. Facilitation occurred for the children in the last two conditions—but only when the dimensions were size and color. Pretaining was of no help in learning to categorize stimuli on the basis of form.

Experience in differentiating the dimensions on which stimuli differ may be helpful for later concept learning if the same dimensions are represented in both the pretraining and concept learning problems. Comprehending the rule that reward always is associated with a particular stimulus may aid discrimination learning, but has a negligible influence on tasks involving the abstraction of concepts. These are the conclusions that may be reached for children of below-average intelligence. Whether social class, independent of intelligence, has a general effect on concept learning will have to be investigated in later studies.

HYPOTHESIS TESTING

In previous discussions we have characterised children as hypothesis generators. It is of interest now to look at several developmental studies that were designed for the express purpose of investigating the formation of hypotheses by children.

The operation of hypotheses can be detected relatively easily if care is given to the order in which stimuli are presented. Sequences of trials can be constructed so that certain patterns of response must represent the application of particular hypotheses. Assume that there are four possible bases of response: response to color, form, size, or position. The detection of a position hypothesis is immediately apparent. Detecting the operation of other hypotheses requires analysis of performance over blocks of trials. For example, over a particular block of four trials the sequence may be constructed so that the large stimulus is on the left on Trials 1 and 2 and on the right on Trials 3 and 4. The stimulus on the left is red on Trials 1 and 3, and the stimulus on the right is red on Trials 2 and 4. We deduce that the child must be responding on the basis of size if his pattern of responses is LLRR and to form if his pattern is LRLR. The deductions are strengthened as more and more blocks of trials are analysed.

Eimas (1969) has constructed such sequences with stimuli differing in two values of each of the dimensions indicated above. Eight such problems were given to children in grades 2, 4, 6, and 8. Information about the correctness of the child's responses was provided on four "outcome" trials in each block of 16 trials, leaving 12 blank trials that could be used to detect the operation of hypotheses. The information was independent of the actual choices made by the children on the four "outcome" trials. The percentage of responses in the 12 blank trials that conformed to one of the eight possible simple hypotheses (two for each of four dimensions) varied from 71% to 79%. These values were significantly above chance, indicating the operation of hypotheses at each age level.

A very similar procedure was used by Ingalls and Dickerson (1969) with children at grades 5, 8, and 10. Size, color, letter, and shape were the dimensions represented in the stimuli. In contrast to the previous study, reinforcement was dependent upon the choices made on the outcome trials. The proportion of blank trials revealing evidence of the application of hypotheses varied between .81 and .86. There was a strong tendency to retain a hypothesis after an outcome was confirmed (.89 to .94) and to discard a hypothesis after nonconfirmation (.07 to .09). Hypotheses were not reinstated rapidly; less than 14% of the responses within two trials after a nonconfirmation conformed to the hypothesis that preceded the nonconfirmed outcome.

The number of hypotheses employed by the children decreased as training progressed. Finding that one hypothesis was not relevant, the child discarded it and applied one of the possible alternatives. After one nonconfirmation there were, of course, four remaining hypotheses (i.e., those related to the second value of each of the dimensions represented in the nonconfirmed choice). An example will clarify this point. Assume that there are two stimuli, differing in shape, color, size, and position. On the left is a large black X, on the right, a small white T. If a choice of the left stimulus is not reinforced, four logical alternatives remain: the stimulus on the right, the small stimulus, the white stimulus, or a T rather than an X. After two nonconfirmations only two alternative hypotheses were appropriate, and after three nonconfirmations, only one hypothesis remained. The optimal strategy would be to sample from four hypotheses after one nonconfirmed outcome, from two hypotheses after two outcomes, and to select the correct hypothesis after three nonconfirmed outcomes. There was an increasing tendency with increasing age for the subjects to approximate this optimal strategy. When imperfect strategies were used, it appeared to be due to children's failure to consider all possible hypotheses or to their forgetting the information received on earlier trials. Nearly half of the fifth graders and one-third of the tenth graders failed to include all possible hypotheses.

Several conclusions can be drawn from these studies. Children appear to go about solving concept learning problems through the successive application of hypotheses. As the trials progress they sample from smaller and smaller numbers of hypotheses and, with increasing age, approximate what would be considered the optimal strategy of response.

Olson (1966) investigated children's use of optimal strategies in a different way. Children were to select one of two patterns that was "correct." Alternative patterns were created by illuminating small light bulbs arranged in 3 by 3 or 5 by 5 matrices. For example, the top row of lights was illuminated to form one pattern, and the top row and middle column to form a second pattern. A comparable matrix of bulbs, all unlit, was in front of the child. The child could discover which pattern was correct by pressing bulbs on his panel. If the bulb conformed to one of the patterns, it would light up. With two patterns, only one choice was necessary to solve the problem. The optimal strategy was to press one of the bulbs in the middle column.

Children of three, five, seven, and nine years were presented two two-pattern problems. Half were permitted an unrestricted choice of bulbs and half were allowed to press only one bulb at a time, with the instruction that they were to select the bulb that would tell them which pattern was correct.

Even three-year-olds did not make random choices. They attempted a somewhat orderly search of the board, but their choices were not directed by the patterns before them. Being told to select one bulb at a time did not produce more efficient search. By five, choices were restricted to those appearing in each pattern, but the children tried to match the models completely. Seven-year-olds, primarily those in the constrained condition, were able to restrict their choices more completely to those that would yield the critical information. Age was less crucial than condition, however, for five-year-olds applied an optimal strategy as frequently in the constrained condition as nine-year-olds did in the "free" condition.

Here, again, we see the nonrandom, but ineffectual behavior of pre-schoolers, the emergence of relevant if inefficient strategies by five-year-olds left to their own resources, and the productive and economical application of optimal strategies at ages seven and nine.

An All-or-none Model

The results of the preceding studies suggest an all-or-none model of concept learning. We assume that children's responses in a concept learning task are directed by hypotheses and that hypotheses are sampled successively. As hypotheses are applied and discarded after nonconfirmation, performance remains at a chance level. Suddenly, the child finds that a particular hypothesis proves to be correct. Performance changes abruptly and the problem is solved. The net effect is to produce one trial learning.

Suppes and Rosenthal-Hill (1968) have tested this model with kindergarteners and discussed its applicability to a number of different concept learning problems. Analyses of learning curves generally supported the model. However, sometimes there was an indication of improvement prior to the trial of the last error, but this tended to be restricted to the few preceding trials. The authors concluded that the "all-or-none model provides a first approximation to the response data from a wide variety of concept formation experiments with children" (Suppes & Rosenthal-Hill, 1968, p. 229.) But they also point out that the model tells us nothing about how children learn new concepts. This is, as the authors concede, a "profound limitation," for the model is applicable only to tasks in which the concepts already are available to the child and his efforts are directed at ascertaining which of the alternative concepts is relevant.

CONCLUSIONS

As a topic for research, concept learning lies somewhere in the hazy region that differentiates the efforts of psychologists interested in cognitive processes from those of psychologists interested in learning. Cognitive psychologists, notably Piaget and his colleagues, have spent considerable time testing children to chart the ages at which children are able to demonstrate the operation of certain concepts. While these normative data give a rich description of what children are able to do, they are of little help in clarifying how concepts are learned. Laboratory studies also fail to give us a coherent account of concept learning. These studies are more appropriately designated as studies of concept utilization or concept identification than concept learning. In the typical experiment children have been required to discover the relevance of concepts they already know, rather than being required to learn new ones.

It has proved to be difficult to produce concepts such as conservation in the laboratory setting. Whether the failure to transform nonconservers into conservers has been due to inadequate techniques, brevity of training, or to basic difficulties in modifying cognitive structures remains unknown. Since there have been some successful efforts, further exploration may be productive.

Hypotheses used by children differ in their sophistication and relevance, but even at the age of three, performance adheres to a defined scheme. Young children tend to respond on the basis of the perceptual characteristics of the stimuli, and their performance is influenced by their preferences and the number of stimuli present. A transitional period occurs around the age of five or six; after this time children cease to respond only to isolated instances and begin to categorize stimuli into classes. This transition cannot be attributed to the development of linguistic competence. Rather, what seems to occur is that children become capable of constructing well-defined internal representations of stimuli that enable them to organize sets of stimuli in terms of their common and distinctive attributes. Brighter children produce more hypotheses and are better able to define the requirements of the task than are children of average intelligence.

Some of the most useful contributions of psychologists may come from studies of concept learning. As of now, these contributions are limited to descriptive statements and models that deal with the application of concepts to relatively simple tasks.

Individual Differences

There are large individual differences in the rate at which children learn. Psychologists know this, for in nearly all of their studies there are children who learn very rapidly and others whose progress is unbelievably slow. Teachers and parents constantly are made aware of differences among children in the ease with which they learn a new skill. Children in a first-grade classroom almost always are assigned to groups such as the Pink Pussycats, the Grizzly Bears, and the Hummingbirds, according to the progress they have made in learning how to read or to do mathematics. Children in the top reading groups "catch on" very rapidly, while those in the low groups may need long periods of practice and a great deal of help. Is this because the rapid learners also are the brightest children? This is unlikely, for children in the top reading group are not necessarily the ones in the top mathematics group. Why should this be the case? If there is such a thing as a general learning ability we would assume that children who learn one type of material easily would be equally effective with other types of material. Is our assumption incorrect? And how can we account for the fact that there are children with above-average IQs who find it impossible to learn to read? These questions open an interesting topic, that of ascertaining the interrelations and correlates of children's learning. [A discussion of individual differences in learning during infancy has been published by Horowitz (1969).]

The first question we will ask is whether learning is a unitary function or a composite of different types of abilities. Thus far we have paid little attention to the possible correlations between scores obtained in different types of tasks. There is a simple reason for this. The common practice has been for an investigator to use a single problem to assess the influence of certain experimental variables, and rarely have the same children been presented more than one type of problem. Data are available, however, concerning the intercorrelations among scores obtained on a variety of learning tasks. These studies generally have been done by persons interested in the analysis of the psychometric structure of learning ability and have attempted to ascertain whether learning is a unitary, global function or whether it is necessary to posit different kinds of learning abilities.

The second major question concerns the relation of learning and intelligence. We know from earlier examples that scores on learning tasks differ for groups differing in level of intelligence. How pervasive and how strong is this relation?

A third question is whether individual differences in learning are associated with differences in children's personality characteristics. Unfortunately, personality characteristics of effective and ineffective learners have not been investigated extensively, despite the practical implications of such information. The effects of level of anxiety on learning has attracted considerable attention, but only small pieces of information are available concerning the relevance of other personality variables.

Finally, we may ask whether the kinds of learning discussed in this book have any relation to learning that occurs in the classroom. Many critics of laboratory research see little relation between what children do in the laboratory and the everyday learning that goes on at home and in school. They look at a laboratory study of paired-associates, for example, and ask whether the rate at which a child learns to associate two nonsense syllables has any implication for how this child will fare in his science class. Without information about the relations between performance in experimental tasks and in school it is impossible to offer an answer to these critics.

INTERRELATIONS IN CHILDREN'S LEARNING

Before the advent of the computer it was very difficult to analyse large masses of data. While a computer can handle the data obtained from several hundred subjects performing a dozen different tasks in a matter of seconds, it would take weeks or months to obtain these analyses by mechanical calculation. Recently, therefore, investigators have been able to approach the study of interrelations in learning in a much more expansive manner than was feasible in earlier decades.

The few early studies of interrelations among learning tasks (e.g., deWeerdt, 1927; Husband, 1941) gave little support to those who posited the existence of a general learning factor. High intercorrelations would strengthen the conception of learning as a unitary ability. Rarely, however, were the intercorrelations above .30. Children who learned one problem easily did not necessarily demonstrate equal competence in learning other types of problems. These studies cannot be given much emphasis, however, for they were conducted with relatively small numbers of subjects and with only a few different types of learning tasks.

Current Studies

An extensive study of 240 seventh graders was reported by Stake (1961), who tested each of the children with twelve learning tasks. The tasks differed on three dimensions, content (verbal versus nonverbal), type (rote memory versus relational learning), and mode of presentation (group versus game-like individual tests). The median of the correlations between the asymptotic level reached on each task and all other tasks varied from .10 to .30. The highest correlations were those between two forms of the same type of task, such as the correlation of .66 between memory for verbs and memory for adjectives, or between various memory and learning tasks, such as the correlation of .36 between memory for a list of verbs and learning to associate pairs of words. In general, Stake's results provide little evidence for a general learning factor.

Duncanson (1964) included tasks of three types: rote memory, paired associates, and concept formation. Materials of three kinds were used in each type of task: verbal, numerical, and figural. All of the nine resulting tasks were given to a sample of 102 sixth graders. The intertask correlation matrix yielded correlations of no greater magnitude than were found in previous studies. There were a number of significant correlations between the various rote memory and paired-associate tasks, but few significant correlations were found either between the concept formation and rote memory or between the concept formation and paired-associates tasks.

Stevenson and Odom (1965a) reported interrelations among performance on paired-associates, two discrimination learning tasks, concept learning, and anagrams. The subjects were 354 fourth and sixth graders. The median correlation among the tasks was .17; however, consistently significant correlations were obtained for particular pairs of tasks, such as the two forms of discrimination learning (r's = .43 to .69) and between paired-associates and anagrams (r's = .38 to .47).

The most extensive study of interrelations in children's learning was reported by Stevenson, Hale, Klein, and Miller (1968). Over 600 children in grades 3 through 7 were presented twelve tasks, including traditional learning tasks such as rote memory, paired associates, discrimination learning, probability learning, incidental learning, and more complex problem solving tasks involving the concept of probability, concept of conservation, and anagrams. In analyses of the data obtained over a broad range of intelligence at grade 7, the median intercorrelation among the tasks was .30. When analyses included samples of children of average ranges of IQ across all grades, the median intercorrelation was .20. The correlations were slightly higher than those found in other studies, but even here fewer than 10% of the correlations were above .50.

Tasks that were identical or highly similar in structure, such as the two paired-associates, the two memory, or the two concept of probability tasks, tended to be significantly related in all analyses. The single most important determinant of significant interrelations was the presence of verbal material. The greatest numbers of significant correlations were produced by paired associates, verbal memory, and anagrams, all of which tasks were highly dependent upon verbal processes. Traditional learning tasks were no more frequently correlated significantly with each other than were learning tasks and tasks that were assumed to be measures of more complex forms of problem solving.

The subjects in the preceding studies were older children. Perhaps learning abilities are less highly differentiated with younger children. That is, even though there is little consistency in the level of performance of older children on various learning tasks, preschool children who perform well on one type of task also may be effective in learning other types of tasks. If this were the case, support would be provided for a position postulating a global learning function in young children and the emergence of more specific abilities with increasing age.

Friedrichs et al. (1970) constructed eight learning and problem-solving tasks that were appropriate for preschool children. The tasks included paired associates, serial memory, oddity learning, concept learning, observational learning, incidental learning, problem solving, and category sorting. As in the Stevenson, Hale, Klein, and Miller study, an effort was made to select tasks that were commonly used in laboratory studies of learning. All tasks were administered to 50 four- and five-year-old middle-class children. The median of the intercorrelations was .17, indicating a high degree of differentiation of learning abilities. The same tasks were administered to 50 four- and five-year-old children from lower-class homes (Stevenson, Williams, & Coleman, 1971). The intercorrelations were comparable to those found for middle-class children. There appears, therefore, to be little merit in assuming that learning abilities become increasingly differentiated with increasing age. Interrelations in performance on learning tasks are of no greater magnitude at age four than they are at age twelve.

The number of studies is small, but the results are consistent. Low positive intercorrelations tend to be found among different learning tasks, except when the tasks are similar in structure, or, in some cases, similar in content. There is little basis for assuming that learning represents a unitary function that operates in a similar manner across different types of learning tasks. A series of factors must be involved, including intellectual and motivational factors as well as ones related to the structure and content of the tasks.

This information is sobering for anyone who is tempted to construct a theory of learning based on children's performance in a restricted sample of problems. Theoretical mechanisms developed to account for performance on one type of problem may have limited applicability in the discussion of other types of problems. We can evaluate this disturbing possibility only through further research in which efforts are made to apply the same experimental variables to groups of children who are required to learn a variety of different problems.

Information about the low interrelations across different types of learning problems may be of significance for educators. If children are not uniformly good at all types of learning, there may be greater need than is now acknowledged to provide children with different kinds of opportunities as they are faced with different kinds of subject matter in their classes at school.

LEARNING AND INTELLIGENCE

The story behind the early development of intelligence tests is well-known but worth repeating. Shortly after public education was established, school authorities became alarmed at the frequency with which children failed in school. Since it was expensive and unproductive to provide regular instruction for slow-learning children, some means had to be devised for deciding which children should be assigned to special classes. Alfred Binet, a psychologist interested in the problems of intelligence, and his colleague, Theodore Simon, were commissioned by Parisian authorities to develop a procedure by which such decisions could be made. The outcome of their efforts was the 1905 Binet-Simon intelligence scale, the prototype of a large number of intelligence tests for children. The scale included a variety of tasks, such as repeating digits, following orders, and distinguishing between abstract terms. It was assumed that this graded series of tasks would provide an indication of the child's intellectual level, according to which predictions could be made about the child's potential success in learning school materials. These tests are used today on the same assumption, in placing children in special classes for the retarded and for children with "learning disabilities."

The success of intelligence tests in predicting school learning is related, in part, to the fact that the ability to carry out many of the tasks in intelligence tests is dependent upon past learning. For example, if a child has learned thoroughly the meaning of two abstract words, he will have little difficulty in explaining their similarities and differences. Other tasks may draw even more directly from past learning. The Wechsler Intelligence Scale for Children, for example, includes subtests such as arithmetic, vocabulary, and general information. Without having learned from appropriate prior experience, the child is unable to respond correctly. The tests do not depend solely on past learning, however. In the Wechsler

Scale the child also is asked to solve problems he has not encountered previously, such as arranging pictures in a logical manner and reproducing designs with colored blocks. Success in these tasks is less reliant upon transfer from relevant prior experience.

Learning in School

Examples of the correlation between IQ and performance in school are presented in Table 23-1. Here, correlations have been computed between IQ and school grades for two groups of seventh graders, the first of above-average and the second of average intelligence. At both levels of ability all the correlations between IQ and one-quarter's grades in four academic subjects were highly significant. Interestingly, the correlations consistently were higher for girls than for boys.

Table 23-1.   Correlations between IQ (Lorge-Thorndike) and grades in school

Group		N	*IQ* M	SD	English	*Subject* Social Studies	Science	Math
1	B	38	121	11	.53	.45	.63	.45
	G	40	119	11	.63	.60	.71	.71
2	B	48	101	13	.57	.48	.65	.39
	G	46	104	14	.76	.82	.75	.68

All p's $< .01$.
Data from H. W. Stevenson, G. A. Hale, R. E. Klein, and L. K. Miller, Interrelations and correlates in children's learning and problem solving. *Monographs of the Society for Research in Child Development*, 1968, 33, 37–38.

Thus intelligence tests continue to be useful in predicting how well the child, at least the middle-class white child, will do in school. But a good deal of what goes on in school at any one time involves extensive transfer from what has been learned in previous years. Will comparable correlations be found when children are required to learn materials in which such transfer is minimized? We can answer this question by looking at the results of studies where scores obtained on various learning tasks are related to IQ.

Learning in the Laboratory

Early studies revealed low correlations between IQ and performance on such laboratory tasks as digit span, associative memory, and letter cancellation (Munn, 1954). These studies were subject to a variety of criticisms, however, and for several decades a good deal of time was spent in trying to develop more sophisticated techniques for investigation. Garrett (1928), for example, suggested that the intelligence tests used in most of the studies had not been difficult enough, but was unable to obtain higher correlations with more demanding tests. Garrison (1928), on the other hand, criticized previous studies for the kinds of material used to assess learning ability, but found only slightly higher correlations when he included more complex tasks such as verbal analogies. Another difficulty in the early studies was the restricted range of ability represented in the groups from which the children had been drawn. Husband (1941) attempted to counter this problem by extending the range of intelligence represented in the sample of children. The results were similar to those obtained with more restricted ranges of intellectual ability. A final problem in the early studies was, according to Woodrow (1940), the confounding of initial level of performance with improvement across repeated presentations of a task. In a review of studies using gain or improvement scores, however, Woodrow found no higher correlations with IQ than had been obtained with other measures. [For a further discussion of these and other early studies see Rapier (1962).]

The prospects of finding strong correlations between learning and intelligence looked rather bleak until several studies were published in the 1960s. The median correlations obtained in these studies varied from the mid .20s to the high .30s (Duncanson, 1964; Stake, 1961; Stevenson & Odom, 1965a; Stevenson, Hale, Klein, & Miller, 1968). The correlations for some tasks were reasonably high. Duncanson, for example, found correlations of .43 and .44 between IQ and verbal paired-associate learning, verbal rote memory, and figural rote memory. Stevenson and Odom found correlations with IQ as high as .57 for paired-associate learning and .49 for anagrams. In the study by Stevenson, Hale, Klein, and Miller, the correlations with IQ obtained for boys in grades 4 through 7 varied between .42 and .46 for paired-associate learning, .49 and .66 for verbal memory, and between .48 and .73 for anagrams. The comparable ranges of correlations for girls were .40 and .67 for paired-associates, .58 and .67 for verbal memory, and .48 and .61 for anagrams. In all of these studies the likelihood of obtaining significant correlations with intelligence was much higher for tasks involving verbal material than for those relying less heavily on verbal functions.

Another group of laboratory studies relating IQ and performance in learning tasks has been reviewed by Zeaman and House (1967). Although these were not correlational studies, level of intelligence was related to learning by comparing the performance of groups of children differing in IQ or MA. Groups differing in IQ differed less frequently in performance on learning tasks than did groups differing in MA. Differences specifically associated with IQ appeared only when the groups differed greatly in intellectual level or when the tasks were very complex.

We conclude that level of intelligence is a significant determinant of performance for some types of learning. The correlations are moderately high when verbal material is to be learned, for tests of the ability to acquire associations, and, not unexpectedly, when the material is similar to that found in intelligence tests. Even so, individual differences in intelligence never are capable of accounting for more than 50% of the variability in rate of learning. It must be pointed out that these conclusions are derived from studies of normal children representing restricted ranges of intelligence. More substantial correlations may be found with samples that represent the full range of intellectual abilities, including low-grade retarded children as well as children who are extremely bright.

LEARNING AND PERSONALITY

Personality characteristics commonly are assumed to exert important influences on learning, and many children seen by clinical and school psychologists confirm this assumption. Some of the most common clinical symptoms of poor learners are tension, restlessness, short attention span and poor motivation. We have relatively little insight into how these effects arise. We know little about the types of learning that are disrupted or facilitated by different personality characteristics, the degree to which the relation between personality and learning is situationally determined, or about possible developmental changes in this relation. The only aspect of personality about which we possess more than a few bits of information is the influence of the child's level of anxiety on his proficiency in learning. When we attempt to discuss other characteristics we are quite ill informed.

Anxiety

Psychologists interested in investigating the relation of anxiety to learning must devise a means of measuring anxiety. A popular approach is to develop a questionnaire in which the child is asked a series of questions tapping various commonly accepted symptoms of anxiety, such as "I worry most of the time," "My hands feel sweaty," "It is hard for me to keep my mind on things," and "When the teacher says she is going to give the class a test, I get a nervous or funny feeling." Two questionnaires have been constructed for use with children, the Children's Manifest Anxiety Scale (Castaneda, McCandless, & Palermo, 1956) and the Test Anxiety Scale for Children (Sarason, et al., 1960). The child's score is determined by the number of statements with which he agrees, and a high score is presumed to reflect a high level of anxiety.

Most of the studies have sought to evaluate the hypothesis derived from a stimulus-response view that anxiety acts as an irrelevant drive, energizing all existing habits. According to this view, the strength of a response is a product of the level of drive and the strength of the habit. High drive, whether the result of deprivation, stress, or anxiety, should result in improved performance for responses that have been well learned. When, however, the strength of the correct response is lower than that of alternative competing responses, high levels of anxiety should impede performance. These arguments can be clarified by several examples.

In a lever-pulling task, which involves well-learned response, highly anxious children are predicted to have faster speeds of response than children with low levels of anxiety. This prediction is supported by several studies. Penney and McCann (1962), for example, tested groups of third and fourth graders who received high and low scores on the Children's Manifest Anxiety Scale. The movement of the lever terminated a loud, unpleasant tone. High anxious children had faster response speeds than low anxious children, as predicted.

Interfering effects of anxiety have been demontrated by Lipsitt and Spears (1965) in a paired-associate learning task. Triads of pairs of stimuli were selected so that one response was strongly associated with three stimulus elements. For example, the tendency to respond "eat" to words such as fork, knife, and spoon is strong for all children. If anxiety energizes the strength of such associations, highly anxious children should have a greater tendency to respond "eat" to all three words than children with lower levels of anxiety. The task was organized, however, so that "eat" was the correct associate for only one of the stimulus elements of the triad: fork-eat, knife-hat, spoon-door. Pairs such as "fork-eat" should be learned rapidly by highly anxious children, but for pairs such as "knife-hat," their tendency to respond to "knife" with the strong associate "eat" should interfere with learning the correct associate "hat." Children with high levels of anxiety did perform less effectively than less anxious children where items had low association values (e.g., knife-hat), but no difference occurred for the high association items, partly because all children learned them very easily.

Another illustrative study is that of Castaneda (1961). Five lights appeared in a horizontal array, and below each light was a response button. Children have a strong tendency to press buttons directly below lights. For some light-button combinations this tendency led to correct response, but other light-button combinations were arranged so that the correct button was not below the light. High levels of anxiety were predicted to result in better performance when the dominant response was correct, but poorer performance when the dominant response was incorrect. In the latter case, the heightened tendency of anxious children to make the dominant, but incorrect response of pressing the button below the light should interfere with learning the correct response. The results revealed a significant interaction between level of anxiety and type of button correct, with each of the differences being in the predicted direction.

While the position just described places great emphasis on the relative strengths of correct and incorrect response tendencies, other studies have reported more general interfering effects of high levels of anxiety. Stevenson and Odom (1965b) related scores on the Test Anxiety Scale for Children to performance on paired-associate learning, discrimination learning, concept learning, and anagrams. The correlations more frequently were significant for boys than for girls. On paired-associate learning, for example, the correlations between scores on the anxiety scale and the incidence of correct response for boys was -.32 at grade 4 and -.28 at grade 6; neither of the correlations was significant for girls. For anagrams, the correlations were significant for girls at both grades 4 and 6 (r's = -.43 and -.28) and for boys at grade 6 (r = -.48). There is a hint in these results that high anxiety may have its most deleterious effects on verbal tasks. This possibility is strengthened when we look at the language and non-language portions of the IQ test (California Test of Mental Maturity) given to these children. The correlations of the language portion of this test with scores on the anxiety questionnaire were significant for both boys and girls at both grades 4 and 6 (r's = -.27 to -.49), while for the nonlanguage IQ score the correlation was significant only for sixth grade boys (r = -.48).

Children's performance in school has been related to their scores on anxiety questionnaires. Two studies with the Test Anxiety Scale for Chil-

Table 23-2.   Correlations between level of anxiety and scores on achievement tests

Grade	Boys		Girls	
	Reading	Arithmetic	Reading	Arithmetic
Hill and Sarason				
4	−.23**	−.30**	−.29**	−.28**
6	−.35**	−.35**	−.36**	−.33**
Stevenson and Odom				
4	−.30*	−.35**	−.22*	−.24*
6	−.29*	−.26*	−.34**	−.26*
Feldhusen and Klausmeier				
5	−.48**	−.47**	−.38**	−.40**

* $p < .05$
** $p < .01$
Data from: K. T. Hill and S. B. Sarason, The relation of test anxiety and defensiveness to test and school performance over the elementary school years: A further longitudinal study. *Monographs of the Society for Research in Child Development*, 1966, 31, 32; H. W. Stevenson and R. D. Odom, Interrelationships in children's learning. *Child Development*, 1965, 36, 1008; J. F. Feldhusen and H. J. Klausmeier, Anxiety, intelligence, and achievement in children of low, average, and high intelligence. *Child Development*, 1962, 33, 407.

dren (Hill & Sarason, 1966; Stevenson & Odom, 1965b) report significant negative correlations for scores on achievement tests in reading and arithmetic. These correlations are presented in Table 23-2, along with those found in a third study using the Children's Manifest Anxiety Scale (Feldhusen & Klausmeier, 1962). Highly anxious children have lower levels of achievement in school. This is reflected both in the results of achievement tests and in school grades. The most ruinous combination found for getting good grades in school was a lower than average level of intelligence and a high level of anxiety (Hill & Sarason, 1966).

The common sense assumption that children who are highly anxious will have difficulty in learning is given rather general support in these studies. The studies tell us that a relation exists between level of anxiety and ease of learning, both in the laboratory and in school, but offer only suggestions about how the effects are mediated. Does anxiety have its major effects through energizing existing habits? Do the internal stimuli produced by high levels of anxiety restrict the child's ability to attend closely to what is taking place in the outside world? Or does anxiety influence unconscious mechanisms so that the child's efforts to respond to certain types of stimuli are distorted and disturbed? These and other possible interpretations have been suggested, but their validity must be evaluated in further research.

Other Characteristics

The most efficient way to describe the relation of other personality characteristics and learning is to list them, along with a brief description of the studies in which the relations were established.

Need for Achievement. Miller and Estes (1961) assessed the need for achievement of nine-year-old boys by means of the Thematic Apperception Test. When the group was dichotomized into high and low scorers, there was a consistent tendency for the high need-achievers to make fewer errors in a two-choice discrimination task, where reinforcement for correct response consisted of knowledge of results, one cent, or fifty cents.

Self-esteem. Lekarczyk and Hill (1969) separated fifth and sixth graders into high and low self-esteem groups on the basis of the Self-Esteem Inventory. Boys with high self-esteem made significantly fewer errors in paired-associate learning than did those with low self-esteem. The difference was not significant for girls.

Need for Approval. Third and sixth graders were separated into upper and lower 30th percentiles on the basis of responses to the Children's Social Desirability Scale (Crowne, Holland, & Conn, 1968). In a concept learning task with one relevant and two irrelevant dimensions selected from form, color, and size, slower learning was found for boys who were rated as having a high need for approval. Again, the difference was not significant for girls.

Hardworking.   Stevenson, Hale, Klein, and Miller (1968) had teachers of seventh graders rate their pupils according to how much effort they put into their school work. The correlations between these ratings were significantly positive for boys for paired-associate learning, incidental learning, verbal memory, concept of probability, and anagrams (r's = .31 to .54). For girls, positive relations were found only for verbal memory and anagrams.

Socially Dependent.   In the Stevenson et al. study the children also were rated by their teachers on how dependent they were upon their teacher. Here, the correlations with learning were more frequently positive for girls than for boys. More independent girls did better in paired-associate learning, discrimination learning, verbal memory, concept of probability, and anagrams (r's = .40 to .65). For boys, the only significant correlation was with discrimination learning.

This sketchy information leads one to be more optimistic than satisfied. Judging from these studies, it should not be especially difficult to obtain a more adequate picture of the relation between personality and learning than now exists. It seems likely, however, that there are sex differences in these relations, with the probability of obtaining significant correlations being greater for boys than for girls.

LEARNING IN THE LABORATORY AND IN SCHOOL

Developmental psychologists who have studied children's learning have not tended to ask themselves whether what they were doing in the laboratory was related to what goes on in school. Some investigators simply have assumed that any information about children's learning in one context would be relevant for discussing learning in other contexts. Others have been interested in theory rather than in application, and have not considered the problem of relating their research to school learning. Information does exist, however, about the relation between the short-term laboratory research and the long-term learning that occurs in school. This information is derived from studies comparing individual differences in learning in the two situations. Three measures of performance in school have been used: teachers' ratings, scores on achievement tests, and grades.

Teachers' Ratings

Teachers have daily experience in evaluating their pupils' proficiency at learning and find it relatively easy to rate their pupils according to their effectiveness in learning. Stevenson, Hale, Klein, and Miller (1968) capitalized on this fact by asking teachers in grades 3 through 7 to rate their pupils according to how rapidly they "caught on," assimilated new material, and grasped new principles. Correlations were computed between these ratings and the children's performance on ten learning and problem solving tasks. Sixty % of the correlations were statistically significant. They were significant for both boys and girls in every grade for paired-associate learning (r's = .39 to .62) and anagrams (r's = .39 to .72), and in all but one grade for incidental learning and verbal memory (r's = .30 to .76). Skills necessary in these types of tasks tend to be ones that teachers are aware of in their daily experience in teaching the children. Correlations less often were significant for tasks that did not require the use of words, such as discrimination learning and probability learning. This should not be surprising, for the classroom typically is a world of words, and the child's success depends on the ease with which he understands and uses language.

Achievement Tests

Children's attainments in school are measured by yearly achievement tests. Among the most popular of these are the Iowa Tests of Basic Skills, which assess children's accomplishments in language, work-study skills, and arithmetic. Stevenson, Friedrichs, and Simpson (1970) have reported the relation of scores obtained on these tests to paired-associate learning,

Table 23-3.   Correlations between scores on Iowa Tests of Basic Skills in grade 7 and performance on experimental tasks in grades 4 and 7

	Total Language			Total Work Study			Total Arithmetic		
	4	7		4	7		4	7	
		Old	New		Old	New		Old	New
1. Paired associates	.33**	.24	.42**	.40**	.23	.40**	.38**	.13	.42**
2. Discrimination learning	.15	.32**	.29*	.17	.17	.24*	.21	.23	.25*
3. Incidental learning	.32*	.31*	.35**	.32*	.24	.37**	.34*	.24	.35**
4. Verbal memory	.51**	.40**	.38**	.48**	.17	.28*	.50**	.42**	.26*
5. Anagrams	.54**	.58**	.53**	.55**	.30*	.52**	.55**	.63**	.52**

* $p < .05$
** $p < .01$
Data from H. W. Stevenson, A. G. Friedrichs and W. E. Simpson, Interrelations and correlates over time in children's learning. *Child Development*, 1970, 41, 683.

discrimination learning, incidental learning, verbal memory, and ana-grams. The study is unique in the fact that the children were tested with the learning tasks at grade 4 and again at grade 7. It was possible, there-fore, to determine whether performance on the learning tasks at grade 4 was related to achievement in school at grade 7, as well as whether per-formance on the learning tasks at grade 7 was related to seventh grade achievement scores. In addition to the 73 subjects in the longitudinal sample, an additional 138 subjects were presented the learning tasks for the first time in grade 7.

Correlations are presented in Table 23-3 for the "old" subjects at both grades 4 and 7, and for the "new" subjects at grade 7. The frequency of significant correlations is high. Perhaps the most remarkable aspects of the results are those involving learning scores at grade 4. The rate at which children learned paired-associates at grade 4, for example, corre-lated between .33 and .40 with achievement test scores obtained in grade 7. The correlations for some of the other tasks were even higher over the three-year period.

Grades

A third measure of learning in school is obtained from the grades as-signed the children. Correlations also were computed in the Stevenson, Friedrichs, and Simpson study between performance on the learning tasks in grades 4 and 7 and grades received in the seventh grade. These correlations are presented in Table 23-4. 80% of the correlations were sig-nificant for the two sets of data collected at grade 7, and 40% of the cor-relations were significant between these grades and performance on the learning tasks given three years earlier.

These sets of results offer evidence that performance in tasks of the types used in laboratory studies of children's learning are significantly related to the kinds of long-term learning that occur in school. Criticisms of experimental studies as having no application for the discussion of what goes on in daily classroom activities appear, therefore, to be inap-propriate. The results offer no excuse for failing to conduct research on learning in the classroom, but they do point out that the overlap between experimental and educational psychology may not be so slight as some-times has been suggested.

CONCLUSIONS

We usually think of individual differences as contributing to variability in performance. Children differ in their rates of learning, as they differ in all other characteristics. Part of this variability must be related to bio-

Table 23-4.   Correlations of performance at grades 4 and 7 with 7th grade grades

	Boys				Girls			
	Eng.	Soc. Stud.	Sci.	Math.	Eng.	Soc. Stud.	Sci.	Math.
Paired associates								
Grade 4	.24	.18	.32	.51*	.31	.32	.26	.33
Grade 7	.26*	.12	.34**	.35**	.16	.24*	.35**	.29*
Discrimination learning								
Grade 4	.25	.30	.20	.24	.20	.30	.25	.44*
Grade 7	.31**	.22*	.45**	.35**	.22	.04	.24*	.27*
Incidental learning								
Grade 4	.32	.51*	.16	.19	.55**	.56*	.50**	.53**
Grade 7	.18	.19	.29**	.26*	.39**	.26*	.13	.13**
Verbal memory								
Grade 4	.14	.16	.38*	.31	.47**	.30	.36*	.32
Grade 7	.23*	.15	.26*	.27**	.54**	.44**	.27*	.50**
Anagrams								
Grade 4	.32	.24	.48**	.43**	.39*	.46**	.37*	.45**
Grade 7	.52**	.22*	.43**	.42**	.53**	.43**	.32**	.42**

* $p < .05$
** $p < .01$
Data from H. W. Stevenson, A. G. Friedrichs and W. E. Simpson, Interrelations and correlates over time in children's learning. *Child Development,* 1970, 41, 654.

logical factors, but about this we have only conjecture and no facts. Instead, psychologists interested in studying individual differences in learning have spent most of their time in assessing the types of individual differences that exist, the relation of individual differences in learning among various kinds of tasks, and in investigating other characteristics of children that contribute to differences in speed of learning.

The major questions that have been asked are (a) whether there is a general learning ability, (b) how performance on learning tasks is related to measures of intelligence and personality, and (c) how individual differences in long-term measures of learning relate to those found in laboratory tasks.

The answer to the first question is essentially negative. There is no evidence for the operation of a single learning ability. Interrelations among learning tasks often are statistically significant, but only a small portion of the variability in performance on one task is related to variability on another task. Rather than being dependent upon a single ability, adequate performance is a product of the combination of many abilities. A fine-grained analysis of any learning situation reveals a host of factors that determine performance, including those related to attention, perception, memory, and motivation.

In their efforts to classify learning abilities, psychologists have tended to give greater emphasis to the structure than to the content of what is learned. It has been assumed, for example, that paired-associate learning and rote memory reflect associative learning, while concept learning and problem solving are dependent upon higher cognitive processes (e.g., Jensen, 1969). Such assumptions are not supported by the results of the studies that have been reviewed. Paired-associate learning is as highly related to performance in a "complex" task such as anagrams as it is to verbal memory. Learning abilities must be classified by the content of what is learned, as well as by the structure imposed upon this content by the requirements of the task.

The assumption that intelligence is the major determinant of rate of learning is challenged by the results of studies with children of average ranges of intelligence. Learning is related to intelligence, but the two are not identical functions. Perhaps higher correlations would be obtained if large numbers of severely retarded or exceptionally gifted children were included in the studies. Even so, this would not help us in understanding why children with above-average IQs often do less well in learning than their duller age-mates.

Some clues to the problem may lie in the relation of learning to personality. It is unfortunate that we have little information about this matter, other than that obtained in studies of anxiety. Anxious children learn more poorly than do children who possess fewer symptoms of anxiety. There are other bits of interesting information, but they do not give us anything like a comprehensive understanding of how personality characteristics influence learning. For example, boys learn more effectively if they have a high need for achievement, high self-esteem, a low need for approval, and are hardworking in school. Girls who are socially independent learn more effectively than those who are less able to function in the absence of other persons. Extending our catalogue of personality correlates of learning is a reasonable goal, but however many of these correlates are uncovered, the question of causality remains unanswered. When we say a child is anxious, has a low need for achievement, or is dependent, does this mean he attends less well, his ability to retain information is impaired, he is unwilling to try new modes of response, that he does not profit from experience? Until we know more about how personality characteristics are represented in behavior and how these behaviors interfere with or facilitate learning, we will have only statistical rather than causal relationships.

Finally, evidence does not support the criticism that laboratory research is remote from everyday learning at home and in school. Children who are judged by their teachers as being effective learners and who attain high scores on achievement tests and high grades in school tend to be the same children who do well in standard laboratory learning tasks. The child apparently does not recognize that learning to associate two nonsense syllables is different from learning his arithmetic or science. Research that isolates reliable information about learning in one context is likely to be a useful source of ideas about the variables that influence learning in other situations.

How simple the learning of lower organisms appears when we look at the child! The accumulated contributions of language, social interactions, and a memory for vast amounts of rich and varied experience increase the difficulties in understanding children's learning exponentially over that of understanding the lever-pressing of the rat or the manipulation of tools by the monkey. There are developmental changes in children's learning; their learning is subject to the influence of all kinds of variables; and to make matters even more complicated, there are large and pervasive differences among individual children that influence how much and how well they learn.

CHAPTER

24

General Conclusions

We know before we start that it is nearly impossible to summarize all the material that has been presented. There are too many studies, too many aspects of learning, and too many theoretical points of view. It is a challenge, however, to ask what kinds of order can be imposed.

Three general headings suggest themselves as focal points. First, "Methodology." Although the experimental method has been used very productively, the account of children's learning it is producing may be less comprehensive than we may wish. We are now in a position to evaluate the merits and weaknesses of the procedures that have been used. Second, "Theoretical Positions." There has been a continuous interplay between theory and research, and although it is not clear yet that any particular theoretical orientation will prove to be most effective, the strengths and limitations of the various positions are becoming increasingly clear. Third, "Developmental Changes." A large majority of the studies yield data which bear on the developmental changes in learning that appear as children mature and have broader experiences in their everyday lives. It is tempting to try to characterize the major developmental changes in the ways children approach and perform in various types of learning tasks.

METHODOLOGY

Child psychologists have been criticized at times for their reliance on the experimental method. It is argued that the atypical environment of the laboratory and the artificiality of the materials restrict the usefulness of the information that is obtained. This criticism can be countered, in part, by pointing out that more rapid advances in knowledge followed the introduction of the experimental method than had occurred in centuries of observation and interaction with children. Even astute philosophers and

340

sensitive parents are unable to have enough experience with enough different children to sort out the effects of variables and their interactions, and thus to test whatever generalizations or questions may have occurred to them.

This is not to say that other approaches are irrelevant or that they may be unproductive. The value of experimental data is enhanced through information obtained by other methods. The contribution of many studies would have been greater if careful observational records had been made while the children performed, or if the children had been questioned closely about their interpretation of the task and how they went about solving it. Clarity might come to many problems if experimenters would leave their laboratories at times and observe children in their everyday environments.

At worst, an experimental study may be a contrived elaboration of the trivial and the obvious. At best, it is a richly productive source of reliable information. It is not satisfying to investigate the trivial. But it often is very hard to separate the trivial from the significant before the results of an experiment have been obtained. In fact, some of our most interesting studies have been those that did *not* turn out to produce effects that were obvious from common sense. It was "obvious," for example, that learning would be improved if rewards of high rather than of low value were used, or if the experimenter told the child which response would be correct. In each case, as we have seen, what was "obvious" was not borne out by experimental data.

Child psychologists have tended to be more interested in laboratory studies than in applied problems of learning. It is true that reinforcement principles have been applied in studies of behavior modification, that Gibson (1965) has related the principles of perceptual learning to the problem of reading, and that Suppes (1966) and Atkinson (1968) have developed programs for computer-assisted instruction in reading, mathematics, and logic, but other than these, there have been relatively few child psychologists working on applied problems of learning. This has been due primarily to the small number of investigators and to the newness of the field, rather than to disinterest or to rigid insistence on laboratory studies. There are indications that this limitation will be short-lived, as more psychologists begin to undertake research that is both practically oriented and soundly planned and executed. Their studies will be the beginnings of a firmly based applied psychology of children's learning.

Information is restricted in several other ways. The subjects, for the most part, have been middle-class children who have a high desire to achieve and to please adults, broad backgrounds of experience in urban society, well-developed strategies for getting along in the world, fluent verbal abilities, and above-average intelligence. They have been test-wise children with extensive prior experience with both formal and informal learning tasks. The findings will have greater generality when children are selected from more diverse social and cultural backgrounds.

There has been a tendency, too, for investigators to stay too long with traditional problems and traditional methodology, rather than to undertake new and innovative approaches to investigation. Up to a point there is value in having a series of studies conducted with the same materials and the same procedure, but after this the studies may begin to yield diminishing returns. There is, moreover, the ever-present possibility that investigators will become so caught up in a particular problem or procedure that they will lose sight of the central questions that initially stimulated the research.

Finally, studies have been small-scale and short-term. We need to know more about whether the effects are durable and will persist over time. There is no reason now why studies cannot be conducted over days, rather than minutes. Studies that would have been too taxing for both experimenter and child with standard one-to-one laboratory procedures can now be conducted by computers and television or in classrooms through the use of film.

It was feared by some that in the search for precise data, the child would be lost in the laboratory. It is true that many early studies were undertaken by persons who were more experienced in working with rats than with children. To them, the child was another subject, and experiments could be conducted equally well with lower animals or human children. It is hard, however, for anyone to maintain this attitude very long. Psychologists soon realized that their studies would be meaningless samples of the child's repertory of behavior if they failed to give careful attention to the characteristics of the organism being studied. Experimenters have found that they can design studies that are particularly appropriate for children without losing the precision and control demanded by the experimental method.

THEORETICAL POSITIONS

Accumulating information is necessary, but after a while it ceases to be much fun. If we looked forward only to an ever more detailed catalogue of significant variables, the study of children's learning would become tiresome. Knowledge is exciting when we begin to see how things fit together and how we can bring order and consistency to large masses of facts.

Psychologists have spent a great deal of effort in building theories and in seeking to establish lawful relations between antecedents and consequences of behavior. The field of learning has been noted, even notorious, for the efforts devoted to theory construction. Large-scale theories have given way to more limited models, but there has been no loss of interest over the years in shaping theories to fit new facts.

The theories that have dealt with the data on children's learning fall into four general categories: associative-mediational, reinforcement, cognitive, and perceptual. These theories differ in the constructs employed to account for behavior, but more important, they represent profoundly different conceptions of the child and how he learns. The first two positions have had the longest history in child psychology and it is possible, therefore, to discuss them more critically than the more recent cognitive and perceptual approaches.

Associative-mediational

The Hull-Spence formulations played an important role in directing the early studies of children's learning, and we turn first to their views. According to this form of associative learning theory, learning is considered to be a continuous and nonselective process. Learning occurs through the gradual strengthening of stimulus-response relations, and each stimulus impinging upon the organism at the time of response shares in this strengthening. The child is viewed as an "empty" but impressionable organism, who responds to the environment in a passive and indiscriminate manner. Growth of behavior is regarded as an ever-expanding accretion of stimulus-response connections. Questions in which adherents of this position have persistently been interested are ones such as (a) How do excitatory and inhibitory tendencies develop and generalize? (b) How do motivational and incentive variables influence the performance of what has been learned? (c) How do neutral stimuli become capable of eliciting responses and functioning as reinforcers?

It is strange that this theory should have had such an influence on research in child psychology, for neither Hull nor Spence had any special interest in children. They sought to develop a comprehensive theory of behavior, but chose to test this theory mainly with the albino rat. The position was influential because its postulates were explicit and its methodology was precise. It was easy to transfer such experiments from the animal laboratory to the nursery school.

Despite the considerable impact of this view, it has proved to be inadequate. It was most applicable to the behavior of the very young. Even here, there were difficulties. As we saw in the study by Papoušek, conditioning of neonates looks less like the "stamping-in" of a response than a gradual accommodation by the whole organism to new stimulus-response contingencies. In other studies, children even as young as two were found to respond to relations among stimuli, rather than to their absolute properties. Reinforcement, except with the very young, often tended to lead children to change their response than to repeat it. One-trial learning was commonly obtained in studies of discrimination learning and concept identification, and "no-trial" learning appeared when children were able to observe the performance of other persons. All stimuli were not equally effective; children responded to preferred or salient cues and demonstrated in other ways that they were selective in directing their attention.

Even more of a problem, perhaps, was the fact that some of the basic constructs of the theory proved to be resistant to experimental demonstration. Secondary reinforcement, primary stimulus generalization, and deleterious effects of delayed reinforcement were not readily established with children.

The theory was amended. What may be appropriate in describing the behavior of animals may be insufficient to account for the behavior of children. Children have language, for example, and animals do not. It was relatively easy to incorporate the acquisition of language into the system by formulating the verbal mediation hypothesis: Words are new and important types of stimuli, capable of acting as mediators between external stimulus and response. The behavior of the young child, as of lower animals, was assumed to be controlled by what goes on in the environment. As the child grows older, internal representations of environmental events become capable of controlling response. Words were thought to function as stimuli first in their overt form, and then through subvocal speech, symbols, or images. The rapidly expanding associative network among words was important in accounting for the growing complexity and generality of behavior.

The verbal mediation hypothesis was to provide a bridge between animal and human psychology. While the hypothesis fared better than some other components of the theory, it proved to be an oversimplified interpretation of the influence of language on behavior. Children who knew words did not produce them at the appropriate times, and once produced, the words often turned out to be incapable of controlling behavior. Older children solved problems whose solutions they could not verbalize. Predictions thought to characterize the mediating child turned out to be confirmed for young children who did not possess relevant words. Language was unnecessary if children were given certain types of pretraining experiences or were trained with multiple examples of the relevant concept. Some versions of the verbal mediation hypothesis proposed that children verbalized response to a dimension, as opposed to individual objects or single attributes. But response to a dimension requires analysis and abstraction of ways in which sets of stimuli differ and are alike, and such analysis depends upon much higher levels of cognitive activity than proponents of this position were willing to discuss.

Mediation may occur through other means than words. The proposal was made that an attentional response also could function as a mediator.

This proposal was even simpler than the verbal mediation hypothesis. Learning was seen as consisting of two stages, the acquisition of an attentional response and its association with the correct stimulus. No developmental changes were posited, and one-trial learning was considered possible.

Findings contradicting the verbal mediation hypothesis often could be construed as support for attentional mediation. Children of any age should be able to demonstrate mediational effects as long as an appropriate attentional response is learned. Sudden improvement in performance and rapid learning were easily accounted for. The hypothesis was weakened, however, when developmental changes in performance were found. As with the verbal mediation hypothesis, it too failed to face the problem of accounting for how a child isolates and attends to a dimension, rather than to particular attributes of a stimulus. Most importantly, it failed to specify with any clarity just what comprised an attentional response. Attention remained an inferred process, some sort of internalized but unspecified activity.

Mediation was supposed to salvage stimulus-response psychology so that it would be relevant to the discussion of human behavior. The success with which it has done this remains open to question. No one doubts that language and attention are important for learning, but it does not seem likely that mediation as it has been used in behavior theory is capable of offering a satisfactory account of the influence of language and attention on learning. Perhaps the concept can be refined, but one suspects that as these refinements are made mediation will look less and less like the mold of simple R's and S's into which it once was cast.

Reinforcement

Important behavioristic accounts of learning have been built around the concept of reinforcement. The most explicit of these is Skinner's discussion of operant conditioning, in which he sets forth a set of procedures for altering behavior through the application and withdrawal of reinforcement. The position has been attractive because it is easily understood and readily applied, and its impact on child psychology, primarily through studies of behavior modification, has been powerful.

The operant view has been carried far by a few, relatively simple principles. Some remarkable effects have been produced when it has been applied to the problems of strengthening or weakening what was already part of the child's repertoire, but its success in producing new types of behavior has been less notable. Many problems have been given only cursory attention or have been ignored, such as developmental changes in learning, the interaction between language and learning, and the learning of higher order concepts.

There is probably unanimous agreement that behavior is influenced by the consequences of response. But is reinforcement as automatic and mechanical as the Skinnerians imply? Should not reinforcement be considered simply as another useful source of information? Are all types of behavior equally susceptible to modification by the application of reinforcement? Why do certain responses deteriorate so rapidly when reinforcement is discontinued? If the system is to cope with such questions, it must be amplified and refined, perhaps in the ways recently suggested by Bandura (1969).

Cognitive

A third, major influence on child psychology has come from the cognitive theory of Piaget. It is hard to imagine two points of view that disagree more completely than do those of Piaget and associative learning theorists. They are sharply divergent conceptual systems, they rely on different methods, and they study different problems. Piaget has criticized tasks used in ordinary studies of learning as producing a temporary change in arbitrary stimulus-response relations rather than any significant modification of the child's cognitive structures. He has sought to assess the current status of these structures through carefully structured questioning rather than through experiments. Associative principles are thought to be too mechanical, and to place too much emphasis on the development of habits, which are considered to be random, passive aspects of behavior. Behaviorists are criticized for their failure to acknowledge the active role the child plays in organizing his experience. Reinforcement is a source of information to the child about the success of certain mental operations, rather than a means of strengthening responses. What is learning? It is the reorganization of the child's cognitive structures, rather than the incremental acquisition of stimulus-response associations. The child learns sets, expectations, hypotheses, and rules; in short, he comes to change his way of thinking rather than his mode of response.

Thus far, little research on learning has been generated by this view. There have been some efforts to train children in certain mental operations, but Piagetians generally have been more interested in describing the changes that occur in the child's cognitive activity than in investigating the specific arrangements and sequences of experience that may produce these changes. However, the ideas recently have been applied in the development of curricula for preschool children and for mathematics and science, and careful evaluation of children's day-to-day performance in these programs may produce useful data about learning. Whether or not Piagetians undertake more extensive programs of research on children's learning, a healthy vitality has been infused into the field by their probing criticisms and constructive proposals.

Perceptual Learning

The newest and one of the most original theoretical discussions of children's learning is Eleanor Gibson's theory of perceptual learning. She shares many of Piaget's doubts about the validity of the stimulus-response position. Unlike Piaget, however, she is more interested in perception than in cognition and has retained the experiment as her preferred method. Perceptual learning is conceived of as an active, adaptive, and self-regulating process through which the child becomes increasingly capable of extracting and differentiating the information that is available in the environment. The child isolates distinctive features of stimuli and invariants of events. Perceptual learning occurs at all ages, although the efficiency with which information is processed improves as the child grows older. Development leads to more complex behavior because the environment becomes more differentiated by the child.

It is too early to know what the long-term influence of this theory will be. Although there needs to be further clarification of some of the central concepts in the system, it already has led to important studies showing how the child is able to sort his experiences in appropriate ways without the necessity of external reinforcement. It has brought the stimulus under close scrutiny and has demonstrated how early experiences with stimuli influence later learning. These are impressive contributions, particularly for a position that is so new.

A psychologist's life is not as simple as it once was. There is no single theory into which all data will fit. We look to the future, however, with the expectation that in studying anything as complex as human behavior there will be a continuing interaction between theory and research, so that theories will become broader and more refined as new information is acquired.

DEVELOPMENTAL CHANGES

What are the most salient developmental changes that occur in children's learning? Learning occurs from the time of earliest infancy and from that time on the effects of prior experience accumulate, so that the manner in which the child approaches a task at one time may not be characteristic of his performance at a later date. Also, there are large individual differences in the rate at which children learn. All children do not perform in the same way, even though they have a relatively common background of earlier experiences, or are of the same age and intellectual level and share many other common features. There always will be exceptions to our generalizations, and we must be aware of this as we begin our discussion.

Children's motivation to learn appears to be high at all ages. The infant or young child may be less highly motivated to learn what the experimenter wants him to learn, than to learn ways in which he can accomplish his own self-defined goals. It does not take long, however, for children (at least the middle-class children who have been studied most frequently) to begin to find gratification in succeeding in tasks that are defined by other persons. After infancy, pleasing the experimenter, and later, pleasing themselves seem to be the most important incentives for children's learning. The high motivation to succeed does not appear to be strongly dependent upon a desire to obtain material rewards, for it is difficult to produce differences in performance by manipulating incentive conditions, except when the responses are already well-learned or the children have been subjected to conditions of deprivation. At times, highly valued incentives may hinder learning by distracting or exciting the child.

External forms of reinforcement have different effects at different ages. The young child is likely to repeat a response that is reinforced, but older children are likely to try new ones. Older children are able to detach themselves from the immediate consequences of response; having found one response to be correct does not necessarily mean that all others would be wrong. For infants and young children, the physical and temporal manner in which reinforcers are presented may influence their rate of learning. Older children, who are better able to remember what they have done, are less dependent upon the immediate delivery of information. At all ages, responses that have led to inconsistent reinforcement are difficult to eliminate.

Verbal instructions, the most common means by which adults attempt to impart information, do not appear to be highly effective for controlling the behavior of young children, especially when the effects of instructions are compared with those resulting from actual performance or observation of the performance of others. Most adults implicitly assume that instructions have the same effect for children that they do for other adults, but this does not seem to be a valid assumption. Young children are influenced less by instructions than by the characteristics of the external situation. Older children are better able to direct their attention and control their responses on the basis of what they have been told, but even they have difficulty in abandoning sets or expectations that are contrary to the instructions they have received.

The relation of language to learning is less simple than was once assumed. When a child can describe a situation meaningfully in words, learning is improved. However, we do not know whether this is because learning is improved through active verbalization or because such verbalization implies that the child already possesses the concepts or has abstracted the relevant aspects of the situation. Language aids in making certain cues distinctive, probably because it focusses attention on cues that otherwise would go unnoticed. When cues are perceptually dominant or when the procedure demonstrates the broad applicability of a response, the ability to verbalize is of little value. In general, the child appears to go through at least three stages in relating words to action: first, he may not have the relevant words; then, he may know the words but fail to use them; finally, he may have the words and use them appropriately. The time at which words can function efficiently in directing response is probably later than had been assumed, for the performance of six- and seven-year-olds does not consistently indicate an ability to control behavior through language.

Young children enter the experimental situation with strong response biases and stimulus preferences which, if in accord with the correct response, lead to rapid learning and otherwise interfere with performance. They have difficulty in abandoning their biases and preferences and tend to retain them in the face of only partial success. Older children are more likely to respond in terms of hypotheses and expectations. If their efforts prove to be incorrect, they rapidly formulate alternative hypotheses. Learning is facilitated by such efforts unless they result in the child's overcomplicating or responding inappropriately to the task.

Two common obstacles to rapid learning are the child's failure to attend to the stimuli and his failure to determine the critical features by which the stimuli differ. Once appropriate attentional and discriminative habits have been developed the child can transfer prior learning to a new situation with ease. Young children are readily distracted by irrelevant cues. They find it difficult to separate what is relevant from what is irrelevant, and to organize their behavior according to the demands of the task. As children gain more experience they are able to define problems more readily and to deploy their attention in selective manners. Their strategies for exploring the environment are efficient; they respond to what is important rather than to what is momentarily interesting.

Social variables, such as the child's relation to the experimenter, the environment in which he has been raised, and his opportunities to use the behavior of others as models for his own behavior, significantly influence the rate at which he will learn. There are hints that these variables may play a greater role in the learning of boys than of girls. Personality characteristics of the child, such as level of anxiety and motivation to achieve, also have significant effects on performance in learning tasks. Again, their effects are more marked for boys than for girls. Although personality-social variables are operative in any task presented to the child, we know less about developmental changes in their influence than we should.

Much of what this seems to add up to is that during the course of infancy and childhood human beings learn how to go about learning. They learn how to structure tasks more readily, to respond to significant cues, to sample relevant responses, and to detach themselves so that they can evaluate more objectively how well their efforts meet the requirements of the task. They are able to encompass a broader range of information and to handle it with greater precision. Their performance becomes more flexible, relevant, and systematic, and they remember with increasing precision the aspects of their environment that were distinctive and useful and the activities that led to effective outcomes. Can we capitalize on such developmental trends to provide children with experiences that will lead them to the most constructive application of what they already know and to develop the techniques in which they are deficient?

References

Abel, L. B. The effects of shift in motivation upon the learning of a sensori-motor task. *Archives of Psychology,* 1936, 29 (205).

Abravanel, E. The development of intersensory patterning with regard to selected spatial dimensions. *Monographs of the Society for Research in Child Development,* 1968, 33 (Serial No. 118). (*a*)

Abravanel, E. Intersensory integration of spatial position during early childhood. *Perceptual and Motor Skills,* 1968, 26, 251–256. (*b*)

Alberts, E., & Ehrenfreund, D. Transposition in children as a function of age. *Journal of Experimental Psychology,* 1951, 41, 30–38.

Aldrich, C. A. A new test for hearing in the newborn: The conditioned reflex. *American Journal of Diseases of Disturbed Children,* 1928, 35, 36–37.

Allen, E. K., Hart, B., Buell, J. S., Harris, F. R., & Wolf, M. M. Effects of social reinforcement on isolate behavior of a nursery school child. *Child Development,* 1964, 35, 511–518.

Allen, S. A., Spear, P. S., & Johnson, J. Experimenter role effects on children's task performance and perception. *Child Development,* 1969, 40, 1–9.

Amsel, A. The role of frustrative nonreward in noncontinuous reward situations. *Psychological Bulletin,* 1958, 55, 102–119.

Amsel, A. Frustrative nonreward in partial reinforcement and discrimination learning: Some recent history and a theoretical extension. *Psychological Review,* 1962, 69, 306–328.

Aronfreed, J. The problem of imitation. In L. P. Lipsitt & H. W. Reese (Eds.), *Advances in child development and behavior,* Vol. 4. New York: Academic Press, 1969. Pp. 209–319.

Atkinson, R. C. Computerized instruction and the learning process. *American Psychologist,* 1968, 23, 225–239.

Azrin, N. H., & Holz, W. C. Punishment. In W. K. Honig (ed.). *Operant behavior: Areas of research and application.* New York: Appleton-Century-Crofts, 1966.

Baer, D. M. Laboratory control of thumbsucking by withdrawal and re-presentation of reinforcement. *Journal of the Experimental Analysis of Behavior,* 1962, 5, 525–528.

Bandura, A. Influence of model's reinforcement contingencies on the acquisition of imitative responses. *Journal of Personality and Social Psychology,* 1965, 1, 589–595.

Bandura, A. *Principles of behavior modification.* New York: Holt-Rinehart-Winston, 1969.

Bandura, A., & Harris, M. B. Modification of syntactic style. *Journal of Experimental Child Psychology,* 1967, 4, 341–352.

Bandura, A., & Huston, A. C. Identification as a process of incidental learning. *Journal of Abnormal and Social Psychology,* 1961, 63, 311–318.

Bandura, A., Ross, D., & Ross, S. A. Transmission of aggression through imitation of aggressive models. *Journal of Abnormal and Social Psychology,* 1961, 63, 575–582.

Bandura, A., Ross, D., & Ross, S. A. Imitation of film-mediated aggressive models. *Journal of Abnormal and Social Psychology,* 1963, 66, 3–11. (*a*)

Bandura, A., Ross, D., & Ross, S. A. Vicarious reinforcement and imitative learning. *Journal of Abnormal and Social Psychology,* 1963, 67, 601–607. (*b*)

Bartoshuk, A. K. Response decrement with repeated elicitation of human neonatal cardiac acceleration to sound. *Journal of Comparative and Physiological Psychology,* 1962, 55, 9–13.

Beatty, W. E., & Weir, M. W. Children's performance on the intermediate-size transposition problem as a function of two different training procedures. *Journal of Experimental Child Psychology,* 1966, 4, 332–340.

Beiswenger, H. Luria's model of the verbal control of behavior. *Merrill-Palmer Quarterly,* 1968, 14, 267–284.

Berman, P. W., & Graham, F. K. Children's response to relative, absolute, and position cues in a two-trial size discrimination. *Journal of Comparative and Physiological Psychology,* 1964, 57, 393–397.

Berman, P. W., Rane, N. G., & Bahow, E. Age changes in children's learning set with win-stay, lose-shift problems. *Developmental Psychology,* 1970, 2, 233–239.

Bernbach, H. A. The effects of labels on short-term memory for colors with nursery school children. *Psychonomic Science,* 1967, 7, 149–150.

Bijou, S. W., & Baer, D. M. *Child Development,* Vol. 1. New York: Appleton-Century-Crofts, 1961.

Bijou, S. W., & Baer, D. M. Some methodological contributions from a functional analysis of child development. In L. P. Lipsitt & C. C. Spiker (Eds.), *Advances in child development and behavior,* Vol. 1. New York: Academic Press, 1963. Pp. 197–231.

Bijou, S. W., & Baer, D. M. (Eds.) *Child development: Readings in experimental analysis.* New York: Appleton-Century-Crofts, 1967.

Bijou, S. W., & Sturges, P. T. Positive reinforcers for experimental studies with children—consumables and manipulatables. *Child Development,* 1959, 30, 151–170.

Bisett, B. M., & Rieber, M. The effects of age and incentive value on discrimination learning. *Journal of Experimental Child Psychology,* 1966, 3, 199–206.

Blank, M. The effects of training and verbalization on reversal and extradimensional learning. *Journal of Experimental Child Psychology,* 1966, 4, 50–57.

Blank, M., & Altman, L. D. Effect of stimulus modality and task complexity on discrimination and reversal learning in preschool children. *Journal of Experimental Child Psychology,* 1968, p. 598–606.

Blank, M., Altman, L. D., & Bridger, W. H. Cross-modal transfer of form discrimination in preschool children. *Psychonomic Science,* 1968, 10, 51–52.

Blank, M., & Bridger, W. H. Cross-modal transfer in nursery-school children. *Journal of Comparative and Physiological Psychology,* 1964, 58, 277–282.

Bloom, R., & Moore, J. Effects of stimulus modality on reversal and nonreversal concept learning in children. *Psychonomic Science,* 1969, 16, 188–189.

Boat, B. M., & Clifton, C. Verbal mediation in four-year-old children. *Child Development,* 1968, 39, 505–514.

Bogartz, R. S., & Witte, K. L. On the locus of the stimulus familiarization effect in young children. *Journal of Experimental Child Psychology,* 1966, 4, 317–331.

Brackbill, Y. Extinction of the smiling response in infants as a function of re-inforcement schedule. *Child Development,* 1958, 29, 115–124.

Brackbill, Y., Fitzgerald, H. E., & Lintz, L. M. A developmental study of classical conditioning. *Monographs of the Society for Research in Child Development,* 1967, 32 (Whole No. 8).

Brackbill, Y. Kappy, M. S., & Starr, R. H. Magnitude of reward and probability learning. *Journal of Experimental Psychology,* 1962, 63, 32–35.

Brackbill, Y., & Koltsova, M. M. Conditioning and learning. In Brackbill, Y. (Ed.) *Infancy and early childhood.* New York: Free Press, 1967. Pp. 207–288.

Brackbill, Y., & O'Hara, J. The relative effectiveness of reward and punishment for discrimination learning in children. *Journal of Comparative and Physiological Psychology,* 1958, 51, 747–751.

Brackbill, Y., Wagner, J., & Wilson, D. Feedback delay and the teaching machine. *Psychology in the Schools,* 1964, 1, 148–156.

Bridger, W. H. Sensory habituation and discrimination in the human neonate. *American Journal of Psychiatry,* 1961, 117, 991–996.

Bronshtein, A. I., Antonova, T. G., Kamenetskaya, N. H., Luppova, V. A., & Sytova, V. A. On the development of the function of analyzers in infants and some animals at the early stage of ontogenesis. *Problems of evolution of physiological functions.* Moscow, U.S.S.R.: Academy of Science, 1958.

Brown, A. L. Subject and experimental variables in the oddity learning of normal and retarded children. *American Journal of Mental Deficiency,* 1970, 75, 141–142.

Brown, A. L. The stability of dimensional preference following oddity training. *Journal of Experimental Child Psychology,* 1970, 9, 239–252. *(b)*

Brown, A. L., & Scott, M. S. Acquisition and reversal of a relational concept. Unpublished manuscript, University of Illinois, 1970.

Brown, L. Developmental differences in the effects of stimulus novelty on discrimination learning. *Child Development,* 1969, 40, 813–822.

Bruning, J. L. Effects of magnitude of reward and percentage of reinforcement on a lever movement response. *Child Development,* 1964, 35, 281–285.

Bruning, J. L. Direct and vicarious effects of a shift in magnitude of reward on performance. *Journal of Personality and Social Psychology,* 1965, 2, 278–282.

Budoff, M., & Quinlan, D. Auditory and visual learning in primary grade children. *Child Development,* 1964, 35, 583–586.

Butterfield, E. C., & Zigler, E. The influence of differing institutional climates on the effectiveness of social reinforcement in the mentally retarded. *American Journal of Mental Deficiency,* 1965, 70, 48–56.

Caldwell, E. C., & Hall, V. C. Distinctive features versus prototype learning reexamined. *Journal of Experimental Psychology,* 1970, 83, 7–12.

Cantor, G. N. Children's "like-dislike" ratings of familiarized and nonfamiliarized visual stimuli. *Journal of Experimental Child Psychology,* 1968, 6, 651–657.

Cantor, G. N. Stimulus familiarization effect and the change effect in children's motor task behavior. *Psychological Bulletin,* 1969, 71, 144–160. (*a*)

Cantor, G. N. Effect of stimulus familiarization on child behavior. In J. P. Hill (Ed.), *Minnesota symposia on child psychology,* Vol. 3, Minneapolis: University of Minnesota Press, 1969. Pp. 3–30. (*b*)

Cantor, G. N., & Cantor, J. H. Effects of conditioned-stimulus familiarization on instrumental learning in children. *Journal of Experimental Child Psychology,* 1964, 1, 71–78.

Cantor, G. N., & Cantor, J. H. Discriminative reaction time performance in preschool children as related to stimulus familiarization. *Journal of Experimental Child Psychology,* 1965, 2, 1–9.

Cantor, G. N., & Spiker, C. C. Effects of nonreinforced trials on discrimination learning in preschool children. *Journal of Experimental Psychology,* 1954, 47, 256–258.

Cantor, J. H. Transfer of stimulus pretraining to motor paired-associate and discrimination learning tasks. In L. P. Lipsitt & C. C. Spiker (Eds.), *Advances in child development and behavior,* Vol. 2. New York: Academic Press, 1965. Pp. 19–58.

Cantor, J. H., & Cantor, G. N. Children's observing behavior as related to amount and recency of stimulus familiarization. *Journal of Experimental Child Psychology,* 1964, 1, 241–247.

Caron, A. J. Far transposition of intermediate-size in preverbal children. *Journal of Experimental Child Psychology,* 1966, 3, 296–311.

Caron, A. J. Intermediate-size transposition at an extreme distance in preverbal children. *Journal of Experimental Child Psychology,* 1967, 5, 186–207.

Caron, A. J. Conceptual transfer in preverbal children as a consequence of dimensional training. *Journal of Experimental Child Psychology,* 1968, 6, 522–542.

Caron, A. J. Discrimination shifts in three-year-olds as a function of dimensional salience. *Developmental Psychology,* 1969, 1, 333–339.

Castaneda, A. Supplementary report: Differential position habits and anxiety in children as determinants of performance in learning. *Journal of Experimental Psychology,* 1961, 61, 257–258.

Castaneda, A., Fahel, L. S., & Odom, R. Associative characteristics of sixty-three adjectives and their relation to verbal paired-associate learning in children. *Child Development,* 1961, 32, 297–304.

Castaneda, A., McCandless, B. R., & Palermo, D. S. The children's form of the manifest anxiety scale. *Child Development,* 1956, 27, 317–326.

Coates, B., & Hartup, W. W. Age and verbalization in observational learning. *Developmental Psychology,* 1969, 1, 556–562.

Cobb, N. J., & Price, L. E. Reversal and nonreversal shift learning in children as a function of two types of pretraining. *Psychological Reports,* 1966, 19, 1003–1010.

Cole, R. E., Dent, H. E., Eguchi, P. E., Fujii, K. K., & Johnson, R. C. Transposition with minimal errors during training trials. *Journal of Experimental Child Psychology,* 1964, 1, 355–359.

Connolly, K., & Stratton, P. An exploration of some parameters affecting classical conditioning in the neonate. *Child Development,* 1969, 40, 431–441.

Crane, N. L., & Ross, L. E. A developmental study of attention to cue redundancy introduced following discrimination learning. *Journal of Experimental Child Psychology,* 1967, 5, 1–15.

Crowne, D. P., Holland, C. H., & Conn, L. K. Personality factors in discrimination learning in children. *Journal of Personality and Social Psychology,* 1968, 10, 420–430.

Das, J. P., & Panda, K. C. Two-choice learning in children and adolescents under reward and nonreward conditions. *Journal of Genetic Psychology,* 1963, 68, 203–211.

Dashkovskaia, V. S. The first conditional reactions in newborn infants under normal and pathological conditions. *Zhurnal Vyshchoi nervnoi Deyatel'nosti.,* 1953, 3, 247–259.

Davidson, R. E. Mediation and ability in paired-associate learning. *Journal of Educational Psychology,* 1964, 55, 352–356.

Davis, J. K. Mediated generalization and interference across five grade levels. *Psychonomic Science,* 1966, 6, 273–274.

Degtiar, E. N. Cited in Y. Brackbilll & M. M. Koltsova, Conditioning and learning. In Y. Brackbilll (Ed.), *Infancy and early childhood.* New York: Free Press, 1967. Pp. 207–286.

Derks, P. L., & Paclisanu, M. Simple strategies in binary prediction by children and adults. *Journal of Experimental Psychology,* 1967, 73, 278–285.

deWeerdt, E. H. A study of improvability of fifth-grade children in certain mental functions. *Journal of Educational Psychology,* 1927, 18, 547–557.

Dickerson, D. J. Performance of preschool children on three discrimination shifts. *Psychonomic Science,* 1966, 4, 417–418.

Dornbush, R. L., & Winnick, W. A. The relative effectiveness of stereometric and pattern stimuli in discrimination learning in children. *Psychonomic Science,* 1966, 5, 301–302.

Druker, J. F., & Hagen, J. W. Developmental trends in the processing of task-relevant and task-irrelevant information. *Child Development,* 1969, 40, 371–382.

Duncanson, J. P. *Intelligence and the ability to learn.* Princeton, N.J.: Educational Testing Service, 1964.

Ebbinghaus, H. Über das gedächtnis. Leipzig, 1885. *Memory: A contribution to experimental psychology,* Teacher's College reprint, No. 3, New York: Teacher's College, 1913.

Eimas, P. D. Stimulus compounding in the discrimination learning of kindergarten children. *Journal of Experimental Child Psychology,* 1965, 2, 178–185.

Eimas, P. D. Effects of overtraining and age on intradimensional and extradimensional shifts in children. *Journal of Experimental Child Psychology,* 1966, 3, 348–355.

Eimas, P. D. Optional shift behavior in children as a function of overtraining, irrelevant stimuli and age. *Journal of Experimental Child Psychology,* 1967, 5, 332–340.

Eimas, P. D. A developmental study of hypothesis behavior and focusing. *Journal of Experimental Child Psychology,* 1969, 8, 160–172.

Endsley, R. C. Effortfulness and blocking at different distances from the goal as determinants of response speed and amplitude. *Journal of Experimental Child Psychology,* 1966, 3, 18–30.

Endsley, R. C. Effects of differential prior exposure on preschool children's subsequent choice of novel stimuli. *Psychonomic Science,* 1967, 7, 411–412.

Endsley, R. C. Effects of forced reward-nonreward ratios on children's performance in a discrimination task. *Journal of Experimental Child Psychology,* 1968, 6, 563–570.

Engen, T., & Lipsitt, L. P. Decrement and recovery of responses to olfactory stimuli in the human neonate. *Journal of Comparative and Physiological Psychology,* 1965, 59, 312–316.

Engen, T., Lipsitt, L. P., & Kaye, H. Olfactory responses and adaptation in the human neonate. *Journal of Comparative and Physiological Psychology,* 1963, 56, 73–77.

Erickson, M. T. Effects of social deprivation and satiation on verbal conditioning in children. *Journal of Comparative and Physiological Psychology,* 1962, 55, 953–958.

Erickson, M. T., & Lipsitt, L. P. Effects of delayed reward on simultaneous and successive discrimination learning in children. *Journal of Comparative and Physiological Psychology,* 1960, 53, 256–260.

Evans, P. K., & Endsley, R. C. Effects of three reward-nonreward ratios on discrimination learning in preschool children. *Journal of Experimental Child Psychology,* 1966, 4, 143–149.

Fagan, J. F., & Witryol, S. L. The effects of instructional set and delay of reward on children's learning in a simultaneous discrimination task. *Child Development,* 1966, 37, 433–438.

Falk, C. T. Object and pattern discrimination learning by young children as a function of availability of cues. *Child Development,* 1968, 39, 923–931.

Faw, T. T., & Nunnally, J. C. The influence of stimulus complexity, novelty, and affective value on children's visual fixations. *Journal of Experimental Child Psychology,* 1968, 6, 141–153.

Feldhusen, J. F., & Klausmeier, H. J. Anxiety, intelligence, and achievement in children of low, average, and high intelligence. *Child Development,* 1962, 33, 403–409.

Ferguson, N. Peers as social agents. Unpublished masters thesis, University of Minnesota, 1964.

Flavell, J. H. *The developmental psychology of Jean Piaget.* Princeton, N.J.: Van Nostrand, 1963.

Flavell, J. H. Developmental studies of mediated memory. In L. P. Lipsitt & H. W. Reese (Eds.), *Advances in child development and behavior.* New York: Academic Press, 1970, 5, 182–211.

Flavell, J. H., Beach, D. R., & Chinsky, J. M. Spontaneous verbal rehearsal in a memory task as a function of age. *Child Development,* 1966, 37, 283–299.

Friedrichs, A. G., Hertz, T. W., Moynahan, E., Simpson, W. E., Arnold, M. R., Christy, M. D., Cooper, C. R., & Stevenson, H. W. Interrelations among learning and performance tasks at the preschool level. *Developmental Psychology,* 1971, 4, 164–172.

Furth, H. G., & Youniss, J. Effect of overtraining on three discrimination shifts in children. *Journal of Comparative and Physiological Psychology,* 1964, 57, 290–293.

Garrett, H. E. The relation of tests of memory and learning to each other and to general intelligence in a highly selected group. *Journal of Educational Psychology,* 1928, 19, 601–613.

Garrison, K. C. The correlation between intelligence test scores and success in certain rational organization problems. *Journal of Applied Psychology,* 1928, 12, 621–630.

Gelfand, D. M., & Hartmann, D. P. Behavior therapy with children: A review and evaluation of research methodology. *Psychological Bulletin,* 1968, 69, 204–215.

Gelman, R. Conservation acquisition: A problem of learning to attend to relevant attributes. *Journal of Experimental Child Psychology,* 1969, 7, 167–187.

Gesell, A., & Thompson, H. Learning and growth in identical infant twins. *Genetic Psychology Monographs,* 1929, 6, 1–123.

Gewirtz, J. L. Deprivation and satiation of social stimuli as determinants of their reinforcing efficacy. In J. P. Hill (Ed.), *Minnesota symposia on child psychology,* Vol. 1. Minneapolis: University of Minnesota Press, 1967. Pp. 3–56.

Gewirtz, J. L., & Baer, D. M. The effect of brief social deprivation on behaviors for a social reinforcer. *Journal of Abnormal and Social Psychology,* 1958, 56, 49–56. (*a*)

Gewirtz, J. L., & Baer, D. M. Deprivation and satiation of social reinforcers as drive conditions. *Journal of Abnormal and Social Psychology,* 1958, 57, 165–172. (*b*)

Gibson, E. Learning to read. *Science,* 1965, 148, 1066–1072.

Gibson, E. J. *Principles of perceptual learning and development.* New York: Appleton-Century-Crofts, 1969.

Gibson, J. J., & Gibson, E. J. Perceptual learning: Differentiation or enrichment? *Psychological Review,* 1955, 62, 32–41.

Ginsberg, H., & Opper, S. *Piaget's theory of intellectual development.* Englewood Cliffs, N.J.: Prentice-Hall, 1969.

Gliner, C. R., Pick, A. D., Pick, H. L. Jr., & Hales, J. J. A developmental investigation of visual and haptic preferences for shape and texture. *Monographs of the Society for Research in Child Development.* 1969, 34 (Whole No. 6).

Gollin, E. S. Solution of conditional discrimination problems by young children. *Journal of Comparative and Physiological Psychology,* 1966, 62, 454–456.

Gollin, E. S., Saravo, A., & Salten, C. Perceptual distinctiveness and oddity problem solving in children. *Journal of Experimental Child Psychology,* 1967, 5, 586–596.

Gollin, E. S., & Shirk, E. J. A developmental study of oddity problem learning in young children. *Child Development,* 1966, 37, 213–217.

Gonzales, R. C., & Ross, S. The basis of solution by preverbal children of the intermediate-size problem. *American Journal of Psychology,* 1958, 71, 742–746.

Goulet, L. R. Verbal learning in children: Implications for developmental research. *Psychological Bulletin*, 1968, 69, 359–376.

Goulet, L. R., & Goodwin, K. S. Development and choice behavior in probabilistic and problem-solving tasks. In H. W. Reese & L. P. Lipsitt (Eds.), *Advances in child development and behavior*, Vol. V. New York: Academic Press, 1970, 5, 214–254.

Graham, F. K., Clifton, R. K., Hattan, H. M. Habituation of heart rate response to repeated auditory stimulation during the first five days of life. *Child Development*, 1968, 39, 35–52.

Graham, F. K., Ernhart, C. B., Craft, M., & Berman, P. W. Learning of relative and absolute size concepts in preschool children. *Journal of Experimental Child Psychology*, 1964, 1, 26–36.

Greene, F. M. Effect of novelty on choices made by preschool children in a simple discrimination task. *Child Development*, 1964, 35, 1257–1264.

Gruen, G. E., Ottinger, D., & Zigler, E. F. Level of aspiration and the probability learning of middle- and lower-class children. Unpublished manuscript, Yale University, 1969.

Gruen, G. E., & Weir, M. W. Effect of instructions, penalty, and age on probability learning. *Child Development*, 1964, 35, 265–273.

Gruen, G. E., & Zigler, E. F. Expectancy of success and the probability learning of middle-class, lower-class and retarded children. *Journal of Abnormal Psychology*, 1968, 73, 343–352.

Gullickson, G. R. A note on children's selection of novel auditory stimuli. *Journal of Experimental Child Psychology*, 1966, 4, 158–162.

Hagen, J. W. The effect of distraction on selective attention. *Child Development*, 1967, 38, 685–694.

Hagen, J. W., & Kingsley, P. R. Labeling effects in short-term memory. *Child Development*, 1968, 39, 113–121. (*a*)

Hagen, J. W., & Kingsley, P. R. Developmental studies of verbal labeling effects on memory. Paper presented at Midwestern Psychological Association. May, 1968. (*b*)

Hagen, J. W., & Sabo, R. A. A developmental study of selective attention. *Merrill-Palmer Quarterly*, 1967, 13, 159–172.

Hale, G. A. Discrimination shift performance in children. Unpublished manuscript. University of Minnesota, 1968.

Hale, G. A., Miller, L. K., & Stevenson, H. W. Incidental learning of film content: A developmental study. *Child Development*, 1968, 39, 69–77.

Hall, G. Association of neutral objects with rewards: Persistence of effect upon verbal evaluation. *Journal of Verbal Learning and Verbal Behavior*, 1967, 6, 291–294.

Hansen, B., & Cole, M. Discriminability and transposition in the intermediate size problem. *Journal of Experimental Child Psychology*, 1968, 6, 174–180.

Harlow, H. F. The formation of learning sets. *Psychological Review*, 1949, 56, 51–65.

Harris, L. The effects of relative novelty on children's choice behavior. *Journal of Experimental Child Psychology*, 1965, 2, 297–305.

Harris, L. The effects of stimulus setting and of variability in delayed reinforcement on children's visual orientation and speed of lever movement. *Journal of Experimental Child Psychology*, 1967, 5, 350–361.

Harter, S. Discrimination learning set in children as a function of IQ and MA. *Journal of Experimental Child Psychology*, 1965, 2, 31–43.

Harter, S. Mental age, IQ, and motivational factors in the discrimination learning set of normal and retarded children. *Journal of Experimental Child Psychology*, 1967, 5, 123–141.

Hartup, W. W. Friendship status and the effectiveness of peers as reinforcing agents. *Journal of Experimental Child Psychology*, 1964, 1, 154–162.

Hartup, W. W., & Coates, B. Imitation of a peer as a function of reinforcement from the peer group and rewardingness of the model. *Child Development*, 1967, 38, 1003–1016.

Heal, L. W. The role of the cue value, cue novelty, and overtraining in the discrimination shift performance of retardates and normal children of comparable discrimination ability. *Journal of Experimental Child Psychology*, 1966, 4, 126–142.

Hebert, J. A., & Krantz, D. L. Transposition: A reevaluation. *Psychological Bulletin*, 1965, 63, 244–257.

Helson, H. *Adaptation-level theory.* New York: Harper & Row, 1964.

Hess, R. D., & Bear, R. M. (Eds.) *Early education.* Chicago: Aldine, 1968.

Hetherington, E. M., & Banta, T. J. Incidental and intentional learning in normal and mentally retarded children. *Journal of Comparative and Physiological Psychology*, 1962, 55, 402–404.

Hicks, D. J. Imitation and retention of film-mediated aggressive peer and adult models. *Journal of Personality and Social Psychology*, 1965, 2, 97–100.

Hicks, D. J. Effects of co-observer's sanctions and adult presence on imitative aggression. *Child Development*, 1968, 39, 303–309.

Hicks, V. C., & Carr, H. A. Human reactions in a maze. *Journal of Animal Psychology*, 1912, 2, 98–125.

Hilgard, J. R. Learning and maturation in preschool children. *Journal of Genetic Psychology*, 1932, 41, 31–56.

Hill, K. T., & Sarason, S. B. The relation of test anxiety and defensiveness to test and school performance over the elementary school years: A further longitudinal study. *Monographs of the Society for Research in Child Development*, 1966, 31, (Serial No. 104).

Hill, S. D. The performance of young children on three discrimination-learning tasks. *Child Development*, 1965, 36, 425-435. (*a*)

Hill, S. D. Transfer in discrimination learning. *Child Development*, 1965, 36, 749–760. (*b*)

Hill, S. D., & Hecker, E. E. Auditory and visual learning of a paired-associate task by second grade children. *Perceptual Motor Skills*, 1966, 23, 814–820.

Hochman, S. H. The effects of overtraining on a reversal and nonreversal shift. *Psychonomic Science*, 1966, 4, 235–236.

Holton, R. B. Amplitude of instrumental response following cessation of reward. *Child Development*, 1961, 32, 107–116.

Horowitz, F. D. Social reinforcement effects on child behavior. In W. W. Hartup & N. L. Smothergill (Eds.), *The young child.* Washington, D. C.; National Association for the Education of Young Children, 1967. Pp. 27–41.

Horowitz, F. D. Infant learning and development: Retrospect and prospect. *Merrill-Palmer Quarterly*, 1968, 14, 101–120.

Horowitz, F. D. Learning, developmental research, and individual differences. In L. P. Lipsitt & H. W. Reese (Eds.), *Advances in child development and behavior,* Vol. 4. New York: Academic Press, 1969, Pp. 83–126.

Houck, E. V., Gardner, D. B., & Ruhl, D. Effects of auditory and visual pretraining on performance in a tactile discrimination task. *Perceptual and Motor Skills,* 1965, 20, 1057–1063.

Hull, C. L. The conflicting psychologies of learning—a way out. *Psychological Review,* 1935, 42, 491–516.

Hunter, I. M. L. An experimental investigation of the absolute and relative theories of transposition behavior in children. *British Journal of Psychology,* 1952, 43, 113–128.

Hunter, W. S. Delayed reactions in animals and children. *Behavioral Monographs,* 1913, 2 (No. 6).

Hurlock, E. B. The psychology of incentives. *Journal of Social Psychology,* 1931, 2, 261–290.

Husband, R. W. Intercorrelations among learning abilities, IV: Effects of age and spread of intelligence upon relationships. *Journal of Genetic Psychology,* 1941, 58, 431–434.

Ingalls, R. P., & Dickerson, D. J. Development of hypothesis behavior in human concept identification. *Developmental Psychology,* 1969, 1, 707–716.

Jarvis, P. E. Verbal control of sensory-motor performance. A test of Luria's hypotheses. *Human Development,* 1968, 11, 172–183.

Jeffrey, W. E. Variables affecting reversal-shifts in young children. *American Journal of Psychology,* 1965, 78, 589–595.

Jeffrey, W. E. The orienting reflex and attention in cognitive development. *Psychological Review,* 1968, 75, 323–334.

Jeffrey, W. E., & Cohen, L. B. Effect of spatial separation of stimulus, response, and reinforcement on selective learning in children. *Journal of Experimental Psychology,* 1964, 67, 577–580.

Jeffrey, W. E., & Cohen, L. B. Response tendencies of children in a two-choice situation. *Journal of Experimental Child Psychology,* 1965, 2, 248–254.

Jeffrey, W. E., & Skager, R. W. Effect of incentive conditions on stimulus generalization in children. *Child Development,* 1962, 33, 865–870.

Jensen, A. R. How much can we boost IQ and scholastic achievement? *Harvard Educational Review,* 1969, 39, 1–123.

Jensen, A. R., & Rohwer, W. D., Jr. Syntactical mediation of serial and paired-associate learning as a function of age. *Child Development,* 1965, 36, 601–608.

Johnson, P., & Bailey, D. E. Some determinants of the use of relationships in discrimination learning. *Journal of Experimental Psychology,* 1966, 71, 365–372.

Johnson, P. J., & White, R. M., Jr. Concept of dimensionality and reversal shift performance in children. *Journal of Experimental Child Psychology,* 1967, 5, 223–227.

Johnson, R. C., & Zara, R. C. Relational learning in young children. *Journal of Comparative and Physiological Psychology,* 1960, 53, 594–597.

Jones, M. C. A laboratory study of fear: The case of Peter. *Pedagogical Seminary,* 1924, 31, 308–315. (*a*)

Jones, M. C. The elimination of children's fears. *Journal of Experimental Psychology,* 1924, 7, 382–390. (*b*)

Jones, M. H., & Liverant, S. Effects of age differences on choice behavior. *Child Development,* 1960, 31, 673–680.

Kass, N. Resistance to extinction as a function of age and schedules of reinforcement. *Journal of Experimental Psychology,* 1962, 64, 249–252.

Kass, N. Risk in decision-making as a function of age, sex, and probability preference. *Child Development,* 1964, 35, 577–582.

Kass, N., Beardshall, A., & Wilson, H. The effects of schedules of training upon the development of a conditioned reinforcer. *Psychonomic Science,* 1966, 6, 183–184.

Kass, N., & Wilson, H. Resistance to extinction as a function of percentage of reinforcement, number of training trials, and conditioned reinforcement. *Journal of Experimental Psychology,* 1966, 71, 355–357.

Katz, P. A. Effects of labels on children's perception and discrimination learning. *Journal of Experimental Psychology,* 1963, 66, 423–428.

Katz, P. A., & Zigler, E. F. Effects of labels on perceptual transfer: Stimulus and developmental factors. *Journal of Experimental Psychology,* 1969, 80, 73–77.

Kausler, D. H., Laughlin, P. R., & Trapp, E. P. Effects of incentive-set on relevant and irrelevant (incidental) learning in children. *Child Development,* 1963, 34, 195–199.

Kaye, H. The conditioned Babkin reflex in human newborns. *Psychonomic Science,* 1965, 2, 287–288.

Keen, R. Effects of auditory stimuli on sucking behavior in the human neonate. *Journal of Experimental Child Psychology,* 1964, 1, 348–354.

Keeney, T. J., Cannizzo, S. R., & Flavell, J. H. Spontaneous and induced verbal rehearsal in a recall task. *Child Development,* 1967, 38, 953–966.

Kendler, H. H., & Kendler, T. S. Effect of verbalization on discrimination reversal shifts in children. *Science,* 1961, 134, 1619–1620.

Kendler, H. H., & Kendler, T. S. Vertical and horizontal processes in problem solving. *Psychological Review,* 1962, 69, 1–16.

Kendler, H. H., & Kendler, T. S. Reversal-shift behavior: Some basic issues. *Psychological Bulletin,* 1969, 72, 229–232.

Kendler, H. H., Kendler, T. S., & Marken, R. S. Developmental analysis of reversal and half reversal shifts. *Developmental Psychology,* 1969, 1, 318–326.

Kendler, T. S. Development of mediating responses in children. In J. C. Wright & J. Kagan (Eds.), *Basic cognitive processes in children. Monographs of the Society for Research in Child Development,* 1963, 28 (No. 2), 33–52.

Kendler, T. S. Verbalization and optional reversal shifts among kindergarten children. *Journal of Verbal Learning and Verbal Behavior,* 1964, 3, 428–436.

Kendler, T. S., & Kendler, H. H. Reversal and nonreversal shifts in kindergarten children. *Journal of Experimental Psychology,* 1959, 58, 56–60.

Kendler, T. S., & Kendler, H. H. Optional shifts of children as a function of number of training trials on the initial discrimination. *Journal of Experimental Child Psychology,* 1966, 3, 216–224.

Kendler, T. S., & Kendler, H. H. Experimental analysis of inferential behavior in children. In L. P. Lipsitt & C. C. Spiker (Eds.), *Advances in child development and behavior*, Vol. 3. New York: Academic Press, 1967. Pp. 157–190.

Kendler, T. S. & Kendler, H. H. An otogeny of optional shift behavior. *Child Development*, 1970, 41, 1–27.

Kendler, T. S., Kendler, H. H., & Carrick, M. Verbal labels and inferential problem solution of children. *Child Development*, 1966, 37, 749–764.

Kendler, T. S., Kendler, H. H., & Learnard, B. Mediated responses to size and brightness as a function of age. *American Journal of Psychology*, 1962, 75, 571–586.

Kendler, T. S., Kendler, H. H., & Wells, D. Reversal and nonreversal shifts in nursery school children. *Journal of Comparative and Physiological Psychology*, 1960, 53, 83–88.

Keppel, G. Verbal learning in children. *Psychological Bulletin*, 1964, 61, 63–80.

Kerpelman, L. C. Stimulus dimensionality and manipulability in visual perceptual learning. *Child Development*, 1967, 38, 563–572.

Kessen, W., & Kessen, M. L. Behavior of young children in a two-choice guessing problem. *Child Development*, 1961, 32, 779–788.

Kier, R. J., & Zigler, E. F. Probability learning strategies of lower- and middle-class children and the expectancy of success hypothesis. Unpublished manuscript, Yale University, 1970.

Kinnamon, A. J. Mental life of two *Macacus rhesus* monkeys in captivity. *American Journal of Psychology*, 1902, 13, 98–148, 173–218.

Klinger, N. N., & Palermo, D. S. Aural paired-associate learning in children as a function of free-associative strength. *Child Development*. 1967, 38, 1143–1152.

Kobasigawa, A. Observation of failure in another person as a determinant of amplitude and speed of a simple motor response. *Journal of Personality and Social Psychology*, 1965, 1, 626–630.

Koch, M. B., & Meyer, D. R. A relationship of mental age to learning-set formation in the preschool child. *Journal of Comparative and Physiological Psychology*, 1959, 52, 387–389.

Kofsky, E., & Osler, S. F. Free classification in children. *Child Development*, 1967, 38, 927–937.

Kohler, W. *Gestalt psychology*. New York: Liveright, 1929.

Koltsova, M. M. The physiological mechanisms underlying the development of generalization in the child. In Y. Brackbill & G. G. Thompson (Eds.), *Behavior in infancy and early childhood: A book of readings*. New York: Free Press, 1967. Pp. 250–258.

Krachkovskaia, M. V. Conditioned leukocytosis in newborn infants. In Y. Brackbill & G. G. Thompson (Eds.), *Behavior in infancy and early childhood: A book of readings*. New York: Free Press, 1967. Pp. 240–245.

Krasner, L., & Ullman, L. P. (Eds.) *Research in behavior modification*. New York: Holt, Rinehart, & Winston, 1965.

Krasnogorski, N. I. Opyt polucheniia iskusstvennykn uslovnykn refleksor u detei rannego vosrastra. *Russkii Vrach*, 1907, 26, 1245–1246. Translated and reprinted in Y. Brackbill & G. G. Thompson (Eds.), *Behavior in in-*

fancy and early childhood: A book of readings. New York: Free Press, 1967. Pp. 237–239.

Kuenne, M. R. Experimental investigation of the relation of language to transposition behavior in young children. *Journal of Experimental Psychology,* 1946, 36, 471–490.

Kuhn, D. F., Madsen, C., Jr., & Becker, W. C. Effects of exposure to an aggressive model and "frustration" on children's aggressive behavior. *Child Development,* 1967, 38, 739–745.

Lee, L. C. Concept utilization in preschool children. *Child Development,* 1965, 36, 221–227.

Leff, R. Behavior modification and the psychoses of childhood. *Psychological Bulletin,* 1968, 69, 396–409.

Lekarczyk, D. T., & Hill, K. T. Self-esteem, test anxiety, stress, and verbal learning. *Developmental Psychology,* 1969, 1, 147–154.

Lent, J. R. Mimosa Cottage: Experiment in hope. *Psychology Today,* 1968, 2, 51–58.

Leont'ev, A. N. Learning as a problem in psychology. In N. O'Connor (Ed.), *Recent Soviet Psychology.* New York: Liveright, 1961. Pp. 227–246.

Levinson, B., & Reese, H. W. Patterns of discrimination learning set in preschool children, fifth-graders, college freshmen, and the aged. *Monographs of the Society for Research in Child Development,* 1967, 32 (Whole No. 7).

Lewis, M., Wall, A. M., & Aronfreed, J. Developmental changes in the relative values of social and nonsocial reinforcement. *Journal of Experimental Psychology,* 1963, 66, 133–137.

Liebert, R. M., Odom, R. D., Hill, J. H., & Huff, R. L. Effects of age and rule familiarity on the production of modeled language constructions. *Developmental Psychology,* 1969, 1, 108–112.

Lintz, L. M. The delay-retention effect with auditory presentations. *Child Development,* 1968, 39, 933–943.

Lintz, L. M., Fitzgerald, H. E., & Brackbill, Y. Conditioning the eyeblink response to sound in infants. *Psychonomic Science,* 1967, 7, 405–406.

Lipsitt, L. P. Learning in the human infant. In H. W. Stevenson, E. H. Hess, & H. L. Rheingold (Eds.), *Early behavior: Comparative and developmental approaches.* New York: Wiley, 1967. Pp. 225–247.

Lipsitt, L. P., Kaye, H., & Bosack, T. N. Enhancement of neonatal sucking through reinforcement. *Journal of Experimental Child Psychology,* 1966, 4, 163–168.

Lipsitt, L. P., & Serunian, S. A. Oddity-problem learning in young children. *Child Development,* 1963, 34, 201–206.

Lipsitt, L. P., & Spears, W. C. Effects of anxiety and stress on children's paired-associate learning. *Psychonomic Science,* 1965, 3, 553–554.

Longstreth, L. E. Frustration and secondary reinforcement concepts as applied to human conditioning and extinction. *Psychological Monographs,* 1966, 80 (Whole No. 619).

Lovaas, O. I. A program for the establishment of speech in psychotic children. In J. K. Wing (Ed.), *Early childhood autism.* New York: Pergamon Press, 1966. Pp. 115–144.

Lovaas, O. I. A behavior therapy approach to the treatment of childhood schizophrenia. In J. P. Hill (Ed.), *Minnesota symposia in child psychology*, Vol. 1. Minneapolis: University of Minnesota Press, 1967. Pp. 108–159.

Lovaas, O. I., Freitag, G., Gold, V. J., Kassorla, I. C. Experimental studies in childhood schizophrenia: Analysis of self-destructive behavior. *Journal of Experimental Child Psychology*, 1965, 2, 67–84.

Lovaas, O. I., Schaeffer, B., & Simmons, J. Q. Experimental studies in childhood schizophrenia: Building social behavior in autistic children by use of electric shock. *Journal of Experimental Research in Personality*, 1966, 1, 99–109.

Lubker, B. J. Irrelevant stimulus dimensions and children's performance on simultaneous discrimination problems. *Child Development*, 1967, 38, 119–125.

Lubker, B. J. The role of between- and within-setting irrelevant dimensions in children's simultaneous discrimination learning. *Child Development*, 1969, 40, 957–964.

Lubker, B. J., & Small, M. Y. Children's performance on dimension-abstracted oddity problems. *Developmental Psychology*, 1969, 1, 35–39.

Luria, A. R. The role of language in the formation of temporary connections. In B. Simon (Ed.), *Psychology in the Soviet Union*. Stanford: Stanford University Press, 1957. Pp. 115–129.

Luria, A. R. The genesis of voluntary movements. In N. O'Connor (Ed.), *Recent Soviet Psychology*. New York: Liveright, 1961. Pp. 165–185.

Maccoby, E. E., & Hagen, J. W. Effect of distraction upon central versus incidental recall: Developmental trends. *Journal of Experimental Child Psychology*, 1965, 2, 280–289.

Mackintosh, N. J. Selective attention in animal discrimination learning. *Psychological Bulletin*, 1965, 64, 124–150.

Madsen, C., Jr. Nurturance and modeling in preschoolers. *Child Development*, 1968, 39, 221–236.

Marquis, D. P. Can conditioned responses be established in the newborn infant? *Journal of Genetic Psychology*, 1931, 39, 479–492.

Marquis, D. P. Learning in the neonate: The modification of behavior under three feeding conditions. *Journal of Experimental Psychology*, 1941, 29, 263–282.

Marsh, C., & Sherman, M. Verbal mediation of transposition as a function of age level. *Journal of Experimental Child Psychology*, 1966, 4, 90–98.

Marsh, G. Effect of overtraining on reversal and nonreversal shifts in nursery school children. *Child Development*, 1964, 35, 1367–1372.

Marshall, H. H. Learning as a function of task interest, reinforcement, and social class variables. *Journal of Educational Psychology*, 1969, 60, 133–137.

Mateer, F. *Child behavior: A critical and experimental study of young children by the method of conditioned reflexes*. Boston: Badger, 1918.

McConnell, O. L. Perceptual versus verbal mediation in the concept learning of children. *Child Development*, 1964, 35, 1373–1383.

McCoy, N., & Zigler, E. Social reinforcer effectiveness as a function of the relationship between child and adult. *Journal of Personality and Social Psychology*, 1965, 1, 604–612.

McCullers, J. C. Effects of associative strength, grade level, and interpair interval in verbal paired-associate learning. *Child Development,* 1961, 32, 773–778.

McGraw, M. B. *Growth: A study of Johnny and Jimmy.* New York: Appleton-Century, 1935.

Mednick, S. A., & Lehtinen, L. E. Stimulus generalization as a function of age in children. *Journal of Experimental Psychology,* 1957, 53, 180–183.

Mendel, G. Children's preferences for differing degrees of novelty. *Child Development,* 1965, 36, 453–465.

Miller, L. B., & Estes, B. W. Monetary reward and motivation in discrimination learning. *Journal of Experimental Psychology,* 1961, 61, 501–504.

Miller, S., Shelton, L. J., & Flavell, J. H. A test of Luria's hypothesis concerning the development of verbal self-regulation. *Child Development,* 1970, 41, 651–655.

Morse, P. A., & Shepp, B. E. The effects of overt verbalization and overtraining on dimensional shifts. In B. E. Shepp (Ed.), *Studies of discriminative learning and transfer in normal and retarded children.* Progress Report, Brown University, 1967.

Mumbauer, C. C., & Odom, R. D. Variables affecting the performance of preschool children in intradimensional, reversal and extradimensional shifts. *Journal of Experimental Psychology,* 1967, 75, 180–187.

Munn, N. L. Learning in children. In L. Carmichael (Ed.), *Manual of child psychology,* 2nd Ed. New York: Wiley, 1954. Pp. 374–458.

Murphy, J. V., & Miller, R. E. Spatial contiguity of cue, reward, and response in discrimination learning by children. *Journal of Experimental Psychology,* 1959, 58, 485–489.

Mussen, P. H. (ed.). *Carmichael's manual of child psychology,* 3rd ed. New York: Wiley, 1970.

Mussen, P. H., & Parker, A. L. Mother nurturance and girls' incidental imitative learning. *Journal of Personality and Social Psychology,* 1965, 2, 94–97.

Nelson, F. B., Reid, I. E., & Travers, R. M. W. Effect of electric shock as a reinforcer of the behavior of children. *Psychological Reports,* 1965, 16, 123–126.

Nikkel, N., & Palermo, D. S. Effects of mediated associations in paired-associate learning of children. *Journal of Experimental Child Psychology,* 1965, 2, 92–101.

Norcross, K. J. Effects on discrimination performance of similarity of previously acquired stimulus names. *Journal of Experimental Psychology,* 1958, 56, 305–309.

Norcross, K. J., & Spiker, C. C. The effects of type of stimulus pretraining on discrimination performance in preschool children. *Child Development,* 1957, 28, 79–84.

Norcross, K. J., & Spiker, C. C. Effects of mediated association on transfer in paired-associate learning. *Journal of Experimental Psychology,* 1958, 55, 129–134.

Nunnally, J. C., Duchnowski, A. J., & Parker, R. K. Association of neutral objects with rewards: Effect on verbal evaluation, reward expectancy, and selective attention. *Journal of Personality and Social Psychology,* 1965, 1, 270–274.

Nunnally, J. C., & Faw, T. T. The acquisition of conditioned reward value in discrimination learning. *Child Development,* 1968, 39, 159–166.

Nunnally, J. C., Knott, P. D., & Duchnowski, A. J. Association of neutral objects with rewards: Effects of different numbers of conditioning trials and of anticipated reward versus actual reward. *Journal of Experimental Child Psychology,* 1967, 5, 249–262.

Nunnally, J. C., Stevens, D. A., & Hall, G. H. Association of neutral objects with rewards: Effect on verbal evaluation and eye movements. *Journal of Experimental Child Psychology,* 1965, 2, 44–57.

Odom, R. D. Effects of auditory and visual stimulus deprivation and satiation on children's performance in an operant task. *Journal of Experimental Child Psychology,* 1964, 1, 16–25.

Odom, R. D. Concept identification and utilization among children of different ages. *Journal of Experimental Child Psychology,* 1967, 4, 309–316.

Odom, R. D. Problem-solving strategies as a function of age and socio-economic level. *Child Development,* 1967, 38, 747–752.

Odom, R. D., & Coon, R. C. The development of hypothesis testing. *Journal of Experimental Child Psychology,* 1966, 4, 285–291.

Odom, R. D., Liebert, R. M., & Hill, J. H. The effects of modeling cues, reward, and attentional set on the production of grammatical and ungrammatical syntactic constructions. *Journal of Experimental Child Psychology,* 1968, 6, 131–140.

Olson, D. R. On conceptual strategies. In J. S. Bruner, R. R. Olver, P. M. Greenfield et al. *Studies in cognitive growth.* New York: Wiley, 1966. Pp. 135–167.

Osler, S. F., & Fivel, M. W. Concept attainment: I. The role of age and intelligence in concept attainment by induction. *Journal of Experimental Psychology,* 1961, 62, 1–8.

Osler, S. F., & Kofsky, E. Stimulus uncertainty as a variable in the development of conceptual ability. *Journal of Experimental Child Psychology,* 1965, 2, 264–279.

Osler, S. F., & Kofsky, E. Structure and strategy in concept learning. *Journal of Experimental Child Psychology,* 1966, 4, 198–209.

Osler, S. F., & Scholnick, E. K. The effect of stimulus differentiation and inferential experience on concept attainment in disadvantaged children. *Journal of Experimental Child Psychology,* 1968, 6, 658–666.

Osler, S. F., & Shapiro, S. L. Studies in concept attainment. IV. The role of partial reinforcement as a function of age and intelligence. *Child Development,* 1964, 35, 623–633.

Osler, S. F., & Trautman, G. E. Concept attainment: II. Effect of stimulus complexity upon concept attainment at two levels of intelligence. *Journal of Experimental Psychology,* 1961, 62, 9–13.

Osler, S. F., & Weiss, S. R. Studies in concept attainment. III. Effect of instructions at two levels of intelligence. *Journal of Experimental Psychology,* 1962, 63, 528–533.

Otto, W. The acquisition and retention of paired-associates by good, average, and poor readers. *Journal of Educational Psychology*, 1961, 52, 241–248.

Paivio, A., & Yuille, J. C. Word abstractness and meaningfulness, and paired-associates learning in children. *Journal of Experimental Child Psychology*, 1966, 4, 81–89.

Palermo, D. S. Mediated association in a paired-associate transfer task. *Journal of Experimental Psychology*, 1962, 64, 234–238.

Palermo, D. S. Word associations and children's verbal behavior. In L. P. Lipsitt & C. C. Spiker (Eds.), *Advances in child development and behavior*, Vol. 1. New York: Academic Press, 1963. Pp. 31–68.

Palermo, D. S. Mediated association in the paired-associate learning of children using heterogeneous and homogeneous lists. *Journal of Experimental Psychology*, 1966, 71, 711–717.

Palermo, D. S., Flamer, G. B., & Jenkins, J. J. Association value of responses in the paired-associate learning of children and adults. *Journal of Verbal Learning and Verbal Behavior*, 1964, 3, 171–175.

Palermo, D. S., & Jenkins, J. J. *Word-association norms: Grade school through college*. Minneapolis: University of Minnesota Press, 1964.

Papoušek, H. Experimental studies of appetitional behavior in human newborns and infants. In H. W. Stevenson, E. Hess, & H. L. Rheingold (Eds.), *Early behavior: Comparative and developmental approaches*. New York: Wiley, 1967. Pp. 249–278. (*a*)

Papoušek, H. Conditioning during early postnatal development. In Y. Brackbill & G. G. Thompson (Eds.), *Behavior in infancy and early childhood*. New York: Free Press, 1967. Pp. 259–274. (*b*)

Parten, D. A., & Fouts, G. T. Effects of stimulus-response similarity and dissimilarity on children's matching performance. *Journal of Experimental Child Psychology*, 1969, 8, 461–468.

Penney, R. K. The effects of nonreinforcement on response strength as a function of number of previous reinforcements. *Canadian Journal of Psychology*, 1960, 14, 206–215.

Penney, R. K. Children's escape performance as a function of schedules of delay of reinforcement. *Journal of Experimental Psychology*, 1967, 73, 109–112.

Penney, R. K., & Lupton, A. A. Children's discrimination learning as a function of reward and punishment. *Journal of Comparative and Physiological Psychology*, 1961, 54, 449–451.

Penney, R. K., & McCann, B. The instrumental escape conditioning of anxious and nonanxious children. *Journal of Abnormal and Social Psychology*, 1962, 65, 351–354.

Pick, A. D. Improvement of visual and tactual form discrimination. *Journal of Experimental Psychology*, 1965, 69, 331–339.

Pick, A. D., Pick, H. L., Jr., & Thomas, M. L. Cross-modal transfer and improvement of form discrimination. *Journal of Experimental Child Psychology*, 1966, 3, 279–288.

Pick, H. L., Jr., Pick, A. D., & Klein, R. E. Perceptual integration in children. In L. P. Lipsitt & C. C. Spiker (Eds.), *Advances in child development and behavior*. Vol. 3. New York: Academic Press, 1967. Pp. 191–223.

Postman, L. Short-term memory and incidental learning. In A. W. Melton

(Ed.), *Categories of human learning.* New York: Academic Press, 1964. Pp. 145–201.

Price, L. E. Learning and performance in a verbal paired-associate task with preschool children. *Psychological Reports,* 1963, 12, 847–850.

Prokasy, W. F., & Hall, J. F. Primary stimulus generalization. *Psychological Review,* 1963, 70, 310–322.

Rabinowitz, F. M. Conditioned stimulus duration and delay of reward as variables in a lever pulling situation. *Journal of Experimental Child Psychology,* 1966, 3, 225–234.

Ramiriz, M., III, & Castaneda, A. Paired-associate learning of sociometrically ranked children's names. *Child Development,* 1967, 38, 171–180.

Rapier, J. L. Measured intelligence and the ability to learn. *Acta Psychologica,* 1962, 20, 1–17.

Reese, H. W. Transposition in the intermediate-size problem by preschool children. *Child Development,* 1961, 32, 311–314.

Reese, H. W. The distance effect of transposition in the intermediate-size problem. *Journal of Comparative and Physiological Psychology,* 1962, 55, 528–531.

Reese, H. W. Verbal mediation as a function of age level. *Psychological Bulletin,* 1962, 59, 502–509.

Reese, H. W. Discrimination learning set in children. In L. P. Lipsitt & C. C. Spiker (Eds.), *Advances in child development and behavior.* Vol. 1. New York: Academic Press, 1963. Pp. 115–145.

Reese, H. W. Mediation in young children in the intermediate size problem. Paper read at meetings of Eastern Psychological Association, Philadelphia, April, 1964.

Reese, H. W. Imagery in paired-associate learning in children. *Journal of Experimental Child Psychology,* 1965, 2, 290–296.

Reese, H. W. Intermediate-size transposition in young children. *Journal of Comparative and Physiological Psychology,* 1965, 59, 413–415.

Reese, H. W. Verbal effects in the intermediate-size transposition problem. *Journal of Experimental Child Psychology,* 1966, 3, 123–130.

Reese, H. W. *The perception of stimulus relations: Discrimination learning and transposition.* New York: Academic Press, 1968.

Reese, H. W., & Fiero, P. G. Overlearning and transposition. *Child Development,* 1964, 35, 1361–1365.

Reese, H. W., Paivio, A., Rohwer, W. D., Jr., & Palermo D. S. Imagery in children's learning: A symposium. *Psychological Bulletin,* 1970, 73, 383–421.

Renner, K. E. Delay of reinforcement: A historical review. *Psychological Bulletin,* 1964, 61, 341–361.

Rheingold, H. L., Gewirtz, J. L., & Ross, H. W. Social conditioning of vocalizations in the infant. *Journal of Comparative and Physiological Psychology,* 1959, 52, 68–73.

Rieber, M. The effect of CS presence during delay of reward on the speed of an instrumental response. *Journal of Experimental Psychology,* 1961, 61, 290–294. (*a*)

Rieber, M. Shifts in response-reward interval and its effect upon response speed. *Psychological Reports,* 1961, 60, 393–398. (*b*)

Rieber, M. Delay of reward and discrimination learning in children. *Child Development,* 1964, 35, 559–568.

Rieber, M. Response alternation in children under different schedules of reinforcement. *Psychonomic Science,* 1966, 4, 149–150.

Rieber, M., & Johnson, B. M. The relative effects of alternating delayed reinforcement and alternating nonreinforcement on response speeds of children. *Journal of Experimental Child Psychology,* 1964, 1, 174–181.

Riley, D. A., McKee, J. P., Bell, D. D., & Schwartz, C. R. Auditory discrimination in children: The effect of relative and absolute instructions on retention and transfer. *Journal of Experimental Psychology,* 1967, 73, 581–588.

Riley, D. A., Sherman, M., & McKee, J. P. A comment on intermediate-size discrimination and adaptation level theory. *Psychological Review,* 1966, 78, 252–256.

Risley, T. Learning and lollipops. *Psychology Today,* 1968, 2, 21–31, 62–65.

Rohwer, W. D., Jr. Constraint, syntax, and meaning in paired-associate learning. *Journal of Verbal Learning and Verbal Behavior,* 1968, 5, 541–547.

Rohwer, W. D., Jr., & Levin, J. R. Action, meaning, and stimulus selection in paired-associate learning. *Journal of Verbal Learning and Verbal Behavior,* 1968, 7, 137–141.

Rohwer, W. D., Jr., & Lynch, S. Semantic constraint in paired-associate learning. *Journal of Educational Psychology,* 1966, 57, 271–278.

Rohwer, W. D., Jr., Lynch, S., Levin, J. R., & Suzuki, N. Pictorial and verbal factors in the efficient learning of paired-associates. *Journal of Educational Psychology,* 1967, 58, 278–284.

Rohwer, W. D., Jr., Lynch S., Suzuki, N., & Levin, J. R. Verbal and pictorial facilitation of paired-associate learning. *Journal of Experimental Child Psychology,* 1967, 5, 294–302.

Rosenbaum, M. E. The effect of verbalization of correct responses by performers and observers on retention. *Child Development,* 1967, 38, 615–622.

Rosenbaum, M. E., & Bruning, J. L. Direct and vicarious experience of variations in percentage of reinforcement. *Child Development,* 1966, 37, 959–966.

Rosenblith, J. F. Learning by imitation in kindergarten children. *Child Development,* 1959, 30, 69–80.

Rosenhan, D. L. Effects of social class and race on responsiveness to approval and disapproval. *Journal of Personality and Social Psychology,* 1966, 4, 253–259.

Rosenthal, R. *Experimenter effects in behavioral research.* New York: Appleton-Century-Crofts, 1966.

Ross, D. Relationship between dependency, intentional learning, and incidental learning in preschool children. *Journal of Personality and Social Psychology,* 1966, 4, 374–381.

Ross, L. E. Classical conditioning and discrimination research with the mentally retarded. In N. R. Ellis (Ed.), *International review of research in mental retardation.* New York: Academic Press, 1966, 1, Pp. 21–54.

Routh, D. K., & Wischner, G. J. Effect of verbal pretraining and single-problem mastery on Weigl learning set formation in children. *Developmental Psychology,* 1970, 2, 176–180.

Rudel, R. G. Transposition of response by children trained in intermediate-size problems. *Journal of Comparative and Physiological Psychology,* 1957, 50, 292–295.

Rudel, R. G. Transposition of response to size in children. *Journal of Comparative and Physiological Psychology,* 1958, 51, 386–390.

Ryan, T. J., & Watson, P. Frustrative nonreward theory applied to children's behavior. *Psychological Bulletin,* 1968, 69, 111–125.

Ryan, T. J. The effects of nonreinforcement and incentive value on response speed. *Child Development,* 1965, 36, 1067–1081.

Ryan, T. J. Instrumental performance as related to several reward schedules and age. *Journal of Experimental Child Psychology,* 1966, 3, 398–404.

Ryan, T. J., & Cantor, G. N. Response speed in children as a function of reinforcement schedule. *Child Development,* 1962, 33, 871–878.

Ryan, T. J., & Moffitt, A. R. Response speed as a function of age, incentive value, and reinforcement schedule. *Child Development.* 1966, 37, 103–113.

Ryan, T. J., & Strawbridge, J. E. Effects of observer condition, instructional set, reward schedule, and sex of subject upon performer and observer. *Developmental Psychology,* 1969, 1, 474–481.

Ryan, T. J., & Voorhoeve, A. C. A parametric investigation of reinforcement schedule and sex of S as related to acquisition and extinction of an instrumental response. *Journal of Experimental Child Psychology,* 1966, 4, 189–197.

Sameroff, A. J. Can conditioned responses be established in the newborn infant: 1971? *Developmental Psychology,* 1971, 5, 1–12.

Sanders, B., Ross, L. E., & Heal, I. W. Reversal and nonreversal shift learning in normal children and retardates of comparable mental age. *Journal of Experimental Psychology,* 1965, 69, 84–88.

Sarason, S. B., Davidson, K. S., Lighthall, F. F., Waite, R. R., & Ruebush, B. K. *Anxiety in elementary school children.* New York: Wiley, 1960.

Saravo, A. Effect of number of variable dimensions on reversal and nonreversal shifts. *Journal of Comparative and Physiological Psychology,* 1967, 64, 93–97.

Saravo, A., & Gollin, E. S. Oddity learning and learning sets in children. *Journal of Experimental Child Psychology,* 1969, 7, 541–552.

Scholnick, E. K., Osler, S. F., & Katzenellenbogen, R. Discrimination learning and concept identification in disadvantaged and middle-class children. *Child Development,* 1968, 39, 15–26.

Schroth, M. L. The function of stimulus predifferentiation pretraining in complex problem-solving. *Psychonomic Science,* 1968, 10(4), 123–124.

Schusterman, R. J. The use of strategies in two-choice behavior of children and chimpanzees. *Journal of Comparative and Physiological Psychology,* 1963, 56, 96–100.

Shapiro, S. I., & Palermo, D. S. Mediation in children's aural paired-associate learning. *Child Development,* 1968, 39, 569–577.

Shapiro, S. S. Paired-associate learning in children. *Journal of Verbal Learning and Verbal Behavior,* 1965, 4, 170–174.

Shapiro, S. S. Aural paired-associate learning in grade school children. *Child Development,* 1966, 37, 417–424.

Shepp, B. E. Some cue properties of incentives: Discrimination of distinct rewards by retardates. *Journal of Comparative and Physiological Psychology,* 1963, 56, 1078–1080.

Sherman, M., & Strunk, J. Transposition as a function of single versus double discrimination training. *Journal of Comparative and Physiological Psychology,* 1964, 58, 449–450.

Sidowski, J. B., Kass, N., & Wilson, H. Cue and secondary reinforcement effects with children. *Journal of Experimental Psychology,* 1965, 69, 340–342.

Siegel, A. W. Variables affecting incidental learning in children. *Child Development,* 1968, 39, 957–968.

Siegel, A. W., & Corsini, D. A. Attentional differences in children's incidental learning. *Journal of Educational Psychology,* 1969, 60, 65–70.

Siegel, A. W., & Stevenson, H. W. Incidental learning: A developmental study. *Child Development,* 1966, 37, 811–817.

Siegel, S., & Andrews, J. M. Magnitude of reinforcement and choice behavior in children. *Journal of Experimental Psychology,* 1962, 63, 337–341.

Sigel, I. E. The attainment of concepts. In M. L. Hoffman & L. W. Hoffman (Eds.), *Review of child development research,* Vol. 1. New York: Russell Sage, 1964. Pp. 209–248.

Silverman, I. W. Effect of verbalization on reversal shifts in children. *Journal of Experimental Child Psychology,* 1966, 4, 1–8.

Siqueland, E. R. Reinforcement patterns and extinction in human newborns. *Journal of Experimental Child Psychology,* 1968, 6, 431–442.

Siqueland, E. R., & Lipsitt, L. P. Conditioned head turning in human newborns. *Journal of Experimental Child Psychology,* 1966, 3, 356–376.

Skinner, B. F. *The behavior of organisms: An experimental analysis.* New York: Appleton-Century-Crofts, 1938.

Slamecka, N. J. A methodological analysis of shift paradigms in human discrimination learning. *Psychological Bulletin,* 1968, 69, 423–438.

Smedslund, J. The acquisition of conservation of substance and weight in children: III. Extinction of conservation of weight acquired "normally" and by means of empirical controls on a balance. *Scandinavian Journal of Psychology,* 1961, 2, 85–87.

Smiley, S. S., & Weir, M. W. Role of dimensional dominance in reversal and nonreversal shift behavior. *Journal of Experimental Child Psychology,* 1966, 4, 296–307.

Sokolov, Y. N. *Perception and the conditional reflex.* Translated by S. W. Waydenfeld. New York: Pergamon, 1963.

Spence, J. T., & Segner, L. L. Verbal versus nonverbal reinforcement combinations in the discrimination learning of middle- and lower-class children. *Child Development,* 1967, 38, 29–38.

Spence, K. W. The differential response in animals to stimuli varying within a single dimension. *Psychological Review,* 1937, 44, 430–444.

Spence, K. W. The basis of solution by chimpanzees of the intermediate-size problem. *Journal of Experimental Psychology,* 1942, 31, 257–271.

Spiker, C. C. The stimulus generalization gradient as a function of the intensity of stimulus lights. *Child Development,* 1956, 27, 85–98.

Spiker, C. C. Experiments with children on the hypotheses of acquired distinctiveness and equivalence of cues. *Child Development,* 1956, 27, 253–263.

Spiker, C. C. Performance on a difficult discrimination following pretraining with distinctive stimuli. *Child Development*, 1959, 30, 513–522.

Spiker, C. C. Associative transfer in verbal paired-associate learning. *Child Development*, 1960, 31, 73–88.

Spiker, C. C., Gerjuoy, I. R., & Shepard, W. O. Children's concept of middle-sizedness and performance on the intermediate size problem. *Journal of Comparative and Physiological Psychology*, 1956, 49, 416–419.

Spiker, C. C., & Holton, R. B. Associative transfer in motor paired-associate learning as a function of amount of first task practice. *Journal of Experimental Psychology*, 1958, 56, 123–132.

Spiker, C. C., & Norcross, K. J. Effects of previously acquired stimulus names on discrimination performance. *Child Development*, 1962, 33, 859–864.

Stake, R. Learning parameters, aptitudes, and achievements. *Psychometric Monographs*, 1961, (No. 9).

Statten, P., & Wishart, D. E. S. Pure-tone audiometry in young children: Psycho-galvanic-skin-resistance and peepshow. *Annuals of Otolaryngology, Rhinology, and Laryngology*, 1956, 65, 511–534.

Steigman, M. J., & Stevenson, H. W. The effect of pretraining reinforcement schedules on children's learning. *Child Development*, 1960, 31, 53–58.

Stevenson, H. W. Latent learning in children. *Journal of Experimental Psychology*, 1954, 47, 17–21.

Stevenson, H. W. Social reinforcement with children as a function of CA, sex of E, and sex of S. *Journal of Abnormal and Social Psychology*, 1961, 63, 147–154.

Stevenson, H. W. Social reinforcement of children's behavior. In L. P. Lipsitt & C. Spiker (Eds.), *Advances in child development and behavior*, Vol. 2. New York: Academic Press, 1965. Pp. 97–126.

Stevenson, H. W. Studies of children's learning: A bibliography. *Psychonomic Monograph Supplements*, 1968, 2 (No. 11, Whole No. 27).

Stevenson, H. W. Learning in children. In P. H. Mussen (Ed.), *Carmichael's manual of child psychology*, 3rd ed. Vol. 1. New York: Wiley, 1970. Pp. 849–983.

Stevenson, H. W., & Bitterman, M. E. The distance-effect in the transposition of intermediate size by children. *American Journal of Psychology*, 1955, 68, 274–279.

Stevenson, H. W., Friedrichs, A. G., & Simpson, W. E. Interrelations and correlates over time in children's learning. *Child Development*, 1970, 41, 625–637.

Stevenson, H. W., Hale, G. A., Klein, R. E., & Miller, L. K. Interrelations and correlates in children's learning and problem solving. *Monographs of the Society for Research in Child Development*, 1968, 33 (Serial No. 123).

Stevenson, H. W., & Hill, K. T. Effectiveness of social reinforcement following social and sensory deprivation. *Journal of Abnormal and Social Psychology*, 1964, 68, 579–584.

Stevenson, H. W., & Hoving, K. L. Probability learning as a function of age and incentive. *Journal of Experimental Child Psychology*, 1964, 1, 64–70.

Stevenson, H. W., & Iscoe, I. Overtraining and transposition in children. *Journal of Experimental Psychology*, 1954, 47, 251–255.

Stevenson, H. W., Iscoe, I., & McConnell, C. A developmental study of transposition. *Journal of Experimental Psychology*, 1955, 49, 278–280.

Stevenson, H. W., Keen, R., & Knights, R. M. Parents and strangers as reinforcing agents for children's performance. *Journal of Abnormal and Social Psychology*, 1963, 67, 183–186.

Stevenson, H. W., & Langford, T. Time as a variable in transposition by children. *Child Development*, 1957, 28, 365–370.

Stevenson, H. W., & McBee, G. The learning of object and pattern discriminations by children. *Journal of Comparative and Physiological Psychology*, 1958, 51, 752–754.

Stevenson, H. W., & Odom, R. D. Children's behavior in a probabilistic situation. *Journal of Experimental Psychology*, 1964, 68, 260–268.

Stevenson, H. W., & Odom, R. D. Interrelationships in children's learning. *Child Development*, 1965, 36, 7–19. (*a*)

Stevenson, H. W., & Odom, R. D. The relation of anxiety to children's performance on learning and problem-solving tasks. *Child Development*, 1965, 36, 1003–1012. (*b*)

Stevenson, H. W., & Pirojnikoff, L. A. Discrimination learning as a function of pretraining reinforcement schedules. *Journal of Experimental Psychology*, 1958, 56, 41–44.

Stevenson, H. W., & Siegel, A. Effects of instructions and age on retention of filmed content. *Journal of Educational Psychology*, 1969, 60, 71–74.

Stevenson, H. W., & Weir, M. W. Variables affecting children's performance in a probability learning task. *Journal of Experimental Psychology*, 1959, 57, 403–412.

Stevenson, H. W., & Weir, M. W. The role of age and verbalization in probability-learning. *American Journal of Psychology*, 1963, 76, 299–305.

Stevenson, H. W., Weir, M. W., & Zigler, E. F. Discrimination learning in children as a function of motive-incentive conditions. *Psychological Reports*, 1959, 5, 95–98.

Stevenson, H. W., Williams, A. M., & Coleman, E. Interrelations among learning tasks in disadvantaged children. *Journal of Educational Psychology*, 1971, 62, 179–184.

Stevenson, H. W., & Zigler, E. F. Probability learning in children. *Journal of Experimental Psychology*, 1958, 56, 185–192.

Strain, G. S., Unikel, I. P., & Adams, H. E. Alternation behavior by children from lower socioeconomic status groups. *Developmental Psychology*, 1969, 1, 131–133.

Strong, P. N., Jr. Comparative studies in simple oddity learning: II. Children, adults, and seniles. *Psychonomic Science*, 1966, 6, 439–460.

Suchman, R. G., & Trabasso, T. Color and form preference in young children. *Journal of Experimental Child Psychology*, 1966, 3, 177–187. (*a*)

Suchman, R. G., & Trabasso, T. Stimulus preference and cue function in young children's concept attainment. *Journal of Experimental Child Psychology*, 1966, 3, 188–198. (*b*)

Suppes, P. The uses of computers in education. *Scientific American*, 1966, 215, 206–220.

Suppes, P., & Ginsberg, R. Application of a stimulus sampling model to children's concept formation with and without overt correction responses. *Journal of Experimental Psychology*, 1962, 63, 330–336.

Suppes, P., & Rosenthal-Hill, I. Concept formation by kindergarten children in a card-sorting task. *Journal of Experimental Child Psychology*, 1968, 6, 212–230.

Suzuki, N. S., & Rohwer, W. D. Verbal facilitation of paired-associate learning: Type of grammatical unit versus connective form class. Unpublished manuscript, University of California, Berkeley, 1968.

Suzuki, S. Study on shifts of discrimination learning in children. *Japanese Journal of Educational Psychology*, 1961, 9, 84–91.

Tempone, V. J. Stimulus generalization as a function of mental age. *Child Development*, 1965, 36, 229–235.

Tempone, V. J. Mediational processes in primary stimulus generalization. *Child Development*, 1966, 37, 687–696.

Tempone, V. J. The nature of the stimulus in primary stimulus generalization. *Canadian Journal of Psychology*, 1968, 22, 244–251.

Terrell, G. The role of incentive in discrimination learning in children. *Child Development*, 1958, 29, 231–236.

Terrell, G. Manipulatory motivation in children. *Journal of Comparative and Physiological Psychology*, 1959, 52, 705–709.

Terrell, G. Delayed reinforcement effects. In L. P. Lipsitt & C. C. Spiker (Eds.), *Advances in child development and behavior*, Vol. II. New York: Academic Press, 1965. Pp. 127–158.

Terrell, G., Durkin, K., & Wiesley, M. Social class and the nature of the incentive in discrimination learning. *Journal of Abnormal and Social Psychology*, 1959, 59, 270–272.

Terrell, G., & Ware, R. Role of delay of reward in speed of size and form discrimination learning in children. *Child Development*, 1961, 32, 409–415.

Thorndike, E. L. Animal intelligence. *Psychological Review Monograph Supplements*, 1898, 2 (No. 8).

Thorndike, E. L. *The fundamentals of learning*. New York: Teacher's College, 1932.

Tighe, L. S. Effect of perceptual pretraining on reversal and nonreversal shifts. *Journal of Experimental Psychology*, 1965, 70, 379–385.

Tighe, L. S., & Tighe, T. J. Overtraining and discrimination shift behavior in children. *Psychonomic Science*, 1965, 2, 365–366.

Tighe, L. S., & Tighe, T. J. Discrimination learning: Two views in historical perspective. *Psychological Bulletin*, 1966, 66, 353–370.

Tighe, L. S., & Tighe, T. J. Transfer from perceptual pretraining as a function of number of stimulus values per dimension. *Psychonomic Science*, 1968, 12, 135–136.

Tighe, L. S., & Tighe, T. J. Transfer from perceptual pretraining as a function of number of task dimensions. *Journal of Experimental Child Psychology*, 1969, 8, 494–502.

Tighe, T. J., & Tighe, L. S. Overtraining and optional shift behavior in rats and children. *Journal of Comparative and Physiological Psychology*, 1966, 62, 49–54.

Tighe, T. J., & Tighe, L. S. Discrimination shift performance as a function of age and shift procedure. *Journal of Experimental Psychology*, 1967, 74, 466–470.

Tighe, T. J., & Tighe, L. S. Perceptual learning in the discrimination processes of children: An analysis of five variables in perceptual pretraining. *Journal of Experimental Psychology*, 1968, 77, 125–134.

Tighe, T. J., & Tighe, L. S. Perceptual variables in the transposition behavior of children. *Journal of Experimental Child Psychology*, 1969, 7, 566–577.

Tighe, T. J., & Tighe, L. S. Facilitation of transposition and reversal learning in children by prior perceptual training. *Journal of Experimental Child Psychology*, 1969, 8, 366–374.

Tiktin, S., & Hartup, W. W. Sociometric status and the reinforcing effectiveness of children's peers. *Journal of Experimental Child Psychology*, 1965, 2, 306–315.

Todd, G. A., & Palmer, B. Social reinforcement of infant babbling. *Child Development*, 1968, 39, 591–596.

Tolman, E. C. *Purposive behavior in animals and men.* New York: Appleton-Century-Crofts, 1932.

Trabasso, T., Deutsch, J. A., & Gelman, R. Attention and discrimination learning of young children. *Journal of Experimental Child Psychology*, 1966, 4, 9–19.

Trabasso, T., Stave, M., & Eichberg, R. Attribute preference and discrimination shifts in young children. *Journal of Experimental Child Psychology*, 1969, 8, 195–209.

Turnure, J. E. Children's reactions to distractors in a learning situation. *Developmental Psychology*, 1970, 2, 115–122.

Ullman, L. P., & Krasner, L. (Eds.) *Case studies in behavior modification.* New York: Holt, Rinehart, & Winston, 1965.

Vaughan, M. E. Clustering, age, and incidental learning. *Journal of Experimental Child Psychology*, 1968, 6, 323–334.

Vaughter, R. M., & Cross, H. A. Discrimination reversal performance in children as a function of pre-reversal experience and overlearning. *Psychonomic Science*, 1965, 2, 363–364.

Viney, W., & Varner, G. A. The effects of overtraining and delay on reversal and nonreversal shifts in kindergarten children. *Psychonomic Science*, 1967, 8, 407–408.

Vurpillot, E. The development of scanning strategies and their relation to visual differentiation. *Journal of Experimental Child Psychology*, 1968, 6, 632–650.

Walk, R. D., & Saltz, E. J. Discrimination learning with varying numbers of positive and negative stimuli by children of different ages. *Psychonomic Science*, 1965, 2, 95–96.

Walters, R. H., & Foote, A. A study of reinforcer effectiveness with children. *Merrill-Palmer Quarterly*, 1962, 8, 149–157.

Ware, R., & Terrell, G. Effects of delayed reinforcement on associative and incentive factors. *Child Development*, 1961, 32, 789–793.

Watson, J. B. What the nursery has to say about instincts. In C. Murchison (Ed.), *Psychologies of 1925.* Worcester: Clark University Press, 1926.

Watson, J. B., & Raynor, R. Conditioned emotional reactions. *Journal of Experimental Psychology*, 1920, 3, 1–14.

Weir, M. W. Effects of age and instructions on children's probability learning. *Child Development*, 1962, 33, 729–735.

Weir, M. W. Developmental changes in problem-solving strategies. *Psychological Review*, 1964, 71, 473–490.

Weir, M. W., & Gruen, G. E. Role of incentive level, number of choices, and type of task in children's probability learning. *Journal of Experimental Child Psychology*, 1965, 2, 121–134.

Weir, M. W., & Stevenson, H. W. The effect of verbalization in children's learning as a function of chronological age. *Child Development*, 1959, 30, 143–149.

Weisberg, P. Social and nonsocial conditioning of infant vocalization. *Child Development*, 1963, 34, 377–388.

Wenger, M. A. An investigation of conditioned responses in human infants. *University of Iowa Studies in Child Welfare*, 1936, 12 (No. 1), 7–90.

White, S. H. Generalization of an instrumental response with variation in two attributes of the CS. *Journal of Experimental Psychology*, 1958, 56, 339–343.

White, S. H. Learning. In H. W. Stevenson (Ed.), *Child psychology: 62nd yearbook of the National Society for the Study of Education,* Part I. Chicago: University of Chicago Press, 1963. Pp. 196–235.

White, S. H. Discrimination learning with ever-changing positive and negative cues. *Journal of Experimental Child Psychology*, 1965, 2, 154–162.

White, S. H. Evidence for a hierarchical arrangement of learning processes. In L. P. Lipsitt & C. C. Spiker (Eds.), *Advances in child development and behavior,* Vol. 2. New York: Academic Press, 1965. Pp. 187–220.

White, S. H. Age differences in reaction to stimulus variation. In O. J. Harvey (Ed.), *Experience, structure, and adaptability.* New York: Springer, 1966. Pp. 95-122.

White, S. H., & Plum, G. E. Eye movement photography during children's learning. *Journal of Experimental Child Psychology*, 1964, 1, 327–338.

White, S. H., & Spiker, C. C. The effect of a variable conditioned stimulus upon the generalization of an instrumental response. *Child Development*, 1960, 31, 313–319.

White, S. H., Spiker, C. C., & Holton, R. B. Associative transfer as shown by response speeds in motor paired-associate learning. *Child Development*, 190, 1960, 31, 609–616.

Whitehurst, G. J. Discrimination learning in children as a function of reinforcement condition, task complexity, and chronological age. *Journal of Experimental Child Psychology*, 1969, 7, 314–325.

Wickens, D. D., & Wickens, C. A study of conditioning in the neonate. *Journal of Experimental Psychology*, 1940, 26, 94–102.

Wickland, D. A., Palermo, D. S., & Jenkins, J. J. The effects of associative strength and response hierarchy on paired-associate learning. *Journal of Verbal Learning and Verbal Behavior*, 1964, 3, 413–420.

Wilder, L. The role of speech and other extra-signal feedback in the child's sensorimotor behavior. Paper presented at annual meeting of the Speech Association of America, December, 1968.

Willer, H. I. The effect of interpolated training on reversal and nonreversal shifts in grade school children. Doctoral dissertation, State University of Iowa, 1963.

Wilson, W. C. Imitation and the learning of incidental cues by preschool children. *Child Development,* 1958, 29, 393–397.

Wohlwill, J. F., & Lowe, R. C. Experimental analysis of the development of the conservation of number. *Child Development,* 1962, 33, 153–167.

Wolf, T. H. *Persisting behavior of kindergarten children.* Minneapolis: University of Minnesota Press, 1938.

Wolff, J. L. The role of dimensional preferences in discrimination learning. *Psychonomic Science,* 1966, 5, 455–456.

Wolff, J. L. Concept shift and discriimnation-reversal learning in humans. *Psychological Bulletin,* 1967, 68, 369–408.

Woodrow, H. Interrelations of measures of learning. *Journal of Psychology,* 1940, 10, 49–73.

Wozniak, R. H. Verbal regulation of motor behavior. Soviet research and non-Soviet replications. *Human Development,* 1971 (in press).

Wray, N. P. Some factors in the concurrent intentional and incidental learning of children. *Journal of Experimental Child Psychology,* 1968, 6, 13–21.

Wunderlich, R. A., Nazzaro, J., & Youniss, J. Stimulus, response, and reward contiguity in pattern discrimination by children. *Journal of Experimental Child Psychology,* 1968, 6, 556–562.

Youniss, J. Concept transfer as a function of shifts, age, and deafness. *Child Development,* 1964, 35, 695–700.

Youniss, J., & Furth, H. G. Discrimination shifts as a function of degree of training in children. *Journal of Experimental Psychology,* 1965, 70, 424-427.

Zaporozhets, A. V. The development of perception in the preschool child. In P. H. Mussen (Ed.), *European research in cognitive development. Monographs of the Society for Research in Child Development,* 1965, 30 (Serial No. 100). Pp. 82–101.

Zeaman, D., & House, B. J. The role of attention in retardate discrimination learning. In N. R. Ellis (Ed.), *Handbook of mental deficiency.* New York: McGraw-Hill, 1963. Pp. 159–223.

Zeaman, D., & House, B. J. The relation of IQ and learning. In R. M. Gagné (Ed.), *Learning and individual differences.* Columbus, Ohio: Charles E. Merrill, 1967. Pp. 192–212.

Zeiler, M. D. The ratio theory of intermediate-size discrimination. *Psychological Review,* 1963, 70, 516–533. (*a*)

Zeiler, M. D. New dimensions of the intermediate-size problem: Neither absolute nor relational response. *Journal of Experimental Psychology,* 1963, 66, 588–595. (*b*)

Zeiler, M. D. Solution of the two-stimulus transposition problem by four- and five-year-old children. *Journal of Experimental Psychology,* 1966, 71, 576–579. (*a*)

Zeiler, M. D. The stimulus in the intermediate size problem. *Psychological Review,* 1966, 73, 257–261. (*b*)

Zeiler, M. D., & Salten, C. S. Individual gradients of transposition and absolute choice. *Journal of Experimental Child Psychology,* 1967, 5, 172–185.

Zigler, E. F. Social deprivation and rigidity in the performance of feeble-minded children. *Journal of Abnormal and Social Psychology,* 1961, 62, 413–421.

Zigler, E. F. Rigidity and social reinforcement effects in the performance of institutionalized and non-institutionalized normal and retarded children. *Journal of Personality,* 1963, 31, 258–270.

Zigler, E. F., & Williams, J. Institutionalization and the effectiveness of social reinforcement: A three year follow-up study. *Journal of Abnormal and Social Psychology,* 1963, pp. 197–206.

Author Index

Subject Index